THE DIABETIC COOKBOOK FOR BEGINNERS

700+5 Recipes for Prediabetes and Type 2 Diabetes Newly Diagnosed With 30-Day Meal Plan to Manage Your Healthy Lifestyle and To Control Your Sugar

© Copyright 2022 - All rights reserved.

The content contained within this book may not be reproduced, duplicated or transmitted without direct written permission from the author or the publisher.
Under no circumstances will any blame or legal responsibility be held against the publisher, or author, for any damages, reparation, or monetary loss due to the information contained within this book. Either directly or indirectly.

Legal Notice:

This book is copyright protected. This book is only for personal use. You cannot amend, distribute, sell, use, quote or paraphrase any part, or the content within this book, without the consent of the author or publisher.

Disclaimer Notice:

Please note the information contained within this document is for educational and entertainment purposes only. All effort has been executed to present accurate, up to date, and reliable, complete information. No warranties of any kind are declared or implied. Readers acknowledge that the author is not engaging in the rendering of legal, financial, medical or professional advice. The content within this book has been derived from various sources. Please consult a licensed professional before attempting any techniques outlined in this book.
By reading this document, the reader agrees that under no circumstances is the author responsible for any losses, direct or indirect, which are incurred because of the use of information contained within this document, including, but not limited to, errors, omissions, or inaccuracies.

Table of Contents

INTRODUCTION		9
DIFFERENCE BETWEEN TYPE 1 AND 2 DIABETES		10
30-DAY MEAL PLAN		12
BREAKFAST		**14**
1.	Bell Peppered Rings with Egg and Avocado Salsa	14
2.	Apple Cinnamon Chia Pudding	14
3.	Veggie Fillets Omelets	15
4.	Raspberry Choco Oatmeal	15
5.	Salad with Salsa Verde Vinaigrette	15
6.	Cottage Pancakes	16
7.	Greek Yogurt and Oat Pancakes	16
8.	Apple and Pumpkin Waffles	16
9.	Buckwheat Crêpes	16
10.	Mushroom Frittata	17
11.	Tropical Yogurt Kiwi Bowl	17
12.	Banana Crêpe Cakes	17
13.	Tacos with Pico De Gallo	18
14.	Portobello and Chicken Sausage Frittata	18
15.	Egg Salad Sandwiches	18
16.	Shrimp with Scallion Grits	19
17.	Breakfast Cheddar Zucchini Casserole	19
18.	Banana and Zucchini Bread	19
19.	Breakfast Grain Porridge	20
20.	Tomato Waffles	20
21.	Breakfast Homemade Poultry Sausage	20
22.	Sausage and Pepper Burrito	21
23.	Gouda Egg Casserole	21
24.	Asparagus and Salmon Quiche Cups	21
25.	Swiss chard Shakshuka	21
26.	Tropical Fruity Steel Cut Oats	22
27.	Farro with Walnuts and Berries	22
28.	Cranberry Grits	22
29.	Super Grain Porridge	23
30.	Coconut Berry Smoothie	23
31.	Goat Cheese and Avocado Toast	23
32.	Oat Granola with Walnut	24
33.	Simple Cottage Cheese Pancakes	24
34.	Almond Berry Smoothie	24
35.	Spinach and Cheese Breakfast Tacos	24
36.	Blueberry and Banana Breakfast Cookies	25
37.	Fresh Huevos Rancheros	25
38.	Feta Brussels sprouts and Scrambled Eggs	26
39.	Breakfast Vegetable and Okra Hash	26
40.	Easy and Creamy Grits	26
41.	Carrot and Oat Pancakes	26
42.	Savory Breakfast Egg Bites	27
43.	Simple Grain-Free Biscuits	27
44.	Brussels Sprout with Fried Eggs	27
45.	Vanilla Coconut Pancakes	28
46.	Cheesy Spinach, Artichoke, and Egg Casserole	28
47.	Scrumptious Orange Muffins	28
48.	Easy Turkey Breakfast Patties	29
49.	Quick Breakfast Yogurt Sundae	29
50.	Peanut Butter and Berry Oatmeal	29
51.	Caprese Quiche	29
52.	Spicy Pork on Whole Wheat Rolls	30
53.	Avocado and Egg on a Whole Wheat Toast with Chili Oil	30
54.	Scalloped Potatoes	30
55.	Blended Berry Oats	31
56.	Veggie-Stuffed Omelet	31
57.	Rice Breakfast Bake	31
58.	Potato, Egg and Sausage Frittata	32
59.	Yogurt Sundae	32
60.	Avocado Goat Cheese Toast	32
61.	Cinnamon Walnut Granola	32
62.	Chocolate Zucchini Muffins	33
63.	Carrot Oat Pancakes	33
64.	Breakfast Egg Bites	33
65.	Broccoli Cheese Breakfast Casserole	34
66.	Egg-Stuffed Tomatoes	34
67.	Summer Veggie Scramble	34
68.	Ratatouille Baked Eggs	35
69.	Cottage Cheese Almond Pancakes	35
70.	Greek Yogurt Cinnamon Pancakes	35
71.	Pumpkin Apple Waffles	36
72.	Buckwheat Crêpes with Fruit and Yogurt	36
73.	Golden Potato Cakes	36
74.	Wild Mushroom Frittata	36
75.	Tomato and Broccoli	37
LUNCH		**38**
76.	Green Salad with Berries and Sweet Potatoes	38
77.	Three Bean and Scallion Salad	39
78.	Rainbow Bean Salad	39
79.	Warm Barley and Squash Salad	39
80.	Citrus and Chicken Salad	40
81.	Blueberry and Chicken Salad	40
82.	Joseph's Bacon	40
83.	Texas Goulash	40
84.	Roasted Chickpea	41
85.	Coconut Meringue Cake	41
86.	Banana Nut Bread	41
87.	Oyster Stew	41
88.	Pecan-Oatmeal Pancakes	42
89.	Basic Bread Stuffing	42
90.	Dill Pickle Dip	42
91.	Funnel Cakes	43
92.	Shrimp Burgers	43
93.	Whole Wheat Chapatti	43
94.	Sugar Free Strawberry Cheesecake	43
95.	Shrimps Saganaki	44
96.	Jelly Cookies and Peanut Butter	44
97.	Gorgonzola Tofu Scramble	44
98.	Mushroom Bread	44
99.	Chicken Sandwiches	45
100.	Kohl Slaw	45
101.	Sandwich Filling	45
102.	Berry Burrito	45
103.	Caesar Salad	46
104.	Spinach Frittata	46
105.	Chegg Salad Sandwich	46
106.	Bean Beef Burritos	46
107.	Roasted Persimmon Burrata Focaccia	47
108.	Spicy Ahi Poke Salad	47
109.	Peaches with Creamy Chicken Salad	47
110.	Asian Frittata	47
111.	Baked Cheese and Macaroni with Tomato	48
112.	Swiss and Crab Melts	48
113.	Flapjack	48

#	Recipe	Page
114.	Biryani	49
115.	Veggie and Mustard Pasta Salad	49
116.	Mashed Garlicky Potatoes	49
117.	Toffee Nut Cookies	50
118.	Nutella-Like Brioche Star	50
119.	Barbecue Beef	50
120.	Hamburger Muffins	50
121.	Brie Quesadillas with Pears	51
122.	Chocolate Fudge	51
123.	Zhug Chicken	51
124.	Spicy Tuna Sandwich	52
125.	Sunny Poutine	52
126.	Pancetta and Mushrooms	52
127.	Blueberry Bake	52
128.	Grilled Catfish	53
129.	Bacon and Fiddlehead Omelet	53
130.	Hollow Chicken Salad Supreme	53

DINNER 54

#	Recipe	Page
131.	Cilantro and Lime Broccoli Rice	54
132.	Spicy Garlic Pasta	54
133.	Simple Beef Roast	55
134.	Honey Garlic Butter Roasted Carrots	55
135.	Colorful vegetable casserole	55
136.	Lentil snack with tomato salsa	55
137.	Clear soup with liver dumplings	56
138.	Beef steaks with green asparagus	56
139.	Broccoli Omelet	57
140.	Apple Cinnamon Oatmeal	57
141.	Nutty Steel-cut Oatmeal with Blueberries	57
142.	Slow "Roasted" Tomatoes	57
143.	Tomato-Herb Omelet	58
144.	Mouth-Watering Egg Casserole	58
145.	Amazing Overnight Apple and Cinnamon Oatmeal	59
146.	Zoodles with Pea Pesto	59
147.	Shrimp Peri-Peri	59
148.	Halibut with Lime and Cilantro	59
149.	Autumn Pork Chop with Red Cabbage and Apples	60
150.	Orange-Marinated Pork Tenderloin	60
151.	Vegetarian Chipotle Chili	60
152.	Wild Rice	60
153.	Stuffed Bell Peppers with Quinoa	61
154.	Mediterranean Burrito	61
155.	Prosciutto Wrapped Mozzarella Balls	61
156.	Garlic Chicken Balls	61
157.	Monkey Salad	62
158.	Jarlsberg Lunch Omelet	62
159.	Mu Shu Lunch Pork	62
160.	Fiery Jalapeno Poppers	62
161.	Bacon and Chicken Patties	63
162.	Cheddar Bacon Burst	63
163.	Prosciutto Spinach Salad	63
164.	Riced Cauliflower and Curry Chicken	63
165.	Lasagna Spaghetti Squash	63
166.	Pork Salad	64
167.	Pork with Bell Peppers	64
168.	Roasted Pork Shoulder	64
169.	Pork Chops in Peach Glaze	65
170.	Ground Pork with Spinach	65
171.	Red Wine Pot Roast with Winter Vegetables	65
172.	Salisbury Steaks with Seared Cauliflower	66
173.	Blue Cheese Chicken Wedges	66
174.	'Oh, so Good' Salad	66
175.	Low Carb Pumpkin Pie Pudding	67
176.	Red Cabbage Mix	67
177.	Irish Lamb Stew	67
178.	Vegetables in Half and Half	67
179.	Creamy Broccoli and Ham	68
180.	Glazed Carrots and Cauliflower	68
181.	Broth-Braised Cabbage	68
182.	Shredded BBQ Cream Cheese Chicken	68
183.	Ranch Dump Style Pork Chops	69
184.	Instant Pot Cinnamon Apricot and Pears	69
185.	Beets Dijon	69

MEAT 70

#	Recipe	Page
186.	Pork Medallions with Cherry Sauce	70
187.	Pork Chops Pomodoro	70
188.	Meatballs Barley Soup	71
189.	Beef Massaman Curry	71
190.	Old Fashioned Beef Soup with Vegetables	71
191.	Beef and Red Bean Chili	72
192.	Cider Pork Stew	72
193.	Cuban Pulled Pork Sandwich	73
194.	Sunday Pot Roast	73
195.	Broccoli Beef Stir-Fry	73
196.	Beef and Pepper Fajita Bowls	74
197.	Meat skewers with polenta	74
198.	Chipotle Chili Pork Chops	74
199.	Lime-Parsley Lamb Cutlets	75
200.	Traditional Beef Stroganoff	75
201.	Smothered Sirloin	75
202.	Loaded Cottage Pie	76
203.	Fresh Pot Pork Butt	76
204.	Pork Diane	76
205.	Autumn Pork Chops	77
206.	Roasted Pork Loin with Carrots	77
207.	Herbed Meatballs	77
208.	Roasted Beef with Shallot Sauce	78
209.	Beef Stroganoff	78
210.	Pulled Pork Sandwiches with Apricot Jelly	78
211.	Beef and Mushroom Cauliflower Wraps	79
212.	Zucchini Carbonara	79
213.	Steak and Broccoli Bowls	79
214.	Cauliflower and Beef Fajita	79
215.	Lamb Kofta with Cucumber Salad	80
216.	Mustard Pork Chops	80
217.	Parmesan Golden Pork Chops	80
218.	Mango Pork Tenderloin	81
219.	Steak Sandwich	81
220.	Easy Beef Roast with Green Peppercorn Sauce	81
221.	Coffeed and Herbed Steak	82
222.	Pork Loin, Carrot, and Gold Tomato Roast	82
223.	Sloppy Joes	82
224.	Lemony Dijon Meat Loaf	82
225.	Mushroom, Beef, and Cauliflower Rice in Lettuce	83
226.	Beef Fajitas	83
227.	Beef and Mushroom Barley Soup	83
228.	Roasted Beef with Peppercorn Sauce	84
229.	Italian Pork Chops	84
230.	Pork Rind Nachos	84
231.	Jamaican Jerk Pork	84
232.	Pork Souvlakia with Tzatziki Sauce	85
233.	Beef, Tomato, and Pepper Tortillas	85
234.	Spiced Leg of Lamb	85
235.	Baked Lamb and Spinach	86
236.	Beef with Barley and Veggies	86
237.	Beef with Broccoli	86
238.	Barbecue Beef Brisket	87
239.	Lamb and Chickpeas	87
240.	Classic Stroganoff	87
241.	Ritzy Beef Stew	88
242.	Slow Cooked Beef and Vegetables Roast	88
243.	Easy Lime Lamb Cutlets	88
244.	Sumptuous Lamb and Pomegranate Salad	88
245.	Easy Pot Roast and Vegetables	89
246.	Couscous and Sweet Potatoes with Pork	89
247.	Easy Beef Curry	89
248.	Bunless Sloppy Joes	90
249.	Beef Curry	90
250.	Asian Grilled Beef Salad	90
251.	Mustard Glazed Pork Chop	91
252.	Parmesan-Crusted Pork Chops	91
253.	Pork Tenderloin Roast with Mango Glaze	91

#	Recipe	Page
254.	Curried Pork and Vegetable Skewers	92
255.	Lamb Burgers with Mushrooms and Cheese	92
256.	Cherry-Glazed Lamb Chops	92
257.	Lamb and Vegetable Stew	92
258.	Beef and Butternut Squash Stew	93
259.	Corned Beef and Cabbage Soup	93
260.	Rosemary-garlic Lamb Racks	94

POULTRY 95

#	Recipe	Page
261.	Turkey Chili	95
262.	Barbecue Turkey Burger Sliders	95
263.	Turkey and Quinoa Caprese Casserole	96
264.	Turkey Divan Casserole	96
265.	Spiced Chicken Breast	97
266.	Seasoned Chicken Breast	97
267.	Bruschetta Chicken	97
268.	Chicken with Caper Sauce	97
269.	Yogurt and Parmesan Chicken Bake	98
270.	Pesto Chicken Bake	98
271.	Chicken and Broccoli Bake	98
272.	Chicken and Veggies Bake	98
273.	Chicken with Olives	99
274.	Chicken with Bell Peppers	99
275.	Chicken with Bok Choy	99
276.	Chicken with Cabbage	100
277.	Chicken with Mushrooms	100
278.	Chicken with Broccoli and Mushroom	100
279.	Chicken with Zucchini Noodles	100
280.	Chicken with Yellow Squash	101
281.	Chicken in Veggie Sauce	101
282.	Chicken with Cranberries	101
283.	Chicken Kabobs	102
284.	Chicken and Grape Kabobs	102
285.	Chicken and Zucchini Kabobs	102
286.	Chicken and Broccoli Kabobs	103
287.	Chicken and Veggie Kabobs	103
288.	Chicken and Zucchini Soup	103
289.	Chicken and Spinach Stew	103
290.	Chicken and Bell Pepper Stew	104
291.	Chicken and Tomato Curry	104
292.	Chicken and Cauliflower Curry	104
293.	Chicken and Broccoli Curry	105
294.	Chicken and Spinach Curry	105
295.	Chicken and Sweet Potato Curry	105
296.	Green Chicken and Veggies Curry	106
297.	Ground Chicken and Tofu Soup	106
298.	Gingered Ground Chicken	106
299.	Chicken Meatballs Curry	106
300.	Spicy Chicken Burger	107
301.	Turkey and Veggie Salad	107
302.	Turkey Lettuce Wraps	107
303.	Seasoned Turkey Legs	108
304.	Turkey with Mushrooms	108
305.	Ground Turkey in Tomato Sauce	108
306.	Ground Turkey with Asparagus	108
307.	Ground Turkey with Pumpkin	109
308.	Turkey Stuffed Zucchini	109
309.	Turkey Meatballs Kabobs	109
310.	Turkey, Apple and Veggies Burgers	109
311.	Turkey and Pumpkin Meatloaf	110
312.	Duck Breast	110
313.	Spiced Quail	110
314.	White chicken chili	111
315.	Ritzy Jerked Chicken Breasts	111
316.	Roasted Chicken with Root Vegetables	111
317.	Roasted Vegetable and Chicken Tortillas	112
318.	Chicken with Carrot, and Kale	112
319.	Turkey Meatball and Vegetable Kabobs	112
320.	Shredded Buffalo Chicken	113
321.	Herbed Whole Turkey Breast	113
322.	Garlic Galore Rotisserie Chicken	113
323.	Buttery Lemon Chicken	114
324.	Chicken in Wine	114
325.	Greek Chicken	114
326.	Chicken Casablanca	115
327.	Mexican Turkey Tenderloin	115
328.	Chicken Zoodle Soup	115
329.	Turkey and Spaghetti Squash	115
330.	Thai Green Turkey Curry	116
331.	Duck in Orange Sauce	116
332.	Lemon Cilantro Chicken	116
333.	Chicken Liver Curry	116
334.	Balsamic Turkey Breast	116
335.	Almond crusted chicken	117

FISH AND SEAFOOD 118

#	Recipe	Page
336.	Salmon Cakes	118
337.	Coconut Shrimp	118
338.	Crispy Fish Sticks	119
339.	Honey-Glazed Salmon	119
340.	Basil-Parmesan Crusted Salmon	119
341.	Cajun Shrimp	120
342.	Crispy Air Fryer Fish	120
343.	Air Fryer Lemon Cod	120
344.	Salmon Fillets	120
345.	Fish and Chips	120
346.	Grilled Salmon with Lemon	121
347.	Fish Nuggets	121
348.	Garlic Rosemary Grilled Prawns	121
349.	Cajun Catfish	121
350.	Cajun Flounder and Tomatoes	122
351.	Cajun Shrimp and Roasted Vegetables	122
352.	Cilantro Lime Grilled Shrimp	122
353.	Crab Frittata	122
354.	Crunchy Lemon Shrimp	123
355.	Grilled Tuna Steaks	123
356.	Red Clam Sauce and Pasta	123
357.	Salmon Milano	123
358.	Shrimp and Artichoke Skillet	124
359.	Tuna Carbonara	124
360.	Mediterranean Fish Fillets	124
361.	Lemony Salmon	124
362.	Shrimp with Green Beans	125
363.	Crab Curry	125
364.	Mixed Chowder	125
365.	Mussels in Tomato Sauce	125
366.	Citrus Salmon	125
367.	Herbed Salmon	126
368.	Salmon in Green Sauce	126
369.	Braised Shrimp	126
370.	Shrimp Coconut Curry	126
371.	Trout Bake	127
372.	Sardine Curry	127
373.	Swordfish Steak	127
374.	Lemon Sole	127
375.	Tuna Sweet corn Casserole	127
376.	Lemon Pepper Salmon	128
377.	Almond Crusted Baked Chili Mahi Mahi	128
378.	Salmon and Asparagus	128
379.	Halibut with Spicy Apricot Sauce	129
380.	Popcorn Shrimp	129
381.	Shrimp Lemon Kebab	129
382.	Grilled Herbed Salmon with Raspberry Sauce and Cucumber Dill Dip	129
383.	Tarragon Scallops	130
384.	Garlic Shrimp and Spinach	130
385.	Herring and Veggies Soup	130
386.	Salmon Soup	131
387.	Salmon Curry	131
388.	Salmon with Bell Peppers	131
389.	Shrimp Salad	131
390.	Shrimp and Veggies Curry	132

VEGGIES 133

#	Recipe	Page
391.	Baked Zucchini Recipe from Mexico	133

#	Recipe	Page
392.	Banana Pepper Stuffed with Tofu 'n Spices	134
393.	Baked Potato Topped with Cream cheese 'n Olives	134
394.	Brussels sprouts with Balsamic Oil	134
395.	Bell Pepper-Corn Wrapped in Tortilla	134
396.	Black Bean Burger with Garlic-Chipotle	135
397.	Vegan Edamame Quinoa Collard Wraps	135
398.	Baked Eggplant with Marinara	135
399.	Crispy-Topped Baked Vegetables	136
400.	Creamy Spinach and Mushroom Lasagna	136
401.	Zucchini Parmesan Chips	136
402.	Roasted Squash Puree	137
403.	Roasted Root Vegetables	137
404.	Hummus	137
405.	Thai Roasted Veggies	137
406.	Cheesy Cauliflower Fritters	138
407.	Crispy Jalapeno Coins	138
408.	Jicama Fries	138
409.	Air Fryer Brussels sprouts	138
410.	Spaghetti Squash Tots	139
411.	Cinnamon Butternut Squash Fries	139
412.	Carrot and Zucchini Muffins	139
413.	Curried Cauliflower Florets	139
414.	Oat and Chia Porridge	139
415.	Feta and Mushroom Frittata	140
416.	Butter Glazed Carrots	140
417.	Spinach with Tomatoes	140
418.	Lemony Kale	140
419.	Kale with Cranberries and Pine Nuts	141
420.	Broccoli with Bell Pepper	141
421.	Kale with Carrot	141
422.	Bok Choy and Mushroom Stir-Fry	141
423.	Mushroom with Brussels Sprout	142
424.	Bell Peppers and Zucchini Stir Fry	142
425.	Stir Fried Veggie Noodles	142
426.	Ratatouille	142
427.	Yellow Squash and Bell Pepper Bake	143
428.	Curried Veggies Bake	143
429.	Veggie Casserole	143
430.	Mushrooms Curry	144
431.	Veggies and Walnut Loaf	144
432.	Veggie Stuffed Bell Peppers	144
433.	Veggie Kabobs	144
434.	Sweet Potato and Spinach Stew	145
435.	Cabbage and Carrot Stew	145
436.	Tofu Lettuce Wraps	145
437.	Tofu and Veggie Burger	146
438.	Tofu with Kale	146
439.	Tofu with Broccoli	146
440.	Tofu with Brussels Sprout	147
441.	Tofu with Peas	147
442.	Tofu and Spinach Soup	147
443.	Tofu and Bell Pepper Stew	147
444.	Tofu and Veggies Curry	148
445.	Potatoes with Parsley	148
446.	Peas with Mushrooms and Thyme	148
447.	Sautéed Mixed Vegetables	149
448.	Zucchini Noodles with Lime-Basil Pesto	149
449.	Spaghetti Squash with Sun-Dried Tomatoes	149
450.	Sun-Dried Tomato Brussels Sprouts	149
451.	Pico de Gallo Navy Beans	150
452.	Fennel and Chickpeas	150
453.	Italian Roasted Vegetables	150
454.	Roasted Eggplant with Goat Cheese	150
455.	Roasted Cinnamon Celery Root	151
456.	Roasted Beets, Carrots, and Parsnips	151
457.	Vegetable Medley	151
458.	Best Brown Rice	151
459.	Vegetable Curry	152
460.	Parmesan Cauliflower Mash	152
461.	Lemony Brussels Sprouts with Poppy Seeds	152
462.	Corn on the Cob	153
463.	Parmesan-Topped Acorn Squash	153
464.	Wild Rice Salad with Cranberries and Almonds	153
465.	Tempeh in Tomato Sauce	154

SNACKS **155**

#	Recipe	Page
466.	Chicken and Mushrooms	155
467.	Cheeseburger Pie	156
468.	Salmon Feta and Pesto Wrap	156
469.	Salmon Cream Cheese and Onion on Bagel	156
470.	Melon Cucumber Salad	156
471.	Greek Baklava	157
472.	Glazed Bananas in Phyllo Nut Cups	157
473.	Salmon Apple Salad Sandwich	157
474.	Smoked Salmon and Cheese on Rye Bread	157
475.	Pan-Fried Trout	158
476.	Lemon Cream Fruit Dip	158
477.	Greek Salad Kabobs	158
478.	Green Goddess White Bean Dip	158
479.	Vietnamese Meatball Lollipops with Dipping Sauce	159
480.	Blackberry Baked Brie	159
481.	Creamy Spinach Dip	159
482.	Pesto Veggie Pizza	160
483.	Apple Leather	160
484.	French bread Pizza	160
485.	Candied Pecans	161
486.	Cauliflower Hummus	161
487.	Cheese Crisp Crackers	161
488.	Cheesy Onion Dip	161
489.	Cheesy Pita Crisps	162
490.	Cheesy Taco Chips	162
491.	Chewy Granola Bars	162
492.	Chili Lime Tortilla Chips	162
493.	Chocolate Chip Blondie's	163
494.	Cinnamon Apple Chips	163
495.	Spicy Bruschetta	163
496.	Easy Pizza for Two	163
497.	Bean Salad with Balsamic Vinaigrette	164
498.	Easy Cauliflower Hush Puppies	164
499.	Cauliflower Mash	164
500.	Red Pepper, Goat Cheese, and Arugula Open-Faced Grilled Sandwich	165
501.	Almond Cheesecake Bites	165
502.	Almond Coconut Biscotti	165
503.	Almond Flour Crackers	165
504.	Asian Chicken Wings	166
505.	Banana Nut Cookies	166
506.	BLT Stuffed Cucumbers	166
507.	Buffalo Bites	166
508.	Cinnamon Apple Popcorn	167
509.	Crab and Spinach Dip	167
510.	Cranberry and Almond Granola Bars	167
511.	Cheesy Broccoli Bites	167
512.	Strawberry Smoothie	168
513.	Berry Mint Smoothie	168
514.	Greenie Smoothie	168
515.	Coconut Spinach Smoothie	168
516.	Oats Coffee Smoothie	168
517.	Veggie Smoothie	169
518.	Avocado Smoothie	169
519.	Orange Carrot Smoothie	169
520.	Marinated Green Beans	169
521.	Marinated Vegetable Salad	169
522.	Spinach and Black-Eyed Pea Salad	170
523.	Dried Bean and Cashew Salad	170
524.	Chicken, Bean and Corn Salad	170
525.	Pasta and Kidney Bean Salad	171
526.	Pasta and Artichoke Heart Salad	171
527.	Dilled Cucumbers	171
528.	Barbecue Coleslaw	171
529.	Oriental Coleslaw	172
530.	Banana Cake	172
531.	Chocolate Cake Carrot	172

#	Item	Page
532.	Fruit Slush	172
533.	Lemonade	173
534.	Lime Fizz	173
535.	Mocha Spread	173
536.	Pineapple Kabobs	173
537.	Marbled Cheesecake Muffins	173
538.	Cheesecake	174
539.	Cinnamon Nuts	174
540.	Blackberry Smoothie	174

SIDE DISHES **175**

#	Item	Page
541.	French Lentils	175
542.	Grain-Free Berry Cobbler	175
543.	Coffee-Steamed Carrots	176
544.	Rosemary Potatoes	176
545.	Kale and Cabbage Salad with Peanuts	176
546.	Chili Lime Salmon	176
547.	Collard Greens	177
548.	Mashed Pumpkin	177
549.	Turkey Loaf	177
550.	Mushroom Pasta	177
551.	Garlic Kale Chips	178
552.	Garlic Salmon Balls	178
553.	Onion Rings	178
554.	Crispy Eggplant Fries	178
555.	Charred Bell Peppers	179
556.	Garlic Tomatoes	179
557.	Mushroom Stew	179
558.	Cheese and Onion Nuggets	179
559.	Spiced Nuts	179
560.	Keto French Fries	180
561.	Fried Garlic Green Tomatoes	180
562.	Garlic Cauliflower Tots	180
563.	Chicken Tikka Masala	180
564.	Tomato and Roasted Cod	181
565.	Ravioli	181
566.	Cabbage Wedges	181
567.	Buffalo Cauliflower Wings	181
568.	Sweet Potato Cauliflower Patties	182
569.	Okra	182
570.	Creamed Spinach	182
571.	Eggplant Parmesan	183
572.	Cauliflower Rice	183
573.	Air-Fried Brussels sprouts	183
574.	Green Beans	184
575.	Asparagus Avocado Soup	184
576.	Asparagus and Bacon Salad	184
577.	Quinoa Tabbouleh	184
578.	Black Bean, Quinoa, and Mango Salad	185
579.	Low Fat Roasties	185
580.	Roasted Parsnips	185
581.	Lower Carb Hummus	186
582.	Sweet and Sour Red Cabbage	186
583.	Pinto Beans	186
584.	Cucumber and Kidney Bean Salad	186
585.	Steamed Asparagus	186
586.	Squash Medley	187
587.	Eggplant Curry	187
588.	Lentil and Eggplant Stew	187
589.	Tofu Curry	187
590.	Lentil and Chickpea Curry	187
591.	Split Pea Stew	188
592.	Kidney Bean Stew	188
593.	Fried Tofu Hotpot	188
594.	Chili Sin Carne	188
595.	Brussels sprouts	188

APPETIZER **190**

#	Item	Page
596.	Calico Slaw	190
597.	Simple Appetizer Meatballs	190
598.	Chicken Souvlaki Salad	191
599.	Celery with Chickpea Feta Salad	191
600.	Basil Vinaigrette with Summer Corn Salad	191
601.	Lemon Vinaigrette with Sugar Snap Pea Salad	192
602.	Green Dressing with Shrimp Avocado Salad	192
603.	Beans with Pearl Couscous	192
604.	Blackened Chicken Breast with Jalapeno Caesar Salad	193
605.	Ginger Dressing with Kale Chicken Salad	193
606.	Asian Cucumber Salad	193
607.	Pecans with Blackberry Ginger Beet Salad	193
608.	Blueberry Watermelon Salad	194
609.	Orange Vinaigrette with Roasted Beets	194
610.	Blueberries with Nectarines Spinach Salad	194
611.	Taco Slaw	195
612.	Egg Fried Veg	195
613.	Bone Broth	195
614.	Cauliflower and Celeriac Soup	195
615.	Mushroom and Eggs	195
616.	Carrot and Cilantro Soup	196
617.	Tomato Eggs	196
618.	Herb Crusted Chicken	196
619.	Carrot Hummus	196
620.	Mushroom Tofu Scramble	197
621.	Lentil Soup	197
622.	Stuffed Mushrooms	197
623.	Eggplant Tofu Scramble	197
624.	Spinach Dip	197
625.	Spinach and Orange Salad with Oil Drizzle	198
626.	Fruit Salad with Coconut-Lime Dressing	198
627.	Cranberry and Brussels sprouts With Dressing	198
628.	Parsnip, Carrot, and Kale Salad with Dressing	198
629.	Tomato Toasts	199
630.	Everyday Salad	199
631.	Super-Seedy Salad with Tahini Dressing	199
632.	Vegetable Salad	199
633.	Greek Salad	200
634.	Alkaline Spring Salad	200
635.	Fresh Tuna Salad	200
636.	Roasted Portobello Salad	200
637.	Shredded Chicken Salad	201
638.	Broccoli Salad	201
639.	Cherry Tomato Salad	201
640.	Ground Turkey Salad	201
641.	Celery Apple Salad	202
642.	Cauliflower Tofu Salad	202
643.	Scallop Caesar Salad	202
644.	Chicken Avocado Salad	203
645.	California Wraps	203
646.	Chicken Salad in Cucumber Cups	203
647.	Sunflower Seeds and Arugula Garden Salad	203
648.	Supreme Caesar Salad	204
649.	Tabbouleh- Arabian Salad	204
650.	Aromatic Toasted Pumpkin Seeds	204

DESSERT **205**

#	Item	Page
651.	Strawberry Chiffon Pie	205
652.	Strawberry Fruit Squares	205
653.	Copper Penny Carrots	206
654.	Poached Pears	206
655.	Carrot Cake	206
656.	Bran Muffins	207
657.	Frozen Mocha Milkshake	207
658.	Baked Berry Cups with Crispy Cinnamon Wedges	207
659.	Berry Smoothie Pops	207
660.	Instant Pot Tapioca	208
661.	Oatmeal Cookies	208
662.	Raspberry Nice Cream	208
663.	Chocolate Baked Bananas	208
664.	Greek Yogurt Berry Smoothie Pops	209
665.	Grilled Peach and Coconut Yogurt Bowls	209
666.	Frozen Chocolate Peanut Butter Bites	209
667.	Dark Chocolate Almond Butter Cups	209
668.	No-Bake Carrot Cake Bites	209
669.	Creamy Strawberry Crepes	210
670.	Swirled Cream Cheese Brownies	210

671.	Maple Oatmeal Cookies	210		690.	Cinnamon Cake	216
672.	Ambrosia	211		691.	Choco Peppermint Cake	216
673.	Banana Pudding	211		692.	Ice Cream Brownie Cake	217
674.	Pineapple Nice Cream	211		693.	Strawberry Shortcake	217
675.	Spiced Orange Rice Pudding	211		694.	Chocolate Cake	217
676.	Strawberry Cream Cheese Crepes	212		695.	Berry Coffee Cake	217
677.	Cream Cheese Swirl Brownies	212		696.	Pound Cake	218
678.	Greek Yogurt Sundae	212		697.	Dark Chocolate Cake	218
679.	Cinnamon Baked Apples	213		698.	Berry Cobbler	218
680.	Lemon Berry Chiffon	213		699.	Lemon Cheesecake	219
681.	Flourless Chocolate Cake	213		700.	Banana Coffee Cake	219
682.	Raspberry Cake with White Chocolate Sauce	213		701.	Fruitcake	219
683.	Lava Cake	214		702.	Angel Food Cake	220
684.	Roasted Mango	214		703.	Chocolate Lava Cake	220
685.	Cake with Whipped Cream Icing	214		704.	Decadent Three-Layered Chocolate Cream Cake	220
686.	Walnut-Fruit Cake	215		705.	Carrot Cake with Cream Cheese Frosting	221
687.	Ginger Cake	215		**INDEX**		**222**
688.	Orange Cake	215		**CONCLUSION**		**226**
689.	Lemon Cake	216				

Introduction

Diabetes is a disease caused by either insufficient hormone insulin or the body's inability to react to insulin. Some of the known symptoms of diabetes are excessive thirst, weight loss or gain, blurred vision, frequent urination, and slow healing wounds. Type 2 diabetes accounts for approximately 95% of all cases of diabetes. Type 2 Diabetes usually develops in adults and can last for a lifetime. It was once thought that diabetes only affected older people. However, this is not true. Both type 1 and 2 diabetes can begin at any age. The risk of developing diabetes increases as the person ages, so the condition is more common in adults. Type 2 Diabetes develops from a lack of insulin from the pancreas or insulin resistance of the body's cells. A combination of facts may play a role in causing this disease, including genetics, lifestyle habits, infections, and age. Diabetes is also linked with obesity. Type 2 Diabetes is led by an imbalance between the amount of insulin produced by the pancreas and the body's cells. The cell's insulin receptors are not working as efficiently as they should, so the body cannot utilize the insulin being formed by the pancreas. Too much sugar promotes up in the blood, which leads to other complications.

Prevention of the development of type 2 diabetes is possible if one adheres to a healthy lifestyle. Losing excess weight can help to prevent type 2 diabetes. Exercise, a healthy diet, and proper sleep each day contribute to good health. Controlling risk factors that lead to type 2 diabetes can also help keep this disease at bay. Risk factors include:

High cholesterol levels.

High blood pressure.

High blood sugar levels.

Being overweight or obese.

Life for someone with diabetes is not easy. With the help of this book, your body will learn to use stored fat as energy and eventually begin using the sugar circulating in your blood. Once you manage your blood sugar levels naturally, you'll be able to reduce or even eliminate your diabetes medications. You can retrieve control of your metabolism and reach optimal health. Healthy foods will be easy to include in your diet. Your body will begin to role at its optimal weight and become more energy efficient. You will feel more energetic and become more aware of what your body needs. This book aims to make your life easier by showing you how simple it can be. If you are existing with or caring for someone with diabetes, this book has information that will help you stay healthy and happy along the way. This cookbook will show you how to use healthy ingredients to create delicious, satisfying meals for the entire family.

After reading this book, you will apprehend how Type 2 diabetes develops and make better choices for yourself. The recipes in this cookbook will assist you prepare creative, great-tasting meals that are healthy and easy on your budget. What are you waiting for? Now is the time to make a transform, and these recipes are your guide to helping your diabetes improve.

Difference between Type 1 and 2 Diabetes

When you first hear the term "Type 2 Diabetes", it may seem like some new disease only recently discovered. Still, Type 1 and Type 2 diabetes are two different diseases with different symptoms and complications.
Diabetes is usually either type 1 or type 2, although these two subtypes can also be concurrent within an individual.
Type 1 diabetes (known as insulin-dependent diabetes) has nothing to do with insulin. Still, it is an autoimmune disease where the immune system destroys the beta cells in the pancreas. Type 1 is usually diagnosed before 20 years of age, and it requires daily injections of insulin to stay alive. Unlike Type 2, this is led by genetics and lifestyle factors, Type 1 results from a genetic defect in the pancreas. This means that there will be no danger of complications even if patients discontinue their insulin.
Type 2 diabetes (previously called non-insulin-dependent or adult-onset diabetes) happens more commonly in adults over 40 years. This may be taught that adult-onset diabetes is associated with weight gain and a sedentary lifestyle.

How to Prevent Diabetes and Control Sugar Level
Preventing diabetes sounds like an obvious statement to make, but it is also one of the most important ways to reduce your risk. Lowering your body weight and maintaining a healthy diet will help you prevent diabetes. One of the most common causes of high blood sugar levels is eating too many carbohydrates. So, reducing the intake of carbohydrates will help you reduce your blood sugar level within a few days.
As long as you manage a healthy lifestyle, there are no reasons to take medications or supplements that may cause further complications in the future.

Additional Information Regarding Nutritional Goals for Type 2 Diabetic Patients
People with type 2 diabetes are also encouraged to maintain physical activity to reduce the risk of long-term complications of this disease. Another way to gain effective control of blood sugar levels is by restricting your calorie intake. This means that you should maximize the number of foods that are rich in carbohydrates. Fruits and vegetables are essential parts of a healthy diet. So, if you want to lower the risk of several diseases, including type 2 diabetes, you should insert these foods into your daily meals. By following a healthy diet and maintaining a healthy lifestyle, people with type 2 diabetes can slow down the development of complications and prevent long-term side effects.

The Relationship between Nutrients and Diabetes
By eating healthy foods, you can reduce your risk of complications caused by diabetes. Nutrients have a significant impact on blood sugar levels, which is the leading cause of complications of this disease. While it is recommended to eat healthy foods, some individuals rely solely on medications or supplements to manage their blood sugar levels. Dietary therapy aims to establish a nutrition plan that lowers blood sugar levels and maintains healthy cells. To support this goal, you can use several sources of carbohydrates while still managing your sugar level.

What to Avoid and What to Eat
Forbidden foods are not recommended for people who have diabetes. The most common foods considered forbidden are sugar (including beverages), alcohol, and trans-fat, while carbohydrates should be limited to 250-275 grams per day. Some other food items that are high in calories and can be dangerous for the diabetic individual are meats and cheese. The list of these foods is long, but there are a few unusual examples that we will look at:

- Sweetened beverages: They contain sugar, sometimes a lot of sugar. So, they a must no. Replace with just water or unsweetened tea.
- Coffee: Coffee is another item that is forbidden in the diet of a diabetic person. Coffee contains caffeine which can increase blood sugar levels in the body. In addition to caffeine, coffee also has high carbs, making it a wrong food choice for people who have diabetes.
- Bacon: Bacon is another meat item not recommended for people with diabetes. Bacon contains a lot of saturated fat, which can be dangerous for people with diabetes. In general fish and white meat (not canned!) are more friendly to people suffering from diabetes.
- Processed Cheese (or processed cheese products): Processed cheese companies use artificial ingredients to manufacture their products and thus are not advised for people with diabetes. Unfortunately, there is no substitute for processed cheese, so this is something that most diabetics must avoid at all costs. Better low fat and fresh cheese.

- Red Meat: Red meats are considered forbidden foods for people with diabetes. Red meat contains a lot of cholesterol which on digestion turns into lousy cholesterol in the body. Harmful cholesterol levels may lead to the formation of blood clots in the body.
- White Rice: White rice is packed with carbohydrates, and not much fiber or other nutrition value is found in white rice. These properties make white rice a forbidden food for people with diabetes.
- Fried Potato: The fried potato is not suitable for people with diabetes because fried potatoes contain many calories and carbohydrates. Fried potato is not as bad as white rice, but it should be avoided like any other food item in the diet of a diabetic person.

Superfoods for Diabetic- Superfoods are any food item that contains high nutrition and low carbohydrate content. These foods are healthy and nutritious and must be included in the diabetic diet plan.

These are the foods that can be included in the diet of a diabetic person.

- Fish- Fish is a high protein and low carbohydrate food. Fish contains omega-3 fatty acids, which are suitable for the cardiovascular system.
- Salmon- This is a perfect fish recommended for people with diabetes because salmon contains omega-3 fatty acids, which are suitable for the blood sugar level of a person with diabetes.
- Nuts and Nut butter- Nuts are one of the best and most healthy food items. Many people with diabetes prefer to have nuts because they contain a lot of fat which is a suitable type of fat that helps lower cholesterol levels in the body.
- Avocados- Avocados are rich in fiber which can be very good for health due to their high fiber content.
- Green Tea- Green tea contains antioxidants which can be very good for the health of diabetic people.
- Oatmeal- Oatmeal is one of the best food items for people with diabetes. Oatmeal is low in calories, contains a lot of fiber, and is a good source of vitamins and minerals.
- Whole grains are another excellent food item that has become very popular these days because they taste so good and are very nutritious as well. Whole grains contain more fiber which helps in keeping blood sugar levels under control.
- Mushrooms- Mushrooms contain minimal amount of carbohydrates and are very high in nutrition value.
- Yogurt- White and low-fat yogurt is also a good food item for people with diabetes. It contains probiotics, which are suitable for gut health in general. Probiotics are good bacteria that help maintain a healthy digestive system.
- Olive Oil- Olive oil contains monounsaturated fats, considered the best type of fat for a person who has diabetes. Monounsaturated fats help in reducing the cholesterol level in the blood of a diabetic person.
- Broccoli- Broccoli is included in the list of superfoods because it contains rich amounts of vitamins and minerals and is very low in carbohydrates.

Discouraged or limited food- Many foods may have limited or unwanted effects on the body, but this does not mean that they are entirely inappropriate for people with diabetes. When eating foods that are considered discouraged, it is essential that the nutritionist knows about all possible interactions caused by diabetics in advance.

The following foods are discouraged or limited from the menu of a diabetic person:

- Fruits- Diabetic person should take at least 2 servings of fruit daily. It is recommended that fruits that are rich in fiber and low in sugar be eaten during the day. Better to avoid dried, canned, sirup fruits.
- Fats- It is advised that a diabetic person must limit his consumption of fats to less than 30% of his calorie intake per day. Also, foods that contain trans-fat should be avoided at all costs.
- Carbohydrates. They should be limited to 250-275 gr per day and better if coming from not processed flours.
- Sweeteners- It is advised that diabetic individuals use sweeteners like Splenda and Stevia instead of the traditional table sugar.
- Eggs- Eggs are a good source of protein and vitamin B12. A diabetic person should take at least one egg per day.

30-Day Meal Plan

DAY	BREAKFAST	LUNCH	DINNER	SNACK
Day-1	Bell Peppered Rings with Egg and Avocado Salsa	Green Salad with Berries and Sweet Potatoes	Cilantro and Lime Broccoli Rice	Chicken and Mushrooms
Day-2	Apple Cinnamon Chia Pudding	Three Bean and Scallion Salad	Spicy Garlic Pasta	Cheeseburger Pie
Day-3	Veggie Fillets Omelets	Rainbow Bean Salad	Simple Beef Roast	Salmon Feta and Pesto Wrap
Day-4	Raspberry Choco Oatmeal	Warm Barley and Squash Salad	Honey Garlic Butter Roasted Carrots	Salmon Cream Cheese and Onion on Bagel
Day-5	Salad with Salsa Verde Vinaigrette	Citrus and Chicken Salad	Colorful vegetable casserole	Melon Cucumber Salad
Day-6	Cottage Pancakes	Blueberry and Chicken Salad	Lentil snack with tomato salsa	Greek Baklava
Day-7	Greek Yogurt and Oat Pancakes	Joseph's Bacon	Clear soup with liver dumplings	Glazed Bananas in Phyllo Nut Cups
Day-8	Apple and Pumpkin Waffles	Texas Goulash	Beef steaks with green asparagus	Salmon Apple Salad Sandwich
Day-9	Buckwheat Crêpes	Roasted Chickpea	Broccoli Omelet	Smoked Salmon and Cheese on Rye Bread
Day-10	Mushroom Frittata	Coconut Meringue Cake	Apple Cinnamon Oatmeal	Pan-Fried Trout
Day-11	Tropical Yogurt Kiwi Bowl	Banana Nut Bread	Nutty Steel-cut Oatmeal with Blueberries	Lemon Cream Fruit Dip
Day-12	Banana Crêpe Cakes	Oyster Stew	Slow "Roasted" Tomatoes	Greek Salad Kabobs
Day-13	Tacos with Pico De Gallo	Pecan-Oatmeal Pancakes	Tomato-Herb Omelet	Green Goddess White Bean Dip
Day-14	Portobello and Chicken Sausage Frittata	Basic Bread Stuffing	Mouth-Watering Egg Casserole	Vietnamese Meatball Lollipops with Dipping Sauce
Day-15	Egg Salad Sandwiches	Dill Pickle Dip	Amazing Overnight Apple and Cinnamon Oatmeal	Blackberry Baked Brie
Day-16	Shrimp with Scallion Grits	Funnel Cakes	Zoodles with Pea Pesto	Creamy Spinach Dip
Day-17	Breakfast Cheddar Zucchini Casserole	Shrimp Burgers	Shrimp Peri-Peri	Pesto Veggie Pizza
Day-18	Banana and Zucchini Bread	Whole Wheat Chapatti	Halibut with Lime and Cilantro	Apple Leather
Day-19	Breakfast Grain Porridge	Sugar Free Strawberry Cheesecake	Autumn Pork Chop with Red Cabbage and Apples	French bread Pizza
Day-20	Tomato Waffles	Shrimps Saganaki	Orange-Marinated Pork Tenderloin	Candied Pecans

Day-21	Breakfast Homemade Poultry Sausage	Jelly Cookies and Peanut Butter	Vegetarian Chipotle Chili	Cauliflower Hummus
Day-22	Sausage and Pepper Burrito	Gorgonzola Tofu Scramble	Wild Rice	Cheese Crisp Crackers
Day-23	Gouda Egg Casserole	Mushroom Bread	Stuffed Bell Peppers with Quinoa	Cheesy Onion Dip
Day-24	Asparagus and Salmon Quiche Cups	Chicken Sandwiches	Mediterranean Burrito	Cheesy Pita Crisps
Day-25	Swiss chard Shakshuka	Sandwich Filling	Prosciutto Wrapped Mozzarella Balls	Cheesy Taco Chips
Day-26	Tropical Fruity Steel Cut Oats	Sandwich Filling	Garlic Chicken Balls	Chewy Granola Bars
Day-27	Farro with Walnuts and Berries	Berry Burrito	Monkey Salad	Chili Lime Tortilla Chips
Day-28	Cranberry Grits	Caesar Salad	Jarlsberg Lunch Omelet	Chocolate Chip Blondie's
Day-29	Super Grain Porridge	Spinach Frittata	Mu Shu Lunch Pork	Cinnamon Apple Chips
Day-30	Coconut Berry Smoothie	Chegg Salad Sandwich	Fiery Jalapeno Poppers	Spicy Bruschetta

Breakfast

1. Bell Peppered Rings with Egg and Avocado Salsa

Preparation Time: 20 minutes **Cooking Time:** 40 minutes **Servings:** 12

Ingredients:
- 2 tomatoes, seeded and diced
- Juice of 1 lime
- ¾ teaspoon of salt, divided
- 2 teaspoons of olive oil, divided
- 8 large eggs
- 2 bell peppers of any color
- 1 avocado, diced
- ½ cup of diced red onion
- 1 jalapeño pepper, minced
- ½ cup plus more for garnish of chopped fresh cilantro
- ¼ teaspoon of ground pepper, divided

Directions:
1. Slice the bottoms and tops off bell peppers, and then finely dice.
2. Remove and discard membranes and seeds.
3. Slice each pepper into four half-inch thick rings.
4. Combine the diced pepper with onion, avocado, cilantro, jalapeno, lime juice, tomatoes, and half a teaspoon of salt in a medium bowl.
5. In a large nonstick skillet, warmth about 1 teaspoon of oil over medium heat.
6. Add 4 bell pepper rings, and then crack about 1 egg into the middle of each ring.
7. Season with ⅛ teaspoon of each pepper and salt.
8. Cook and flip gentle. Transfer into serving plates.
9. Repeat with the rest of the pepper rings and eggs.
10. Serve and enjoy!

Nutrition:
Calories: 285 Carbohydrates: 14.2g Sugar: 5.9g
Protein: 15.1g Dietary Fiber: 5.9g Fat: 19.5g

2. Apple Cinnamon Chia Pudding

Preparation Time: 10 minutes **Cooking Time:** 8 hours (refrigerate) **Servings:** 1

Ingredients:
- ¼ teaspoon of vanilla extract
- ¼ teaspoon of ground cinnamon
- ½ cup of diced apple, divided
- ½ cup of unsweetened milk or other nondairy milk
- 2 tablespoons of chia seeds
- 2 teaspoons of pure maple syrup
- 1 tablespoon of chopped toasted pecans, divided

Directions:
1. In a small bowl, stir chia, almond milk (or other non-dairy milk), maple syrup, chia, cinnamon, and vanilla.
2. Cover and refrigerate for about 8 hours and up to 3 days.
3. Stir well when ready to serve.
4. Spoon about half of the pudding into a serving bowl or glass.
5. Top with half the pecans and apple.
6. Add the rest of the pudding.
7. Top with the rest of the pecans and apples.

8. Serve and enjoy!

Nutrition:
Calories: 233　　Carbohydrates: 27.7g　　Sugar: 14.4g
Protein: 4.8g　　Dietary Fiber: 10.1g　　Fat: 12.7g

3. Veggie Fillets Omelets

Preparation Time: 5 minutes　　**Cooking Time:** 30 minutes　　**Servings:** 4

Ingredients:
- ½ ripe avocado, pitted, peeled, and chopped
- 2 eggs
- 1 cup of refrigerated or frozen egg product,
- 2 tablespoons of water
- 1 snipped fresh chive
- 1 teaspoon of dried basil, crushed
- ¼ teaspoon of salt
- ½ cup of no-salt-added diced tomatoes with garlic, basil, and oregano, well-drained
- ½ cup of cucumber, chopped and seeded
- ½ cup of yellow summer squash
- ¼ teaspoon of ground black pepper
- Nonstick cooking spray
- ¼ cup of shredded reduced-fat Monterey Jack cheese with jalapeño chili peppers

Directions:
For the filling:
1. Mix the tomatoes, cucumber, squash, and avocado in a bowl and set aside.

For each of the omelets:
1. Use the cooking spray in a non-stick skillet.
2. Heat it over medium heat and add about ⅓ cup of the egg mixture.
3. Stir the eggs immediately and continuously until the mixture resembles cooked egg pieces surrounded by liquid eggs.
4. Cook until done for about 30 to 60 seconds.
5. Spoon about ½ cup of the filling onto one side of the omelet.
2. Whisk together the eggs, salt, water, basil, and pepper in a medium bowl.
6. Fold the omelet over the filling and remove the omelet from the pan.
7. Repeat to make about 4 omelets total, wiping the pan between each omelet.
8. Sprinkle about a tbsp. of cheese over each omelet (to taste). Garnish with chives, then serve and enjoy!

Nutrition:
Calories: 128　　Carbohydrates: 6.7g　　Sugars: 4.1g
Protein: 12.3g　　Dietary Fiber: 3.5g　　Fat 6.1g

4. Raspberry Choco Oatmeal

Preparation Time: 10 minutes　　**Cooking Time:** 20 minutes　　**Servings:** 4

Ingredients:
- 3 cups of unsweetened almond milk
- 1 cup of fresh red raspberries
- 1-½ cups of regular rolled oats
- 2 tablespoons of unsweetened cocoa powder
- ½ teaspoon of salt
- 4 teaspoons of sugar-free chocolate-flavor syrup (Optional)

Directions:
1. Mix the salt, oats, and cocoa powder in a saucepan.
2. Add the almonds and milk.
3. Set to a boil over medium heat, stirring occasionally.
4. Lower the heat and simmer until thick, about 5 to 7 minutes, stirring.
5. Cover and remove from heat.
6. Allow resting for about 3 minutes.
7. Divide the oatmeal mixture among 4 bowls.
8. Set each serving with about ¼ cup raspberries.
9. On top of each serving, sprinkle with 1 teaspoon of chocolate syrup (to taste). Serve and enjoy!

Nutrition:
Calories: 157　　Carbohydrates: 26.2g　　Sugars: 2.2g
Protein: 5.4g　　Dietary Fiber: 6.6g　　Fat: 4.7g

5. Salad with Salsa Verde Vinaigrette

Preparation Time: 10 minutes　　**Cooking Time:** 0 minutes　　**Servings:** 1

Ingredients:
- 2 cups of mesclun / other salad greens
- 8 blue corn tortilla chips, set into large pieces
- ½ cup of canned red kidney beans, rinsed
- ¼ avocado, sliced
- 3 tablespoons of salsa verde, such as Frontera brand
- 1 tablespoon plus 1 teaspoon of extra-virgin olive oil, divided
- 2 tablespoons of chopped cilantro, plus more for garnish
- 1 large egg

Directions:
1. Blend the sauce, cilantro and use foil in a small bowl.
2. Mix about half of the mixture with the mesclun in a bowl.
3. Layer the chips, beans, and avocado on top of the salad.
4. Over medium-high heat, heat 1 teaspoon oil in a small nonstick skillet.
5. Add the egg and fry for about ⅔ minutes until the white is cooked, but the yolk is still slightly runny.
6. Serve the egg on top of the salad.
7. Drizzle with the rest of the vinaigrette.
8. Sprinkle with the rest of the cilantro (to taste). Serve and enjoy!

Nutrition:
Calories: 526　　Carbohydrates: 36g　　Sugars: 3g
Protein: 17g　　Dietary Fiber: 14g　　Fat: 33g

6. Cottage Pancakes

Preparation Time: 10 minutes **Cooking Time:** 20 minutes **Servings:** 4

Ingredients:
- 2 cups low-fat cottage cheese
- 4 egg whites
- 2 eggs
- 1 tablespoon pure vanilla extract
- 1½ cups almond flour
- Nonstick cooking spray

Directions:
1. Set the cottage cheese, egg whites, eggs, and vanilla in a blender and pulse to combine.
2. Attach the almond flour to the blender and blend until smooth.
3. Set a large nonstick skillet and lightly coat it with cooking spray.
4. Set ¼ cup of batter per pancake, 4 at a time, into the skillet. Cook the pancakes until the bottoms are firm and golden, about 4 minutes.
5. Flip and cook the other side until they are cooked through, about 3 minutes.
6. Detach the pancakes to a plate and repeat with the remaining batter.
7. Serve with fresh fruit.

Nutrition:
Calories: 345
Fat: 22.1g
Protein: 29.1g
Carbohydrates: 11.1g
Fiber: 4.1g
Sugar: 5.1g
Sodium: 560mg

7. Greek Yogurt and Oat Pancakes

Preparation Time: 5 minutes **Cooking Time:** 20 minutes **Servings:** 4

Ingredients:
- 1 cup 2 percent plain Greek yogurt
- 3 eggs
- 1½ teaspoons pure vanilla extract
- 1 cup rolled oats
- 1 tablespoon granulated sweetener
- 1 teaspoon baking powder
- 1 teaspoon ground cinnamon
- Pinch ground cloves
- Nonstick cooking spray

Directions:
1. Set the yogurt, eggs, and vanilla in a blender and pulse to combine.
2. Add the oats, sweetener, baking powder, cinnamon, and cloves to the blender and blend until the batter is smooth.
3. Set a large skillet and lightly coat it with cooking spray.
4. Spoon ¼ cup of batter per pancake, 4 at a time, into the skillet. Cook the pancakes until the bottoms are firm and golden, about 4 minutes.
5. Flip the pancakes over and cook the other side until they are cooked through, about 3 minutes.
6. Detach the pancakes to a plate and repeat with the remaining batter.
7. Serve with fresh fruit.

Nutrition:
Calories: 244
Fat: 8.1g
Fiber: 4.0g
Protein: 13.1g
Carbohydrates: 28.1g
Sugar: 3.0g
Sodium: 82mg

8. Apple and Pumpkin Waffles

Preparation Time: 10 minutes **Cooking Time:** 20 minutes **Servings:** 6

Ingredients:
- 2¼ cups whole-wheat pastry flour
- 2 tablespoons granulated sweetener
- 1 tablespoon baking powder
- 1 teaspoon ground cinnamon
- 1 teaspoon ground nutmeg
- 4 eggs
- 1¼ cups pure pumpkin purée
- 1 apple, peeled, cored, and finely chopped
- Melted coconut oil, for cooking

Directions:
1. In a large bowl, merge together the flour, sweetener, baking powder, cinnamon, and nutmeg.
2. In a small bowl, set together the eggs and pumpkin.
3. Attach the wet ingredients to the dry and whisk until smooth.
4. Stir the apple into the batter.
5. Cook the waffles based to the waffle maker manufacturer's directions, brushing your waffle iron with melted coconut oil, until all the batter is gone.
6. Serve immediately.

Nutrition:
Calories: 232
Fat: 4.1g
Protein: 10.9g
Carbohydrates: 40.1g
Fiber: 7.1g
Sugar: 5.1g
Sodium: 52mg

9. Buckwheat Crêpes

Preparation Time: 10 minutes **Cooking Time:** 20 minutes **Servings:** 5

Ingredients:
- 1½ cups skim milk
- 3 eggs
- 1 tsp. extra-virgin olive oil, plus more for the skillet
- 1 cup buckwheat flour
- ½ cup whole-wheat flour
- ½ cup 2 percent plain Greek yogurt
- 1 cup sliced strawberries
- 1 cup blueberries

Directions:
1. In a large bowl, merge together the milk, eggs, and 1 teaspoon of oil until well combined.
2. Into a medium bowl, sift together the buckwheat and whole-wheat flours. Attach the dry ingredients to the wet ingredients and whisk until well combined and very smooth.
3. Set the batter to rest for at least 2 hours before cooking.
4. Place a large skillet or crêpe pan over medium-high heat and lightly coat the bottom with oil.
5. Set about ¼ cup of batter into the skillet. Swirl the pan until the batter completely coats the bottom.
6. Cook the crêpe for about 1 minute, then flip it over. Cook the other side of the crêpe for another minute, until lightly browned. Transfer the cooked crêpe to a plate and cover with a clean dish towel to keep warm.
7. Redo until the batter is used up; you should have about 10 crêpes.
8. Spoon 1 tablespoon of yogurt onto each crêpe and place two crêpes on each plate.
9. Top with berries and serve.

Nutrition:
Calories: 330
Fat: 6.9g
Protein: 15.9g
Carbohydrates: 54.1g
Fiber: 7.9g
Sugar: 11.1g
Sodium: 100mg

10. Mushroom Frittata
Preparation Time: 10 minutes   **Cooking Time:** 15 minutes   **Servings:** 4

Ingredients:
- 8 large eggs
- ½ cup skim milk
- ¼ teaspoon ground nutmeg
- Sea salt and freshly ground black pepper
- 2 teaspoons extra-virgin olive oil
- 2 cups sliced wild mushrooms (cremini, oyster, shiitake, portobello, etc.)
- ½ red onion, chopped
- 1 teaspoon minced garlic
- ½ cup goat cheese, crumbled

Directions:
1. Preheat the broiler.
2. In a medium bowl, merge together the eggs, milk, and nutmeg until well combined. Flavor the egg mixture lightly with salt and pepper and set it aside.
3. Set an ovenproof skillet over medium heat and add the oil, coating the bottom completely by tilting the pan.
4. Sauté the mushrooms, onion, and garlic until translucent, about 7 minutes.
5. Pour the egg mixture into the skillet and cook until the bottom of the frittata is set, lifting the edges of the cooked egg to allow the uncooked egg to seep under.
6. Set the skillet to boil until the top is set about 1 minute.
7. Sprinkle the goat cheese on the frittata and broil until the cheese is melted, about 1 minute more.
8. Remove from the oven. Cut into 4 wedges to serve.

Nutrition:
Calories: 227
Fat: 15.1g
Protein: 17.1g
Carbohydrates: 5.1g
Fiber: 0.9g
Sugar: 4.1g
Sodium: 224mg

11. Tropical Yogurt Kiwi Bowl
Preparation Time: 5 minutes   **Cooking Time:** 0 minutes   **Servings:** 2

Ingredients:
- 1½ cups plain low-fat Greek yogurt
- 2 kiwis, peeled and sliced
- 2 tablespoons shredded unsweetened coconut flakes
- 2 tablespoons halved walnuts
- 1 tablespoon chia seeds
- 2 teaspoons honey, divided (optional)

Directions:
1. Divide the yogurt between two small bowls.
2. Top each serving of yogurt with half of the kiwi slices, coconut flakes, walnuts, chia seeds, and honey (if using).

Nutrition:
Calories: 261
Fat: 9.1g
Protein: 21.1g
Carbohydrates: 23.1g
Fiber: 6.1g
Sugar: 14.1g
Sodium: 84mg

12. Banana Crêpe Cakes
Preparation Time: 10 minutes   **Cooking Time:** 0 minutes   **Servings:** 1

Ingredients:
- Avocado oil cooking spray
- 4 ounces (113 g) reduced-fat plain cream cheese, softened
- 2 medium bananas
- 4 large eggs
- ½ teaspoon vanilla extract
- ⅛ teaspoon salt

Directions:
1. Heat a large skillet over low heat. Coat the cooking surface with cooking spray and allow the pan to heat for another 2 to 3 minutes.
2. Meanwhile, in a medium bowl, mash the cream cheese and bananas together with a fork until combined. The bananas can be a little chunky.
3. Set the eggs, vanilla, and salt, and mix well.
4. For each cake, drop 2 tablespoons of the batter onto the warmed skillet and use the bottom of a large spoon or ladle to spread it thin. Let it cook for 7 to 9 minutes.
5. Flip the cake over and cook briefly, about 1 minute.

Nutrition:
Calories: 176
Fat: 9.1g
Protein: 9.1g
Carbohydrates: 15.1g
Fiber: 2.1g
Sugar: 8.1g
Sodium: 214mg

13. Tacos with Pico De Gallo

Preparation Time: 10 minutes **Cooking Time:** 10 minutes **Servings:** 4

Ingredients:
For the Taco Filling:
- Avocado oil cooking spray
- 1 medium green bell pepper, chopped
- 8 large eggs
- ¼ cup shredded sharp Cheddar cheese
- 4 (6-inch) whole-wheat tortillas
- 1 cup fresh spinach leaves
- ½ cup Pico de Gallo
- Scallions, chopped, for garnish (optional)
- Avocado slices, for garnish (optional)

For the Pico De Gallo:
- 1 tomato, diced
- ½ large white onion, diced
- 2 tablespoons chopped fresh cilantro
- ½ jalapeño pepper, stemmed, seeded, and diced
- 1 tablespoon freshly squeezed lime juice
- ⅛ teaspoon salt

Directions:
To Make the Taco Filling
1. Heat a medium skillet over medium-low heat. When hot, coat the cooking surface with cooking spray and put the pepper in the skillet. Cook for 4 minutes.
2. Meanwhile, set the eggs in a medium bowl, then add the cheese and whisk to combine. Pour the eggs and cheese into the skillet with the green peppers and scramble until the eggs are fully cooked, about 5 minutes.
3. Microwave the tortillas very briefly, about 8 seconds.
4. For each serving, top a tortilla with one-quarter of the spinach, eggs, and pico de gallo. Garnish with scallions and avocado slices (if using).

To Make the Pico De Gallo
1. In a medium bowl, merge the tomato, onion, cilantro, pepper, lime juice, and salt. Mix well and serve.

Nutrition:
Calories: 277
Fat: 12.1g
Protein: 16.1g
Carbohydrates: 28.1g
Fiber: 2.9g
Sugar: 8.1g
Sodium: 563mg

14. Portobello and Chicken Sausage Frittata

Preparation Time: 10 minutes **Cooking Time:** 15 minutes **Servings:** 4

Ingredients:
- Avocado oil cooking spray
- 1 cup roughly chopped portobello mushrooms
- 1 medium green bell pepper, diced
- 1 medium red bell pepper, diced
- 8 large eggs
- ¾ cup half-and-half
- ¼ cup unsweetened almond milk
- 6 links maple-flavored chicken or turkey breakfast sausage, cut into ¼-inch pieces

Directions:
1. Preheat the oven to 375F (190C).
2. Warmth a large, oven-safe skillet over medium-low heat. When hot, coat the cooking surface with cooking spray.
3. Heat the mushrooms, green bell pepper, and red bell pepper in the skillet. Cook for 5 minutes.
4. Meanwhile, in a medium bowl, set the eggs, half-and-half, and almond milk.
5. Add the sausage to the skillet and cook for 2 minutes.
6. Set the egg mixture into the skillet, then transfer the skillet from the stove to the oven and set to bake for 15 minutes until the middle is firm and spongy.

Nutrition:
Calories: 281
Fat: 17.1g
Protein: 20.9g
Carbohydrates: 10.1g
Fiber: 2.1g
Sugar: 7.1g
Sodium: 445mg

15. Egg Salad Sandwiches

Preparation Time: 10 minutes **Servings:** 4
Cooking Time: 0 minutes

Ingredients:
- 8 large hardboiled eggs
- 3 tablespoons plain low-fat Greek yogurt
- 1 tablespoon mustard
- ½ teaspoon freshly ground black pepper
- 1 teaspoon chopped fresh chives
- 4 slices 100% whole-wheat bread
- 2 cups fresh spinach, loosely packed

Directions:
1. Skin the eggs and cut them in half.
2. In a large bowl, mash the eggs with a fork, leaving chunks.
3. Add the yogurt, mustard, pepper, and chives, and mix.
4. For each portion, layer 1 slice of bread with one-quarter of the egg salad and spinach.

Nutrition:
Calories: 278
Fat: 12.1g
Protein: 20.1g
Carbohydrates: 23.1g
Fiber: 2.9g
Sugar: 3.1g
Sodium: 365mg

16. Shrimp with Scallion Grits

Preparation Time: 10 minutes **Cooking Time:** 20 minutes **Servings:** 6-8

Ingredients:
- 1½ cups fat-free milk
- 1½ cups water
- 2 bay leaves
- 1 cup stone-ground corn grits
- ¼ cup seafood broth
- 2 garlic cloves, diced
- 2 scallions, white and green parts, thinly diced
- 1 pound (454 g) medium shrimp, shelled and deveined
- ½ teaspoon dried dill
- ½ teaspoon smoked paprika
- ¼ teaspoon celery seeds

Directions:
1. In a medium stockpot, merge the milk, water, and bay leaves and bring to a boil over high heat.
2. Gradually put in the grits, stirring continuously.
3. Set the heat to low, cover, and cook for 5 to 7 minutes, stirring often until the grits are soft and tender. Detach from the heat and discard the bay leaves.
4. In a skillet, bring the broth to boil over medium heat.
5. Attach the garlic and scallions, and sauté for 3 to 5 minutes until softened.
6. Attach the shrimp, dill, paprika, and celery seeds and cook for about 7 minutes until the shrimp is light pink but not overcooked.
7. Set each dish with ¼ cup of grits, topped with shrimp.

Nutrition:
Calories: 198
Fat: 1.0g
Protein: 20.1g
Carbohydrates: 24.9g
Fiber: 1.0g
Sugar: 3.1g
Sodium: 204mg

17. Breakfast Cheddar Zucchini Casserole

Preparation Time: 10 minutes **Cooking Time:** 35 minutes **Servings:** 12-15

Ingredients:
- Nonstick cooking spray
- 6 medium brown eggs
- 8 medium egg whites
- 1 green bell pepper, chopped
- ½ small yellow onion, chopped
- 1 zucchini, finely grated, with water pressed out
- 1 cup shredded reduced-fat Cheddar cheese
- 1 teaspoon paprika
- ½ teaspoon garlic powder

Directions:
1. Preheat the oven to 350F (180C). Set a large cast iron skillet with cooking spray.
2. In a medium bowl, whisk the eggs and egg whites together.
3. Add the bell pepper, onion, zucchini, cheese, paprika, and garlic powder, mix well, and pour into the prepared skillet.
4. Bring the skillet to the oven and bake for 35 minutes. Remove from the oven and let rest for 5 minutes before serving with Broccoli Stalk Slaw.

Nutrition:
Calories: 79
Fat: 4.1g
Protein: 8.1g
Carbohydrates: 2.1g
Fiber: 1.1g
Sugar: 1.2g
Sodium: 133mg

18. Banana and Zucchini Bread

Preparation Time: 15 minutes **Cooking Time:** 45 minutes **Servings:** 4

Ingredients:
- 1½ cups gluten-free all-purpose flour
- 1 cup almond meal
- ½ cup chickpea flour
- 1 teaspoon salt
- 1 teaspoon baking powder
- 1 teaspoon baking soda
- ½ teaspoon ground nutmeg
- ½ teaspoon ground cinnamon
- 3 medium brown eggs
- ¼ cup sunflower seed oil
- 2 ripe bananas, mashed
- 2 zucchinis, grated, with water squeezed out
- 2 teaspoons almond extract

Directions:
1. Preheat the oven to 350F (180C). Line a baking pan with parchment paper.
2. In a large bowl, merge the gluten-free flour, almond meal, chickpea flour, salt, baking powder, baking soda, nutmeg, and cinnamon.
3. In a separate large bowl, set the eggs, oil, bananas, zucchini, and almond extract together well.
4. Set the dry ingredients into the wet ingredients, stir until well combined, and pour into the prepared pan.
5. Bring the pan to the oven and bake for 40 to 45 minutes until a butter knife inserted into the center comes out clean. Remove from the oven and let the bread rest for 15 minutes before serving.

Nutrition:
Calories: 204
Fat: 11.1g
Protein: 6.1g
Carbohydrates: 21.1g
Fiber: 4.1g
Sugar: 4.1g
Sodium: 324mg

19. Breakfast Grain Porridge

Preparation Time: 5 minutes   **Cooking Time:** 35 minutes   **Servings:** 8

Ingredients:
- 1 cup teff
- 1 cup stone-ground corn grits
- 1 cup quinoa
- ¼ teaspoon whole cloves
- 1 tablespoon sunflower seed oil
- 5 cups water
- 2 cups roughly chopped fresh fruit
- 2 cups unsalted crushed nuts

Directions:
1. In an electric pressure cooker, combine the teff, grits, quinoa, and cloves.
2. Add the oil and water, mixing with a fork.
3. Choose the Porridge setting and cook for 20 minutes.
4. Once cooking is complete, allow the pressure to release naturally. Carefully remove the lid.
5. Serve each portion with ¼ cup fresh fruit and ¼ cup nuts of your choice.

Nutrition:
Calories: 418
Fat: 19.1g
Protein: 13.2g
Carbohydrates: 49.1g
Fiber: 9.1g
Sugar: 5.1g
Sodium: 6mg

20. Tomato Waffles

Preparation Time: 15 minutes   **Cooking Time:** 40 minutes   **Servings:** 8

Ingredients:
- 2 cups low-fat buttermilk
- ½ cup crushed tomato
- 1 medium egg
- 2 medium egg whites
- 1 cup gluten-free all-purpose flour
- ½ cup almond flour
- ½ cup coconut flour
- 2 teaspoons baking powder
- ½ teaspoon baking soda
- ½ teaspoon dried chives
- Nonstick cooking spray

Directions:
1. Heat a waffle iron.
2. In a medium bowl, whisk the buttermilk, tomato, egg, and egg whites together.
3. In another bowl, whisk the all-purpose flour, almond flour, coconut flour, baking powder, baking soda, and chives together.
4. Put in the wet ingredients to the dry ingredients.
5. Lightly spray the waffle iron with cooking spray.
6. Gently pour ¼- to ½-cup portions of batter into the waffle iron. Cook time for waffles will vary depending on the kind of waffle iron you use, but it is usually 5 minutes per waffle. (Note: Once the waffle iron is hot, the cooking process is a bit faster.) Repeat until no batter remains.
7. Enjoy the waffles warm with Dandelion Greens with Sweet Onion.

Nutrition:
Calories: 144
Fat: 4.1g
Protein: 7.1g
Carbohydrates: 21.2g
Fiber: 5.1g
Sugar: 2.9g
Sodium: 171mg

21. Breakfast Homemade Poultry Sausage

Preparation Time: 15 minutes   **Cooking Time:** 15 minutes   **Servings:** 10

Ingredients:
- ½ red bell pepper, minced
- ½ orange bell pepper, minced
- ½ jalapeño pepper, minced
- 1 cup roughly chopped tomatoes
- 1 garlic clove, minced
- 1 pound (454 g) ground chicken
- 1 pound (454 g) ground turkey
- ¼ teaspoon smoked paprika
- ¼ teaspoon ground cumin
- 1 tablespoon Worcestershire sauce

Directions:
1. Preheat the oven to 350F (180C).
2. In a large bowl, merge the red bell pepper, orange bell pepper, jalapeño pepper, tomatoes, garlic, chicken, turkey, paprika, cumin, and Worcestershire sauce. Gently fold together until well mixed.
3. With clean hands, take about ⅓-cup portions, and shape into balls about the size of a golf ball.
4. Gently press the balls into flat disks, and place on a rimmed baking sheet in a single layer at least 1 inch apart. Repeat with the remaining meat. You should have 10 patties.
5. Place the baking sheet to the oven and cook for 5 to 7 minutes.
6. Flip the patties and cook for 5 to 7 minutes, or until the juices run clear.
7. Serve with Not-So-Traditional Gravy and Veggie Hash.

Nutrition:
Calories: 125
Fat: 5.1g
Protein: 19.1g
Carbohydrates: 2.1g
Fiber: 0g
Sugar: 1.1g
Sodium: 70mg

22. Sausage and Pepper Burrito

Preparation Time: 10 minutes   **Cooking Time:** 15 minutes   **Servings:** 4

Ingredients:
- 8 ounces (227 g) bulk pork breakfast sausage
- ½ onion, chopped
- 1 green bell pepper, seeded and chopped
- 8 large eggs, beaten
- 4 (6-inch) low-carb tortillas
- 1 cup shredded pepper Jack cheese
- ½ cup sour cream (optional, for serving)
- ½ cup prepared salsa (optional, for serving)

Directions:
1. In a nonstick skillet, cook the sausage, crumbling it with a spoon, until browned, about 5 minutes. Add the onion and bell pepper. Cook and stir until the veggies are fluffy, about 3 minutes. Add the eggs and cook, stirring, until eggs are set, about 3 minutes more.
2. Spoon the egg mixture onto the 4 tortillas. Top each with the cheese and fold into a burrito shape.
3. Serve with sour cream and salsa, if wished.

Nutrition:
Calories: 487   Carbohydrates: 13.1g   Sodium: 811mg
Fat: 36.1g   Fiber: 7.9g
Protein: 31.8g   Sugar: 5.1g

23. Gouda Egg Casserole

Preparation Time: 12 minutes   **Cooking Time:** 20 minutes   **Servings:** 4

Ingredients:
- Nonstick cooking spray
- 1 slice whole grain bread, toasted
- ½ cup shredded smoked Gouda cheese
- 3 slices Canadian bacon, chopped
- 6 large eggs
- ¼ cup half-and-half
- ¼ teaspoon kosher salt
- ¼ teaspoon freshly ground black pepper
- ¼ teaspoon dry mustard

Directions:
1. Spray a cake pan with cooking spray.
2. Set the toast into the bottom of the pan. Set with the cheese and Canadian bacon.
3. In a medium bowl, merge together the egg, salt, pepper, and dry mustard.
4. Spill the egg mixture into the pan. Loosely cover the pan with aluminum foil.
5. Set 1½ cups water into the electric pressure cooker and insert a wire rack or trivet. Set the covered pan on top of the rack.
6. Set and lock the lid of the pressure cooker. Set the valve to sealing. Cook on high pressure.
7. When the cooking is processed, hit Cancel and quick release the pressure.
8. Once the pin drops, unlock and detach the lid.
9. Carefully place the pan from the pressure cooker to a cooling rack and let it sit for 5 minutes.
10. Cut into 4 wedges and serve.

Nutrition:
Calories: 248   Carbohydrates: 7.9g   Sodium: 718mg
Fat: 15.1g   Fiber: 1.2g
Protein: 20.1g   Sugar: 1.1g

24. Asparagus and Salmon Quiche Cups

Preparation Time: 15 minutes   **Cooking Time:** 15 minutes   **Servings:** 2

Ingredients:
- cooking spray
- 4 asparagus spears diced into ½-inch pieces
- 2 tbsp. finely chopped onion
- 3 ounces (85 g) smoked salmon, chopped
- 3 large eggs
- 2 tablespoons 2% milk
- ¼ teaspoon dried dill
- Pinch ground white pepper

Directions:
1. Spill 1½ cups of water into the electric pressure cooker and set a wire rack or trivet.
2. Set the bottom and sides of the ramekins with nonstick cooking spray. Set the asparagus, onion, and salmon between the ramekins.
3. In a measuring cup with a spout, merge together the eggs, milk, dill, and white pepper. Spill half of the egg mixture into each ramekin. Loosely set the ramekins with aluminum foil.
4. Carefully bring the ramekins inside the pot on the rack.
5. Set and lock the lid of the pressure cooker. Set the valve to sealing. Cook on high pressure.
6. When the cooking is processed, hit Cancel and quick release the pressure.
7. Once the pin drops, detach and remove the lid.
8. Carefully remove the ramekins from the pot. Cool and covered.
9. Set a small silicone spatula or a knife around the edge of each ramekin. Set each quiche onto a small plate and serve.

Nutrition:
Calories: 182   Carbohydrates: 2.9g   Sodium: 645mg
Fat: 9.1g   Fiber: 1.0g
Protein: 20.1g   Sugar: 1.1g

25. Swiss chard Shakshuka

Preparation Time: 15 minutes   **Cooking Time:** 20 minutes   **Servings:** 4

Ingredients:
- 4 ounces (113 g) Swiss chard
- 2 tablespoons extra-virgin olive oil

- ½ medium onion, chopped
- ½ teaspoon kosher salt
- ½ teaspoon freshly ground black pepper
- ½ tablespoon Italian seasoning
- 2 teaspoons minced garlic
- 1½ cups Marinara Sauce with Red Lentils or tomato-based pasta sauce
- 4 large eggs
- 1 tablespoon chopped fresh parsley
- 2 tablespoons freshly grated Parmesan cheese

Directions:
1. Detached the stems from the leaves of the Swiss chard. Finely diced the stems; you'll need about ½ cup. Stack the leaves, slice into thin strips, and then chop.
2. Set the cooker to the Sauté setting. When the pot is set, spill in the olive oil.
3. Add the Swiss chard stems, onion, salt, pepper, and Italian seasoning to the pot, and sauté for 3 to 5 minutes.
4. Attach the Swiss chard leaves and garlic, and sauté for more minutes.
5. Hit Cancel. Attach the pasta sauce and let the pot cool.
6. Set 4 evenly spaced indentions in the sauce mixture. Gently crack an egg into a custard cup, and then spill it into one of the indentions. Redo with the remaining eggs.
7. Set and lock the lid of the pressure cooker. Set the valve to sealing. Select low pressure.
8. When the cooking is processed, hit Cancel and quick release the pressure.
9. Once the pin drops, unlock and detach the lid.
10. Set with parsley and Parmesan and serve immediately.

Nutrition:
Calories: 183
Fat: 12.1g
Protein: 8.1g
Carbohydrates: 11.1g
Fiber: 2.9g
Sugar: 5.9g
Sodium: 850mg

26. Tropical Fruity Steel Cut Oats
Preparation Time: 5 minutes **Cooking Time:** 20 minutes **Servings:** 4

Ingredients:
- 1 cup steel cut oats
- 1 cup unsweetened almond milk
- 2 cups coconut water
- ¾ cup chopped peaches
- ¾ cup mango chunks
- 1 (2-inch) vanilla bean, scraped
- Ground cinnamon
- ¼ cup chopped unsalted macadamia nuts

Directions:
1. In the electric pressure cooker, merge the oats, almond milk, coconut water, peaches, mango chunks, and vanilla bean seeds and pod. Mix well. Set and lock the lid of the pressure cooker. Set the valve to sealing.
2. Cook on high pressure for 5 minutes.
3. When the cooking is processed, allow the pressure to release naturally for 10 minutes, then quick release any remaining pressure. Hit Cancel.
4. Once the pin drops, unlock and detach the lid.
5. Discard the vanilla bean pod and mix well.
6. Set the oats into 4 bowls. Place each serving with a sprinkle of cinnamon and 1 tbsp. of the macadamia nuts.

Nutrition:
Calories: 126
Fat: 7.1g
Protein: 1.9g
Carbohydrates: 14.2g
Fiber: 2.9g
Sugar: 8.1g
Sodium: 166mg

27. Farro with Walnuts and Berries
Preparation Time: 8 minutes **Cooking Time:** 15 minutes **Servings:** 6

Ingredients:
- 1 cup farro, rinsed and drained
- 1 cup unsweetened almond milk
- ¼ teaspoon kosher salt
- ½ teaspoon pure vanilla extract
- 1 teaspoon ground cinnamon
- 1 tablespoon pure maple syrup
- 1½ cups fresh blueberries, raspberries, or strawberries (or a combination)
- 6 tablespoons chopped walnuts

Directions:
1. In the electric pressure cooker, combine the farro, almond milk, 1 cup of water, salt, vanilla, cinnamon, and maple syrup.
2. Close and lock the lid. Set the valve to sealing. Cook on high pressure.
3. When the cooking is processed, allow the pressure to release naturally for 10 minutes, then quick release any remaining pressure. Hit Cancel.
4. Once the pin drops, unlock and detach the lid.
5. Stir the farro. Set into bowls and top each serving with ¼ cup of berries and 1 tablespoon of walnuts.

Nutrition:
Calories: 190
Fat: 4.9g
Protein: 5.1g
Carbohydrates: 31.9g
Fiber: 2.9g
Sugar: 6.0g
Sodium: 112mg

28. Cranberry Grits
Preparation Time: 10 minutes **Cooking Time:** 15 minutes **Servings:** 5

Ingredients:
- ¾ cup stone-ground grits or polenta (not instant)
- ½ cup unsweetened dried cranberries
- Pinch kosher salt
- 1 tablespoon unsalted butter or ghee (optional)
- 1 tablespoon half-and-half
- ¼ cup sliced almonds, toasted

Directions:
1. In the electric pressure cooker, stir together the grits, cranberries, salt, and 3 cups of water.
2. Close and lock the lid. Set the valve to sealing.
3. Cook on high pressure for 10 minutes.
4. When the cooking is done, hit Cancel and quick release the pressure.
5. Once the pin drops, unlock and detach the lid.
6. Add the butter (if using) and half-and-half. Stir until the mixture is creamy, adding more half-and-half if necessary.
7. Spoon into serving bowls and sprinkle with almonds.

Nutrition:
Calories: 219
Fat: 10.2g
Protein: 4.9g
Carbohydrates: 32.1g
Fiber: 4.1g
Sugar: 6.9g
Sodium: 30mg

29. Super Grain Porridge
Preparation Time: 5 minutes **Cooking Time:** 40 minutes **Servings:** 7

Ingredients:
- ½ cup steel cut oats
- ½ cup short-grain brown rice
- ½ cup millet
- ½ cup barley
- ⅓ cup wild rice
- ¼ cup corn grits or polenta (not instant)
- 3 tablespoons ground flaxseed
- ½ teaspoon salt
- Ground cinnamon (optional)
- Unsweetened almond milk (optional)
- Berries (optional)
- Sliced almonds or chopped walnuts (optional)

Directions:
1. In the electric pressure cooker, merge the oats, brown rice, millet, barley, wild rice, grits, flaxseed, salt, and 8 cups of water.
2. Set and lock the lid of the pressure cooker. Set the valve to sealing. Cook on high pressure.
3. When the cooking is processed, hit Cancel and allow the pressure to release naturally for 15 minutes, and then set to release any remaining pressure.
4. Once the pin drops, unlock and detach the lid. Stir.
5. Serve with any combination of cinnamon, almond milk, berries, and nuts (if using).

Nutrition:
Calories: 265
Fat: 3.1g
Protein: 7.9g
Carbohydrates: 50.9g
Fiber: 7.1g
Sugar: 0.5g
Sodium: 141mg

30. Coconut Berry Smoothie
Preparation Time: 10 minutes **Cooking Time:** 0 minutes **Servings:** 2

Ingredients:
- ½ cup mixed berries (blueberries, strawberries, blackberries)
- ½ cup leafy greens (kale, spinach)
- ¼ cup unsweetened vanilla nonfat yogurt
- ½ cup unsweetened plain coconut milk
- 2 tablespoons unsweetened coconut flakes
- 1 tablespoon ground flaxseed
- ½ cup ice

Directions:
1. Process the mixed berries, leafy greens, yogurt, coconut milk, coconut flakes, flaxseed, and ice in a blender until all ingredients are combined into a smooth mixture. Pour the mixture into two smoothie glasses.
2. Serve chilled or at room temperature.

Nutrition:
Calories: 183
Fat: 15.3g
Protein: 6.2g
Carbohydrates: 8.2g
Fiber: 4.1g
Sugar: 3.2g
Sodium: 26mg

31. Goat Cheese and Avocado Toast
Preparation Time: 10 minutes **Cooking Time:** 5 minutes **Servings:** 2

Ingredients:
- 2 slices whole-wheat bread, thinly sliced
- ½ avocado
- 2 tablespoons goat cheese, crumbled
- Salt, to taste
- 2 slices of crumbled bacon, for topping (optional)

Directions:
1. Toast the bread slices in a toaster for 2 to 3 minutes on each side until golden brown.
2. Using a large spoon set the avocado flesh out of the skin and transfer to a medium bowl. Smash the flesh until it has a spreadable consistency.
3. Spoon the mashed avocado onto the bread slices and evenly spread it all over.
4. Scatter with crumbled goat cheese and lightly season with salt.
5. Serve topped with crumbled bacon, if desired.

Nutrition:
Calories: 140
Fat: 6.2g
Protein: 5.2g
Carbohydrates: 18.2g
Fiber: 5.1g
Sugar: 0g
Sodium: 197mg

32. Oat Granola with Walnut

Preparation Time: 10 minutes **Cooking Time:** 30 minutes **Servings:** 16

Ingredients:
- 4 cups rolled oats
- ½ cup pepitas
- 1 cup walnut pieces
- 1 teaspoon ground ginger
- 1 teaspoon ground cinnamon
- ¼ teaspoon salt
- ½ cup melted coconut oil
- ½ cup unsweetened applesauce
- 1 teaspoon vanilla extract
- ½ cup dried cherries

Directions:
1. Warmth the oven to 350F and line a baking sheet with parchment paper. Set aside.
2. Mix the oats, pepitas, walnut pieces, ginger, cinnamon, and salt in a large bowl. Gently toss to combine well.
3. In a separate bowl, merge together the melted coconut oil, applesauce, and vanilla extract until completely mixed. Pour into the bowl of dry mixture and stir until the oats are coated in the oil mixture.
4. Set out the mixture on the prepared baking sheet. Bake in the preheated oven for 30 minutes, stirring once halfway through, or until the oats are toasted.
5. Remove the granola from the oven to a wire rack. Allow to sit undisturbed until completely cooled.
6. When cooled, break the granola into small pieces. Stir in the dried cherries and serve.

Nutrition:
Calories: 194
Fat: 13.5g
Protein: 6g
Carbohydrates: 12.2g
Fiber: 4.5g
Sugar: 1.8g
Sodium: 39mg

33. Simple Cottage Cheese Pancakes

Preparation Time: 5 minutes **Cooking Time:** 10 minutes **Servings:** 2

Ingredients:
Batter:
- ½ cup low-fat cottage cheese
- ¼ cup oats
- ⅓ cup egg whites (about 2 egg whites)
- 1 tablespoon stevia
- 1 teaspoon vanilla extract
- Olive oil cooking spray
- Berries or sugar-free jam, for topping (optional)

Directions:
1. Add the cottage cheese, oats, egg whites, stevia and vanilla extract to a food processor. Pulse into a smooth and thick batter.
2. Set a large skillet with cooking spray and place it over medium heat.
3. Slowly pour half of the batter into the pan, tilting the pan to spread it evenly. Cook until the pancake turns golden brown around the edges. Gently flip the pancake and cook.
4. Bring the pancake to a plate and repeat with the remaining batter.
5. Top with the berries or sugar-free jam and serve, if desired.

Nutrition:
Calories: 188
Fat: 1.6g
Protein: 24.6g
Carbohydrates: 18.9g
Fiber: 1.9g
Sugar: 2g
Sodium: 258mg

34. Almond Berry Smoothie

Preparation Time: 5 minutes **Cooking Time:** 0 minutes **Servings:** 4

Ingredients:
- 2 cups frozen berries of choice
- 1 cup plain low-fat Greek yogurt
- 1 cup unsweetened vanilla almond milk
- ½ cup natural almond butter

Directions:
1. In a blender, add the berries, almond milk, yogurt, and almond butter. Process until fully mixed and creamy. Pour into four smoothie glasses.
2. Serve chilled or at room temperature.

Nutrition:
Calories: 279
Fat: 18.2g
Protein: 13.4g
Carbohydrates: 19.1g
Fiber: 6.1g
Sugar: 11.1g
Sodium: 138mg

35. Spinach and Cheese Breakfast Tacos

Preparation Time: 5 minutes **Cooking Time:** 10 minutes **Servings:** 4

Ingredients:
Taco:
- Avocado oil cooking spray
- 1 medium green bell pepper, chopped
- 8 large eggs
- ¼ cup sharp Cheddar cheese, shredded
- 4 (6-inch) whole-wheat tortillas
- 1 cup fresh spinach leaves
- ½ cup Pico de Gallo (see below)
- Chopped scallions, for garnish (optional)
- Avocado slices, for garnish (optional)

Pico De Gallo:
- 1 tomato, diced
- ½ large white onion, diced
- ½ jalapeño pepper, stemmed, seeded, and diced
- 2 tablespoons fresh cilantro, chopped

- 1 tablespoon freshly squeezed lime juice
- ⅛ teaspoon salt

Directions:
Make the Tacos
1. Warmth a skillet over medium-low heat until hot, then spray the skillet with cooking spray.
2. Add the chopped bell pepper and sauté for 4 minutes until tender, stirring occasionally.
3. Meanwhile, whisk together the eggs and shredded cheese in a medium bowl until well blended.
4. Slowly pour the egg mixture into the skillet with the bell pepper. Scramble for about 5 minutes until the eggs are soft and the cheese melts.

Make the Pico De Gallo
1. Mix the tomato, onion, pepper, cilantro, lime juice, and salt in a bowl. Stir well with a fork to incorporate.

5. Remove the egg mixture from the pan to a platter and set aside.
6. Set the tortillas on a plate and microwave for 8 seconds until warm and pliable.
7. Top each tortilla evenly with ¼ cup of spinach leaves and scrambled eggs, followed by the Pico de Gallo.
8. Sprinkle the scallions and avocado slices on top for garnish before serving, if desired.

Nutrition:
Calories: 279
Fat: 15.3g
Protein: 16.2g
Carbohydrates: 28.3g
Fiber: 3.1g
Sugar: 8.2g
Sodium: 560mg

36. Blueberry and Banana Breakfast Cookies
Preparation Time: 10 minutes **Cooking Time:** 15 minutes **Servings:** 4

Ingredients:
- 4 tablespoons unsalted butter, at room temperature
- 2 medium bananas
- 4 large eggs, whisked
- ½ cup unsweetened applesauce
- 1 teaspoon vanilla extract
- ⅔ cup coconut flour
- ¼ teaspoon salt
- 1 cup fresh or frozen blueberries

Directions:
1. Preheat the oven to 375C (190C). Set a baking sheet with parchment paper and set aside.
2. With the back of a fork, mash the butter and bananas in a large bowl until a uniform consistency is achieved.
3. Add the whisked eggs, applesauce, and vanilla extract. Stir to combine well. Add the coconut flour and salt and give the mixture a good stir, then fold in the blueberries.
4. Using a cookie scoop to drop about 2 tablespoons of the mixture onto the prepared baking sheet and flatten each into a rounded biscuit shape with the back of a spoon.
5. Bake in the preheated oven for about 12 minutes, or until the cookies are firm to the touch and lightly browned.
6. Detach from the oven and let the cookies cool for 5 minutes before serving.

Nutrition:
Calories: 307
Fat: 18.2g
Protein: 8.1g
Carbohydrates: 28.1g
Fiber: 7.3g
Sugar: 15.3g
Sodium: 220mg

37. Fresh Huevos Rancheros
Preparation Time: 5 minutes **Cooking Time:** 15 minutes **Servings:** 4

Ingredients:
- Huevos Rancheros:
- 1 cup low-sodium black beans
- ½ cup jarred salsa verde
- Avocado oil cooking spray
- 8 large eggs
- 1 cup fresh Pico de Gallo (see below)
- 4 lime wedges
- Pico De Gallo:
- 1 tomato, diced
- ½ large white onion, diced
- ½ jalapeño pepper, stemmed, seeded, and diced
- 2 tablespoons fresh cilantro, chopped
- 1 tablespoon freshly squeezed lime juice
- ⅛ teaspoon salt

Directions:
Make the Huevos Rancheros
1. In a small saucepan, add the black beans and salsa verde. Cover, and cook over low heat for 10 minutes until the black beans are heated through.
2. Meantime heat a skillet over medium-low heat until hot. Coat the skillet with cooking spray.

3. One at a time, crack the eggs into the skillet and fry about 4 to 5 minutes, or until the eggs white are opaque and the yolks are firm.
4. Remove the black bean and fried eggs from the heat to a plate.
5. To serve, place ¼ of the cooked black beans and pico de gallo on top of two fried eggs, finished by the juice squeezed from the lime wedges.

Make the Pico De Gallo
1. Mix the tomato, onion, pepper, cilantro, lime juice, and salt in a bowl. Stir well with a fork to incorporate.

Nutrition:
Calories: 212
Fat: 9.6g
Protein: 15.2g
Carbohydrates: 18.2g
Fiber: 5.2g
Sugar: 4.2g
Sodium: 440mg

38. Feta Brussels sprouts and Scrambled Eggs

Preparation Time: 5 minutes **Cooking Time:** 15 minutes **Servings:** 4

Ingredients:
- Avocado oil cooking spray
- 4 slices low-sodium turkey bacon
- 20 Brussels sprouts, halved lengthwise
- 8 large eggs, whisked
- ¼ cup crumbled feta cheese

Directions:
1. Warmth a large skillet over medium heat until hot. Coat the skillet with cooking spray.
2. Fry the bacon slices for about 8 minutes until evenly crisp, flipping occasionally.
3. With a slotted spoon, set the bacon to a paper towel-lined plate to drain and cool. Leave the bacon grease in the skillet.
4. Add the Brussels sprouts to the bacon grease in the skillet and cook as you stir for about 6 minutes until browned on both sides.
5. Push the Brussels sprouts to one side of the skillet, add the whisked eggs and scramble until almost set.
6. Once the bacon is cooled, crumble into small pieces.
7. Divide the Brussels sprouts and scrambled eggs among four serving plates. Scatter the tops with crumbled bacon pieces and garnish with feta cheese before serving.

Nutrition:
Calories: 255 Carbohydrates: 10.2g Sodium: 340mg
Fat: 15.3g Fiber: 4.2g
Protein: 21.3g Sugar: 4.2g

39. Breakfast Vegetable and Okra Hash

Preparation Time: 15 minutes **Cooking Time:** 30 minutes **Servings:** 6-8

Ingredients:
- 2 tablespoons extra-virgin olive oil
- 2 garlic cloves, minced
- 1 small yellow onion, finely chopped
- 4 russet potatoes, cut into 1-inch cubes
- 2 tablespoons Creole seasoning
- ¼ cup low-sodium broth
- 1 zucchini, roughly chopped
- 1 green bell pepper, roughly chopped
- 2 cups okra, cut into 1-inch rounds

Directions:
1. Warmth the oil in a skillet over medium-low heat.
2. Toss in the garlic and onion and sauté for 4 minutes, or until the onion is translucent.
3. Add the potatoes, Creole seasoning, and broth and stir well. Cover and cook until the potatoes are pierced easily with the tip of a sharp knife.
4. Add the zucchini, bell pepper, and okra into the skillet. Mix well, and cook uncovered for 7 to 10 minutes, stirring frequently, or until the zucchini is fork-tender.
5. Remove from the heat and serve on plates.

Nutrition:
Calories: 168 Carbohydrates: 30g Sodium: 286mg
Fat: 2.3g Fiber: 5.5g
Protein: 6.7g Sugar: 3.7g

40. Easy and Creamy Grits

Preparation Time: 5 minutes **Cooking Time:** 10 minutes **Servings:** 4

Ingredients:
- 1 cup fat-free milk
- 2 cups water
- 1 cup stone-ground corn grits

Directions:
1. Spill the milk and water into a saucepan over medium heat, then bring to a simmer until warmed through.
2. Add the corn grits and stir well. Set the heat to low and cook, whisking continuously, or until the grits become tender.
3. Remove from the heat and serve warm.

Nutrition:
Calories: 168 Carbohydrates: 33.8g Sodium: 33mg
Fat: 1.1g Fiber: 1.1g
Protein: 6.2g Sugar: 2.8g

41. Carrot and Oat Pancakes

Preparation Time: 10 minutes **Cooking Time:** 8 minutes **Servings:** 4

Ingredients:
- ¼ cup plain Greek yogurt
- 1 tablespoon pure maple syrup
- 1 cup rolled oats
- 1 cup low-fat cottage cheese
- 1 cup shredded carrots
- ½ cup unsweetened plain almond milk
- 2 eggs
- 1 teaspoon baking powder
- 2 tablespoons ground flaxseed
- ½ teaspoon ground cinnamon
- 2 teaspoons canola oil, divided

Directions:
1. Set together the yogurt and maple syrup in a small bowl and set aside.
2. Grind the oats in a blender, or until they are ground into a flour-like consistency.
3. Make the batter: Add the cheese, carrots, almond milk, eggs, baking powder, flaxseed, and cinnamon to the blender, and process until fully mixed and smooth.
4. Heat 1 teaspoon of canola oil in a large skillet over medium heat.

5. Make the pancakes: Pour ¼ cup of batter into the skillet and swirl the pan so the batter covers the bottom evenly. Cook until bubbles form on the surface. Gently flip the pancake and cook until the pancake turns golden brown around the edges. Repeat with the remaining canola oil and batter.
6. Top the pancakes with the maple yogurt and serve warm.

Nutrition:
Calories: 227
Fat: 8.1g
Protein: 14.9g
Carbohydrates: 24.2g
Fiber: 4.0g
Sugar: 7.0g
Sodium: 403mg

42. Savory Breakfast Egg Bites

Preparation Time: 10 minutes **Cooking Time:** 20 minutes **Servings:** 8

Ingredients:
- 6 eggs, beaten
- ¼ cup unsweetened plain almond milk
- ¼ cup crumbled goat cheese
- ½ cup sliced brown mushrooms
- 1 cup chopped spinach
- ¼ cup sliced sun-dried tomatoes
- 1 red bell pepper, diced
- Salt and freshly ground black pepper
- Nonstick cooking spray

Special Equipment:
- An 8-cup muffin tin

Directions:
1. Preheat the oven to 350F (180C). Grease an 8-cup muffin tin with nonstick cooking spray.
2. Make the egg bites: Mix the beaten eggs, almond milk, cheese, mushroom, spinach, tomatoes, bell pepper, salt, and pepper, and stir to mix.
3. Spoon the mixture into the prepared muffin cups, filling each about three-quarters full.
4. Bake for 25 minutes until the topmost is golden brown and a fork comes out clean.
5. Let the egg bites sit for 5 minutes until slightly cooled. Detach from the muffin tin and serve warm.

Nutrition:
Calories: 68
Fat: 4.1g
Protein: 6.2g
Carbohydrates: 2.9g
Fiber: 1.1g
Sugar: 2.0g
Sodium: 126mg

43. Simple Grain-Free Biscuits

Preparation Time: 10 minutes **Cooking Time:** 15 minutes **Servings:** 4

Ingredients:
- 2 tablespoons unsalted butter
- ¼ cup plain low-fat Greek yogurt
- Pinch salt
- 1½ cups finely ground almond flour

Directions:
1. Preheat the oven to 375F (190C). Set a baking sheet with parchment paper and set aside.
2. Place the butter in a microwave-safe bowl and microwave for 15 to 20 seconds, or until it is just enough to soften.
3. Add the yogurt and salt to the bowl of butter and blend well.
4. Slowly pour in the almond flour and keep stirring until the mixture just comes together into slightly sticky, shaggy dough.
5. Use a ¼-cup measuring cup to mound balls of dough onto the parchment-lined baking sheet and flatten each into a rounded biscuit shape, about 1 inch thick.
6. Bake in the preheated oven for 13 to 15 minutes, or until the biscuits are lightly golden brown.
7. Let the biscuits cool before serving.

Nutrition:
Calories: 309
Fat: 28.1g
Protein: 9.9g
Carbohydrates: 8.7g
Fiber: 5.1g
Sugar: 2.0g
Sodium: 31mg

44. Brussels Sprout with Fried Eggs

Preparation Time: 10 minutes **Cooking Time:** 15 minutes **Servings:** 4

Ingredients:
- 3 teaspoons extra-virgin olive oil, divided
- 1 pound (454 g) Brussels sprouts, sliced
- 2 garlic cloves, thinly sliced
- ¼ teaspoon salt
- Juice of 1 lemon
- 4 eggs

Directions:
1. Heat 1½ teaspoons of olive oil in a large skillet over medium heat.
2. Add the Brussels sprouts and sauté for 6 to 8 minutes until crispy and tender, stirring frequently.
3. Set in the garlic and cook until fragrant. Sprinkle with the salt and lemon juice.
4. Detach from the skillet to a plate and set aside.
5. Warmth the remaining oil in the skillet over medium-high heat. Crack the eggs one at a time into the skillet and fry for about 3 minutes. Flip the eggs and continue cooking, or until the egg whites are set and the yolks are cooked to your liking.
6. Serve the fried eggs over the crispy Brussels sprouts.

Nutrition:
Calories: 157
Fat: 8.9g
Protein: 10.1g
Carbohydrates: 11.8g
Fiber: 4.1g
Sugar: 4.0g
Sodium: 233mg

45. Vanilla Coconut Pancakes

Preparation Time: 5 minutes **Cooking Time:** 15 minutes **Servings:** 4

Ingredients:
- ½ cup coconut flour
- 1 teaspoon baking powder
- ½ teaspoon ground cinnamon
- ⅛ teaspoon salt
- 8 large eggs
- ⅓ cup unsweetened almond milk
- 2 tablespoons avocado or coconut oil
- 1 teaspoon vanilla extract

Directions:
1. Set together the flour, baking powder, cinnamon, and salt in a large bowl. Set aside.
2. Beat the eggs with the almond milk, oil, and vanilla in a medium bowl until fully mixed.
3. Warmth a large nonstick skillet over medium-low heat.
4. Make the pancakes: Pour ⅓ cup of batter into the hot skillet, tilting the pan to spread it evenly. Cook until bubbles form on the surface. Flip the pancake and cook for about 3 minutes until the pancake is browned around the edges and cooked through. Repeat with the remaining batter.
5. Serve the pancakes on a plate while warm.

Nutrition:
Calories: 269
Fat: 17.8g
Protein: 13.9g
Carbohydrates: 10.1g
Fiber: 5.1g
Sugar: 1.9g
Sodium: 324mg

46. Cheesy Spinach, Artichoke, and Egg Casserole

Preparation Time: 5 minutes **Cooking Time:** 35 minutes **Servings:** 8

Ingredients:
- 1 (10-ounce / 284-g) package frozen spinach, thawed and drained
- 1 (14-ounce / 397-g) can artichoke hearts, drained
- ¼ cup chopped red bell pepper
- 8 eggs, lightly beaten
- ¼ cup unsweetened plain almond milk
- 2 garlic cloves, minced
- ½ teaspoon salt
- ½ teaspoon freshly ground black pepper
- ½ cup crumbled goat cheese
- Nonstick cooking spray

Directions:
1. Preheat the oven to 375F (190C). Set a baking dish with nonstick cooking spray and set aside.
2. Mix the spinach, artichoke hearts, bell peppers, beaten eggs, almond milk, garlic, salt, and pepper in a large bowl, and stir to incorporate.
3. Spill the mixture into the greased baking dish and scatter the goat cheese on top.
4. Bake in the preheated oven for 35 minutes, or until the top is lightly golden around the edges and eggs are set.
5. Remove from the oven and serve warm.

Nutrition:
Calories: 105
Fat: 4.8g
Protein: 8.9g
Carbohydrates: 6.1g
Fiber: 1.7g
Sugar: 1.0g
Sodium: 486mg

47. Scrumptious Orange Muffins

Preparation Time: 15 minutes **Cooking Time:** 15 minutes **Servings:** 8

Ingredients:

Dry Ingredients:
- 2½ cups finely ground almond flour
- ½ teaspoon baking powder
- ½ teaspoon ground cardamom
- ¾ teaspoon ground cinnamon
- ¼ teaspoon salt

Wet Ingredients:
- 2 large eggs
- 4 tablespoons avocado or coconut oil
- 1 tablespoon raw honey
- ¼ teaspoon vanilla extract
- Grated zest and juice of 1 orange

Special Equipment:
- An 8-cup muffin tin

Directions:
1. Warmth the oven to 375F (190C) and line an 8-cup muffin tin with paper liners.
2. Stir together the almond flour, baking powder, cardamom, cinnamon, and salt in a large bowl. Set aside.
3. Whisk together the eggs, oil, honey, vanilla, zest and juice in a medium bowl. Spill the mixture into the bowl of dry ingredients and stir.
4. Pour the batter into the prepared muffin cups, filling each about three-quarters full.
5. Bake in the oven.
6. Let the muffins cool before serving.

Nutrition:
Calories: 287
Fat: 23.5g
Protein: 7.9g
Carbohydrates: 15.8g
Fiber: 3.8g
Sugar: 9.8g
Sodium: 96mg

48. Easy Turkey Breakfast Patties

Preparation Time: 10 minutes **Cooking Time:** 10 minutes **Servings:** 8

Ingredients:
- 1 pound (454 g) lean ground turkey
- ½ teaspoon dried thyme
- ½ teaspoon dried sage
- ½ teaspoon salt
- ½ teaspoon freshly ground black pepper
- ¼ teaspoon ground fennel seeds
- 1 teaspoon extra-virgin olive oil

Directions:
1. Mix the ground turkey, thyme, sage, salt, pepper, and fennel in a large bowl, and stir until well combined.
2. Form the turkey mixture into 8 equal-sized patties with your hands.
3. In a skillet, heat the olive oil over medium-high heat. Cook the patties per side.
4. Transfer the patties to a plate and serve hot.

Nutrition:
Calories: 91
Fat: 4.8g
Protein: 11.2g
Carbohydrates: 0.1g
Fiber: 0.1g
Sugar: 0g
Sodium: 155mg

49. Quick Breakfast Yogurt Sundae

Preparation Time: 5 minutes **Cooking Time:** 0 minutes **Servings:** 1

Ingredients:
- ¾ cup plain Greek yogurt
- ¼ cup mixed berries (blueberries, strawberries, blackberries)
- 2 tablespoons cashew, walnut, or almond pieces
- 1 tablespoon ground flaxseed
- 2 fresh mint leaves, shredded

Directions:
1. Pour the yogurt into a tall parfait glass and scatter the top with the berries, cashew pieces, and flaxseed.
2. Sprinkle the mint leaves on top for garnish and serve chilled.

Nutrition:
Calories: 238
Fat: 11.2g
Protein: 20.9g
Carbohydrates: 15.8g
Fiber: 4.1g
Sugar: 8.9g
Sodium: 63mg

50. Peanut Butter and Berry Oatmeal

Preparation Time: 5 minutes **Cooking Time:** 5 minutes **Servings:** 2

Ingredients:
- 1½ cups unsweetened vanilla almond milk
- ¾ cup rolled oats
- 1 tablespoon chia seeds
- 2 tablespoons natural peanut butter
- ¼ cup fresh berries, divided (optional)
- 2 tablespoons walnut pieces, divided (optional)

Directions:
1. Add the almond milk, oats, and chia seeds to a small saucepan and bring to a boil.
2. Cover and continue cooking, stirring often, or until the oats have absorbed the milk.
3. Add the peanut butter and keep stirring until the oats are thick and creamy.
4. Divide the oatmeal into two serving bowls. Serve topped with the berries and walnut pieces, if desired.

Nutrition:
Calories: 260
Fat: 13.9g
Protein: 10.1
Carbohydrates: 26.9g
Fiber: 7.1g
Sugar: 1.0g
Sodium: 130mg

51. Caprese Quiche

Preparation Time: 15 minutes **Cooking Time:** 60 minutes **Servings:** 8

Ingredients:
- 10 leaves of chopped fresh basil
- ¼ teaspoon of salt
- 1 pinch of ground black pepper
- 2 tomatoes, diced
- 1 (12 ounces) package of fresh mozzarella cheese
- 1 (9 inches) refrigerated pie crust
- 2 tablespoons of olive oil
- ¼ cup of diced onion
- 8 large eggs
- ¼ teaspoon of lemon juice

Directions:
1. Preheat oven to 350F.
2. Place the crust on an ovenproof dish.
3. Warmth the oil in a skillet.
4. Cook and stir the onion until softened.
5. Set the heat to medium-low. Cook and stir until onion is very gentle.
6. Set mozzarella cheese and tomatoes over the bottom of the pie crust. Whisk eggs, salt, black pepper, lemon juice, basil, and caramelized onion in a large bowl.
7. Pour mixture over cheese and tomatoes.
8. Bake for about 30-40 minutes.
9. Serve and enjoy!

Nutrition:
Calories: 231
Protein: 17.4g
Carbohydrates: 12.6g
Fat: 19.7g
Cholesterol: 213.2mg

52. Spicy Pork on Whole Wheat Rolls
Preparation Time: 30 minutes **Cooking Time:** 30 minutes **Servings:** 1
Ingredients:
- 1 cucumber, sliced and peeled thin
- 1 handful of basil, julienned
- Lettuce
- 1 pound of marinated boneless pork chops
- 1 red pepper, sliced very thin
- Rice Papers for rolling
- (Note: You can add tons of things to these rolls like other herbs, bean sprouts, etc.)

Marinade:
- 3 cloves garlic, minced
- 2 tablespoons of soy sauce (gluten-free)
- 1 teaspoon of Splenda brown sugar
- 2 tablespoons of sesame oil
- 1 shallot, minced
- 2 Thai chilies, diced (or a jalapeno)
- 1 tablespoon of fish sauce
- 2 teaspoons of freshly ground black pepper

Dipping sauce:
- 2 cloves garlic, crushed
- 1 tablespoon of rice vinegar
- 1 tablespoon of sriracha
- ½ cup of hoisin sauce (gluten-free)
- ¼ cup of smooth peanut butter

Directions:
For marinade:
1. Add all ingredients in a bowl, and then add pork chops in a plastic bag with marinade. Let it sit for 1 hour.
2. Grill or cook in a skillet to cook the pork chops for about 4 to 5 minutes per side, depending on the pork chop's thickness.

For the dipping sauce:
1. Add all ingredients to a food processor. Pulse for some time to combine (you can just mix everything well in a bowl if you don't have a food processor).

Making the rolls:
1. Start by pouring some warm water into a large plate.
2. Add a spring roll wrapper into the plate and flip it over once or maybe twice until it becomes flexible and relaxes, probably about 15 to 20 seconds.
3. Move wrapper into a clean work surface.

3. Let it rest before slicing into them for about 10 minutes. Slice them thinly.
4. Prep all over the veggies for rolls and be sure to spend time slicing evenly and thinly.

4. Add some strips of pork and some strips of all other veggies to the wrapper - make sure you don't add the fillings to the middle of the wrapper.
5. Fold the wrapper over the filling, staying away from you, then fold the edges in, and go ahead with making the rolls.
6. Slice them in half once you have all the rolls wrapped.
7. Serve them with the sauce and enjoy it.

Nutrition:
Calories: 314
Fat: 13.4g
Protein: 9.9g
Sodium: 1083.2mg
Sugar: 9.7g

53. Avocado and Egg on a Whole Wheat Toast with Chili Oil
Preparation Time: 0 minutes **Cooking Time:** 10 minutes **Servings:** 1
Ingredients:
- ¼ avocado
- 1 slice whole-wheat bread, toasted
- 1 large egg, fried
- Chili oil for drizzling
- 1 teaspoon of Sriracha
- ¼ teaspoon of ground pepper
- ⅛ teaspoon of garlic powder
- 1 tablespoon of scallion, sliced

Directions:
1. Combine pepper, avocado, and garlic powder in a small bowl.
2. Gently mash together.
3. Top the toast with the avocado mixture, fried egg, and lastly, with a light drizzling of chili oil.

Nutrition:
Calories: 301
Fat: 22.3g
Saturated fat: 4.7g
Protein: 14.1g
Fiber: 8.1g
Sodium: 1167mg
Sugar: 3.1g

54. Scalloped Potatoes
Preparation Time: 50 minutes **Cooking Time:** 0 minutes **Servings:** 1
Ingredients:
- 1 Nonstick cooking spray
- 1 medium yellow onion (set into thin strips)
- ¼ teaspoon of black pepper
- 1 cup of fat-free half-and-half
- ¼ teaspoon of salt (optional)
- 6 medium russet potatoes
- ½ cup of cheddar cheese (reduced-fat, shredded sharp, divided)

Directions:
1. Preheat oven to 400 F.
2. Skin the potatoes and rip them into thin rounds.
3. Use cooking spray to coat a large nonstick skillet.

4. Then sauté potatoes and onions over medium-high heat until the onions turn clear.
   5. Use cooking spray to spray a pie pan and place a thick layer of potatoes and onion in the bottom of the pan.
   6. Add pepper and salt to half-and-half.
   7. Pour half cup of the half-and-half over the potatoes.
   8. Whisk ¼ cup of the cheese on top, and add the potatoes left, then pour a half cup of half-and-half over the potatoes.
   9. Top with the cheese left and bake until potatoes are soft, for about 40 minutes. Serve.

Nutrition:
Calories: 29
Fat: 2.5g
Saturated fat: 1.5g
Protein: 6g
Fiber: 2g
Sodium: 120mg
Potassium: 550mg
Sugar: 5g

55. Blended Berry Oats
Preparation Time: 5 minutes **Cooking Time:** 0 minutes **Servings:** 2
Ingredients:
- ½ cup rolled oats
- 1 tablespoon ground chia seeds
- 4 or 5 pitted dates
- ⅛ teaspoon cinnamon or nutmeg
- ¼ teaspoon almond extract (optional)
- Pinch of sea salt
- 1 cup + 2-3 tablespoons low-fat nondairy milk
- 1¼ cups raspberries, fresh or frozen

Directions:
1. In a blender, combine the oats, chia, dates, cinnamon, almond extract (if using), salt, and 1 cup of the milk. Puree until just combined. Add 1 cup of the raspberries and puree again just to combine.
2. Transfer the mixture to a bowl or jar using a spatula and stir in the remaining ¼ cup berries.
3. Secure and refrigerate overnight (or for several hours, if eating as a snack). Before eating, add the additional 2 to 3 tablespoons of milk to thin, if desired.

Nutrition:
Calorie: 267
Fat: 5g
Protein: 8g
Carbs: 53g
Fiber: 16g
Sugars: 1g
Sodium: 199mg

56. Veggie-Stuffed Omelet
Preparation Time: 15 minutes **Cooking Time:** 10 minutes **Servings:** 1
Ingredients:
- 1 tsp. olive or canola oil
- 2 tbsp. chopped red bell pepper
- 1 tbsp. sliced onion
- ¼ cup sliced mushrooms
- 1 cup loosely packed fresh spinach leaves, washed
- ½ cup fat-free egg product
- 1 tbsp. water
- Pinch salt and pepper
- 1 tbsp. shredded reduced-fat Cheddar cheese

Directions:
1. In 8-inch nonstick skillet, warmth oil and attach bell pepper, onion and mushrooms. Cook until onion is tender. Whisk in spinach and continue cooking.
2. Set vegetables from pan to small bowl. In a bowl, beat egg product, water, salt and pepper with fork or whisk until well mixed.
3. Warmth same skillet over medium-high heat. Quickly spill egg mixture into pan.
4. Stir with spatula to spread eggs continuously as they thicken.
5. Gently slide out of pan onto plate. Serve immediately.

Nutrition:
Calorie: 140
Fat: 5g
Protein: 16g
Carbs: 6g
Sugars: 2g
Fiber: 2g
Sodium: 470mg

57. Rice Breakfast Bake
Preparation Time: 10 minutes **Cooking Time:** 20 minutes **Servings:** 4
Ingredients:
- 1¼ cups vanilla low-fat nondairy milk
- 1 tablespoon ground chia seeds
- 2½ cups cooked short-grain brown rice
- 2 cups sliced ripe (but not overripe) banana (2–2½ medium bananas)
- 1 cup chopped apple
- 2–3 tablespoons raisins (optional)
- 1 teaspoon cinnamon
- ½ teaspoon pure vanilla extract
- ¼ teaspoon freshly grated nutmeg (optional)
- Rounded ⅛ teaspoon sea salt
- 2 tablespoons almond meal (or 1 tablespoon tigernut flour, for nut-free option)
- 2 tablespoons of sugar replacement (like stevia)

Directions:
1. Preheat the oven to 400F.
2. In a blender or food processor, merge the milk, ground chia, and 1 cup of the rice. Puree until smooth. In a bowl, combine the blended mixture, bananas, apple, raisins (if using), cinnamon, vanilla, nutmeg (if using), salt, and the remaining 1½ cups rice.
3. Stir to fully combine.
4. Transfer the mixture to a baking dish (8" x 8" or similar size). In a bowl, merge the almond meal and sugar, and sprinkle it over the rice mixture. Secure with foil and bake for 15 minutes, then remove the foil and bake for another 5 minutes.
5. Detach and let it cool for 5 to 10 minutes, and then serve.

Nutrition:
Calorie: 334
Fat: 5g
Protein: 7g
Carbs: 69g
Sugars: 2g
Fiber: 7g
Sodium: 145mg

58. Potato, Egg and Sausage Frittata
Preparation Time: 30 minutes **Cooking Time:** 20 minutes **Servings:** 4
Ingredients:
- 4 frozen soy-protein breakfast sausage links
- 1 tsp. olive oil
- 2 cups frozen shredded hash brown potatoes
- 4 - 8 egg whites
- ¼ cup fat-free (skim) milk
- ¼ teaspoon salt
- ⅛ teaspoon dried basil leaves
- ⅛ teaspoon dried oregano leaves
- 1½ cups chopped tomatoes
- ½ cup shredded mozzarella
- Pepper
- Chopped green onion

Directions:
1. Divide each sausage link into 8 pieces. Coat 10-inch nonstick skillet with oil; warmth over medium heat. Attach sausage and potatoes; cook 6 to 8 minutes, stirring occasionally, until potatoes are golden brown.
2. In small bowl, set eggs and milk with fork or whisk until well blended. Spill egg mixture over potato mixture. Cook uncovered over medium-low heat. Cook until eggs are thickened; avoid constant stirring.
3. Set salt, basil, oregano, tomatoes and cheese over eggs. Set heat to low; cover and cook about 5 minutes or until center is set and cheese is melted. Sprinkle with pepper and green onion.

Nutrition:
Calorie: 280
Fat: 12g
Protein: 17g
Carbs: 26g
Sugars: 5g
Fiber: 3g
Sodium: 590mg

59. Yogurt Sundae
Preparation Time: 5 minutes **Cooking Time:** 0 minutes **Servings:** 1
Ingredients:
- ¾ cup plain nonfat Greek yogurt
- ¼ cup mixed berries (blueberries, strawberries, blackberries)
- 2 tablespoons cashew, walnut, or almond pieces
- 1 tablespoon ground flaxseed
- 2 fresh mint leaves, shredded

Directions:
1. Spoon the yogurt into a small bowl.
2. Top with the berries, nuts, and flaxseed.
3. Garnish with the mint and serve.

Nutrition:
Calories: 238
Fat: 11g
Protein: 21g
Carbs: 16g
Sugars: 3g
Fiber: 4g
Sodium: 64mg

60. Avocado Goat Cheese Toast
Preparation Time: 5 minutes **Cooking Time:** 10 minutes **Servings:** 2
Ingredients:
- 2 slices whole-wheat thin-sliced bread
- ½ avocado
- 2 tablespoons crumbled goat cheese
- Salt, to taste

Directions:
1. In a toaster or broiler, toast the bread until browned.
2. Remove the flesh from the avocado. In a medium bowl, set a fork to mash the avocado flesh. Spread it onto the toast.
3. Sprinkle with the goat cheese and season lightly with salt.
4. Add any toppings and serve.

Nutrition:
Calories: 137
Fat: 6g
Protein: 5g
Carbs: 18g
Sugars: 0g
Fiber: 5g
Sodium: 195mg

61. Cinnamon Walnut Granola
Preparation Time: 10 minutes **Cooking Time:** 30 minutes **Servings:** 6
Ingredients:
- 4 cups rolled oats
- 1 cup walnut pieces
- ½ cup pepitas
- ¼ teaspoon salt
- 1 teaspoon ground cinnamon
- 1 teaspoon ground ginger
- ½ cup coconut oil, melted
- ½ cup unsweetened applesauce
- 1 teaspoon vanilla extract
- ½ cup dried cherries

Directions:
1. Preheat the oven to 350F (180C). Line a baking sheet with parchment paper.
2. In a large bowl, set the oats, walnuts, pepitas, salt, cinnamon, and ginger.
3. In a large measuring cup, combine the coconut oil, applesauce, and vanilla. Spill over the dry mixture and mix well.
4. Transfer the mixture to the prepared baking sheet. Cook for 30 minutes. Detach from the oven and let the granola sit

undisturbed until completely cool. Break the granola into pieces and whisk in the dried cherries.

Nutrition:
Calories: 224
Fat: 15g
Protein: 5g
Carbs: 20g
Sugars: 5g
Fiber: 3g

5. Set to an airtight container, and store at room temperature for up to 2 weeks.

Sodium: 30mg

62. Chocolate Zucchini Muffins

Preparation Time: 15 minutes **Cooking Time:** 20 minutes **Servings:** 12

Ingredients:
- 1½ cups grated zucchini
- 1½ cups rolled oats
- 1 teaspoon ground cinnamon
- 2 teaspoons baking powder
- ¼ teaspoon salt
- 1 large egg
- 1 teaspoon vanilla extract
- ¼ cup coconut oil, melted
- ½ cup unsweetened applesauce
- ¼ cup honey
- ¼ cup dark chocolate chips

Directions:
1. Preheat the oven to 350F (180C). Set the cups of a 12-cup muffin tin or line with paper baking liners. Set aside.
2. Set the zucchini in a colander over the sink to drain.
3. In a blender jar, process the oats until they resemble flour. Set to a medium mixing bowl and add the cinnamon, baking powder, and salt. Mix well.
4. In another large mixing bowl, merge the egg, vanilla, coconut oil, applesauce, and honey. Stir to combine.
5. Press the zucchini into the colander, draining any liquids, and add to the wet mixture.
6. Set the dry mixture into the wet mixture and mix until no dry spots remain. Fold in the chocolate chips.
7. Set the batter to the muffin tin, filling each cup a little over halfway. Cook for 16 to 18 minutes until the muffins are lightly browned and a toothpick inserted in the center comes out clean.
8. Set in an airtight container, refrigerated, for up to 5 days.

Nutrition:
Calories: 121
Fat: 7g
Protein: 2g
Carbs: 16g
Sugars: 1g
Fiber: 2g

Sodium: 106mg

63. Carrot Oat Pancakes

Preparation Time: 10 minutes **Cooking Time:** 20 minutes **Servings:** 4

Ingredients:
- 1 cup rolled oats
- 1 cup shredded carrots
- 1 cup low-fat cottage cheese
- 2 eggs
- ½ cup unsweetened plain almond milk
- 1 teaspoon baking powder
- ½ teaspoon ground cinnamon
- 2 tablespoons ground flaxseed
- ¼ cup plain nonfat Greek yogurt
- 1 tablespoon pure maple syrup
- 2 teaspoons canola oil, divided

Directions:
1. In a blender jar, process the oats until they resemble flour. Add the carrots, cottage cheese, eggs, almond milk, baking powder, cinnamon, and flaxseed to the jar. Process until smooth.
2. In a small bowl, merge the yogurt and maple syrup and stir well. Set aside.
3. In a large skillet, warmth 1 teaspoon of oil over medium heat. Using a measuring cup, add ¼ cup of batter per pancake to the skillet. Cook until bubbles form on the surface and flip the pancakes. Cook until the pancakes are browned and cooked through. Repeat with the remaining 1 teaspoon of oil and remaining batter.
4. Serve warm topped with the maple yogurt.

Nutrition:
Calories: 227
Fat: 8g
Protein: 14g
Carbs: 24g
Sugars: 3g
Fiber: 4g

Sodium: 402mg

64. Breakfast Egg Bites

Preparation Time: 10 minutes **Cooking Time:** 25 minutes **Servings:** 8

Ingredients:
- Nonstick cooking spray
- 6 eggs, beaten
- ¼ cup unsweetened plain almond milk
- 1 red bell pepper, diced
- 1 cup chopped spinach
- ¼ cup crumbled goat cheese
- ½ cup sliced brown mushrooms
- ¼ cup sliced sun-dried tomatoes
- Salt and ground black pepper, to season

Directions:
1. Preheat the oven to 350F (180C). Spray 8 muffin cups of a 12-cup muffin tin with nonstick cooking spray. Set aside.
2. In a large mixing bowl, merge the eggs, almond milk, bell pepper, spinach, goat cheese, mushrooms, and tomatoes. Season with salt and pepper.
3. Set the prepared muffin cups three-fourths full of the egg mixture. Bake for 20 to 25 minutes until the eggs are set. Let cool slightly and remove the egg bites from the muffin tin.
4. Serve warm, or store in an airtight container in the refrigerator for up to 5 days.

Nutrition:
Calories: 68
Fat: 4g
Protein: 6g
Carbs: 3g
Sugars: 2g
Fiber: 1g
Sodium: 126mg

65. Broccoli Cheese Breakfast Casserole

Preparation Time: 10 minutes **Cooking Time:** 40 minutes **Servings:** 4

Ingredients:
- 2 tablespoons extra-virgin olive oil
- 1 cup sliced button mushrooms
- ½ sweet onion, chopped
- 1 teaspoon minced garlic
- 1 cup chopped broccoli
- 8 large eggs
- ¼ cup skim milk
- 1 tablespoon chopped fresh basil
- 1 cup shredded fat-free Cheddar cheese
- Sea salt
- Freshly ground black pepper

Directions:
1. Preheat the oven to 375F.
2. Set an ovenproof skillet over medium-high heat and add the olive oil.
3. Sauté the mushrooms, onion, and garlic until tender, about 5 minutes.
4. Add the broccoli and sauté for 5 minutes.
5. In a small bowl, whisk together the eggs, milk, and basil.
6. Detach the skillet from the heat and pour the egg mixture evenly over the vegetables.
7. Sprinkle the cheese over the casserole and bake, uncovered, until the eggs are puffy, about 30 minutes.
8. Season with salt and pepper. Serve hot or cold.

Nutrition:
Calories: 273
Fat: 19g
Cholesterol: 429mg
Sodium: 342mg
Carbohydrates: 5g
Sugar: 3g

66. Egg-Stuffed Tomatoes

Preparation Time: 20 minutes **Cooking Time:** 15 minutes **Servings:** 4

Ingredients:
- 1 teaspoon extra-virgin olive oil
- 4 large tomatoes
- ¼ tsp. sea salt, plus more for seasoning
- 1 cup shredded kale
- 2 tablespoons heavy (whipping) cream
- ¼ cup shredded low-fat Swiss cheese
- 4 large eggs
- 1 tablespoon chopped fresh parsley
- Freshly ground black pepper

Directions:
1. Preheat the oven to 375F.
2. Lightly grease an 8-by-8-inch baking dish with the olive oil and set it aside.
3. Cut the tops off the tomatoes and carefully scoop out the insides, leaving the outer shells intact.
4. Whisk the insides of the tomatoes with ¼ teaspoon of salt and set them cut-side down on paper towels for 30 minutes.
5. Place the tomatoes in the baking dish, hollow-side up, and evenly divide the kale between them.
6. Divide the cream and cheese between the tomatoes. Crack and set an egg on top of the cheese in each tomato.
7. Bake the tomatoes until the eggs are set, about 15 minutes.
8. Serve the stuffed tomatoes topped with parsley and seasoned lightly with salt and pepper.

Nutrition:
Calories: 161
Fat: 10g
Cholesterol: 223mg
Sodium: 145mg
Carbohydrates: 10g
Sugar: 5g
Fiber: 3g
Protein: 10g

67. Summer Veggie Scramble

Preparation Time: 10 minutes **Cooking Time:** 10 minutes **Servings:** 4

Ingredients:
- 1 teaspoon extra-virgin olive oil
- 1 scallion, white and green parts, minced
- ½ yellow bell pepper, seeded and minced
- ½ zucchini, diced
- 8 large eggs, beaten
- 1 tomato, cored, seeded, and diced
- 2 teaspoons chopped fresh oregano
- Sea salt
- Freshly ground black pepper

Directions:
1. Set a skillet over medium heat and attach the olive oil.
2. Add the scallion, bell pepper, and zucchini to the skillet and sauté for about 5 minutes.
3. Spill in the eggs and, using a wooden spoon or spatula, scramble them until thick and the eggs are cooked through.
4. Add the tomato and oregano to the skillet and stir to incorporate.
5. Serve seasoned with salt and pepper.

Nutrition:
Calories: 196
Fat: 11g
Cholesterol: 432mg
Sodium: 156mg
Carbohydrates: 4g
Sugar: 2g
Fiber: 1g
Protein: 13g

68. Ratatouille Baked Eggs

Preparation Time: 20 minutes   **Cooking Time:** 50 minutes   **Servings:** 4

Ingredients:
- 2 teaspoons extra-virgin olive oil
- ½ sweet onion, finely chopped
- 2 teaspoons minced garlic
- ½ small eggplant, peeled and diced
- 1 green zucchini, diced
- 1 yellow zucchini, diced
- 1 red bell pepper, seeded and diced
- 3 tomatoes, seeded and chopped
- 1 tablespoon chopped fresh oregano
- 1 tablespoon chopped fresh basil
- Pinch red pepper flakes
- Sea salt
- Freshly ground black pepper
- 4 large eggs

Directions:
1. Preheat the oven to 350F.
2. Set an ovenproof skillet over medium heat and add the olive oil.
3. Toast the onion and garlic until softened and translucent, about 3 minutes. Stir in the eggplant and sauté for about 10 minutes, stirring occasionally. Stir in the zucchini and pepper and sauté for 5 minutes.
4. Reduce the heat to low and cover. Cook until the vegetables are soft.
5. Stir in the tomatoes, oregano, basil, and red pepper flakes, and cook 10 minutes more. Season the ratatouille with salt and pepper.
6. With the use of a spoon, create four wells in the mixture. Crack an egg into each well.
7. Bring the skillet in the oven and bake until the eggs are firm, about 5 minutes.
8. Remove from the oven. Serve the eggs with a generous scoop of vegetables.

Nutrition:
Calories: 147
Fat: 8g.
Cholesterol: 211mg
Sodium: 98mg
Carbohydrates: 13g
Sugar: 2.3g
Fiber: 4g
Protein: 9g

69. Cottage Cheese Almond Pancakes

Preparation Time: 10 minutes   **Cooking Time:** 20 minutes   **Servings:** 4

Ingredients:
- 2 cups low-fat cottage cheese
- 4 egg whites
- 2 eggs
- 1 tablespoon pure vanilla extract
- 1½ cups almond flour
- Nonstick cooking spray

Directions:
1. Place the cottage cheese, egg whites, eggs, and vanilla in a blender and pulse to combine.
2. Attach the almond flour to the blender and blend until smooth.
3. Set a nonstick skillet overheat and lightly coat it with cooking spray.
4. Set ¼ cup of batter per pancake, 4 at a time, into the skillet. Cook the pancakes until the bottoms are firm and golden, about 4 minutes.
5. Roll the pancakes over and cook the other side until they are cooked through, about 3 minutes.
6. Detach the pancakes to a plate and repeat with the remaining batter.
7. Serve with fresh fruit.

Nutrition:
Calories: 344
Fat: 22g
Cholesterol: 110mg
Sodium: 559mg
Carbohydrates: 11g
Sugar: 5g
Fiber: 4g
Protein: 29g

70. Greek Yogurt Cinnamon Pancakes

Preparation Time: 5 minutes   **Cooking Time:** 20 minutes   **Servings:** 4

Ingredients:
- 1 cup 2 percent plain Greek yogurt
- 3 eggs
- 1½ teaspoons pure vanilla extract
- 1 cup rolled oats
- 1 tablespoon granulated sweetener
- 1 teaspoon baking powder
- 1 teaspoon ground cinnamon
- Pinch ground cloves
- Nonstick cooking spray

Directions:
1. Set the yogurt, eggs, and vanilla in a blender and pulse to combine.
2. Add the oats, sweetener, baking powder, cinnamon, and cloves to the blender and blend until the batter is smooth.
3. Set a nonstick skillet and lightly coat it with cooking spray.
4. Set ¼ cup of batter per pancake, 4 at a time, into the skillet. Cook the pancakes until the bottoms are firm and golden, about 4 minutes.
5. Roll the pancakes over and cook the other side until they are cooked through, about 3 minutes.
6. Detach the pancakes to a plate and repeat with the remaining batter.
7. Serve with fresh fruit.

Nutrition:
Calories: 243
Fat: 8g
Cholesterol: 169mg
Sodium: 81mg
Carbohydrates: 28g
Sugar: 3g
Fiber: 4g
Protein: 13g

71. Pumpkin Apple Waffles

Preparation Time: 10 minutes **Cooking Time:** 20 minutes **Servings:** 6

Ingredients:
- 2¼ cups whole-wheat pastry flour
- 2 tablespoons granulated sweetener
- 1 tablespoon baking powder
- 1 teaspoon ground cinnamon
- 1 teaspoon ground nutmeg
- 4 eggs
- 1¼ cups pure pumpkin purée
- 1 apple, peeled, cored, and finely chopped
- Melted coconut oil, for cooking

Directions:
1. In a large bowl, set together the flour, sweetener, baking powder, cinnamon, and nutmeg.
2. In a small bowl, whisk together the eggs and pumpkin.
3. Attach the wet ingredients to the dry and whisk until smooth.
4. Stir the apple into the batter.
5. Cook the waffles based to the waffle maker manufacturer's directions, brushing your waffle iron with melted coconut oil, until all the batter is gone.
6. Serve.

Nutrition:
Calories: 231
Fat: 4g
Cholesterol: 141mg
Sodium: 51mg
Carbohydrates: 40g
Sugar: 5g
Fiber: 7g
Protein: 11g

72. Buckwheat Crêpes with Fruit and Yogurt

Preparation Time: 20 minutes **Cooking Time:** 20 minutes **Servings:** 5

Ingredients:
- 1½ cups skim milk
- 3 eggs
- 2 tsp. extra-virgin olive oil
- 1 cup buckwheat flour
- ½ cup whole-wheat flour
- ½ cup 2 percent plain Greek yogurt
- 1 cup sliced strawberries
- 1 cup blueberries

Directions:
1. In a large bowl, set together the milk, eggs, and 1 teaspoon of oil until well combined.
2. Into a medium bowl, sift together the buckwheat and whole-wheat flours. Attach the dry ingredients to the wet ingredients and whisk until well combined and very smooth.
3. Allow the batter to rest before cooking.
4. Place a large skillet or crêpe pan over medium-high heat and lightly coat the bottom with oil.
5. Spill about ¼ cup of batter into the skillet. Swirl the pan until the batter completely coats the bottom.
6. Cook the crêpe for about 1 minute, then flip it over. Cook the other side of the crêpe for another minute, until lightly browned. Set the cooked crêpe to a plate and cover with a clean dish towel to keep warm.
7. Redo until the batter is used up; you should have about 10 crêpes.
8. Spoon 1 tablespoon of yogurt onto each crêpe and place two crêpes on each plate.
9. Top with berries and serve.

Nutrition:
Calories: 329
Fat: 7g
Cholesterol: 130mg
Sodium: 102mg
Carbohydrates: 54g
Sugar: 11g
Fiber: 8g
Protein: 16g

73. Golden Potato Cakes

Preparation Time: 10 minutes **Cooking Time:** 25 minutes **Servings:** 4

Ingredients:
- ½ pound russet potatoes, peeled, shredded, rinsed, and patted dry
- ¼ sweet onion, chopped
- 1 teaspoon extra-virgin olive oil
- 1 teaspoon chopped fresh thyme
- Sea salt
- Freshly ground black pepper
- Nonstick cooking spray
- 1 cup unsweetened applesauce

Directions:
1. Place the potatoes, onion, oil, and thyme in a large bowl and stir to mix well.
2. Season the potato mixture generously with salt and pepper.
3. Place a large skillet over medium heat and lightly coat it with cooking spray.
4. Set about ¼ cup of potato mixture per cake into the skillet and press down with a spatula, about 4 cakes per batch.
5. Cook about 5 to 7 minutes, then roll the cake over. Cook the other side.
6. Remove the cakes to a plate and repeat with the remaining mixture.
7. Serve with the applesauce.

Nutrition:
Calories: 106
Fat: 3g
Cholesterol: 0mg
Sodium: 6mg
Carbohydrates: 18g
Sugar: 7g
Fiber: 2g
Protein: 1g

74. Wild Mushroom Frittata

Preparation Time: 10 minutes **Cooking Time:** 15 minutes **Servings:** 4

Ingredients:
- 8 large eggs
- ½ cup skim milk

- ¼ teaspoon ground nutmeg
- Sea salt
- Freshly ground black pepper
- 2 teaspoons extra-virgin olive oil
- 2 cups sliced wild mushrooms (cremini, oyster, shiitake, portobello, etc.)
- ½ red onion, chopped
- 1 teaspoon minced garlic
- ½ cup goat cheese, crumbled

Directions:
1. Preheat the broiler.
2. In a bowl, merge together the eggs, milk, and nutmeg until well combined. Flavor the egg mixture lightly with salt and pepper and set it aside.
3. Set an ovenproof skillet over medium heat and add the oil, coating the bottom completely by tilting the pan.
4. Sauté the mushrooms, onion, and garlic until translucent, about 7 minutes.
5. Pour the egg mixture into the skillet and cook until the bottom of the frittata is set, lifting the edges of the cooked egg to allow the uncooked egg to seep under.
6. Set the skillet under the broiler about 1 minute.
7. Sprinkle the goat cheese on the frittata and broil until the cheese is melted, about 1 minute more.
8. Remove from the oven. Cut into 4 wedges to serve.

Nutrition:
Calories: 226
Fat: 15g
Fiber: 1g
Cholesterol: 430mg
Sodium: 223mg
Protein: 17g
Carbohydrates: 5g
Sugar: 4g

75. Tomato and Broccoli

Preparation Time: 15 minutes **Cooking Time:** 10 minutes **Servings:** 2

Ingredients:
- 1lb chopped broccoli
- 1lb cherry tomato
- 1 cup low sodium broth
- 1tbsp dry basil
- 1 minced onion

Directions:
1. Mix all the ingredients in your Instant Pot.
2. Cook on Stew for 10 minutes.
3. Release the pressure naturally.

Nutrition:
Calories: 130
Carbohydrates: 6g
Sugar: 3g
Fat: 10g
Protein: 6g

Lunch

76. Green Salad with Berries and Sweet Potatoes

Preparation Time: 15 minutes **Cooking Time:** 20 minutes **Servings:** 4

Ingredients:

For the vinaigrette
- 1-pint blackberries
- 2 tablespoons red wine vinegar
- 1 tablespoon honey
- 3 tablespoons extra-virgin olive oil
- ¼ teaspoon salt
- Freshly ground black pepper

For the salad
- 1 sweet potato, cubed
- 1 teaspoon extra-virgin olive oil
- 8 cups salad greens (baby spinach, spicy greens, romaine)
- ½ red onion, sliced
- ¼ cup crumbled goat cheese

Directions:

For vinaigrette
1. In a blender jar, combine the blackberries, vinegar, honey, oil, salt, and pepper, and process until smooth. Set aside.

For salad
1. Preheat the oven to 425F. Line a baking sheet with parchment paper.
2. Mix the sweet potato with the olive oil. Bring to the prepared baking sheet and roast, stirring once halfway through, until tender. Remove and cool for a few minutes.
3. In a large bowl, set the greens with the red onion and cooled sweet potato, and drizzle with the vinaigrette. Serve topped with 1 tablespoon of goat cheese per serving.

Nutrition:
Calories: 168
Fat: 1.1g
Protein: 6.2g
Carbohydrates: 33.8g
Fiber: 1.1g
Sugar: 2.8g
Sodium: 33mg

77. Three Bean and Scallion Salad

Preparation Time: 10 minutes **Cooking Time:** 0 minute **Servings:** 8

Ingredients:
- 1 (15-ounce) can low-sodium chickpeas
- 1 (15-ounce) can low-sodium kidney beans
- 1 (15-ounce) can low-sodium white beans
- 1 red bell pepper
- ¼ cup chopped scallions
- ¼ cup finely chopped fresh basil
- 3 garlic cloves, minced
- 2 tablespoons extra-virgin olive oil
- 1 tablespoon red wine vinegar
- 1 teaspoon Dijon mustard
- ¼ teaspoon freshly ground black pepper

Directions:
1. Toss chickpeas, kidney beans, white beans, bell pepper, scallions, basil, and garlic gently.
2. Blend together olive oil, vinegar, mustard, and pepper. Toss with the salad.
3. Wrap and chill for 1 hour.

Nutrition:
Calories: 183
Fat: 12.1g
Protein: 8.1g
Carbohydrates: 11.1g
Fiber: 2.9g
Sugar: 5.9g
Sodium: 850mg

78. Rainbow Bean Salad

Preparation Time: 15 minutes **Cooking Time:** 0 minute **Servings:** 5

Ingredients:
- 1 (15-ounce) can low-sodium black beans
- 1 avocado, diced
- 1 cup cherry
- 3 tomatoes, halved
- 1 cup chopped baby spinach
- ½ cup red bell pepper
- ¼ cup jicama
- ½ cup scallions
- ¼ cup fresh cilantro
- 2 tablespoons lime juice
- 1 tablespoon extra-virgin olive oil
- 2 garlic cloves, minced
- 1 teaspoon honey
- ¼ teaspoon salt
- ¼ teaspoon freshly ground black pepper

Directions:
1. Mix black beans, avocado, tomatoes, spinach, bell pepper, jicama, scallions, and cilantro.
2. Blend lime juice, oil, garlic, honey, salt, and pepper. Add to the salad and toss.
3. Chill for 1 hour before serving.

Nutrition:
Calories: 244
Fat: 8.1g
Protein: 13.1g
Carbohydrates: 28.1g
Fiber: 4.0g
Sugar: 3.0g
Sodium: 82mg

79. Warm Barley and Squash Salad

Preparation Time: 20 minutes **Cooking Time:** 40 minutes **Servings:** 8

Ingredients:
- 1 small butternut squash
- 3 tablespoons extra-virgin olive oil
- 2 cups broccoli florets
- 1 cup pearl barley
- 1 cup toasted chopped walnuts
- 2 cups baby kale - ½ red onion, sliced
- 2 tablespoons balsamic vinegar
- 2 garlic cloves, minced
- ½ teaspoon salt
- ¼ teaspoon black pepper

Directions:
1. Preheat the oven to 400F. Line a baking sheet with parchment paper.
2. Peel off the squash, and slice into dice. In a large bowl, toss the squash with 2 teaspoons of olive oil. Set to the prepared baking sheet and roast for 20 minutes.
3. While the squash is roasting, toss the broccoli in the same bowl with 1 teaspoon of olive oil. After 20 minutes, flip the squash and push it to one side of the baking sheet. Attach the broccoli to the other side and continue to roast for 20 more minutes until tender.
4. While the veggies are roasting, in a pot, cover the barley with several inches of water. Boil, then adjust heat, cover, and simmer for 30 minutes until tender. Drain and rinse.
5. Transfer the barley to a large bowl, and toss with the cooked squash and broccoli, walnuts, kale, and onion.
6. In a small bowl, merge the remaining 2 tablespoons of olive oil, balsamic vinegar, garlic, salt, and pepper. Drizzle dressing over the salad and toss.

Nutrition:
Calories: 176
Fat: 9.1g
Protein: 9.1g
Carbohydrates: 15.1g
Fiber: 2.1g
Sugar: 8.1g
Sodium: 214mg

80. Citrus and Chicken Salad

Preparation Time: 10 minutes **Cooking Time:** 0 minute **Servings:** 4

Ingredients:
- 4 cups baby spinach
- 2 tablespoons extra-virgin olive oil
- 1 tablespoon lemon juice
- ⅛ teaspoon salt
- 2 cups chopped cooked chicken
- 2 mandarin oranges
- ½ peeled grapefruit, sectioned
- ¼ cup sliced almonds

Directions:
1. Toss spinach with the olive oil, lemon juice, salt, and pepper.
2. Add the chicken, oranges, grapefruit, and almonds to the bowl. Toss gently.
3. Arrange on 4 plates and serve.

Nutrition:
Calories: 157
Protein: 5.4g
Carbohydrates: 26.2g
Dietary Fiber: 6.6g
Sugars: 2.2g
Fat: 4.7g

---

81. Blueberry and Chicken Salad

Preparation Time: 10 minutes **Cooking Time:** 0 minute **Servings:** 4

Ingredients:
- 2 cups chopped cooked chicken
- 1 cup fresh blueberries
- ¼ cup almonds
- 1 celery stalk
- ¼ cup red onion
- 1 tablespoon fresh basil
- 1 tablespoon fresh cilantro
- ½ cup plain, vegan mayonnaise
- ¼ teaspoon salt
- ¼ teaspoon freshly ground black pepper
- 8 cups salad greens

Directions:
1. Toss chicken, blueberries, almonds, celery, onion, basil, and cilantro.
2. Blend yogurt, salt, and pepper. Stir chicken salad to combine.
3. Situate 2 cups of salad greens on each of 4 plates and divide the chicken salad among the plates to serve.

Nutrition:
Calories: 265
Fat: 3.1g
Protein: 7.9g
Carbohydrates: 50.9g
Fiber: 7.1g
Sugar: 0.5g
Sodium: 141mg

---

82. Joseph's Bacon

Preparation Time: 10 minutes **Cooking Time:** 15 minutes **Servings:** 6

Ingredients:
- 1 (16 ounces) package of thick-cut bacon

Directions:
1. Set a large baking sheet with 2 sheets of aluminum foil, ensuring the pan is completely covered.
2. Pile the bacon strips on the prepared baking sheet, keeping at least ½-inch space between strips.
3. Set a pan in the cold oven. Heat oven to 425 degrees F
4. Cook bacon for 14 minutes.
5. Place cooked bacon on a paper towel.
6. Let warm for 5 minutes for bacon to firm.
7. Serve and enjoy!

Nutrition:
Calories: 91
Fat: 4.8g
Protein: 11.2g
Carbohydrates: 0.1g
Fiber: 0.1g
Sugar: 0g
Sodium: 155mg

---

83. Texas Goulash

Preparation Time: 25 minutes **Cooking Time:** 60 minutes **Servings:** 6

Ingredients:
- 2 tablespoons of water
- 3 teaspoons of chili powder, or to taste
- 2 teaspoons of white sugar replacement (like stevia)
- ¼ teaspoon of salt
- ¼ teaspoon of ground black pepper
- 1 (8 ounces) package of dry elbow macaroni
- 1 pound of ground beef
- ¼ cup of bell pepper green, hashed
- ¼ cup of chopped onion
- 1-½ cups of canned pinto beans, rinsed and drained
- ¾ cup of tomato paste
- 2 cups of water

Directions:
1. Cook and whisk ground beef, bell pepper, and onion in a large pot over medium-high heat until beef is ready and vegetables are tender, 5 to 7 minutes.
2. Spill pinto beans into a saucepan and cook over medium heat until heated for about 5 minutes. Stir in tomato paste.
3. Combine 2 cups plus 2 tablespoons of water, salt, chili powder, sugar, and pepper in a small bowl.
4. Whisk into the beef mixture. Attach pinto bean mixture. Secure and parboil for 20 minutes.
5. While goulash cooks, set a large pot of lightly salted water to a boil. Cook elbow macaroni in the boiling water, occasionally stirring, until tender yet firm to the bite, about 8 minutes. Drain.
6. Mix cooked macaroni into the goulash, cover.
7. Simmer for 30 minutes to 1 hour.
8. Serve and enjoy!

Nutrition:
Calories: 68
Fat: 4.1g
Protein: 6.2g
Carbohydrates: 2.9g
Fiber: 1.1g
Sugar: 2.0g
Sodium: 126mg

84. Roasted Chickpea
Preparation Time: 10 minutes **Cooking Time:** 40 minutes **Servings:** 4
Ingredients:
- ¼ tsp. of salt to taste
- ground black pepper to taste
- 1 (15 ounces) can of garbanzo beans, drained and rinsed
- 2 teaspoons of olive oil

Directions:
1. Preheat oven to 425F.
2. Set garbanzo beans in a baking dish and pat dry with a paper towel.
3. Bake in the warmth oven, stirring halfway through, for about 22 minutes. Whisk with olive oil, salt, and pepper in a bowl.
4. Bring to the baking dish.
5. Continue baking chickpeas, stirring halfway through, until ready and dry outside, about 22 minutes more.
6. Serve and enjoy!

Nutrition:
Calories: 168
Fat: 1.1g
Protein: 6.2g
Carbohydrates: 33.8g
Fiber: 1.1g
Sugar: 2.8g
Sodium: 33mg

85. Coconut Meringue Cake
Preparation Time: 20 minutes **Cooking Time:** 30 minutes **Servings:** 9
Ingredients:
- 1 teaspoon of vanilla extract
- 3 egg whites
- 1 tablespoon of white sugar replacement (like stevia)
- 1-½ cups of flaked coconut
- ½ cup of butter, softened
- 1 teaspoon of white sugar replacement (like stevia)
- 3 egg yolks
- 1 cup of all-purpose flour
- 1-½ teaspoons of baking powder
- ¼ teaspoon of salt
- ⅓ cup of milk

Directions:
1. Preheat oven to 350F.
2. Grease a 9x9-inch baking pan. Beat butter and 1 tablespoon white sugar until light and fluffy. Beat in egg yolks.
3. Combine flour, baking powder, and salt in a bowl.
4. Attach flour mixture to butter mixture in two parts, alternating with milk and vanilla, beginning and ending with flour mixture.
5. Spread in the prepared pan.
6. For the topping, set the egg whites until soft peaks form. Add 1 teaspoon of the white sugar gradually and beat until egg whites are stiff.
7. Fold in the coconut.
8. Bake in warmth oven until meringue topping starts to brown and a toothpick inserted in the center comes out clean, for about 30 to 35 minutes.

Nutrition:
Calories: 190
Fat: 4.9g
Protein: 5.1g
Carbohydrates: 31.9g
Fiber: 2.9g
Sugar: 6.0g
Sodium: 112mg

86. Banana Nut Bread
Preparation Time: 25 minutes **Cooking Time:** 75 minutes **Servings:** 10
Ingredients:
- 1-½ teaspoons of baking powder
- ½ teaspoon of baking soda
- 1 cup of chopped walnuts
- 2 ripe bananas, mashed
- 1 package of cream cheese, softened
- 1 teaspoon of white sugar replacement (like stevia)
- ½ cup of butter
- 2 eggs, well-beaten
- 2-¼ cups of all-purpose flour

Directions:
1. Preheat an oven to 350F.
2. Grease a 9x5-inch loaf pan.
3. Beat together the cream cheese, eggs, sugar, butter, and banana in a large bowl until smooth.
4. Spill in the flour, baking soda, baking powder, and walnuts until just combined.
5. Spill the batter into the prepared loaf pan.
6. Bake in the warmth oven until a toothpick inserted into the center comes out clean, about 1 hour and 15 minutes.
7. Serve and enjoy!

Nutrition:
Calories: 321
Protein: 7.8g
Carbohydrates: 49.3g
Fat: 25.9g
Cholesterol: 81.8mg

87. Oyster Stew
Preparation Time: 15 minutes **Cooking Time:** 20 minutes **Servings:** 6
Ingredients:
- 2 pints of half-and-half
- 1 teaspoon of dried parsley
- salt and ground black pepper to taste
- 1 (12 ounces) can think of oysters
- 2 dashes of Louisiana-style hot sauce
- ¼ cup of butter

- 1 cup of finely chopped celery
- ½ cup of chopped green onion
- ½ cup of hashed red bell pepper

Directions:
1. Dissolve the butter in a saucepan over medium heat until it begins to foam.
2. Cook and stir the onion, celery, and red bell pepper in the hot butter until soft, about 8 to 10 minutes.
3. Attach the parsley and season with salt and black pepper.
4. Continue cooking until the mixture begins to bubble. Attach the oysters and any liquid from the can lead to the stew along with the Louisiana-style hot sauce.
5. Set the mixture to a simmer and cook until the oysters begin to curl, 10 to 15 minutes.
6. Detach the saucepan from heat and allow the stew to sit 5 minutes before serving.

Nutrition:
Calories: 53
Protein: 9.2g
Carbohydrates: 11.8g
Fat: 30.3g
Cholesterol: 114.2mg

88. Pecan-Oatmeal Pancakes

Preparation Time: 10 minutes **Cooking Time:** 15 minutes **Servings:** 6

Ingredients:
- 1 cup quick cooking oats
- 1½ teaspoons baking powder
- 2 eggs
- ⅓ cup mashed banana
- ⅓ cup skim milk
- ½ teaspoon vanilla extract
- 2 tablespoons chopped pecans
- 1 tablespoon canola oil

Directions:
1. Press the oats in a food processor until they are ground into a powder-like consistency.
2. Transfer the ground oats to a small bowl, along with the baking powder. Mix well.
3. Whisk together the eggs, mashed banana, skim milk, and vanilla in another bowl. Spill into the bowl of dry ingredients and stir with a spatula just until well incorporated. Add the chopped pecans and mix well.
4. In a large nonstick skillet, warmth the canola oil over medium heat.
5. Spoon ¼ cup of batter for each pancake onto the hot skillet, swirling the pan so the batter covers the bottom evenly. Cook until bubbles set on top of the pancake. Flip the pancake and cook for an additional 1 to 2 minutes, or until the pancake is browned and cooked through. Repeat with the remaining batter.
6. Remove from the heat and serve on a plate.

Nutrition:
Calories: 131
Fat: 6.9g
Protein: 5.2g
Carbohydrates: 13.1g
Fiber: 2.0g
Sugar: 2.9g
Sodium: 120mg

89. Basic Bread Stuffing

Preparation Time: 40 minutes **Cooking Time:** 10 minutes **Servings:** 12

Ingredients:
- 6 cups of diced whole-grain bread
- 1 tablespoon of paprika
- ¼ cup of egg substitute
- 2-½ cups of low fat, low sodium chicken broth
- 3 onions, diced
- salt and pepper to flavor

Directions:
1. In a skillet over medium-high warmth, heat ½ cup of the chicken broth.
2. Attach onions and cook for 10 minutes until softened.
3. Combine the remaining broth, cooked onions, bread, egg replacer, paprika, salt, and pepper in a bowl. Stir
4. Set mixture inside the cavity of a turkey.
5. If stuffing is to be baked separately from the turkey, set stuffing in a preheated 350-degree oven and bake for 45 minutes. Serve.

Nutrition:
Calories: 67
Protein: 3.9g
Carbohydrates: 10.7g
Fat: 1.1g
Cholesterol: 0.1mg

90. Dill Pickle Dip

Preparation Time: 10 minutes **Cooking Time:** 15 minutes **Servings:** 12

Ingredients:
- 2 tablespoons of pickle juice, or more to taste
- 1 teaspoon of dried dill weed
- ½ teaspoon of kosher salt
- 1 pinch of ground black pepper
- 1 (8 ounces) package of cream cheese, at room temperature
- 1 cup of chopped dill pickles, or more to taste
- ¼ cup of chopped sweet onion

Directions:
1. Spill cream cheese in a bowl with a wooden spoon until smooth.
2. Stir in dill pickles, onion, pickle juice, dill weed, salt, and pepper until evenly distributed.
3. Refrigerate before serving, at least 1 hour.

Nutrition:
Calories: 79
Protein: 2.5g
Carbohydrates: 2.4g
Fat: 5.5g
Cholesterol: 20.5mg

91. Funnel Cakes

Preparation Time: 15 minutes **Cooking Time:** 10 minutes **Servings:** 4

Ingredients:
- 1 tablespoon of baking powder
- 1 teaspoon of vanilla extract
- ½ teaspoon of salt
- ¼ cup of vegetable oil for frying or as needed
- 1-¼ cups of all-purpose flour, or more if needed
- 1 teaspoon of white sugar replacement (like stevia)
- ½ cup of water
- ½ cup of milk
- 1 egg

Directions:
1. Pour oil into a frying pan.
2. Heat over medium-high heat.
3. Mix sugar, flour, water, egg, milk, baking powder, vanilla extract and salt in a blender until smooth.
4. Attach more flour if the batter is too watery.
5. Place your finger over the hole in a funnel and fill the funnel with the batter.
6. Place the filled funnel on top of the pan, release your finger.
7. Swirl batter in hot oil; cook until golden brown, about 4 to 5 minutes per side. Serve.

Nutrition:
Calories: 56   Carbohydrates: 46.1g   Cholesterol: 48.9mg
Protein: 8.6g   Fat: 2.5g

92. Shrimp Burgers

Preparation Time: 35 minutes **Cooking Time:** 10 minutes **Servings:** 3

Ingredients:
- 1 teaspoon of seafood seasoning (such as Old Bay®)
- ground black pepper to taste
- 2 tablespoons of frozen butter cut into small pieces
- 2 tablespoons of canola oil, or as needed
- ¾ pound of raw, peeled shrimp
- 1 egg, beaten
- ¼ cup of breadcrumbs
- 1 small lemon, juiced
- 1 tablespoon of lemon zest

Directions:
1. Set to chop 3 or 4 shrimp and place in a bowl.
2. Pulse remaining shrimp in a food processor and transfer them to the bowl with the sliced shrimp.
3. Combine egg, breadcrumbs, lemon juice, lemon zest, seafood seasoning, and black pepper in a bowl.
4. Add shrimp and butter. Form mixture into three patties and refrigerate for at least 30 minutes.
5. Warmth oil in a skillet over medium heat.
6. Cook patties until browned, 4 to 5 minutes.

Nutrition:
Calories: 89   Carbohydrates: 6.4g   Cholesterol: 254.6mg
Protein: 21g   Fat: 20.1g

93. Whole Wheat Chapatti

Preparation Time: 10 minutes **Cooking Time:** 2 minutes **Servings:** 4

Ingredients:
- 1 tablespoon of olive oil
- ¼ cup of water
- 1 cup of whole wheat flour
- 1 pinch of salt

Directions:
1. Spill together the flour and salt in a bowl.
2. Whisk in olive oil and water, and then knead until firm and elastic.
3. Set into four balls and roll as flat as possible with a rolling pin.
4. Heat a frying pan over medium-high heat.
5. Cook the chapatti on both sides until golden brown.
6. If desired, drizzle with additional olive oil before serving. Serve and enjoy!

Nutrition:
Calories: 123   Carbohydrates: 22.8g
Protein: 3.1g   Fat: 2.9g

94. Sugar Free Strawberry Cheesecake

Preparation Time: 10 minutes **Cooking Time:** 60 minutes **Servings:** 1

Ingredients:
- 1 package of cream cheese, softened
- 1-½ cups of milk
- 1 (1 ounce) package of cheesecake flavor sugar-free instant pudding mix
- 2 pints of fresh strawberries, sliced
- ¾ cup of graham cracker crumbs
- 3 tablespoons of butter, melted
- ¼ teaspoon of ground cinnamon
- ¼ teaspoon of ground nutmeg

Directions:
1. Mix graham cracker crumbs, cinnamon, melted butter and nutmeg in a bowl.
2. Press the mixture into a cake pan. Refrigerate while you prepare the filling.
3. Merge the cream cheese in a bowl with an electric mixer on medium speed until softened.
4. Set the speed to low, and gradually attach the milk, a little at a time (the mixture will be watery).
5. Beat in pudding mix until filling is thick and smooth.
6. Spread half of the cream cheese filling into the bottom of the graham cracker crust.
7. Spread half of the strawberries on top of the filling.
8. Repeat cheesecake layer and strawberry layer.
9. Chill the pie in the refrigerator until cold, at least 1 hour. Serve and enjoy!

Nutrition:
Calories: 269
Protein: 5.4g
Carbohydrates: 24.2g
Fat: 16.4g
Cholesterol: 58.2mg

95. Shrimps Saganaki

Preparation Time: 10 minutes **Cooking Time:** 35 minutes **Servings:** 4

Ingredients:
- 1 can of diced tomatoes, drained
- ¼ teaspoon of garlic powder (Optional)
- ¼ cup of olive oil
- 1 (8 ounces) package of feta cheese, cubed
- 1 pound of medium shrimp, with shells
- 1 onion, chopped
- 2 tablespoons of chopped fresh parsley
- 1 cup of white wine
- 1 pinch of salt and pepper to flavor

Directions:
1. Set about 2 inches of water to a boil in a large saucepan.
2. Attach the shrimp; the water should just cover them.
3. Boil for 5 minutes, then drain, keeping the liquid, and set aside.
4. Heat about 2 tbsp. of oil in a saucepan.
5. Attach the onions; cook and stir until the onions are soft.
6. Merge in the parsley, wine, tomatoes, garlic powder, and remaining olive oil.
7. Simmer, occasionally stirring, for about 30 minutes.
8. While the sauce is broiling, the shrimps should have become cool enough to handle.
9. First, detach the legs, and then pull off the shells, parting the head and tail.
10. When the sauce is thickened, spill in the shrimp stock and shrimp. Bring to a parboil and cook for about 5 minutes.
11. Attach the feta cheese and remove it from the heat. Let stand until the cheese starts to dissolve.
12. Serve warm and enjoy!

Nutrition:
Calories: 357
Protein: 24.8g
Carbohydrates: 11.1g
Fat: 19.6g
Cholesterol: 223.1mg

96. Jelly Cookies and Peanut Butter

Preparation Time: 30 minutes **Cooking Time:** 30 minutes **Servings:** 54

Ingredients:
- 1-¼ cups of all-purpose flour
- ¾ teaspoon of baking soda
- ½ teaspoon of baking powder
- ¼ teaspoon of salt
- ½ cup of any flavor fruit jam
- ½ cup of shortening
- ½ cup of peanut butter
- 1 tablespoon of white sugar replacement (like stevia)
- 1 tablespoon of packed Splenda brown sugar
- 1 egg

Directions:
1. In a mixing bowl, merge the peanut butter and sugars.
2. Beat in egg. Combine dry ingredients. Gradually add to creamed mixture.
3. Cover and chill for 1 hour.
4. Roll into 1 inch balls. Set 2 inches distant on greased baking sheets. Flatten slightly.
5. Bake at 375 F for 10 minutes.
6. Cool on the wire rack, spread jam on the bottom of half of the cookie.
7. Top with remaining cookie half.
8. Serve and enjoy!

Nutrition:
Calories: 66
Protein: 1g
Carbohydrates: 8.6g
Fat: 3.2g
Cholesterol: 3.4mg

97. Gorgonzola Tofu Scramble

Preparation Time: 15 minutes **Cooking Time:** 10 minutes **Servings:** 2

Ingredients:
- ⅔ cup of sliced white mushrooms
- 1 cup of packed fresh spinach
- 3 tablespoons of crumbled Gorgonzola cheese
- 1-½ tablespoons of olive oil
- ⅓ (12 ounces) package of extra-firm tofu, cut into cubes
- ¼ cup of chopped red onion
- 1 clove garlic, minced

Directions:
1. Warmth olive oil in a skillet; cook and spill the tofu, onion, and garlic until onion is tender, 5 to 10 minutes.
2. Attach mushrooms; cook and stir until mushrooms are tender and tofu is lightly browned, for about 5 to 10 minutes.
3. Remove skillet from heat.
4. Mix spinach and Gorgonzola cheese into the tofu mixture until spinach begins to wilt and the cheese dissolves from the heat of the tofu mixture.

Nutrition:
Calories: 210
Protein: 9.7g
Carbohydrates: 5.1g
Fat: 17.5g
Cholesterol: 17mg

98. Mushroom Bread

Preparation Time: 15 minutes **Cooking Time:** 15 minutes **Servings:** 12

Ingredients:
- 2 cups of shredded mozzarella cheese
- 6 green onions, chopped
- 3 cloves of garlic, minced
- 1 loaf of Italian bread

- ½ cup of softened butter

Directions:
1. Preheat an oven to 400F.
2. Diced bread in half horizontally. Set out most of the soft bread to form a shell.
3. Keep the pulled-out bread for another use.
4. Mix cheese, green onions, butter, mushrooms, and garlic.

- 1 pound of sliced fresh mushrooms

5. Drizzle the mixture on both cut sides of the bread.
6. Place the bread, cut sides up on the baking sheet.
7. Bake in warmth oven until the cheese has melted, for about 10 to 15 minutes. Cut in wedges to serve.

Nutrition:
Calories: 226
Protein: 12.9g
Carbohydrates: 19.6g
Fat: 10.8g
Cholesterol: 32.4mg

99. Chicken Sandwiches

Preparation Time: 20 minutes **Cooking Time:** 20 minutes **Servings:** 12

Ingredients:
- 1 (8 ounces) container of pineapple cream cheese spread
- 6 large leaves Boston lettuce, halved
- 1 (16 ounces) package of fresh strawberries, hulled and diced
- 3 cups of diced, cooked chicken breast meat
- 3 green onions, minced
- ½ cup of refrigerated poppy seed salad dressing, or to taste
- 12 Hawaiian sweet bread rolls, sliced in half horizontally

Directions:
1. Mix chicken with green onions in a bowl. Moisten with poppy seed salad dressing.
2. Spread both cut sides of each Hawaiian roll with pineapple cream cheese. Place a half leaf of lettuce on the bottom half of each roll.
3. Top with ¼ cup of chicken mixture and about 2 tablespoons of strawberries.
4. Place tops on rolls to serve.

Nutrition:
Calories: 121
Protein: 22.9g
Carbohydrates: 38g
Fat: 11.1g
Cholesterol: 82.8mg

100. Kohl Slaw

Preparation Time: 15 minutes **Cooking Time:** 15 minutes **Servings:** 4

Ingredients:
- 1 teaspoon of Dijon mustard (optional)
- salt and ground black pepper to taste
- 2 crisp apples, shredded
- 2 kohlrabi bulbs, peeled and shredded
- 4 carrots, shredded
- 2 tablespoons of cherry vinegar
- 1 tablespoon of vegan mayonnaise
- 1 tablespoon of agave nectar
- 1 tablespoon of brown mustard seeds

Directions:
1. Whisk vinegar, mustard seeds, Dijon mustard, salt, vegan mayonnaise, agave nectar, and pepper together in a bowl until dressing is smooth.
2. Stir the kohlrabi, apples and carrots into the dressing until coated.
3. Cover the bowl with plastic wrap.
4. Refrigerate to let the flavors blend for 1 hour.

Nutrition:
Calories: 96
Protein: 3.2g
Carbohydrates: 29.4g
Fat: 2.6g

101. Sandwich Filling

Preparation Time: 25 minutes **Cooking Time:** 10 minutes **Servings:** 8

Ingredients:
- ¼ cup of chopped pimento peppers
- 1 (8 ounces) can of mushrooms, drained and chopped
- 8 ounces of extra-sharp Cheddar cheese, shredded
- 1-½ teaspoons of chili powder
- salt and ground black pepper to taste
- ½ pound of lean ground beef
- 8 ounces of tomato sauce
- ½ cup of finely chopped onion
- ½ cup of chopped black olives
- 4 hamburger buns, split

Directions:
1. Preheat oven to 400 F.
2. Cook and spill the ground beef in a large skillet until well browned, about 10 minutes; drain fat.
3. Place cooked beef in a large bowl.
4. Stir in tomato sauce, mushrooms, Cheddar cheese, chili powder, onion, black olives, pimentos, salt, and black pepper.
5. Spoon sandwich filling on hamburger bun bottoms, spreading to the edges. The filling should be approximately ½-inch thick in the center of the sandwich.
6. Bake in the warmth oven until the edges start to bubble for about 5-10 minutes. Bring in the oven to broil and continue to cook. Serve and enjoy!

Nutrition:
Calories: 2622
Protein: 15.6g
Carbohydrates: 16.2g
Fat: 15.1g
Cholesterol: 49.5mg

102. Berry Burrito

Preparation Time: 10 minutes **Cooking Time:** 10 minutes **Servings:** 4

Ingredients:
- 1 cup of fresh blueberries
- 1 cup of diced fresh strawberries
- 4 Mission® Large/Burrito-size of Flour Tortillas
- 8 tablespoons of JIF® Peanut Butter

- 4 tablespoons of SMUCKER'S® Strawberry Jam

Directions:
1. Spread each tortilla with ¼ of each ingredient.
2. Roll into a burrito and cut in half.
3. Serve immediately or wrap in plastic wrap.
4. Place in refrigerator for later use. Serve and enjoy!

Nutrition:
Calories: 184
Protein: 14.5g
Carbohydrates: 64.4g
Fat: 21.2g
Sodium: 780.8mg

---

103. Caesar Salad

Preparation Time: 10 minutes
Cooking Time: 60 minutes
Servings: 2

Ingredients:
- ⅓ cup of grated Parmesan cheese
- ¼ cup of half-and-half
- 2 tablespoons of fresh lemon juice
- 1 tablespoon of Dijon mustard
- 2 anchovy fillets
- 2 cloves garlic, chopped, or to taste
- 1 cup of mayonnaise
- 2 teaspoons of Worcestershire sauce

Directions:
1. Merge the anchovy fillets with garlic in a food processor.
2. Pulse several times to form a paste.
3. Process mayonnaise, lemon juice, Dijon mustard, Parmesan cheese, half-and-half, and Worcestershire sauce with anchovy mixture until dressing is smooth.
4. Refrigerate for 1 hour before serving.

Nutrition:
Calories: 48
Protein: 0.4g
Carbohydrates: 0.4g
Fat: 4.9g
Cholesterol: 3.3mg

---

104. Spinach Frittata

Preparation Time: 25 minutes
Cooking Time: 10 minutes
Servings: 3

Ingredients:
- salt and pepper to taste
- 1 pinch of ground nutmeg
- 3 tablespoons of butter
- 2 packages of frozen chopped spinach
- 3 matzo crackers
- 4 eggs, beaten
- 2 tablespoons of Parmesan cheese

Directions:
1. Warmth the spinach in a saucepan with ½ cup of water until completely thawed.
2. Strain the spinach, keeping half the amount of liquid.
3. Set the matzo into a medium-size mixing bowl and spill the spinach and the remaining liquid over them.
4. Merge thoroughly until the matzo is softened.
5. Attach the Parmesan, eggs, salt, nutmeg, and pepper.
6. Heat the margarine in a 12-inch skillet and attach the spinach mixture.
7. Cook on medium heat, unsealed for 5 minutes on each side.
8. Set with grated Parmesan and serve immediately.

Nutrition:
Calories: 153
Protein: 18.7g
Carbohydrates: 29.8g
Fat: 15.3g
Cholesterol: 280.5mg

---

105. Chegg Salad Sandwich

Preparation Time: 25 minutes
Cooking Time: 20 minutes
Servings: 5

Ingredients:
- 10 slices of sandwich bread
- 5 lettuce leaves
- 5 slices of ripe tomato
- 2 avocados, sliced
- 5 slices of Monterey Jack cheese
- 2 (10 ounces) cans of chunk chicken, drained
- ⅓ cup of mayonnaise
- ⅓ cup of coleslaw dressing
- 4 hard-cooked eggs, chopped
- ¼ cup of Parmesan curls, shaved with a vegetable peeler
- ¼ cup of chopped pine nuts
- 2 tablespoons of sweet dill pickle relish
- ¼ cup of chopped white onion
- salt and freshly ground black pepper to flavor

Directions:
1. Lightly combine the canned chicken, eggs, chopped onion, mayonnaise, coleslaw dressing, Parmesan cheese, pine nuts, pickle relish, salt, and pepper to season in a large bowl.
2. Cover and refrigerate for 30 minutes to blend the flavors.
3. To assemble sandwiches, spread a generous serving on each of 5 slices of sandwich bread, place lettuce leaves, sliced tomato, sliced avocado, and Monterey Jack cheese slices over the salad.
4. Top with remaining sandwich bread slices.

Nutrition:
Calories: 310
Protein: 45.6g
Carbohydrates: 30.4g
Fat: 57.1g
Cholesterol: 280.4mg

---

106. Bean Beef Burritos

Preparation Time: 25 minutes
Cooking Time: 10 minutes
Servings: 10

Ingredients:
- 1 (4 ounces) can of chopped green chilies, drained
- 10 flour tortillas
- 1 (16 ounces) package of shredded mild Cheddar cheese
- 1 pound of lean ground beef
- 1 small onion, chopped
- 2 cloves garlic, minced, or to taste

- 1 (16 ounces) can of refried beans
- 1 (1 ounce) package of burrito seasoning

Directions:
1. Warmth a large skillet; cook and spill the beef in the skillet.
2. Add onion and garlic. Drain and discard grease. Add refried beans and a burrito seasoning packet.
3. Attach the green chilies and heat over low heat, occasionally stirring, until heated through, about 5 minutes more.
4. Set tortillas in a damp paper towel and cook in a microwave oven until warmed through, about 10 seconds.
5. Spoon about 2 tablespoons of beef mixture into a warm tortilla.
6. Add a tablespoon or more of Cheddar cheese.
7. Fold both sides in, then fold and roll over mixture to seal burrito.
8. Repeat with remaining tortillas, filling, and cheese.
9. Wrap burritos in waxed paper or place them in plastic bags.
10. Store in the freezer for use in lunch boxes.

Nutrition:
Calories: 102　　Carbohydrates: 37.8g　　Cholesterol: 82.2mg
Protein: 26.6g　　Fat: 16.5g

107. Roasted Persimmon Burrata Focaccia

Preparation Time: 10 minutes　　**Cooking Time:** 40 minutes　　**Servings:** 2

Ingredients:
- ½ teaspoon of salt
- 2 sprigs of fresh rosemary, leaves stripped
- ½ cup of burrata cheese
- 1 precooked 9-inches focaccia flatbread
- 1 Fuyu persimmon, skinned and sliced into ¼-inch rounds
- 4 teaspoons of olive oil, divided

Directions:
1. Preheat the oven to 350F.
2. Set a baking sheet with parchment paper.
3. Set persimmon slices onto the prepared baking sheet.
4. Drizzle with 2 tsp. of olive oil and sprinkle salt on top.
5. Sprinkle ½ of the rosemary leaves over the persimmon slices.
6. Roast in the warmth oven for 20 minutes. Turn persimmon slices over and roast.
7. Detach the baking sheet from the oven. Increase the temperature to 200 C. Place focaccia on a baking sheet.
8. Bake focaccia until warmed through. Remove from oven. Set focaccia with roasted persimmon slices.
9. Tear burrata cheese and lay evenly on the focaccia, avoiding the persimmon slices.
10. Reserve about 1 tablespoon of rosemary leaves and sprinkle the rest on top.
11. Return focaccia to the hot oven. Bake until warmed, and burrata cheese has dissolved slightly for about 5 minutes.
12. Set with reserved fresh rosemary leaves and drizzle the remaining 2 teaspoons olive oil on top.
13. Slice and serve hot. Enjoy!

Nutrition:
Calories: 387　　Carbohydrates: 78.9g　　Cholesterol: 45.1mg
Protein: 28.1g　　Fat: 21.1g

108. Spicy Ahi Poke Salad

Preparation Time: 15 minutes　　**Cooking Time:** 73 minutes　　**Servings:** 5

Ingredients:
- 1 pound of ahi tuna, cut into ½-inch cubes
- ¼ cup of minced green onion
- 1 teaspoon of minced fresh ginger
- 1 teaspoon of red pepper flakes
- 1 teaspoon of sriracha sauce, or to taste
- 2 tablespoons of ground roasted macadamia nuts
- 2 tablespoons of chopped fresh cilantro, or more to taste
- 1 tablespoon of fresh lime juice
- 2 teaspoons of sesame oil, or more to taste

Directions:
1. Combine the tuna, green onion, sesame oil, ginger, red pepper flakes, macadamia nuts, cilantro, lime juice and sriracha sauce in a bowl
2. Refrigerate for about 2 hours.

Nutrition:
Calories: 144　　Carbohydrates: 1.6g　　Cholesterol: 40.9mg
Protein: 21.7g　　Fat: 5.5g

109. Peaches with Creamy Chicken Salad

Preparation Time: 15 minutes　　**Cooking Time:** 10 minutes　　**Servings:** 4

Ingredients:
- ¼ cup of chopped walnuts (optional)
- 1 tablespoon of chopped green onions
- 2 ounces of cream cheese, softened
- 1 tablespoon of poppy seed salad dressing
- ¾ cup of diced cooked chicken
- ½ fresh peach, diced

Directions:
1. Merge the cream cheese and poppy seed dressing together in a bowl.
2. Set in peach, walnuts, chicken, and green onions until well coated.

Nutrition:
Calories: 125　　Carbohydrates: 5.5g　　Cholesterol: 71.1mg
Protein: 15.8g　　Fat: 25.3g

110. Asian Frittata

Preparation Time: 25 minutes　　**Cooking Time:** 10 minutes　　**Servings:** 6

Ingredients:
- 4 eggs
- 8 egg whites

- 2 tablespoons of light soy sauce
- 1 cup of fresh bean sprouts
- 1 cup of trimmed and halved snow peas
- 1 tablespoon of sesame seeds
- 1 tablespoon of peanut oil
- 3 green onions, minced
- 2 teaspoons of grated fresh ginger
- 2 cloves of garlic, minced
- 1 cup of diced red bell pepper

Directions:
1. Preheat oven to 350 F.
2. In a large nonstick, warmth the oil. Add the scallions, ginger, and garlic and sauté for 1 to 2 minutes.
3. Add the red pepper and sauté for 3 minutes.
4. In a medium-size mixing bowl, merge together the eggs and soy sauce. Attach to the skillet.
5. Cook until eggs are inserted on the bottom.
6. Set the bean sprouts and snow peas over the eggs. Sprinkle with sesame seeds.
7. Set in the oven at 350 degrees F, and bake just until the top is set, about 8 to 10 minutes.
8. Observe that eggs are just cooked and do not become tough.
9. Set oven to broil.
10. Broil the frittata for 30 seconds just to give it a nice browned color.
11. Serve in wedges and enjoy!

Nutrition:
Calories: 125
Protein: 11g
Carbohydrates: 6.1g
Fat: 6.5g
Cholesterol: 32mg

111. Baked Cheese and Macaroni with Tomato
Preparation Time: 35 minutes **Cooking Time:** 45 minutes **Servings:** 6

Ingredients:
- 8 tablespoons of butter, divided
- ¼ cup of dry breadcrumbs
- 1 pound of macaroni
- 1 can of condensed tomato soup
- 1-¼ cups of milk
- 3 cups of shredded Cheddar cheese

Directions:
1. Preheat oven to 350 F.
2. Set a pot of salted water to a boil.
3. Spill in pasta and cook for 8 to 10 minutes or until al dente; drain.
4. In a large bowl, combine macaroni, soup, milk, cheese, and six tablespoons of butter. Pour into 9 by 13 baking dish.
5. Set with breadcrumbs and dot with remaining butter.
6. Bake for 45 minutes until golden brown and bubbly. Serve and enjoy!

Nutrition:
Calories: 240
Protein: 28.3g
Carbohydrates: 71.4g
Fat: 37.9g
Cholesterol: 104.1mg

112. Swiss and Crab Melts
Preparation Time: 10 minutes **Cooking Time:** 15 minutes **Servings:** 4

Ingredients:
- hot pepper sauce to taste
- 4 thick slices of Italian bread, cut in half
- 1½ cups of Swiss cheese
- 1 (8 ounces) package of cream cheese
- 1 cup of cooked crabmeat
- 1 clove garlic, chopped
- salt and pepper to taste
- 1 tbsp. of chopped fresh parsley for garnish

Directions:
1. Preheat oven to 425 F.
2. Whisk in a medium bowl until frothy.
3. Stir in cream cheese, crab, salt, garlic, pepper and hot sauce.
4. Spread on bread slices and top with Swiss cheese.
5. Place on a baking sheet.
6. Bake for about 10 to 15 minutes in the preheated oven until the cheese has melted and browned slightly.
7. Sprinkle with parsley. Serve and enjoy!

Nutrition:
Calories: 163
Protein: 39.1g
Carbohydrates: 22g
Fat: 46.4g

113. Flapjack
Preparation Time: 10 minutes **Cooking Time:** 30 minutes **Servings:** 10

Ingredients:
- 3 cups of rolled oats
- ¼ cup of raisins
- ½ cup of butter or margarine
- 1 teaspoon of packed Splenda brown sugar
- 4 tablespoons of golden syrup or corn syrup

Directions:
1. Preheat the oven to 350 F.
2. In a saucepan over low heat, combine the butter, brown sugar, and golden syrup.
3. Cook, occasionally stirring until butter and sugar have melted.
4. Stir in the oats and raisins until coated.
5. Pour into a 7 or 8-inch square baking pan.
6. The mixture should be about 1 inch thick.
7. Bake for 30 minutes in the warmth oven or until the top is golden.
8. Cut into squares, then leave to cool completely before removing from the pan. Serve.

Nutrition:
Calories: 241
Protein: 4.4g
Carbohydrates: 28.7g
Fat: 8.8g
Cholesterol: 23.4mg

114. Biryani

Preparation Time: 20 minutes **Cooking Time:** 35 minutes **Servings:** 6

Ingredients:

Mixed Masala Paste:
- 4 whole black peppercorns
- 4 dried red chili peppers
- ½ inch of piece ginger
- 2 whole cloves
- 1 piece of cinnamon stick

Rice:
- 1 cup of French-fried onions
- 1 cup of finely chopped fresh cilantro

Vegetables:
- ¼ cup of peas
- 4 tablespoons of vegetable oil
- ½ teaspoon of ground cumin
- ½ teaspoon of ground coriander
- salt to taste
- 2 tomatoes, chopped
- 2 onions, chopped
- 15 cloves garlic, minced
- 1½ cups of basmati rice
- 2 cups of water
- 1 cup of water
- ¼ cup of chopped potatoes
- ¼ cup of chopped cauliflower
- ¼ cup of chopped French-style green beans

Directions:
1. In a food processor, combine tomatoes, dried peppers, ginger, cloves, cinnamon, onions, garlic, peppercorns, and salt.
2. Grind to a fine paste and set to a bowl.
3. Place rice in a bowl with water until covered. Allow soaking for 15 minutes.
4. Place 2 cups of water to a boil in a saucepan, add drained rice and a pinch of salt.
5. Cook until the rice begins to soften, about 10 minutes.
6. Drain and transfer to a bowl. Add the cilantro, fried onions, and salt.
7. Set 1 cup of water to a boil in a saucepan.
8. Add the cauliflower, potatoes, green beans, and peas. Cook until the vegetables begin to become soft, 3 to 4 minutes. Then drain.
9. Heat the oil in a skillet. Add 1 tablespoon masala paste mixture and sauté for 1 minute.
10. Add the partially cooked vegetables and 1 pinch of salt; Then stir.
11. Add the cilantro, cumin and ½ teaspoon masala paste.
12. Stir and add a little water. Cook for 5 minutes.
13. Seal and cook until vegetables are tender, about 4 minutes longer.
14. Distribute the partially cooked rice. Then loosen over the vegetables in the pan, leaving small spaces for steam to escape.
15. Cover and cook until rice is tender, about 10 minutes.

Nutrition:
Calories: 315
Protein: 4.5g
Carbohydrates: 64.4g
Fat: 21.7g

115. Veggie and Mustard Pasta Salad

Preparation Time: 10 minutes **Cooking Time:** 20 minutes **Servings:** 4

Ingredients:
- ½ cup of chopped fresh tomato
- ½ cup of hashed red bell pepper
- 3 tablespoons of prepared Dijon-style mustard
- 2 tablespoons of Italian-style salad dressing
- 1 tablespoon of balsamic vinaigrette salad dressing
- ½ teaspoon of celery seed, crushed
- 2 cups of macaroni
- ½ cup of frozen peas, thawed
- ½ cup of chopped fresh broccoli
- ½ cup of julienned carrots
- ½ cup of canned yellow corn
- 1 tablespoon of Splenda brown sugar

Directions:
1. In a pot of salted boiling water.
2. Cook pasta until al dente, wash under cold water and drain.
3. Combine the pasta, peas, broccoli, carrot, corn, tomatoes, and bell peppers in a large bowl.
4. Prepare the dressing by whisking together the Italian, vinegar, brown sugar, celery seed, mustard, and basil.
5. Pour over salad and mix well.
6. Refrigerate until chilled.

Nutrition:
Calories: 302
Protein: 9.2g
Carbohydrates: 56.5g
Fat: 4.5g

116. Mashed Garlicky Potatoes

Preparation Time: 5 minutes **Cooking Time:** 45 minutes **Servings:** 50-100

Ingredients:
- 3 cups of chopped garlic
- ½ cup of salt
- ½ cup of dried oregano
- 50 pounds of unpeeled red potatoes, quartered
- 8 pounds of butter, room temperature
- 3 pounds of Romano cheese, grated

Directions:
1. Set a pot of salted water to a simmer.
2. Attach potatoes and cook until tender but still firm for about 45 minutes.
3. Whisk in butter, cheese, garlic, salt, and oregano.
4. Smash with a potato masher or with electric mixer. Serve and enjoy!

Nutrition:
Calories: 243
Protein: 8.8g
Carbohydrates: 43.2g
Fat: 33.4g
Cholesterol: 92.3mg

117. Toffee Nut Cookies

Preparation Time: 15 minutes **Cooking Time:** 15 minutes **Servings:** 24

Ingredients:
- 1 teaspoon of vanilla extract
- 1 cup of semisweet chocolate chips
- 1 cup of chopped walnuts (optional)
- 1 cup of butter
- 1 teaspoon of packed brown sugar
- 1 egg yolk
- 2 cups of sifted all-purpose flour

Directions:
1. Set together butter or margarine and brown sugar.
2. Attach 1 egg yolk, sifted flour, and vanilla. The batter will be stiff.
3. Spread on a greased 13 x 9-inch cookie sheet.
4. Bake at 375 degrees F for 12-15 minutes until golden brown.
5. While still warm, add 1 cup of semi-sweet chocolate chips to the top of the cookie until melted.
6. Spread with a knife until the top is covered.
7. Add chopped nuts, if desired.
8. Let cool, then cut into squares.

Nutrition:
Calories: 201 Carbohydrates: 1g Cholesterol: 28.9mg
Protein: 4.3g Fat: 10.3g

---

118. Nutella-Like Brioche Star

Preparation Time: 40 minutes **Cooking Time:** 20 minutes **Servings:** 8

Ingredients:
- 2 large eggs, separated
- 2 tablespoons of unsalted butter, melted
- 1 teaspoon of vegetable oil, or as needed
- 1 cup of sugar-free chocolate-hazelnut spread
- 3⅓ cups of bread flour
- 1 teaspoon of white sugar
- 2 teaspoons of active dry yeast
- 1 pinch of salt
- ¾ cup of milk, warmed

Directions:
1. Set bread flour, sugar, yeast, and salt in the bowl of a stand mixer.
2. Mix with a fork. Add milk, butter, and egg yolks.
3. Attach the dough hook and knead until dough forms a ball and feels smooth and elastic, about 10 minutes.
4. Pour vegetable oil into a large bowl. Add dough. Wrap around to coat with oil.
5. Seal with a damp cloth and let rise in a warm place until doubled, 1 to 2 hours.
6. Place dough to a flat work surface.
7. Form gently to knock the air out. Set dough into a flat oblong shape then rolls into a log.
8. Cut the dough into 4 equal pieces.
9. Keep the dough sealed with a damp cloth while you work with 1 piece at a time.
10. Dust work surface with a little flour.
11. With a rolling pin, roll out the first piece of dough.
12. Set a round 8-inch pan or plate on top. Use a knife to cut dough into an 8-inch circle.

Nutrition:
Calories: 412 Carbohydrates: 44.2g Cholesterol: 46mg
Protein: 11.7g Fat: 12g

---

119. Barbecue Beef

Preparation Time: 5 minutes **Cooking Time:** 2 hours 45 minutes **Servings:** 16

Ingredients:
- 2 tablespoons of brown sugar
- 1 teaspoon of mustard powder
- 2 tablespoons of Worcestershire sauce
- ½ tsp. of ground black pepper
- 1 teaspoon of salt
- 4 pounds of boneless chuck roast
- 1 onion, chopped
- 2 tablespoons of butter
- 3 tablespoons of distilled white vinegar
- 12 ounces of chili sauce
- ⅛ teaspoon of ground cayenne pepper
- 3 cloves garlic, minced

Directions:
1. Place roast in a large covered pan.
2. Roast at 325 F for 2 hours until the meat falls apart and shreds easily.
3. In a large skillet, dissolve butter over medium heat.
4. Add onions, and sauté until onions become translucent.
5. Stir in vinegar and chili sauce.
6. Fill empty chili sauce bottle with water, shake, and pour liquid into skillet.
7. Mix in mustard, Worcestershire sauce, black pepper, brown sugar, salt, cayenne pepper, and garlic.
8. Cook sauce over low heat, often stirring, until thickened.
9. With two forks, shred roasted beef.
10. Stir meat into the sauce in the skillet.
11. Simmer for 30 minutes, serve and enjoy!

Nutrition:
Calories: 200 Carbohydrates: 4.9g Cholesterol: 52.9mg
Protein: 14.4g Fat: 13.3g

---

120. Hamburger Muffins

Preparation Time: 10 minutes **Cooking Time:** 30 minutes **Servings:** 12

Ingredients:
- 1 small onion, chopped
- 1 (10.75 ounces) can of condensed cream of mushroom soup
- salt and pepper to taste
- 3 tablespoons of butter, softened
- 12 slices of white bread
- 1¼ pound of ground beef

- 1 egg

Directions:
1. Preheat the oven to 350 F.
2. Set a butter one side of each slice of bread and press each slice butter-side down into the cups of a muffin tin.
3. In a medium bowl, merge the onion, cream of mushroom soup, ground beef, egg, salt, and pepper until well blended.
4. Fill each bread cup with the mixture.
5. Sprinkle shredded Cheddar cheese over the tops.
6. Bake for 30 minutes in the warmth oven or until meat is cooked through. Serve and enjoy!

- ¾ cup of shredded Cheddar cheese

Nutrition:
Calories: 300
Protein: 12.9g
Carbohydrates: 15g
Fat: 21g
Cholesterol: 72.4mg

121. Brie Quesadillas with Pears

Preparation Time: 10 minutes **Cooking Time:** 40 minutes **Servings:** 3

Ingredients:
- salt and ground black pepper to taste
- 1 (10 ounces) package of flour tortillas
- cooking spray
- 6 ounces of Brie cheese, cut into ¼-inch slices
- 2 ripe of Danjou pears, sliced ¼-inch thick
- 2 teaspoons of olive oil
- 1 sweet onion, thinly sliced
- 2 tablespoons of honey
- ½ teaspoon of dried thyme

Directions:
1. Heat the oil in a skillet.
2. Cook onion until soft, 10 to 13 minutes. Stir in the thyme, honey, pepper and salt.
3. Continue to cook until golden brown, about 7 minutes longer.
4. Add pears and cook until just softened, 2 minutes. Remove from heat and set aside.
5. Warmth a skillet over medium heat and grease with cooking spray.
6. Place 1 tortilla in the skillet and top with ¼ of the Brie.
7. Add ¼ of the onion and pear mixture and top with a second tortilla.
8. Bake quesadilla in smaller skillet until lightly browned, 2 to 3 minutes.
9. Flip and continue cooking until ready on the other side, 2 to 3 minutes longer. Transfer to a plate.
10. Repeat with remaining tortillas, Brie cheese, and onion-pear mixture.
11. Slice the quesadillas into wedges.

Nutrition:
Calories: 386
Protein: 15.7g
Carbohydrates: 63.4g
Fat: 19.9g
Cholesterol: 42.5mg

122. Chocolate Fudge

Preparation Time: 10 minutes **Cooking Time:** 3 minutes **Servings:** 6

Ingredients:
- 1-½ cups of chopped walnuts (optional)
- 1 cup of miniature marshmallows
- 2 cups of semisweet chocolate chips
- 1 can of sweetened condensed milk
- 2 tsp. of vanilla extract

Directions:
1. Grease an 8x8 inch square pan.
2. Set the chocolate chips and sweetened condensed milk in a microwave-safe bowl.
3. Microwave for 3 minutes, occasionally stirring, until smooth.
4. Stir in vanilla, then add marshmallows and nuts.
5. Spread into the prepared pan.
6. Chill until firm. Serve and enjoy!

Nutrition:
Calories: 223
Protein: 6.5g
Carbohydrates: 22.7g
Fat: 12.6g
Cholesterol: 8.3mg

123. Zhug Chicken

Preparation Time: 10 minutes **Cooking Time:** 45 minutes **Servings:** 4

Ingredients:
- 2 bone-in chicken thighs with skin
- 2 whole artichokes
- ½ cup of marinated sun-dried tomatoes, drained
- ½ lemon, juiced
- ¾ cup of zhug sauce, divided
- 1 boneless chicken breast
- 2 chicken legs, bone-in and skin-on
- ½ cup of pitted Kalamata olives, drained

Directions:
1. Spread 1-½ tablespoons zhug sauce over each piece of chicken.
2. Bring to the refrigerator to marinate for at least 2 hours.
3. Remove from refrigerator about 20 minutes before cooking.
4. Remove outer leaves from artichokes.
5. Cut the artichokes into quarters. Set them in a bowl, cover with water and add the lemon juice.
6. Stir in the artichokes and set aside.
7. Preheat the oven to 325F.
8. Set the marinated chicken in a deep baking dish.
9. Drain the artichokes and add them around the chicken.
10. Add the sun-dried tomatoes and olives.
11. Bake sealed until the chicken is no longer pink in the center and the juices run clear, about 45 minutes.

Nutrition:
Calories: 124
Protein: 32.5g
Carbohydrates: 14.4g
Fat: 19.3g
Cholesterol: 119.5mg

124. Spicy Tuna Sandwich

Preparation Time: 15 minutes **Cooking Time:** 15 minutes **Servings:** 2

Ingredients:
- 1 tablespoon of chopped dill pickles
- 2 leaves of lettuce
- 2 slices of Swiss cheese
- 4 slices of bread
- 2 slices of tomato
- 1 (5 ounces) can of tuna, drained
- ¼ cup of mayonnaise
- 1-½ teaspoons of cream-style horseradish sauce
- 2 thin slices of red onion

Directions:
1. Combine the drained tuna, horseradish sauce, mayonnaise, and pickles in a small bowl.
2. Set a slice of Swiss cheese on 2 slices of bread and cover with a lettuce leaf.
3. Spread the tuna mixture over the lettuce leaves.
4. Add the red onion and tomato slices.
5. Finish with the remaining slices of bread. Serve.

Nutrition:
Calories: 312 Carbohydrates: 21.2g Cholesterol: 56.9mg
Protein: 24.3g Fat: 19.7g

---

125. Sunny Poutine

Preparation Time: 10 minutes **Cooking Time:** 35 minutes **Servings:** 4

Ingredients:
- salt and ground black pepper to taste
- ½ cup of prepared hollandaise sauce
- 1 tablespoon of chopped fresh chives
- 1 (16 ounces) package of frozen French fries
- 12 slices of bacon
- cooking spray
- 4 eggs

Directions:
1. Preheat oven to 425F.
2. Set frozen French fries in a single layer on a baking sheet.
3. Bake in the preheated oven until golden, for about 20 minutes; keep warm.
4. Set bacon in a large skillet and cook over medium-high heat, occasionally turning, until evenly browned, for about 10 minutes.
5. Drain bacon slices on paper towels. Crumble when cool enough to handle.
6. Warmth a large skillet over medium heat; spray with cooking spray.
7. Crack eggs into skillet; season with salt and pepper.
8. Reduce heat to medium-low, cover skillet loosely.
9. Cook until egg whites are ready and yolks are still runny for about 3 minutes.
10. Divide French fries onto 4 plates: sprinkle evenly with crumbled bacon
11. Drizzle each serving with hollandaise sauce, sprinkle with chives, and top with an egg. Serve and enjoy!

Nutrition:
Calories: 171 Carbohydrates: 28.9g Cholesterol: 306.2mg
Protein: 20g Fat: 30.8g

---

126. Pancetta and Mushrooms

Preparation Time: 10 minutes **Cooking Time:** 20 minutes **Servings:** 4

Ingredients:
- 1 tablespoon of minced garlic
- ½ cup of heavy cream
- ¼ teaspoon of Italian seasoning
- ¼ cup of grated Parmesan cheese, or to taste
- 1 (12 ounces) package of penne pasta
- 1 (3 ounces) package of pancetta bacon, diced
- 2 tablespoons of butter
- 1 (10 ounces) package of sliced mushrooms

Directions:
1. Set a pot of salted water to a boil.
2. Add pasta and cook for 8 minutes. Drain and set aside.
3. Meanwhile, cook bacon in another skillet until golden brown but not crispy, about 3 minutes.
4. Spill on a paper towel-lined plate and set aside.
5. Set off the bacon fat from the skillet and add the butter.
6. Increase the heat to medium and stir in the sliced mushrooms.
7. Cook and whisk until the mushrooms are tender and released their liquid.
8. Add the minced garlic and cook for an additional 2 minutes.
9. Reduce the heat to medium-low, and then stir in the cream and Italian seasoning.
10. Parboil until the sauce has thickened slightly.
11. To serve, set the cooked penne with the sauce. Sprinkle with Parmesan cheese.

Nutrition:
Calories: 125 Carbohydrates: 39.2g Cholesterol: 65.2mg
Protein: 19.8g Fat: 21.4g

---

127. Blueberry Bake

Preparation Time: 35 minutes **Cooking Time:** 40 minutes **Servings:** 6

Ingredients:
- 2 tablespoons of honey
- 1 tablespoon of white sugar
- 1 tablespoon of cornstarch
- 1 teaspoon of ground cinnamon
- 1 cup of water
- 2 tablespoons of lemon juice
- 1 cup of whole wheat pastry flour
- 1 teaspoon of baking powder

- ½ teaspoon of baking soda
- ½ cup of low-fat buttermilk
- 3 cups of fresh blueberries

Directions:
1. Preheat oven to 400 F.
2. Combine the baking soda, flour, baking powder, and 1 tablespoon of sugar in a medium bowl.
3. Mix well, then stir in buttermilk until all ingredients are moistened, and dough forms a ball. Set it aside.
4. For the filling: In a saucepan, merge the cornstarch, cinnamon, water, honey, and lemon juice.
5. Stir until smooth, then add the berries.
6. Stir gently, until thickened, about 8 minutes.
7. Pour the berry mixture into a nonstick casserole dish.
8. Drop cookie dough over berry mixture with spoonful.
9. Bake in warmth oven until cookies are lightly browned.

Nutrition:
Calories: 109　　Carbohydrates: 35.2g　　Cholesterol: 0.8mg
Protein: 3.3g　　Fat: 0.7g

128. Grilled Catfish

Preparation Time: 10 minutes　　**Cooking Time:** 20 minutes　　**Servings:** 6

Ingredients:
- 6 toothpicks
- 1 tablespoon of dried mint
- 2 tablespoons of olive oil
- 6 (8 ounces) fillets of catfish
- Greek seasoning, or to taste
- 4 ounces of crumbled feta cheese

Directions:
1. Warmth the grill and lightly oil the grill.
2. Season both sides of each fish fillet with the Greek dressing.
3. Sprinkle mint and feta cheese on one side of each fillet.
4. Drizzle oil over the mint and cheese.
5. Starting at a narrower end, tightly roll the fish around the filling and secure with a toothpick.
6. Bake on the preheated grill until the fish flakes easily with a fork, about 20-25 minutes.

Nutrition:
Calories: 298　　Carbohydrates: 2.5g　　Cholesterol: 128.7mg
Protein: 29.6g　　Fat: 16.6g

129. Bacon and Fiddlehead Omelet

Preparation Time: 10 minutes　　**Cooking Time:** 25 minutes　　**Servings:** 2

Ingredients:
- 1 tablespoon of water
- 2 teaspoons of butter
- 2 slices of Gruyere cheese (Optional)
- 1 teaspoon of chopped fresh chives
- 1 cup of fiddleheads
- 2 slices of bacon
- 6 eggs
- salt and ground black pepper to season
- 1 tablespoon of milk

Directions:
1. Carefully rinse each fiddlehead, remove all the brown papery covers and trim the ends.
2. Attach an inch of water to the bottom of a steamer basket. Warmth on high until the water is boiling.
3. Set fiddleheads into the top of the steamer basket. Cover and steam for 10 minutes.
4. Fill a bowl with ice chips and water and set aside.
5. Meanwhile, set the bacon bits into a small nonstick skillet.
6. Add 2 teaspoons of water. Cook on medium heat until crispy, for about 5 minutes. Spill bacon on a paper towel-lined plate.
7. Sink the steamed fiddleheads into the icy water to stop the cooking progress. Detach after 5 minutes and set dry.
8. Break eggs into a bowl and flavor with salt and pepper.
9. Add milk and 1 tablespoon of water: whisk until smooth.
10. Melt 1 tsp. butter in a nonstick skillet. Pour in ½ the egg mixture let partially set.
11. Lift 1 section of the omelet with a spatula and tilt skillet, allowing liquid egg to run underneath.

Nutrition:
Calories: 149　　Carbohydrates: 3.7g　　Cholesterol: 102.4mg
Protein: 31.4g　　Fat: 19.3g

130. Hollow Chicken Salad Supreme

Preparation Time: 10 minutes　　**Cooking Time:** 20 minutes　　**Servings:** 4

Ingredients:
- 1 teaspoon of curry powder
- ⅓ cup of chopped celery
- ½ cup of chopped pecans
- 1 cup of seedless grapes
- 4 cups of boneless whole chicken breasts, cooked and chopped
- ¾ cup of golden raisins
- 1 teaspoon of Dijon-style prepared mustard
- ¾ cup of mayonnaise
- ¾ cup of pineapple tidbits, drained
- 1 head of iceberg lettuce - rinsed, dried, and chopped

Directions:
1. Combine the mustard, mayonnaise, pineapple, curry powder, chicken, raisins, and celery in a large bowl.
2. Mix ingredients and divide among four servings of lettuce.
3. Top with pecans and garnish with grapes.

Nutrition:
Calories: 109　　Carbohydrates: 33.8g　　Cholesterol: 98.7mg
Protein: 41.7g　　Fat: 29.6g

Dinner

131. Cilantro and Lime Broccoli Rice

Preparation Time: 5 minutes 0   **Cooking Time:** 8 minutes   **Servings:** 2

Ingredients:
- 2 ounces broccoli florets, finely chopped
- 2 green onions, white and green part separated
- 2 tablespoons chopped cilantro

Extra:
- ¼ teaspoon cayenne pepper
- ½ teaspoon garlic powder
- 1 teaspoon lime juice
- 1 tablespoon olive oil

Directions:
1. Take a medium skillet pan, set it over medium heat, add oil and when hot, add white parts of green onion and then cook for 1 to 2 minutes until softened.
2. Stir in garlic, add broccoli, stir until mixed, then cover the pan and cook for 4 to 5 minutes until broccoli has turned slightly soft.
3. Add lime juice and cilantro, sprinkle with cayenne pepper, and then cook for 30 seconds.
4. Taste to adjust seasoning and then serve.

Nutrition:
Calories: 241   Carbohydrates: 28.7g   Cholesterol: 23.4mg
Protein: 4.4g   Fat: 8.8g

132. Spicy Garlic Pasta

Preparation Time: 5 minutes   **Cooking Time:** 5 minutes   **Servings:** 2

Ingredients:
- 2 ounces fettuccine pasta, boiled
- 1 tablespoon minced garlic
- ½ teaspoon red chili flakes
- 1 teaspoon lime juice
- 1 ½ tablespoon olive oil

Directions:
1. Take a medium skillet pan, place it over medium heat, add oil and when hot, add garlic and then cook for 1 minute until golden.
2. Stir in chili flakes, cook for 20 seconds, then add pasta and toss to coat.
3. Drizzle lime juice over pasta, cook for 1 minute until hot, and then serve.

Nutrition:
Calories: 310
Protein: 45.6g
Carbohydrates: 30.4g
Fat: 57.1g
Cholesterol: 280.4mg

133. Simple Beef Roast
Preparation Time: 10 minutes **Cooking Time:** 8 hours **Servings:** 8

Ingredients:
- 5 pounds' beef roast
- 2 tablespoons Italian seasoning
- 1 cup beef stock
- 1 tablespoon sweet paprika
- 3 tablespoons olive oil

Directions:
1. In your slow cooker, mix all the ingredients, cover and cook on low for 8 hours.
2. Carve the roast, divide it between plates and serve.

Nutrition:
Calories: 187
Fat: 24.1,
Fiber: 0.3
Carbohydrates: 0.9
Protein: 86.5

134. Honey Garlic Butter Roasted Carrots
Preparation Time: 5 minutes **Cooking Time:** 20 minutes **Servings:** 2

Ingredients:
- 2 carrots
- ½ tablespoon minced garlic
- ⅛ teaspoon salt

Extra:
- ⅛ teaspoon ground black pepper
- ⅔ tablespoon honey
- 1 tablespoon chopped cilantro
- 1⅔ tablespoon butter, unsalted

Directions:
1. Switch on the oven, then set it to 425 F and let it preheat.
2. Meanwhile, prepare the carrot, and for this, peel them and diagonally cut them into 2-inch pieces.
3. Take a medium skillet pan, place it over medium heat, add butter and when it melts, add garlic and then cook for 1 minute until golden.
4. Remove pan from heat, add honey into the pan and then stir until well combined.
5. Add carrots into the pan, season with salt and black pepper and mix until well coated.
6. Set carrots in a single layer on a baking sheet greased with oil and then bake for 15 to 18 minutes until carrots have become tender and golden brown.

Nutrition:
Calories: 53
Protein: 9.2g
Carbohydrates: 11.8g
Fat: 30.3g
Cholesterol: 114.2mg

135. Colorful vegetable casserole
Preparation Time: 20 minutes **Cooking Time:** 1 hour 20 minutes **Servings:** 2

Ingredients:
- 1 organic zucchini
- 300 g of potatoes
- 1 onion, red
- 2 organic beefsteak tomatoes
- olive oil, as needed
- Sea salt and black pepper and thyme, fresh
- 100 g of feta
- 30 g of pitted olives
- Herbs for garnish, e.g., B. parsley, chives

Directions:
1. Wash zucchini and detach the ends, cut into cubes. Peel and wash the potatoes and divide into bite-sized pieces. Peel the onions and cut into slices. Wash tomatoes remove greens and cut into large cubes.
2. Warmth a pan with oil and fry the potatoes with the zucchini and onion. Pre heat the oven to 180F.
3. Wash and dry the thyme, pick off the leaves. Mix the tomatoes and 1 tbsp. thyme, flavor them well with sea salt and pepper. Put everything in a lightly greased casserole dish, cover with baking paper or aluminum foil and cook for about 50-60 minutes.
4. In the meantime, crumble the feta, cut the olives into rings and distribute them evenly on the casserole. Then cook for another 20 minutes.
5. Wash, dry and chop the herbs and finally garnish the casserole with the herbs.

Nutrition:
Calories: 167
Protein: 6.92 g
Fat: 6.85 g
Carbohydrates: 21.35 g

136. Lentil snack with tomato salsa
Preparation Time: 10 minutes **Cooking Time:** 45 minutes **Servings:** 2

Ingredients:
- 100 g of red lentils
- 1 small onion, red
- 80 g of wheat semolina
- 3 tbsp. paprika tomato paste

- 2 tbsp. mixed, chopped herbs (e.g., parsley, chervil, chives) - ½ organic lemon
- Sea salt and black pepper
- 1 organic tomato
- ½ red chili pepper, small
- 1 spring onion
- Olive oil, as needed
- 1 teaspoon rice syrup or maple syrup

Directions:
1. Cook the lentils based to the package instructions. Skin the onion and cut into small cubes. Mix the semolina with the finished lentils and leave to swell (about 3 minutes).
2. In the meantime, wash, dry and chop herbs. Add onion, paprika tomato paste (if you like) and herbs, stir and season with lemon juice, sea salt and pepper, then let cool.
3. For the tomato salsa, wash the tomatoes, remove the greens and cut into small cubes. Wash the chili peppers, cut lengthways, remove the seeds and partitions, wash again and cut into very small pieces.
4. Clean, wash and divide the spring onions into rings. Mix tomatoes, spring onions, chili peppers and a little paprika tomato paste as well as olive oil and rice syrup and season with sea salt and pepper.
5. Shape the lentil mixture into small rolls or balls. Set the oil in a pan and fry it brown all over or prepare it on the grill.
6. Arrange on plates and serve with the tomato salsa.

Nutrition:
Calories: 394
Protein: 20.1 g
Fat: 2.13 g
Carbohydrates: 76.77 g

137. Clear soup with liver dumplings

Preparation Time: 10 minutes **Cooking Time:** 40 minutes **Servings:** 2

Ingredients:
For the dumplings:
- 75 g veal liver
- 1 red onion, small
- Parsley, to taste
- ½ tbsp. olive oil

For the soup:
- 1 organic carrot
- 50 g of celery
- 2 spring onions
- 35 g breadcrumbs
- 1 organic egg size M
- Sea salt and black pepper
- Nutmeg, grated, optional
- ½ tbsp. oil
- Bay leaf, optional
- 500 ml of vegetable stock

Directions:
1. Turn the liver through a meat grinder (or have it made by the butcher).
2. Peel and cut the onion. Wash, dry and chop parsley.
3. Set the oil in a saucepan, sauté the onion briefly, add the parsley and sauté briefly. Then let it cool down.
4. Place the liver with the breadcrumbs in a bowl, add the onion-parsley mixture and egg and knead, salt and pepper. If you like, add some nutmeg and knead. Shape the mixture into about 6 dumplings and place in the refrigerator.
5. Now wash and dry the vegetables for the soup thoroughly. Cut the carrot into slices, cut the celery into bite-sized pieces and finally cut the spring onion into rolls. Warmth a little oil in a saucepan, cook the carrot, celery and spring onion together with the bay leaf for about 5 minutes. Then season with sea salt and pepper. Add the vegetable stock and simmer the soup over medium heat (about 10 minutes).
6. Finally add the dumplings and simmer for another 10 minutes.
7. When the dumplings stay to afloat to the surface, they are done.
8. Serve the soup with the liver dumplings.

Nutrition:
Calories: 217
Protein: 13.41 g
Fat: 13.63 g
Carbohydrates: 10.73 g

138. Beef steaks with green asparagus

Preparation Time: 15 minutes **Cooking Time:** 20 minutes **Servings:** 4

Ingredients:
- 500 g asparagus, green
- 40 g herb butter
- 2 beef fillet steaks (approx. 150 g each)
- 1 dried tomato pickled in oil
- 50 g ricotta
- Sea salt and black pepper
- Herbs, fresh e.g., B. oregano, basil
- 1 tbsp. oil for frying and capers, as desired (optional)
- Also: aluminum foil and toothpicks or small wooden skewers

Directions:
1. Wash the asparagus and skin the lower ends. Prepare two pieces of baking paper or aluminum foil and spread the asparagus on top. Put the herb butter on the asparagus, close the foil tightly, put on the grill for about 10 - 15 minutes.
2. Dab steaks with a little paper towel, cut a pocket. Drain the tomatoes and cut into small pieces. Put the ricotta and capers in a bowl, wash, dry and chop the herbs and add them as well.
3. Mix everything well and season with sea salt and pepper. Pour the finished cream into the steaks and seal the openings with a toothpick.
4. Finally, season the steaks with sea salt and pepper, brush with the oil and grill depending on the degree of cooking required (approx. 5-8 minutes on each side).
5. Arrange the steaks with the asparagus, add the rest of the cream and serve hot.

Nutrition:
Calories: 339
Protein: 18.91 g
Fat: 27.06 g
Carbohydrates: 6.31 g

139. Broccoli Omelet

Preparation Time: 5 minutes
Cooking Time: 1.5-2 hours
Servings: 2

Ingredients:
- 2 garlic cloves, minced
- 3 eggs
- ½ yellow onion, chopped
- ¼ cup milk
- ½ cup broccoli florets
- ¼ teaspoon black pepper
- ½ tomato, chopped
- ⅛ teaspoon chili powder
- ½ tablespoon Parmesan cheese, shredded
- ¾ cups Cheddar cheese, shredded
- ⅛ teaspoon salt
- ⅛ cup green onions, chopped
- ⅛ teaspoon garlic powder

Directions:
1. Spill the eggs, milk, and spices in a bowl.
2. To the egg mixture, add onions along with the garlic, parmesan cheese, and broccoli. Whisk well until combined, and then pour the egg mixture into a slow cooker.
3. Close the lid and cook for about 1 ½ hour to 2 hours on high.
4. Remove the cover when the cooking time is over and then sprinkle the shredded cheddar cheese on top. Close the lid again and then turn off the slow cooker.
5. Let rest for about 10 minutes, until the cheddar cheese has melted.
6. When done, cut the omelet into quarters and then serve.
7. Garnish the servings with chopped green onion and fresh tomato. Enjoy!

Nutrition:
Calories: 423
Fat: 28g
Carbohydrates: 13g
Protein: 29g

140. Apple Cinnamon Oatmeal

Preparation Time: 10 minutes
Cooking Time: 8 hours
Servings: 4

Ingredients:
- 2 peeled and sliced apples
- 1 tbsp. cinnamon

What you'll need from store cupboard:
- Pinch of salt
- ⅓ Cup brown sugar
- 2 cups rolled oats, old-fashioned
- 4 cups water

Directions:
1. Place the apples in the crockpot bottom then add cinnamon and sugar over the apples. Stir to mix.
2. Add the oats over apples evenly then add salt and water. Do not stir.
3. Cover and cook for about 8-9 hours on low or cook overnight.
4. Stir well; making sure oats are not at the bottom.
5. Serve.

Nutrition:
Calories: 232.4
Fat: 3.1g
Carbohydrates: 53g
Protein: 5.2g
Sugars: 20.9g
Fiber: 6g
Sodium: 4.9mg

141. Nutty Steel-cut Oatmeal with Blueberries

Preparation Time: 5 minutes
Cooking Time: 30 minutes
Servings: 2

Ingredients:
- 1 ½ cups water
- ½ cup steel-cut oats
- 1 ½ tablespoons almond butter
- ½ teaspoon ground cinnamon
- ¼ teaspoon ground nutmeg
- Pinch ground ginger
- ½ cup blueberries
- ¼ cup whole almonds

Directions:
1. Over high-heat, put the water in a medium saucepan, and bring the liquid to a boil.
2. Spill in the oats and reduce the heat to low so they simmer gently.
3. Simmer the oats uncovered for about 20 minutes, until they are tender.
4. Stir in the almond butter, cinnamon, nutmeg, and ginger, and simmer for an additional 10 minutes.
5. Serve topped with blueberries and whole almonds.

Nutrition:
Calories: 246
Carbohydrates: 24g
Fiber: 5g
Protein: 8g
Sodium: 2mg
Fat: 14g

142. Slow "Roasted" Tomatoes

Preparation Time: 5 minutes
Cooking Time: 1 hour 15 minutes
Servings: 2

Ingredients:
- ½ tablespoon balsamic vinegar
- 1 large firm under-ripe tomato, halved crosswise
- 1 garlic clove, minced
- 1 teaspoon olive oil
- ½ teaspoon dried basil, crushed
- ½ cup breadcrumbs, coarse, soft whole-wheat
- Dried rosemary, crushed
- 1 tablespoon Parmesan cheese, grated
- Salt
- ¼ teaspoon dried oregano, crushed
- Chopped fresh basil, optional

Directions:
1. Using cooking spray, coat the unheated slow cooker lightly. Then add tomatoes to the bottom of the slow cooker, cut side up.
2. In a bowl, combine vinegar together with garlic, oil, rosemary, dried basil, and salt, and then spoon the mixture over the tomatoes in the slow cooker evenly.
3. Close the lid and cook for either 2 hours on low, or 1 hour on high.
4. Over medium preheat a skillet, and then add the breadcrumbs. Cook as you stir constantly until lightly browned, for about 2-3 minutes. Remove from heat when done and then stir in the parmesan.
5. When through, remove tomatoes from the slow cooker and put them on the serving plates, and then drizzle over tomatoes with the cooking liquid. Then sprinkle with the breadcrumb mixture and let rest for 10 minutes to absorb the flavors.
6. Garnish with basil if need be and then serve. Enjoy!

Nutrition:
Calories: 96
Fat: 4g
Carbohydrates: 13g
Protein: 3g

143. Tomato-Herb Omelet

Preparation Time: 10 minutes **Cooking Time:** 10 minutes **Servings:** 2

Ingredients:
- 1 tablespoon coconut oil, divided
- 2 scallions, green and white parts, chopped
- 1 teaspoon minced garlic
- 2 tomatoes, chopped, liquid squeezed out
- 6 eggs, beaten
- ½ teaspoon chopped fresh thyme
- ½ teaspoon chopped fresh basil
- ½ teaspoon chopped fresh chives
- ½ teaspoon chopped fresh oregano
- ⅛ teaspoon sea salt
- Pinch ground nutmeg
- Pinch freshly ground black pepper
- Chopped fresh parsley, for garnish

Directions:
1. Put a small saucepan over medium heat before adding 1 teaspoon of coconut oil.
2. Sauté the scallions and garlic for about 3 minutes, until the vegetables are softened.
3. Add the tomatoes and sauté for 3 minutes. Remove the saucepan from the heat and set aside.
4. Spill together the eggs, thyme, basil, chives, oregano, salt, nutmeg, and pepper in a medium bowl.
5. Put a large skillet over medium-high heat before adding the remaining 2 teaspoons of oil. Swirl the oil until it coats the skillet.
6. Spill in the egg mixture, and swirl until the eggs start to firm up- do not stir the eggs. Lift the edges of the firmed eggs to let the uncooked egg flow at the bottom.
7. When the eggs are almost done, spoon the tomato mixture onto one-half of the eggs.
8. Fold the uncovered side over the tomato mixture and cook for a minute longer.
9. Cut the omelet in half, sprinkle with parsley, and serve.

Nutrition:
Calories: 306
Carbohydrates: 13g
Fiber: 6g
Protein: 19g
Sodium: 312mg
Fat: 21g

144. Mouth-Watering Egg Casserole

Preparation Time: 15 minutes **Cooking Time:** 10 hours **Servings:** 2

Ingredients:
- 10oz ham, ½-inch slices
- ½ cup thinly sliced button mushrooms
- 1 tbsp. seeded red capsicum, thinly sliced

What you'll need from store cupboard:
- ¼ cup diced potatoes, cooked
- 1 tbsp. drained tomatoes, sun-dried and chopped up
- ¼ cup thawed and drained spinach, chopped and frozen
- 10oz diced Swiss cheese
- 10oz goat feta cheese
- ¼ cup thawed artichoke hearts, frozen and quartered
- Whole basil leaves, fresh
- 2 eggs
- 1 cup whole milk
- 1 tbsp. Dijon mustard
- Sea salt to taste
- Black pepper freshly cracked to taste

Directions:
1. Place a coated crockpot liner with cooking oil inside a crockpot, 2-qt
2. Grill the ham pieces for about 4 minutes until crisp. Retain the fat.
3. Sauté mushrooms and capsicum in the fat and butter for about 4 minutes until soft.
4. Place potatoes in the crockpot base and on top, then place an even layer of mushroom-capsicum mixture.
5. Add half of artichokes, tomatoes, and spinach in layers then sprinkle with half Swiss cheese, followed by remaining vegetables, then remaining cheese and feta cheese.
6. Meanwhile, combine eggs, milk, and mustard in a bowl then pour over to settle through on the dish.
7. Place ham on top.
8. Seal and cook for about 8 hours on low then use the liner to remove the casserole.
9. Rest for about 10 minutes, then detach the liner.
10. Slice the casserole and garnish with basil leaves.
11. Serve alongside with green salad, leafy.

Nutrition:
Calories: 297
Fat: 17g
Carbohydrates: 20.8g
Protein: 15.8g,
Sugars: 10.2g
Fiber: 2.4g
Sodium: 416mg
Potassium: 617mg

145. Amazing Overnight Apple and Cinnamon Oatmeal

Preparation Time: 10 minutes **Cooking Time:** 7 hours **Servings:** 2

Ingredients:
- ¾ cup coconut milk
- 1 diced whole apple
- ½ cup steel cut oats
- ½ tbsp. raw honey

What you'll need from store cupboard:
- 1 tbsp. coconut oil
- ¾ cup water, fresh
- ¼ tbsp. salt to taste, sea
- 1 tbsp. cinnamon

Directions:
1. Spray your crockpot with cooking oil. This is to prevent food from sticking.
2. Add water, coconut milk, apples, oats, coconut oil, raw honey, salt, and cinnamon. Stir to combine.
3. Cover and cook for about 6-7 hours on low.
4. Serve hot with favorite toppings.

Nutrition:
Calories: 284
Fat: 17.9g
Carbohydrates: 30.3g
Protein: 4.2g
Sugars: 1.3g
Fiber: 4.7g
Sodium: 30mg
Potassium: 90mg

146. Zoodles with Pea Pesto

Preparation Time: 10 minutes **Cooking Time:** 10 minutes **Servings:** 2

Ingredients:
- 1 ½ zucchini
- 1 tablespoon extra-virgin olive oil
- Pinch sea salt
- Pea Pesto

Directions:
1. Cut the zucchini lengthwise into long strips using a vegetable peeler. Use a knife to cut the strips into the desired width. Alternatively, use a spiralizer to cut the zucchini into noodles.
2. In a large skillet, the olive oil is heated until it shimmers over medium-high heat. Add the zucchini and cook until softened for about 3 minutes. Add the sea salt.
3. Toss the zucchini noodles with the pesto.

Nutrition:
Calories: 348
Fat: 30g
Sodium: 343mg
Carbohydrates: 13g
Fiber: 1g
Protein: 10g

147. Shrimp Peri-Peri

Preparation Time: 10 minutes **Cooking Time:** 15 minutes **Servings:** 2

Ingredients:
- Peri-Peri Sauce
- ½ lb. large shrimp
- 1 tablespoon extra-virgin olive oil
- Sea salt

Directions:
1. Preheat the oven broiler on high.
2. In a small pot, bring the Peri-Peri Sauce to a simmer.
3. Meanwhile, place the cleaned shrimp on a rimmed baking sheet, deveined-side down. Garnish with olive oil and sprinkle with salt.
4. Broil until opaque, about 5 minutes. Serve with the sauce on the side for dipping or spooned over the top of the shrimp.

Nutrition:
Calories: 279
Fat: 16g
Sodium: 464mg
Carbohydrates: 10g
Fiber: 3g
Protein: 24g

148. Halibut with Lime and Cilantro

Preparation Time: 30 minutes **Cooking Time:** 45 minutes **Servings:** 2

Ingredients:
- 2 tbsp. lime juice
- 1 tbsp. chopped fresh cilantro
- 1 tsp. olive or canola oil
- 1 clove garlic, finely chopped
- 2 halibut or salmon steaks
- Freshly ground pepper
- ½ cup chunky-style salsa

Directions:
1. In a shallow glass or in a resalable food-storage plastic bag, merge lime juice, cilantro, oil, and garlic. Attach halibut, turning several times to coat with marinade. Seal; refrigerate 15 minutes, turning once.
2. Heat gas or charcoal grill. Remove halibut from marinade, discard marinade.
3. Place halibut on the grill over medium heat. Cover grill: cook 10 to 20 minutes, turning once, until halibut flakes easily with a fork. Sprinkle it with pepper. Serve with salsa.

Nutrition:
Calories: 190
Fat: 4.5g
Cholesterol: 90mg
Sodium: 600mg
Carbohydrates: 6g
Fiber: 0g
Sugars: 2g
Protein: 32g

149. Autumn Pork Chop with Red Cabbage and Apples

Preparation Time: 15 minutes **Cooking Time:** 30 minutes **Servings:** 2

Ingredients:
- ⅛ Cup apple cider vinegar
- 1 tablespoon granulated sweetener
- 2 (4 oz.) pork chops, about 1 inch thick
- ½ tablespoon extra-virgin olive oil
- ¼ red cabbage, finely shredded
- ½ sweet onion, thinly sliced
- ½ apple, peeled, cored, and sliced
- ½ teaspoon chopped fresh thyme

Directions:
1. Scourge together the vinegar and sweetener. Set it aside.
2. Season the pork with salt and pepper.
3. Position a big skillet over medium-high heat and add the olive oil.
4. Cook the pork chops until no longer pink, turning once, about 8 minutes per side.
5. Put chops aside.
6. Attach the cabbage and onion to the skillet and sauté until the vegetables have softened about 5 minutes.
7. Add the vinegar mixture and the apple slices to the skillet and bring the mixture to boiling point.
8. Adjust low-heat and simmer for 5 additional minutes.
9. Return the pork chops to the skillet, along with any accumulated juices and thyme, cover, and cook for 5 more minutes.

Nutrition:
Calories: 306 Fiber: 6g Sodium: 312mg
Carbohydrates: 13g Protein: 19g Fat: 21g

150. Orange-Marinated Pork Tenderloin

Preparation Time: 2 hours **Cooking Time:** 30 minutes **Servings:** 2

Ingredients:
- ⅛ Cup freshly squeezed orange juice
- 1 teaspoon orange zest
- 1 teaspoon minced garlic
- ½ teaspoon low-sodium soy sauce
- ½ teaspoon grated fresh ginger
- ½ teaspoon honey
- ¾ pounds pork tenderloin roast
- ½ tablespoon extra-virgin olive oil

Directions:
1. Blend together the orange juice, zest, garlic, soy sauce, ginger, and honey.
2. Pour the marinade into a resalable plastic bag and add the pork tenderloin.
3. Detach as much air as possible and seal the bag. Marinate the pork in the refrigerator, turning the bag a few times, for 2 hours.
4. Preheat the oven to 400F.
5. Pull out tenderloin from the marinade and discard the marinade.
6. Position a big ovenproof skillet over medium-high heat and add the oil.
7. Sear the pork tenderloin on all sides.
8. Position skillet to the oven and roast for 25 minutes.
9. Put aside for 10 minutes before serving.

Nutrition:
Calories: 217 Fat: 13.63 g
Protein: 13.41 g Carbohydrates: 10.73 g

151. Vegetarian Chipotle Chili

Preparation Time: 5 minutes **Cooking Time:** 6 hours **Servings:** 2

Ingredients:
- ¼ onion, diced
- 2 ¼ oz. corn, frozen
- ¾ carrots, diced
- Ground cumin
- 1 garlic clove, minced
- ½ medium sweet potatoes, diced
- ¼ teaspoon chipotle chili powder
- Ground black pepper
- 1 cup kidney beans, cooked from dried beans, or use rinsed canned beans
- ¼ tablespoon salt
- 7 oz. tomatoes, diced, undrained
- ½ avocados, diced

Directions:
1. In a slow cooker, combine all the ingredients except the diced avocados.
2. Cook for 3 hours on high, and then cook for 3 hours on low until done. If desired, you can also cook for 4-5 hours on high or 7-8 hours on low until cooked through.
3. When done, serve with the diced avocado and enjoy!

Nutrition:
Calories: 283 Carbohydrates: 45g
Fat: 8g Protein: 11g

152. Wild Rice

Preparation Time: 5 minutes **Cooking Time:** 2-3 hours **Servings:** 2

Ingredients:
- ¼ cup onions, diced
- ½ cup wild rice, uncooked
- ¾ cups chicken broth, low sodium
- ¼ cup diced green or red peppers
- ⅛ teaspoon pepper
- ½ tablespoon oil
- ⅛ teaspoon salt
- ¼ cup mushrooms, sliced

Directions:
1. In a slow cooker, layer the rice and the vegetables, and then pour oil, pepper, and salt over the vegetables. Stir well.
2. Heat the chicken broth in a pot, and then pour over the ingredients in the slow cooker.

3. Seal the lid and cook for 2 ½-3 hours on high, until the rice has softened and the liquid is absorbed.
4. Serve and enjoy!

Nutrition:
Calories: 157
Fat: 3g
Carbohydrates: 27g
Protein: 6g

153. Stuffed Bell Peppers with Quinoa

Preparation Time: 10 minutes **Cooking Time:** 35 minutes **Servings:** 2

Ingredients:
- 2 bell peppers
- ⅓ cup quinoa
- 3 oz. chicken stock ¼ cup onion, diced
- ½ teaspoon salt
- ¼ teaspoon tomato paste
- ½ teaspoon dried oregano
- ⅓ cup sour cream
- 1 teaspoon paprika

Directions:
1. Trim the bell peppers and take away the seeds.
2. Then combine chicken broth and quinoa in the pan.
3. Add salt and boil the ingredients for 10 minutes or until quinoa will soak all liquid.
4. Then combine cooked quinoa with dried oregano, ingredient, and onion.
5. Set the bell peppers with the quinoa mixture and arrange them in the casserole mold.
6. Add soured cream and bake the peppers for 25 minutes at 365 F.
7. Serve the cooked peppers with soured cream sauce from the casserole mold.

Nutrition:
Calories: 237
Fat: 10.3
Fiber: 4.5
Carbohydrates: 31.3
Protein: 6.9g

154. Mediterranean Burrito

Preparation Time: 10 minutes **Cooking Time:** 0 minutes **Servings:** 2

Ingredients:
- 2 wheat tortillas
- 2 oz. red kidney beans, canned, drained
- 2 tablespoons hummus
- 2 teaspoons tahini sauce
- 1 cucumber
- 2 lettuce leaves
- 1 tablespoon lime juice
- 1 teaspoon olive oil
- ½ teaspoon dried oregano

Directions:
1. Mash the red kidney beans until you get a puree.
2. Then spread the wheat tortillas with beans mash from one side.
3. Add hummus and tahini sauce.
4. Cut the cucumber into the wedges and place them over tahini sauce.
5. Then add lettuce leaves.
6. Make the dressing: misunderstanding together vegetable oil, dried oregano, and juice.
7. Drizzle the lettuce leaves with the dressing and wrap the wheat tortillas in burritos' shape.

Nutrition:
Calories: 288
Fat: 10.2
Fiber: 14.6
Carbohydrates: 38.2
Protein: 12.5

155. Prosciutto Wrapped Mozzarella Balls

Preparation Time: 10 minutes **Cooking Time:** 10 minutes **Servings:** 4

Ingredients:
- 8 mozzarella balls, cherry size
- 4 oz. bacon, sliced
- ¼ teaspoon ground black pepper
- ¾ teaspoon dried rosemary
- 1 teaspoon butter

Directions:
1. Sprinkle the sliced bacon with ground black pepper and dried rosemary.
2. Wrap every mozzarella ball in the sliced bacon and secure them with toothpicks.
3. Melt butter.
4. Brush wrapped mozzarella balls with butter.
5. Line the tray with the baking paper and arrange mozzarella balls in it.
6. Bake the meal for 10 minutes at 365F.

Nutrition:
Calories: 323
Fat: 26.8
Fiber: 0.1
Carbohydrates: 0.6
Protein: 20.6

156. Garlic Chicken Balls

Preparation Time: 15 minutes **Cooking Time:** 10 minutes **Servings:** 4

Ingredients:
- 2 cups ground chicken
- 1 teaspoon minced garlic
- 1 teaspoon dried dill
- ⅓ carrot, grated
- 1 egg, beaten
- 1 tablespoon olive oil
- ¼ cup coconut flakes
- ½ teaspoon salt

Directions:
1. In the mixing bowl, mix up together ground chicken, minced garlic, dried dill, carrot, egg, and salt.
2. Stir the chicken mixture with the assistance of the fingertips until homogeneous.

3. Then, make medium balls from the mixture.
4. Coat every chicken ball in coconut flakes.
5. Heat vegetable oil in the skillet.
6. Add chicken balls and cook them for 3 minutes from all sides. The cooked chicken balls will have a golden-brown color.

Nutrition:
Calories: 200
Fat: 11.5
Fiber: 0.6
Carbohydrates: 1.7
Protein: 21.9

157. Monkey Salad
Preparation Time: 4 minutes **Cooking Time:** 7 minutes **Servings:** 1

Ingredients:
- 2 tablespoons of butter
- 1 cup unsweetened coconut flakes
- 1 cup raw, unsalted cashews
- 1 cup raw, unsalted s
- 1 cup 90% dark chocolate shavings

Directions:
1. In a skillet, dissolve the butter on medium heat.
2. Add the cashews and s and sauté for 3 minutes. Remove from the warmth and sprinkle with bittersweet chocolate shavings.
3. Serve!

Nutrition:
Calories: 321 Carbohydrates: 5 g
Fat: 12 g
Protein: 6 g
Fiber: 5 g

158. Jarlsberg Lunch Omelet
Preparation Time: 5 minutes **Cooking Time:** 10 minutes **Servings:** 2

Ingredients:
- 4 medium mushrooms, sliced, 2 oz.
- 1 green onion, sliced
- 2 eggs, beaten
- 1 oz. Jarlsberg or Swiss cheese, shredded
- 1 oz. ham, diced

Directions:
1. In a skillet, cook the mushrooms and scallion until tender.
2. Add the eggs and blend well.
3. Drizzle with salt and top with the mushroom mixture, cheese, and therefore the ham.
4. When the egg is set, bend the plain side of the omelet on the filled side.
5. Close up the heat and let it stand until the cheese has melted.
6. Serve!

Nutrition:
Calories: 288
Carbohydrates: 22 g
Fat: 12 g
Protein: 27 g
Fiber: 6 g

159. Mu Shu Lunch Pork
Preparation Time: 5 minutes **Cooking Time:** 10 minutes **Servings:** 2

Ingredients:
- 4 cups coleslaw mix, with carrots
- 1 small onion, sliced thin
- 1 lb. cooked roast pork, cut into ½ cubes
- 2 tablespoon hoisin sauce
- 2 tablespoon soy sauce

Directions:
1. In a large skillet, warmth the oil on high heat.
2. Spill the cabbage and onion for 4 minutes until tender.
3. Add the pork, hoisin, and soy.
4. Cook until browned. Enjoy!

Nutrition:
Calories: 188
Carbohydrates: 16 g
Fat: 21 g
Protein: 25 g
Fiber: 16 g

160. Fiery Jalapeno Poppers
Preparation Time: 10 minutes **Cooking Time:** 40 minutes **Servings:** 4

Ingredients:
- 5 oz. cream cheese
- ¼ cup mozzarella cheese
- 8 medium jalapeno peppers
- ½ teaspoon Mrs. Dash Table Blend
- 8 slices bacon

Directions:
1. Preheat your fryer to 400F/200C.
2. Cut the jalapenos in half.
3. With a spoon, grate out the insides of the peppers.
4. In a bowl, add together the cheese, mozzarella cheese, and spices of your choice.
5. Pack the cheese mixture into the jalapenos and place the peppers on top.
6. Set each pepper in 1 slice of bacon, ranging from rock bottom and dealing up.
7. Bake for half-hour. Broil for a further 3 minutes. Serve!

Nutrition:
Calories: 238
Carbohydrates: 4 g
Fat: 10 g
Protein: 24 g
Fiber: 14 g

161. Bacon and Chicken Patties

Preparation Time: 5 minutes **Cooking Time:** 15 minutes **Servings:** 2

Ingredients:
- 1 ½ oz. can chicken breast
- 4 slices bacon
- ¼ cup parmesan cheese
- 1 large egg
- 3 tablespoons of flour

Directions:
1. Cook the bacon until ready.
2. Hashed the chicken and bacon together in a food processor until fine.
3. Add in the parmesan, egg, flour, and blend.
4. Set the patties by hand and fry on medium heat in a pan with some oil.
5. Once browned, flip over, continue cooking, and lay them to empty. Serve!

Nutrition:
Calories: 387 Fat: 16 g Fiber: 28 g
Carbohydrates: 13 g Protein: 34 g

162. Cheddar Bacon Burst

Preparation Time: 25 minutes **Cooking Time:** 90 minutes **Servings:** 8

Ingredients:
- 30 slices bacon
- 2 ½ cups cheddar cheese
- 4-5 cups raw spinach
- 1-2 tablespoon Tones Southwest Chipotle Seasoning
- 2 teaspoon Mrs. Dash Table Seasoning

Directions:
1. Preheat your fryer to 375F/190C.
2. Weave the bacon into 15 vertical pieces and 12 horizontal pieces. Cut the additional 3 in half to fill in the rest horizontally.
3. Season the bacon.
4. Add the cheese to the bacon.
5. Add the spinach and depress to compress.
6. Tightly roll up the woven bacon.
7. Set a baking sheet with kitchen foil and add salt to it.
8. Put the bacon on top of a cooling rack and put that on top of your baking sheet.
9. Bake for 60-70 minutes.
10. Let cool for 10-15 minutes before 11. Slice and enjoy!

Nutrition:
Calories: 218 Fat: 9 g Fiber: 5 g
Carbohydrates: 20 g Protein: 21 g

163. Prosciutto Spinach Salad

Preparation Time: 5 minutes **Cooking Time:** 5 minutes **Servings:** 2

Ingredients:
- 2 cups baby spinach
- ⅓ lb. prosciutto
- 1 cantaloupe
- 1 avocado
- ¼ cup hashed red onion handful of raw, unsalted walnuts

Directions:
1. Set a cup of spinach on each plate.
2. Top with the diced prosciutto, cubes of melon balls, slices of avocado, a couple of purple onions, and a couple of walnuts.
3. Add some freshly ground pepper if you wish. Serve!

Nutrition:
Calories: 348 Fat: 9 g Fiber: 22 g
Carbohydrates: 11 g Protein: 26 g

164. Riced Cauliflower and Curry Chicken

Preparation Time: 15 minutes **Cooking Time:** 30 minutes **Servings:** 6

Ingredients:
- 2 lbs. chicken (4 breasts)
- 1 packet curry paste
- 3 tablespoon ghee (can substitute with butter)
- ½ cup heavy cream
- 1 head cauliflower (around 1 kg)

Directions:
1. In a large skillet, melt the ghee.
2. Add the curry paste and blend.
3. Once combined, attach a cup of water and simmer for five minutes.
4. Add the chicken, cover the skillet, and parboil for 18 minutes.
5. Set a cauliflower head into florets and blend in a food processor to make the riced cauliflower.
6. When the chicken is cooked, unseal, add the cream and cook for a further 7 minutes. Serve!

Nutrition:
Calories: 267 Fat: 31 g Fiber: 32 g
Carbohydrates: 42 g Protein: 34 g

165. Lasagna Spaghetti Squash

Preparation Time: 30 minutes **Cooking Time:** 90 minutes **Servings:** 6

Ingredients:
- 25 slices mozzarella cheese
- 1 large jar (40 oz.) Rao's Marinara sauce
- 30 oz. whole-milk ricotta cheese
- 2 large spaghetti squash, cooked (44 oz.)
- 4 lbs. ground beef

Directions:
1. Preheat your fryer to 375F/190C.
2. Slice the spaghetti squash and place it face down inside a fryer proof dish. Fill with water until covered.
3. Bake until the skin is soft.
4. Sear the meat until browned.
5. In a large skillet, heat the browned meat and marinara sauce. Put aside when warm.
6. Scrape the flesh off the cooked squash to resemble strands of spaghetti.
7. Layer the lasagna in a large greased pan in alternating layers of spaghetti squash, meat sauce, mozzarella, and ricotta. Repeat until all increases are used.
8. Bake for half-hour and serve!

Nutrition:
Calories: 508
Carbohydrates: 32 g
Fat: 8 g
Protein: 22 g
Fiber: 21 g

166. Pork Salad
Preparation Time: 15 minutes **Cooking Time:** 6 minutes **Servings:** 5

Ingredients:
- 1½ pounds pork tenderloin, trimmed and sliced thinly
- Salt and ground black pepper, as required
- 3 tablespoon olive oil
- 2 carrots, peeled and grated
- 3 cups Napa cabbage, shredded
- 2 scallions, chopped
- 2 tablespoon fresh lime juice
- ¼ cup fresh mint leaves, chopped

Directions:
1. Flavor the pork with salt and black pepper lightly.
2. In a large skillet, warmth the oil over medium heat and cook the pork slices for about 2-3 minutes per sides or until cooked through.
3. Detach from the heat and set aside to cool slightly.
4. In a large bowl, add the pork and remaining ingredients except mint leaves and toss to coat well. Serve with the garnishing of mint leaves.

Nutrition:
Calories: 292
Fat: 13.3 g
Cholesterol: 99 mg
Carbohydrates: 5.7 g
Sugar: 2.7 g
Fiber: 2.1 g
Sodium: 104 mg
Potassium: 760 mg
Protein: 36.6 g

167. Pork with Bell Peppers
Preparation Time: 15 minutes **Cooking Time:** 13 minutes **Servings:** 4

Ingredients:
- 1 tablespoon fresh ginger, chopped finely
- 4 garlic cloves, chopped finely
- 1 cup fresh cilantro, chopped and divided
- ¼ cup plus
- 1 tablespoon olive oil, divided
- 1 pound tender pork, trimmed, sliced thinly
- 2 onions, sliced thinly
- 1 green bell pepper, seeded and sliced thinly
- 1 red bell pepper, seeded and sliced thinly
- 1 tablespoon fresh lime juice

Directions:
1. In a large bowl, merge together ginger, garlic, ½ cup of cilantro and ¼ cup of oil.
2. Add the pork and coat with mixture generously.
3. Refrigerate to marinate for about 2 hours.
4. Heat a large skillet over medium-high heat and stir fry the pork mixture for about 4-5 minutes.
5. Transfer the pork into a bowl. In the same skillet, warmth remaining oil over medium heat and sauté the onion for about 3 minutes. Stir in the bell pepper and stir fry for about 3 minutes.
6. Stir in the pork, lime juice and remaining cilantro and cook for about 2 minutes.
7. Serve hot.

Nutrition:
Calories: 360
Fat: 21.8 g
Cholesterol: 83 mg
Carbohydrates: 11g
Sugar: 5.4g
Fiber: 2.2g
Sodium: 7 mg
Potassium: 706mg
Protein: 31.2g

168. Roasted Pork Shoulder
Preparation Time: 10 minutes **Cooking Time:** 6 hours **Servings:** 12

Ingredients:
- 1 head garlic, peeled and crushed
- ¼ cup fresh rosemary, minced
- 2 tablespoons fresh lemon juice
- 2 tablespoons balsamic vinegar
- 4-pound pork shoulder, trimmed

Directions:
1. In a bowl, attach all the ingredients except pork shoulder and mix well.
2. In a large roasting pan place pork shoulder and coat with marinade generously.
3. With a large plastic wrap, cover the roasting pan and refrigerate to marinate for at least 1-2 hours.
4. Remove the roasting pan from refrigerator.
5. Remove the plastic wrap from roasting pan and keep in room temperature for 1 hour. Preheat the oven to 275 F. Arrange the roasting pan in oven and roast for about 6 hours.
6. Detach from the oven and set aside for about 15-20 minutes. With a sharp knife, cut the pork shoulder into desired slices and serve.

Nutrition:
Calories: 450
Fat: 32.6g
Cholesterol: 136mg
Carbohydrates: 1.5g
Sugar: 0.1g
Fiber: 0.6g
Sodium: 104mg
Potassium: 522mg
Protein: 35.4g

169. Pork Chops in Peach Glaze

Preparation Time: 15 minutes **Cooking Time:** 16 minutes **Servings:** 2

Ingredients:
- 2 (6-ounce) boneless pork chops, trimmed
- Sea Salt and ground black pepper
- ½ of ripe yellow peach, peeled, pitted and chopped
- 1 tablespoon olive oil
- 2 tablespoons shallot, minced
- 2 tablespoons garlic, minced
- 2 tablespoons fresh ginger, minced
- 4-6 drops liquid stevia
- ½ tablespoon balsamic vinegar
- ¼ teaspoon red pepper flakes, crushed
- ¼ cup filtered water

Directions:
1. Flavor the pork chops with sea salt and black pepper generously.
2. In a blender, add the peach pieces and pulse until a puree form.
3. Reserve the remaining peach pieces. In a skillet, warmth the oil over medium heat and sauté the shallots for about 1-2 minutes.
4. Attach the garlic and ginger and sauté for about 1 minute. Stir in the remaining ingredients and bring to a boil.
5. Now, set the heat to medium-low and simmer for about 4-5 minutes or until a sticky glaze form.
6. Remove from the heat and reserve ⅓ of the glaze and set aside. Coat the chops with remaining glaze.
7. Warmth a nonstick skillet over medium-high heat and sear the chops for about 4 minutes per side.
8. Transfer the chops onto a plate and coat with the remaining glaze evenly.
9. Serve immediately.

Nutrition:
Calories 359
Fat 13.5 g
Cholesterol 124 mg
Carbohydrates 12 g
Sugar 3.8 g
Fiber 1.5 g
Sodium 102 mg
Potassium 938 mg
Protein 46.2 g

170. Ground Pork with Spinach

Preparation Time: 15 minutes **Cooking Time:** 15 minutes **Servings:** 4

Ingredients:
- 1 tablespoon olive oil
- ½ of white onion, chopped
- 2 garlic cloves, chopped finely
- 1 jalapeño pepper, chopped finely
- 1 pound lean ground pork
- ½ teaspoon ground coriander
- 1 teaspoon ground cumin
- ½ teaspoon ground turmeric
- ½ teaspoon ground cinnamon
- ½ teaspoon ground fennel seeds
- Salt and ground black pepper, as required
- ½ cup fresh cherry tomatoes, quartered
- 1¼ pounds collard greens leaves, stemmed and chopped
- ½ teaspoon fresh lemon juice

Directions:
1. In a large skillet, warmth the oil over medium heat and sauté the onion for about 4 minutes.
2. Add the garlic and jalapeño pepper and sauté for about 1 minute.
3. Add the pork and spices and cook for about 6 minutes breaking into pieces with the spoon.
4. Stir in the tomatoes and greens and cook, stirring gently for about 4 minutes. Stir in the lemon juice and remove from heat. Serve hot.

Nutrition:
Calories: 316
Fat: 21.8 g
Cholesterol: 0 mg
Carbohydrates: 1.4 g
Sugar: 1.4 g
Fiber: 5.7 g
Sodium: 27 mg
Potassium: 107 mg
Protein: 23 g

171. Red Wine Pot Roast with Winter Vegetables

Preparation Time: 10 minutes **Cooking Time:** 1 hour 35 minutes **Servings:** 6

Ingredients:
- 3-pound boneless beef chuck roast or bottom round roast
- 2 teaspoons fine sea salt
- 1 teaspoon freshly ground black pepper
- 1 tablespoon cold-pressed avocado oil
- 4 large shallots, quartered
- 4 garlic cloves, minced
- 1 cup dry red wine
- 2 tablespoons Dijon mustard
- 2 teaspoons chopped fresh rosemary
- 1 pound parsnips or turnips, cut into ½-inch pieces
- 1 pound carrots, set into ½-inch pcs.
- 4 celery stalks cut into ½-inch pcs.

Directions:
1. Put the beef onto a plate; pat it dry with paper towels, and then season all over with the salt and pepper.
2. Choose the Sauté on the Instant Pot and heat the oil for 2 minutes. Using tongs, set the roast into the pot and sear for about 4 minutes, until browned on the first side. Flip the roast and sear for about 4 minutes more, until browned on the second side. Return the roast to the plate.
3. Attach the shallots to the pot and sauté for about 2 minutes, until they begin to soften. Attach the garlic and sauté for about 1 minute more. Stir in the wine, mustard, and rosemary, using a wooden spoon to nudge any browned bits from the bottom of the pot. Return the roast to the pot, and then spoon some of the cooking liquid over the top.
4. Seal the lid and set the Pressure Release to Sealing. Push the Cancel button to reset the cooking program, then select the Meat/Stew setting and set the cooking time for 1 hour 5 minutes at high pressure.
5. When the cooking program had done, let the pressure release naturally for at least 15 minutes, and then set the Pressure Release to Venting to release any remaining steam. Open the pot and carefully transfer the pot roast to a cutting board. Tent with aluminum foil to keep warm.
6. Attach the parsnips, carrots, and celery to the pot.

7. Seal the lid. Choose the Cancel button to reset the cooking program. Cook for 3 minutes at low pressure.

Nutrition:
Calorie: 448
Fat: 25g
Protein: 26g
Carbohydrates: 26g
Sugars: 7g
Fiber: 6g
Sodium: 945mg

172. Salisbury Steaks with Seared Cauliflower
Preparation Time: 5 minutes **Cooking Time:** 30 minutes **Servings:** 4

Ingredients:
Salisbury Steaks
- 1 pound 95 percent lean ground beef
- ⅓ cup almond flour
- 1 large egg
- ½ teaspoon fine sea salt
- ¼ teaspoon freshly ground black pepper
- 2 tablespoons cold-pressed avocado oil
- 1 small yellow onion, sliced
- 1 garlic clove, chopped
- 8 ounces cremini or button mushrooms, sliced
- ½ teaspoon fine sea salt
- 2 tablespoons tomato paste
- 1½ teaspoons yellow mustard
- 1 cup low-sodium roasted beef bone broth

Seared Cauliflower
- 1 tablespoon olive oil
- 1 head cauliflower, cut into bite-size florets
- 2 tablespoons chopped fresh flat-leaf parsley
- ¼ teaspoon fine sea salt
- 2 teaspoons cornstarch
- 2 teaspoons water

Directions:
1. To make the steaks: In a bowl, combine the beef, almond flour, egg, salt, and pepper and merge with your hands until all the ingredients are evenly distributed. Divide the mixture into four equal portions, and then shape each portion into an oval patty about ½ inch thick.
2. Set the Instant Pot and heat the oil for 2 minutes. Set the oil to coat the bottom of the pot, then add the patties and sear for 3 minutes. Using a thin, flexible spatula, flip the patties and sear the second side for 2 to 3 minutes, until browned. Transfer the patties to a plate.
3. Add the onion, garlic, mushrooms, and salt to the pot and sauté for 4 minutes. Attach the tomato paste, mustard, and broth and stir with a wooden spoon. Set the patties to the pot in a single layer and spoon a bit of the sauce over each one.
4. Seal the lid and set the Pressure Release to Sealing. Push the Cancel button to reset the cooking program, then select the Pressure Cook or Manual setting and cook at high pressure.
5. To make the cauliflower: While the pressure is releasing, in a large skillet over medium heat, warm the oil. Add the cauliflower and stir or toss to coat with the oil, then cook, stirring every minute or two, until lightly browned, about 8 minutes. Turn off the heat, sprinkle in the parsley and salt, and stir to combine. Leave in the skillet, uncovered, to keep warm.
6. Open the pot and using a slotted spatula, transfer the patties to a serving plate. In a small bowl, merge together the cornstarch and water. Push the Cancel button to reset the cooking program, and then select the Sauté setting. When the sauce comes to a simmer, stir in the cornstarch mixture and let the sauce boil for about 1 minute, until thickened.
7. Spoon the sauce over the patties. Serve right away, with the cauliflower.

Nutrition:
Calories: 362
Fat: 21g
Protein: 33g
Carbohydrates: 21g
Sugars: 4g
Fiber: 6g
Sodium: 846mg

173. Blue Cheese Chicken Wedges
Preparation Time: 20 minutes **Cooking Time:** 45 minutes **Servings:** 4

Ingredients:
- Blue cheese dressing
- 2 tablespoons. crumbled blue cheese
- 4 strips of bacon
- 2 chicken breasts (boneless)
- ¾ cup of your favorite buffalo sauce

Directions:
1. Boil in a large pot of salted water.
2. Add two chicken breasts to the pot and cook for 28 minutes.
3. Close up the heat and let the chicken rest for 10 minutes. Using a fork, set out the chicken apart into strips.
4. Cook and funky the bacon strips and put them to the side.
5. On medium heat, combine the chicken and buffalo sauce. Stir until hot.
6. Add the bleu and buffalo pulled chicken. Top with the cooked bacon crumbles.
7. Serve and enjoy.

Nutrition:
Calories: 309
Carbohydrates: 27 g
Fat: 18 g
Protein: 34 g
Fiber: 29 g

174. 'Oh, so Good' Salad
Preparation Time: 5 minutes **Cooking Time:** 10 minutes **Servings:** 2

Ingredients:
- 6 Brussels sprouts
- ½ teaspoon apple cider vinegar
- 1 teaspoon olive/grape seed oil
- 1 grind of salt
- 1 tablespoon freshly grated parmesan

Directions:

1. Slice the clean Brussels sprouts in half.
2. Oppositely cut thin slices.
3. Once sliced, cut the roots off and discard.
4. Toss alongside the apple cider, oil, and salt.
5. Sprinkle with the parmesan cheese, combine and enjoy!

Nutrition:
Calories: 438
Carbohydrates: 31 g
Fat: 23 g
Protein: 24 g
Fiber: 16 g

175. Low Carb Pumpkin Pie Pudding

Preparation Time: 10 minutes **Cooking Time:** 20 minutes **Servings:** 2

Ingredients:
- 3 eggs, whisked
- ⅓ cup of almond milk, whipping
- ¼ cup of stevia sweetener
- 16 ounces of pumpkin puree
- 2 teaspoons pumpkin pie spice

Directions:
1. In a bowl, whisk eggs and add almond milk, stevia, pumpkin puree, and pumpkin pie spice.
2. Grease the oil in a steel pan and then pour egg mixture in it.
3. Pour 2 cups of water inside the instant pot and set trivet in the pot.
4. Place steel pan on top of the trivet. Cover the pan with the aluminum foil.
5. Close the pot and set the timer to 20 minutes at high pressure.
6. Once timer beeps, quick release the steam. Remove the lid of the instant pot.
7. Chill for 2 hours and then serve with whipping cream.

Nutrition:
Calories: 220
Protein: 13.8g
Fat: 15.17g
Carbohydrates: 6.41g

176. Red Cabbage Mix

Preparation Time: 10 minutes **Cooking Time:** 5 minutes **Servings:** 6

Ingredients:
- 4 tablespoons of coconut oil
- 1 teaspoon of butter
- 2 garlic cloves
- 6 cups of red cabbage, shredded
- Salt and black pepper to taste
- ½ cup of water

Directions:
1. Turn on the sauté mode of the instant pot. Add coconut oil and butter to the instant pot.
2. Heat the butter to let it melt. Add salt, pepper, and garlic cloves.
3. Cook until aroma comes. Add cabbage and pour water.
4. Seal the lid and place the timer to 5 minutes.
5. Once timer beeps, release the steam naturally. Serve and enjoy.

Nutrition:
Calories: 109
Protein: 81.01g
Fat: 29.66g
Carbohydrates: 4.39g

177. Irish Lamb Stew

Preparation Time: 10 minutes **Cooking Time:** 45 minutes **Servings:** 6

Ingredients:
- 2 pounds of lamb shank
- 3 cups of chicken broth
- 1 green onion
- ¼ teaspoon of thyme
- ½ cup of green beans, chopped
- Salt and black pepper
- 2 tablespoons of olive oil

Directions:
1. Turn on sauté mode of instant pot and add olive oil.
2. Sear the meat for 3 minutes in oil from both the sides.
3. Add green beans, green onion, and cook for one minute at sautéing mode.
4. Sprinkle salt and black pepper. Pour broth and add thyme to the pot.
5. Turn off the sauté mode and then set the timer to 45 minutes at high pressure.
6. Once timer beeps, release the steam naturally.
7. Open the instant pot and spill the mixture. Then serve.

Nutrition:
Calories: 420
Protein: 59.53g
Fat: 18.59g
Carbohydrates: 2.22g

178. Vegetables in Half and Half

Preparation Time: 10 minutes **Cooking Time:** 8 minutes **Servings:** 4

Ingredients:
- 2 medium parsnips, peeled and cubed
- 1 fennel bulb, sliced
- 3 cloves garlic, minced
- 1 cup chicken broth
- 1 cup half-and-half
- Salt and pepper, to taste

Directions:
1. Add fennel bulbs, parsnip, chicken broth, garlic, salt, and pepper into the instant pot.
2. Lock the lid of the pot. Place timer for 5 minutes at high pressure.
3. Once time beeps, quick release the steam. Turn on the sauté mode and reduce the liquid.
4. Stir occasionally. Next, add half and half and mix well.

5. Stir for 2 more minutes and then serve the dish hot. Enjoy.

Nutrition:
Calories: 212
Protein: 16.57g
Fat: 5.37g
Carbohydrates: 25.42g

179. Creamy Broccoli and Ham

Preparation Time: 10 minutes **Cooking Time:** 10 minutes **Servings:** 4

Ingredients:
- 20 ounces of broccoli
- 12 ounces of ham, smoked and chopped
- 8 ounces of fat-free cream of mushroom soup
- 1 cup almond milk
- 2 cups of Cheddar cheese, shredded
- Salt and black pepper
- 2 teaspoons of olive oil

Directions:
1. Turn on the sauté mode of the instant pot. Add oil and heat it.
2. Then add broccoli and cook for one minute. Next, add ham and season it with salt and pepper. Spill in the cream of mushroom soup and almond milk and lock the lid.
3. Set timer for 4 minutes at high pressure. Once timer beeps, quick release the steam.
4. Reduce the liquid by turning on the sauté mode. Keep stirring.
5. After a few minutes, add cheese and cook for 2 minutes at sauté mode. Once it's done serve.

Nutrition:
Calories: 209
Protein: 20.75g
Fat: 8.65g
Carbohydrates: 14.87g

180. Glazed Carrots and Cauliflower

Preparation Time: 10 minutes **Cooking Time:** 5 minutes **Servings:** 6

Ingredients:
- ⅓ pound of baby carrot
- 1 cauliflower head, small and chopped
- ¾ cup lime juice
- 3 tablespoons butter/olive oil
- ⅓ cup stevia
- ¼ teaspoon ground cinnamon
- Salt and black pepper, to taste

Directions:
1. Merge all the ingredients in the instant pot. Lock the lid and set the timer to 5 minutes.
2. Open timer beeps release the steam quickly. Open the instant pot lid. Stir and serve.

Nutrition:
Calories: 122
Protein: 2.51g
Fat: 4.91g
Carbohydrates: 23.3g

181. Broth-Braised Cabbage

Preparation Time: 10 minutes **Cooking Time:** 5 minutes **Servings:** 4

Ingredients:
- 1 head of cabbage, sliced
- 1 small onion
- 2 garlic cloves, minced
- ⅓ teaspoon star anise seeds
- ¼ cup vegetable broth
- 2 slices of diced bacon
- 2 teaspoons of olive oil
- Salt and black pepper, to taste

Directions:
1. Turn on sauté mode of the instant pot. Add oil and heat it.
2. Then add bacon and cook until crisp.
3. Then add small onions and garlic cloves and cook until aroma comes.
4. Add salt, pepper and anise seed. At the end add cabbage and pour the broth.
5. Cook on high for 3 minutes. Then quickly release the steam.
6. Serve and enjoy.

Nutrition:
Calories: 135
Protein: 4.2g
Fat: 7.73g
Carbohydrates: 14.81g

182. Shredded BBQ Cream Cheese Chicken

Preparation Time: 10 minutes **Cooking Time:** 13 minutes **Servings:** 4

Ingredients:
- 2 pounds of chicken breast
- 1 cup of water
- ½ cup of BBQ sauce, Keto based
- 6 ounces of cream cheese

Directions:
1. Pour water in instant pot. Add chicken and lock the lid.
2. Set timer for 12 minutes at high pressure. Once timer beeps, quick release the steam.
3. Transfer the chicken from the instant pot and place it on the cutting board.
4. Use a fork to scrap the chicken meat. Drain water from the instant pot.
5. Transfer the shredded chicken back to the pot.
6. Next, add cream cheese, and BBQ sauce. Stir and combine all the ingredients.
7. Turn on sauté mode and then cook for one minute. Serve and enjoy.

Nutrition:
Calories: 525
Protein: 50.81g
Fat: 33.2g
Carbohydrates: 3.67g

183. Ranch Dump Style Pork Chops

Preparation Time: 10 minutes **Cooking Time:** 12 minutes **Servings:** 8

Ingredients:
- 4 pounds of pork chops
- 2 ounces of ranch dressing mix
- 18 ounces of cream of chicken soup
- 2 cups of water

Directions:
1. Combine the listed ingredients in the instant pot. Lock the lid of the instant pot and set the timer to 12 minutes at high pressure.
2. Once timer beeps, naturally release the steam for 12 minutes. Then quickly release the steam. Open the pot, stir the ingredients and then serve.

Nutrition:
Calories: 534
Protein: 59.08g
Fat: 30.17g
Carbohydrates: 2.83g

184. Instant Pot Cinnamon Apricot and Pears

Preparation Time: 10 minutes **Cooking Time:** 5 minutes **Servings:** 3

Ingredients:
- ¼ cup of lime juice
- 2 apricots peeled
- 1 teaspoon of cinnamon
- 2 pears, peeled - Salt, pinch
- 2 scoops of stevia powder

Directions:
1. Peel, core, and slice the fruits. Transfer the apricot, cinnamon, pears, salt, and stevia in the instant pot. Pour the lime juice in the instant pot.
2. Lock the lid of the instant pot and set the timer to 2 minutes at high pressure.
3. Once timer beeps, release the steam quickly. Turn on the sauté mode and reduce the liquid.
4. Serve immediately and enjoy.

Nutrition:
Calories: 44
Protein: 0.39g
Fat: 0.07g
Carbohydrates: 12.18g

185. Beets Dijon

Preparation Time: 10 minutes **Cooking Time:** 14 minutes **Servings:** 2

Ingredients:
- 1 pound beets, peeled, cubed (½-inch)
- ⅓ cup finely chopped onion
- ⅓ cup sour cream
- 2 tablespoons Dijon mustard
- 2-3 teaspoons lemon juice
- Salt and white pepper, to taste

Directions:
1. Combine beets, onions, Dijon mustard, lemon juice, salt, and black pepper in a bowl and set aside. Pour water in the instant pot and set trivet inside the pot.
2. Place the heatproof bowl, having beets on a trivet and lock the lid.
3. Set timer to 12 minutes. Once timer beeps, release the steam quickly.
4. Remove the beets bowl from the instant pot. Drain water from pot and turn on sauté mode.
5. Transfer beet to the pot and add sour cream. Cook for 2 minutes and then serve.

Nutrition:
Calories: 297
Protein: 9.24g
Fat: 13.24g
Carbohydrates: 38.71g

Meat

186. Pork Medallions with Cherry Sauce

Preparation Time: 25 minutes **Cooking Time:** 6 to 8 minutes **Servings:** 4

Ingredients:
- 1 pork tenderloin (1 to 1¼ lb.), cut into ½-inch slices
- ½ teaspoon garlic-pepper blend
- 2 teaspoons olive oil
- ¾ cup cherry preserves
- 2 tablespoons chopped shallots
- 1 tablespoon Dijon mustard
- 1 tablespoon balsamic vinegar
- 1 clove garlic, finely chopped

Directions:
1. Drizzle both sides of pork with garlic-pepper blend.
2. In 12-inch skillet, heat 1 tsp. of the oil over medium-high heat. Attach pork; cook 6 to 8 minutes, turning once, until pork is browned and meat thermometer inserted in center reads 145F. Remove pork from skillet; keep warm.
3. In same skillet, mix remaining teaspoon oil, the preserves, shallots, mustard, vinegar and garlic, scraping any brown bits from bottom of skillet. Heat to boiling. Lower heat: simmer uncovered 10 minutes or until reduced to about ½ cup. Serve sauce over pork slices.

Nutrition:
Calories: 330
Fat: 7g
Protein: 23g
Carbohydrates: 44g
Sugars: 30g
Fiber: 1g
Sodium: 170mg

187. Pork Chops Pomodoro

Preparation Time: 0 minutes **Cooking Time:** 30 minutes **Servings:** 6

Ingredients:
- 2 pounds boneless pork loin chops
- ¾ teaspoon sea salt
- ½ tsp. freshly ground black pepper
- 2 tbsp. extra-virgin olive oil
- 2 garlic cloves, hashed
- ½ cup of vegetable broth or chicken broth
- ½ tsp. Italian seasoning
- 1 tbsp. capers, drained
- 2 cups cherry tomatoes
- 2 tbsp. fresh basil or flat-leaf parsley
- Spiralized zucchini noodles
- Lemon wedges for serving

Directions:
1. Set the pork chops dry with paper towels, then flavor them all over with the salt and pepper.
2. Set the Instant Pot and heat 1 tablespoon of the oil for 2 minutes. Set the oil to coat the bottom of the pot. Using tongs, attach half of the pork chops in a single layer and set for about 3 minutes. Set the chops to a plate. Redo with the remaining 1 tbsp. oil and pork chops.
3. Attach the garlic to the pot and sauté for about 1 minute. Spill in the broth, Italian seasoning, and capers. Transfer the pork chops to the pot. Attach the tomatoes in an even layer on top of the chops.
4. Seal the lid and set the Pressure Release to Sealing. Push the Cancel button to reset the cooking program, then select the Pressure Cook at high pressure.
5. Set the tomatoes and some of the cooking liquid on top of the pork chops. Drizzle with the basil and serve right away, with zucchini noodles and lemon wedges on the side.

Nutrition:
Calories: 265
Fat: 13g
Protein: 31g
Carbohydrates: 3g
Sugars: 2g
Fiber: 1g
Sodium: 460mg

188. Meatballs Barley Soup
Preparation Time: 15 minutes **Cooking Time:** 35 minutes **Servings:** 6

Ingredients:
- 2 cups of water
- 1 can of Great Northern beans, washed and drained,
- ½ cup of quick-cooking barley
- 4 cups of fresh baby spinach leaves,
- 1 pound 90% or higher lean ground beef
- 1 tablespoon of olive oil
- 3 medium carrots, peeled and coarsely chopped
- 2 medium yellow and/or red bell peppers, seeded and cut into bite-size strips
- 1 medium onion, chopped
- 2 cups of less-sodium beef stock
- ¾ cup of soft whole-wheat breadcrumbs
- ¼ cup of refrigerated or frozen egg product, thawed, or 1 egg, lightly beaten
- 4 cloves garlic, minced, divided
- 2 tsp. of chopped fresh rosemary, or ½ tsp. of crushed dried rosemary, divided
- ¼ teaspoon of ground pepper

Directions:
1. Preheat oven to 350 F.
2. Combine breadcrumbs, egg, half of the garlic, half of the rosemary, and the ground pepper in a large bowl.
3. Add ground beef; mix well. Shape the meat mixture into a 1 ½-inch meatball.
4. Place the meatballs in a foil-lined 15x10-inch baking pan.
5. Bake for about 15 minutes. Set aside.
6. Warmth oil over medium heat in a large pot. Add carrot, bell pepper, onion, and the remaining garlic; cook for 5 minutes, stirring occasionally.
7. Add beef stock, water, Great Northern beans, barley, and the remaining rosemary.
8. Bring to boiling; reduce heat. Seal and simmer for about 15 minutes or until the barley is tender.
9. Add the meatballs to the barley mixture, heat through. Stir in spinach just before serving.

Nutrition:
Calories: 325
Fat: 8g
Protein: 35g
Carbohydrates: 26g
Sugars: 6g
Fiber: 4g
Sodium: 560mg

189. Beef Massaman Curry
Preparation Time: 10 minutes **Cooking Time:** 2 hours **Servings:** 4

Ingredients:
- 2 onions, roughly chopped
- 4 kaffir lime leaves
- 1.5 tablespoon of tamarind paste
- 1.5 tablespoon of fish sauce
- 75grams of unsalted peanuts
- 400ml of coconut milk
- 3 tablespoons of massaman curry paste
- 550grams of stewing beef steak, diced
- 300grams of potatoes, diced
- 1 red chili, seeds detached and finely sliced, to serve

Directions:
1. Preheat the oven to 200C.
2. Roast the peanuts for 4-5 minutes.
3. Once they have cooled, chop them roughly.
4. Then lower the oven temperature to 200C.
5. Heat 2 tbsp. of coconut cream in a casserole dish that has a lid.
6. Merge in the curry paste and fry for a minute.
7. Set in the beef and cook for about 6 minutes.
8. Attach the remaining coconut cream with half a can of water, the potatoes, onions, fish sauce, kaffir leaves, tamarind paste, and most of the peanuts.
9. Place the lid on the curry. Set in the oven for 2 hours until tender.
10. Sprinkle the sliced chili and the rest of the peanuts.
11. Serve and enjoy!

Nutrition:
Calories: 320
Fat: 4g
Protein: 23g
Carbohydrates: 48g
Sugar: 1.1g
Fiber: 3g
Sodium: 420mg

190. Old Fashioned Beef Soup with Vegetables
Preparation Time: 25 minutes **Cooking Time:** 4 hours 15 minutes **Servings:** 10

Ingredients:
- 1 bay leaf
- ¼ teaspoon of dried marjoram

- ¼ teaspoon of dried oregano
- 2 pounds of beef soup bones
- 1 large carrot, skinned and cut into large chunks
- 1 small green bell pepper, chopped
- 2 tablespoons of butter
- 1 onion, coarsely chopped
- 4 stalks celery, chopped
- ⅓ pound of lean round steak, cut into ½-inch cubes
- 1-quart of beef stock
- 1-quart of water
- ¼ cup of dry black beans
- ¼ cup of dried split peas
- ¼ cup of white rice
- 1 large potato, skinned and cut into large chunks
- ¼ cup of elbow macaroni
- 1 cup of crushed tomatoes in puree
- ¼ cup of chopped cabbage
- 1 cup of red wine
- salt and ground black pepper to taste

Directions:
1. In a large stockpot, dissolve the butter over medium heat; cook the onion, steak, and celery in the melted butter for about 7 to 10 minutes until the onions caramelize.
2. Add the beef, stock, bay leaf, water, oregano, marjoram, and soup bones; lower the heat to medium-low and simmer for about 3 hours.
3. Add the carrot, potato, bell pepper, black beans, rice, split peas, tomatoes in puree, macaroni, red wine, and cabbage to the stockpot.
4. Simmer for about an hour.
5. Remove the soup bones, scraping any meat from them back into the pot.
6. Season with pepper and salt to serve.

Nutrition:
Calories: 140
Fat: 7g
Protein: 18g
Carbohydrates: 3g
Sugars: 1g
Fiber: 1g
Sodium: 141mg

191. Beef and Red Bean Chili

Preparation Time: 10 minutes **Cooking Time:** 6 hours **Servings:** 4

Ingredients:
- 1 cup dry red beans
- 1 tablespoon olive oil
- 2 pounds boneless beef chuck
- 1 large onion, coarsely chopped
- 1 (14 ounce) can beef broth
- 2 chipotle chili peppers in adobo sauce
- 2 teaspoons dried oregano, crushed
- 1 teaspoon ground cumin
- ½ teaspoon salt
- 1 (14.5 ounce) can tomatoes with mild green chilis
- 1 (15 ounce) can tomato sauce
- ¼ cup snipped fresh cilantro
- 1 medium red sweet pepper

Directions:
1. Rinse out the beans and place them into a Dutch oven or big saucepan, then add in water enough to cover them. Allow the beans to boil then drop the heat down. Simmer the beans without a cover for 10 minutes. Take off the heat and keep covered for an hour.
2. In a big fry pan, heat up the oil upon medium-high heat, then cook onion and half the beef until they brown a bit over medium-high heat. Move into a 3 ½- or 4-quart crockery cooker.
3. Do this again with what's left of the beef. Add in tomato sauce, tomatoes (not drained), salt, cumin, oregano, adobo sauce, chipotle peppers, and broth, stirring to blend. Strain out and rinse beans and stir in the cooker.
4. Cook while sealed on a low setting for around 10-12 hours or on high setting for 5-6 hours. Spoon the chili into bowls or mugs and top with sweet pepper and cilantro.

Nutrition:
Calories: 303
Fat: 7g
Protein: 32g
Carbohydrates: 27g
Sugars: 7g
Fiber: 4g
Sodium: 310mg

192. Cider Pork Stew

Preparation Time: 9 minutes **Cooking Time:** 12 hours **Servings:** 3

Ingredients:
- 2 pounds pork shoulder roast
- 3 medium cubed potatoes
- 3 medium carrots
- 2 medium onions, sliced
- 1 cup coarsely chopped apple
- ½ cup coarsely chopped celery
- 3 tablespoons quick-cooking tapioca
- 2 cups apple juice
- 1 teaspoon salt
- 1 teaspoon caraway seeds
- ¼ teaspoon black pepper

Directions:
1. Chop the meat into 1-in. cubes. In the 3.5- 5.5 qt. slow cooker, mix the tapioca, celery, apple, onions, carrots, potatoes and meat. Whisk in pepper, caraway seeds, salt and apple juice.
2. Keep covered and cook over low heat setting for 10-12 hours. If you want, use the celery leaves to decorate each of the servings.

Nutrition:
Calories: 268
Fat: 10g
Protein: 25g
Carbohydrates: 26g
Sugars: 7g
Fiber: 7g
Sodium: 3887mg

193. Cuban Pulled Pork Sandwich

Preparation Time: 6 minutes **Cooking Time:** 5 hours **Servings:** 5

Ingredients:
- 1 teaspoon dried oregano, crushed
- ¾ teaspoon ground cumin
- ½ teaspoon ground coriander
- ¼ teaspoon salt
- ¼ teaspoon black pepper
- ¼ teaspoon ground allspice
- 1 2 to 2½-pound boneless pork shoulder roast
- 1 tablespoon olive oil
- Nonstick cooking spray
- 2 cups sliced onions
- 2 green sweet peppers, cut into bite-size strips
- ½ to 1 fresh jalapeño pepper
- 4 cloves garlic, minced
- ¼ cup orange juice
- ¼ cup lime juice
- 6 heart-healthy wheat hamburger buns, toasted
- 2 tablespoons jalapeño mustard

Directions:
1. Mix allspice, oregano, black pepper, cumin, salt, and coriander together in a small bowl. Press each side of the roast into the spice mixture. On medium-high heat, heat oil in a big non-stick pan; put in roast. Cook for 5mins until both sides of the roast is light brown, turn the roast one time.
2. Using a cooking spray, grease a 3 ½ or 4qt slow cooker; arrange the garlic, onions, jalapeno, and green peppers in a layer. Pour in lime juice and orange juice. Slice the roast if needed to fit inside the cooker; put on top of the vegetables covered or 4 ½-5hrs on high heat setting.
3. Move roast to a cutting board using a slotted spoon. Drain the cooking liquid and keep the jalapeno, green peppers, and onions. Shred the roast with 2 forks then place it back in the cooker. Remove fat from the liquid. Mix half cup of cooking liquid and reserved vegetables into the cooker. Pour in more cooking liquid if desired. Discard the remaining cooking liquid.
4. Slather mustard on rolls. Split the meat between the bottom roll halves. Add avocado on top if desired. Place the roll tops to sandwiches.

Nutrition:
Calories: 321
Fat: 13g
Protein: 11g
Carbohydrates: 42g
Sugars: 7g
Fiber: 11g
Sodium: 412mg

194. Sunday Pot Roast

Preparation Time: 10 minutes **Cooking Time:** 1 hour 45 minutes **Servings:** 10

Ingredients:
- 1 (3- to 4-pound / 1.4- to 1.8-kg) beef rump roast
- 2 teaspoons kosher salt, divided
- 2 tablespoons avocado oil
- 1 large onion, coarsely hashed (about 1½ cups)
- 4 large carrots, each divide into 4 pieces
- 1 tablespoon minced garlic
- 3 cups low-sodium beef broth
- 1 teaspoon freshly ground black pepper
- 1 tablespoon dried parsley
- 2 tablespoons all-purpose flour

Directions:
1. Rub the roast all over with 1 teaspoon of the salt.
2. Warmth the pot and pour in the avocado oil.
3. Carefully set the roast in the pot and sear it for 6 to 9 minutes on each side.
4. Set the roast from the pot to a plate.
5. In order, place the onion, carrots, and garlic in the pot. Form the roast on top of the vegetables along with any juices that accumulated on the plate.
6. In a bowl, whisk together the broth, remaining 1 teaspoon of salt, pepper, and parsley. Pour the broth mixture over the roast.
7. Seal and lock the pressure cooker. Set the valve to sealing.
8. Set on high pressure for 1 hr. and 30 minutes. When the cooking is complete, hit Cancel and allow the pressure to release naturally.
9. Once the pin drops, unseal and remove the lid.
10. Using large slotted spoons, bring the roast and vegetables to a serving platter while you make the gravy.
11. Using a large spoon or fat separator, detach the fat from the juices. Choose the electric pressure cooker to the Sauté setting and set the liquid to a boil.
12. In a small bowl, spill together the flour and 4 tbsp. of water to make a slurry. Spill the slurry into the pot, whisking occasionally, until the gravy is the thickness you like. Season with salt and pepper, if necessary.
13. Serve with the gravy.

Nutrition:
Calories: 245
Fat: 10g
Protein: 33g
Carbohydrates: 6g
Sugars: 2g
Fiber: 1g
Sodium: 397mg

195. Broccoli Beef Stir-Fry

Preparation Time: 10 minutes **Cooking Time:** 15 minutes **Servings:** 4

Ingredients:
- 2 tablespoons extra-virgin olive oil
- 1 pound (454 g) sirloin steak, cut into ¼-inch-thick strips
- 2 cups broccoli florets
- 1 garlic clove, minced
- 1 teaspoon peeled and grated fresh ginger
- 2 tablespoons reduced-sodium soy sauce
- ¼ cup beef broth
- ½ teaspoon Chinese hot mustard
- Pinch red pepper flakes

Directions:
1. In a skillet over medium-high heat, warmth the olive oil until it shimmers. Add the beef. Cook, stirring, until it browns, 3 to 5 minutes. With a slotted spoon, detach the beef from the oil and set it aside on a plate.

2. Add the broccoli to the oil. Cook, stirring, until it is crisp-tender, about 4 minutes.
3. Add the garlic and ginger and cook, stirring constantly, for 30 seconds.
4. Set the beef to the pan, along with any juices that have collected.
5. In a small bowl, whisk together the soy sauce, broth, mustard, and red pepper flakes.
6. Attach the soy sauce mixture to the skillet and cook, stirring, until everything warms through, about 3 minutes.

Nutrition:
Calories: 227
Fat: 11g
Protein: 27g
Carbohydrates: 5g
Sugars: 0g
Fiber: 1g
Sodium: 375mg

196. Beef and Pepper Fajita Bowls
Preparation Time: 10 minutes **Cooking Time:** 15 minutes **Servings:** 4
Ingredients:
- 4 tablespoons extra-virgin olive oil, divided
- 1 head cauliflower, riced
- 1 pound (454 g) sirloin steak, cut into ¼-inch-thick strips
- 1 red bell pepper, seeded and sliced
- 1 onion, thinly sliced
- 2 garlic cloves, minced
- Juice of 2 limes
- 1 teaspoon chili powder

Directions:
1. In a skillet over medium-high heat, warmth 2 tablespoons of olive oil until it shimmers. Attach the cauliflower. Cook and stir.
2. Clean out the skillet. Attach the remaining 2 tablespoons of oil to the skillet and heat it on medium-high until it shimmers. Attach the steak and cook until it browns. Use a slotted spoon to detach the steak from the oil in the pan and set aside.
3. Attach the bell pepper and onion to the pan. Cook and stir until they start to brown, about 5 minutes.
4. Attach d the garlic and cook, stirring constantly, for 30 seconds.
5. Set the beef along with any juices that have collected and the cauliflower to the pan. Attach the lime juice and chili powder. Cook and stir until everything is warmed through, 2 to 3 minutes.

Nutrition:
Calories: 310
Fat: 18g
Protein: 27g
Carbohydrates: 13g
Sugars: 2g
Fiber: 3g
Sodium: 93mg

197. Meat skewers with polenta
Preparation Time: 10 minutes **Cooking Time:** 15 minutes **Servings:** 4
Ingredients:
- 130 g polenta, instant
- Vegetable broth
- 1 organic lemon
- 2 tbsp. parmesan, grated
- Chili flakes, to taste
- 250 g of green asparagus
- 2 carrots, large
- 1 ½ tbsp. oil for frying
- Sea salt and black pepper, fresh
- 4 tbsp. sour cream
- 250 g pork schnitzel
- Paprika powder, noble sweet and parsley, fresh
- Metal skewers

Directions:
1. Prepare the polenta with stock according to the instructions on the packet. Wash the lemon, make zest and squeeze. Season the polenta with 2 teaspoons of lemon juice, a little zest, cheese and chili to taste.
2. Wash and clean the asparagus and carrots, cut lengthways into thin strips with a peeler.
3. Dab the schnitzel with kitchen paper and pound, cut into strips, then slide on skewers in waves, season with sea salt and pepper. Wash, dry and chop parsley.
4. Warmth a pan with oil and fry the skewers for about 5 minutes (the meat should be done).
5. Keep the skewers warm in the oven. Fry the vegetables in oil until al dente, then season with salt and pepper. Pour in a little broth, bring to the boil. And finally stir in the sour cream.
6. Arrange the skewers and vegetables on two plates and sprinkle with the parsley.

Nutrition:
Calories: 200
Fat: 8g
Protein: 30g
Carbohydrates: 1g
Sugars: 1g
Fiber: 0g
Sodium: 394mg

198. Chipotle Chili Pork Chops
Preparation Time: 5 minutes **Cooking Time:** 20 minutes **Servings:** 4
Ingredients:
- Juice and zest of 1 lime
- 1 tablespoon extra-virgin olive oil
- 1 tablespoon chipotle chili powder
- 2 teaspoons minced garlic
- 1 teaspoon ground cinnamon
- Pinch sea salt
- 4 (5-ounce / 142-g) pork chops, about 1 inch thick
- Lime wedges, for garnish

Directions:
1. Combine the lime juice and zest, oil, chipotle chili powder, garlic, cinnamon, and salt in a resalable plastic bag. Add the pork chops. Detach as much air as possible and seal the bag.
2. Marinate the chops in the refrigerator for at least 4 hours, and up to 24 hours, turning them several times.
3. Warmth the oven to 400F (205C) and set a rack on a baking sheet. Let the chops rest, then arrange them on the rack and discard the remaining marinade.
4. Roast the chops until cooked through, turning once, about 10 minutes per side.

5. Serve with lime wedges.

Nutrition:
Calories: 204 Carbohydrates: 1g Sodium: 317mg
Fat: 9g Sugars: 1g
Protein: 30g Fiber: 0g

199. Lime-Parsley Lamb Cutlets

Preparation Time: 10 minutes **Cooking Time:** 10 minutes **Servings:** 4

Ingredients:
- ¼ cup extra-virgin olive oil
- ¼ cup freshly squeezed lime juice
- 2 tablespoons lime zest
- 2 tablespoons chopped fresh parsley
- Pinch sea salt
- Pinch freshly ground black pepper
- 12 lamb cutlets (about 1½ pounds / 680 g total)

Directions:
1. In a medium bowl, merge together the oil, lime juice, zest, parsley, salt, and pepper.
2. Transfer the marinade to a resalable plastic bag.
3. Attach the cutlets to the bag and remove as much air as possible before sealing.
4. Marinate the lamb for about 4 hours, turning the bag several times.
5. Preheat the oven to broil.
6. Detach the chops from the bag and arrange them on an aluminum foil-lined baking sheet. Discard the marinade.
7. Simmer the chops for 4 minutes per side for medium doneness.
8. Let the chops rest before serving.

Nutrition:
Calories: 413 Carbohydrates: 1g Sodium: 100mg
Fat: 29g Sugars: 0g
Protein: 31g Fiber: 0g

200. Traditional Beef Stroganoff

Preparation Time: 10 minutes **Cooking Time:** 30 minutes **Servings:** 4

Ingredients:
- 1 teaspoon extra-virgin olive oil
- 1 pound (454 g) top sirloin, cut into thin strips
- 1 cup sliced button mushrooms
- ½ sweet onion, finely chopped
- 1 teaspoon minced garlic
- 1 tablespoon whole-wheat flour
- ½ cup low-sodium beef broth
- ¼ cup dry sherry
- ½ cup fat-free sour cream
- 1 tablespoon chopped fresh parsley
- Sea salt and freshly ground black pepper

Directions:
1. Set a large skillet with medium-high heat and add the oil.
2. Sauté the beef until browned, about 10 minutes, then remove the beef with a slotted spoon to a plate and set it aside.
3. Attach the mushrooms, onion, and garlic to the skillet and sauté until lightly browned, about 5 minutes.
4. Whisk in the flour and then whisk in the beef broth and sherry.
5. Return the sirloin to the skillet and bring the mixture to a boil.
6. Set the heat to low and simmer until the beef is tender, about 10 minutes.
7. Stir in the sour cream and parsley. Season with salt and pepper.

Nutrition:
Calories: 257 Carbohydrates: 6g Sodium: 141mg
Fat: 14g Sugars: 1g
Protein: 26g Fiber: 1g

201. Smothered Sirloin

Preparation Time: 15 minutes **Cooking Time:** 30 minutes **Servings:** 5

Ingredients:
- 1 pound (454 g) beef round sirloin tip
- 1 teaspoon freshly ground black pepper
- 1 teaspoon celery seeds
- 2 tablespoons extra-virgin olive oil
- 1 medium yellow onion, chopped
- ¼ cup chickpea flour
- 2 cups chicken broth, divided
- 2 celery stalks, thinly sliced
- 1 medium red bell pepper, chopped
- 2 garlic cloves, minced
- 2 tablespoons whole-wheat flour
- Generous pinch cayenne pepper
- Chopped fresh chives, for garnish (optional)
- Smoked paprika, for garnish (optional)

Directions:
1. In a bowl, season the steak on both sides with the black pepper and celery seeds.
2. Select the Sauté setting on an electric pressure cooker and combine the olive oil and onions. Cook and stir until the onions are ready but not burned.
3. Slowly add the chickpea flour, 1 tablespoon at a time, while stirring.
4. Add 1 cup of broth, ¼ cup at a time, as needed.
5. Stir in the celery, bell pepper, and garlic and cook for 3 to 5 minutes, or until softened.
6. Lay the beef on top of vegetables and pour the remaining 1 cup of broth on top.
7. Seal the lid and cook for 20 minutes.
8. Once cooking is complete, quick-release the pressure. Carefully remove the lid.
9. Remove the steak and vegetables from the pressure cooker, reserving the leftover liquid for the gravy base.
10. To make the gravy, add the whole-wheat flour and cayenne to the liquid in the pressure cooker, mixing continuously until thickened.

11. To serve, spoon the gravy over the steak and garnish with the chives (if using) and paprika (if using).

Nutrition:
Calories: 253
Fat: 13g
Protein: 22g
Carbohydrates: 10g
Sugars: 3g
Fiber: 2g
Sodium: 86mg

202. Loaded Cottage Pie
Preparation Time: 15 minutes **Cooking Time:** 60 minutes **Servings:** 6-8

Ingredients:
- 4 large russet potatoes, peeled and halved
- 3 tablespoons extra-virgin olive oil, divided
- 1 small onion, chopped
- 1 bunch collard greens, stemmed and thinly sliced
- 2 carrots, peeled and chopped
- 2 medium tomatoes, chopped
- 1 garlic clove, minced
- 1 pound (454 g) 90 percent lean ground beef
- ½ cup chicken broth
- 1 teaspoon Worcestershire sauce
- 1 teaspoon celery seeds
- 1 teaspoon smoked paprika
- ½ teaspoon dried chives
- ½ teaspoon ground mustard
- ½ teaspoon cayenne pepper

Directions:
1. Preheat the oven to 400F (205C).
2. Set a pot of water to a boil.
3. Attach the potatoes, and boil for 15 to 20 minutes, or until fork-tender.
4. Set the potatoes to a large bowl and mash with 1 tablespoon of olive oil.
5. In a large cast iron skillet, heat the remaining 2 tablespoons of olive oil.
6. Add the onion, collard greens, carrots, tomatoes, and garlic and sauté, stirring often, for 7 to 10 minutes until the vegetables are softened.
7. Add the beef, broth, Worcestershire sauce, celery seeds, and smoked paprika.
8. Spread the meat and vegetable mixture evenly onto the bottom of a casserole dish. Sprinkle the chives, ground mustard, and cayenne on top of the mixture. Drizzle the mashed potatoes evenly over the top.
9. Transfer the casserole dish to the oven, and bake for 30 minutes, or until the top is light golden brown.

Nutrition:
Calories: 440
Fat: 17g
Protein: 27g
Carbohydrates: 48g
Sugars: 6g
Fiber: 9g
Sodium: 107mg

203. Fresh Pot Pork Butt
Preparation Time: 10 minutes **Cooking Time:** 45 minutes **Servings:** 8

Ingredients:
- 2 tablespoons extra-virgin olive oil
- ¼ cup apple cider vinegar
- 1 tablespoon freshly ground black pepper
- 1 tablespoon dried oregano
- 1 small yellow onion, minced
- 2 scallions, white and green parts, minced
- 1 celery stalk, minced
- Juice of 1 lime
- 2 pounds (907 g) boneless pork butt
- 4 garlic cloves, sliced
- 1 cup chicken broth

Directions:
1. In a medium bowl, merge the oil, vinegar, pepper, oregano, onion, scallions, celery, and lime juice. Mix well until a paste is formed.
2. Score the pork with 1-inch-deep cuts in a diamond pattern on both sides. Push the garlic into the slits.
3. Massage the paste all over meat. Secure and refrigerate overnight or for at least 4 hours.
4. Select the Sauté setting on an electric pressure cooker. Cook the meat on each side.
5. Attach the broth, close and lock the lid, and set the pressure valve to sealing.
6. Change to the Manual setting and cook for 20 minutes.
7. Once cooking is complete, allow the pressure to release naturally. Carefully remove the lid.
8. Detach the pork from the pressure cooker and serve with Ranch Dressing.

Nutrition:
Calories: 287
Fat: 22g
Protein: 20g
Carbohydrates: 1g
Sugars: 1g
Fiber: 1g
Sodium: 88mg

204. Pork Diane
Preparation Time: 10 minutes **Cooking Time:** 20 minutes **Servings:** 4

Ingredients:
- 2 teaspoons Worcestershire sauce
- 1 tablespoon freshly squeezed lemon juice
- ¼ cup low-sodium chicken broth
- 2 teaspoons Dijon mustard
- 4 (5-ounce / 142-g) boneless pork top loin chops, about 1 inch thick
- Sea salt and freshly ground black pepper
- 1 teaspoon extra-virgin olive oil

- 2 teaspoons chopped fresh chives
- 1 teaspoon lemon zest

Directions:
1. Combine the Worcestershire sauce, lemon juice, broth, and Dijon mustard in a bowl. Stir to mix well.
2. On a clean work surface, massage the pork chops with salt and ground black pepper.
3. Heat the olive oil in a nonstick skillet over medium-high heat until shimmering.
4. Add the pork chops and sear for 16 minutes or until well browned. Flip the pork halfway through the cooking time. Transfer to a plate and set aside.
5. Pour the sauce mixture in the skillet and cook for 2 minutes or until warmed through and lightly thickened. Mix in the chives and lemon zest.
6. Baste the pork with the sauce mixture and serve immediately.

Nutrition:
Calories: 355
Fat: 27.1g
Protein: 19.8g
Carbs: 5.9g
Fiber: 1.0g
Sugar: 4.0g
Sodium: 200mg

205. Autumn Pork Chops

Preparation Time: 15 minutes **Cooking Time:** 30 minutes **Servings:** 4

Ingredients:
- ¼ cup apple cider vinegar
- 2 tablespoons granulated sweetener
- 4 (4-ounce / 113-g) pork chops, about 1 inch thick
- Sea salt and freshly ground black pepper
- 1 tablespoon extra-virgin olive oil
- ½ red cabbage, finely shredded
- 1 sweet onion, thinly sliced
- 1 apple, peeled, cored, and sliced
- 1 teaspoon chopped fresh thyme

Directions:
1. In a small bowl, merge together the vinegar and sweetener. Set it aside.
2. Season the pork with salt and pepper.
3. Set a large skillet with medium-high heat and add the olive oil.
4. Cook the pork chops, turning once, about 8 minutes per side.
5. Bring the chops to a plate and set aside.
6. Attach the cabbage and onion to the skillet and sauté until the vegetables have softened, about 5 minutes.
7. Add the vinegar mixture and the apple slices to the skillet and bring the mixture to a boil.
8. Set the heat to low and simmer, covered, for 5 additional minutes.
9. Return the pork chops to the skillet, along with any accumulated juices and thyme, cover, and cook for 5 more minutes.

Nutrition:
Calories: 224
Fat: 8.1g
Protein: 26.1g
Carbohydrates: 12.1g
Fiber: 3.1g
Sugar: 8.0g
Sodium: 293mg

206. Roasted Pork Loin with Carrots

Preparation Time: 5 minutes **Cooking Time:** 40 minutes **Servings:** 4

Ingredients:
- 1 pound (454 g) pork loin
- 1 tablespoon extra-virgin olive oil, divided
- 2 teaspoons honey
- ¼ teaspoon freshly ground black pepper
- ½ teaspoon dried rosemary
- 4 (6-inch) carrots, chopped into ½-inch rounds

Directions:
1. Preheat the oven to 350F (180C).
2. Rub the pork loin with ½ tablespoon of oil and the honey. Season with the pepper and rosemary.
3. In a medium bowl, spill the carrots in the remaining ½ tablespoon of oil.
4. Place the pork and the carrots on a baking sheet in a single layer. Cook for 40 minutes.
5. Detach the baking sheet from the oven and let the pork rest for at least 10 minutes before slicing. Divide the pork and carrots into four equal portions.

Nutrition:
Calories: 344
Fat: 10.1g
Protein: 26.1g
Carbohydrates: 25.9g
Fiber: 3.9g
Sugar: 6.0g
Sodium: 110mg

207. Herbed Meatballs

Preparation Time: 10 minutes **Cooking Time:** 15 minutes **Servings:** 4

Ingredients:
- ½ pound (227 g) lean ground pork
- ½ pound (227 g) lean ground beef
- 1 sweet onion, finely chopped
- ¼ cup breadcrumbs
- 2 tablespoons chopped fresh basil
- 2 teaspoons minced garlic
- 1 egg
- Pinch sea salt
- Pinch freshly ground black pepper

Directions:
1. Preheat the oven to 350F (180C).
2. Set a baking tray with parchment paper and set it aside.
3. In a large bowl, mix the pork, beef, onion, breadcrumbs, basil, garlic, egg, salt, and pepper until very well mixed.
4. Roll the meat mixture into 2-inch meatballs. Bake for about 15 minutes.
5. Set with marinara sauce and some steamed green beans.

Nutrition:
Calories: 333　　Carbohydrates: 12.9g　　Sodium: 189mg
Fat: 19.1g　　Fiber: 0.9g
Protein: 24.1g　　Sugar: 2.9g

208. Roasted Beef with Shallot Sauce

Preparation Time: 10 minutes　　**Cooking Time:** 100 minutes　　**Servings:** 4

Ingredients:
- 1½ pounds (680 g) top rump beef roast
- Sea salt and freshly ground black pepper
- 3 teaspoons extra-virgin olive oil, divided
- 3 shallots, minced
- 2 teaspoons minced garlic
- 1 tablespoon green peppercorns
- 2 tablespoons dry sherry
- 2 tablespoons all-purpose flour
- 1 cup sodium-free beef broth

Directions:
1. Heat the oven to 300F (150C).
2. Season the roast with salt and pepper.
3. Set a skillet over medium-high heat and attach 2 teaspoons of olive oil.
4. Brown the beef on all sides, about 10 minutes in total, and transfer the roast to a baking dish.
5. Roast until desired doneness, about 1½ hours for medium.
6. In a saucepan with medium-high heat, sauté the shallots in the remaining 1 teaspoon of olive oil until translucent, about 4 minutes.
7. Stir in the garlic and peppercorns and cook for another minute. Whisk in the sherry to deglaze the pan.
8. Spill in the flour to form a thick paste, cooking for 1 minute and stirring constantly.
9. Spill in the beef broth and whisk until the sauce is thick and glossy, about 4 minutes. Season the sauce with salt and pepper.
10. Serve the beef with a generous spoonful of sauce.

Nutrition:
Calories: 331　　Carbohydrates: 3.9g　　Sodium: 208mg
Fat: 18.1g　　Fiber: 0g
Protein: 36.1g　　Sugar: 1.0g

209. Beef Stroganoff

Preparation Time: 10 minutes　　**Cooking Time:** 30 minutes　　**Servings:** 4

Ingredients:
- 1 teaspoon extra-virgin olive oil
- 1 pound (454 g) top sirloin, cut into thin strips
- 1 cup sliced button mushrooms
- ½ sweet onion, finely chopped
- 1 teaspoon minced garlic
- 1 tablespoon whole-wheat flour
- ½ cup low-sodium beef broth
- ¼ cup dry sherry
- ½ cup fat-free sour cream
- 1 tablespoon chopped fresh parsley
- Sea salt and freshly ground black pepper

Directions:
1. Set a large skillet with medium-high heat and add the oil.
2. Sauté the beef until browned, about 10 minutes, then remove the beef with a slotted spoon to a plate and set it aside.
3. Attach the mushrooms, onion, and garlic to the skillet and sauté until lightly browned, about 5 minutes.
4. Whisk in the flour and then whisk in the beef broth and sherry.
5. Return the sirloin to the skillet and bring the mixture to a boil.
6. Set the heat to low and simmer until the beef is tender, about 10 minutes.
7. Stir in the sour cream and parsley. Season with salt and pepper.

Nutrition:
Calories: 258　　Carbohydrates: 6.1g　　Sodium: 142mg
Fat: 14.1g　　Fiber: 1.1g
Protein: 26.1g　　Sugar: 1.0g

210. Pulled Pork Sandwiches with Apricot Jelly

Preparation Time: 5 minutes　　**Cooking Time:** 15 minutes　　**Servings:** 4

Ingredients:
- Avocado oil cooking spray
- 8 ounces (227 g) store-bought pulled pork
- ½ cup chopped green bell pepper
- 2 slices provolone cheese
- 4 whole-wheat sandwich thins
- 2½ tablespoons apricot jelly

Directions:
1. Heat the pulled pork according to the package instructions.
2. Heat a medium skillet over medium-low heat. When hot, coat the cooking surface with cooking spray.
3. Put the bell pepper in the skillet and cook for 5 minutes. Set to a small bowl and set aside.
4. Meanwhile, tear each slice of cheese into 2 strips, and halves the sandwich thins so you have a top and bottom.
5. Set the heat to low, and place the sandwich thins in the skillet cut-side down to toast, about 2 minutes.
6. Remove the sandwich thins from the skillet. Spread one-quarter of the jelly on the bottom half of each sandwich thin, and then place one-quarter of the cheese, pulled pork, and pepper on top. Seal with the top half of the sandwich thin.

Nutrition:
Calories: 250　　Carbohydrates: 34.1g　　Sodium: 510mg
Fat: 8.1g　　Fiber: 6.1g
Protein: 16.1g　　Sugar: 8.0g

211. Beef and Mushroom Cauliflower Wraps

Preparation Time: 5 minutes **Cooking Time:** 20 minutes **Servings:** 4

Ingredients:
- Avocado oil cooking spray
- ½ cup chopped white onion
- 1 cup chopped Portobello mushrooms
- 1 pound (454 g) 93% lean ground beef
- ½ teaspoon garlic powder
- Pinch salt
- 1 (10-ounce / 283-g) bag frozen cauliflower rice
- 12 iceberg lettuce leaves
- ¾ cup shredded Cheddar cheese

Directions:
1. Heat a large skillet over medium heat. When hot, coat the cooking surface with cooking spray and add the onion and mushrooms. Cook for 5 minutes, stirring occasionally.
2. Add the beef, garlic powder, and salt, stirring and breaking apart the meat as needed. Cook for 5 minutes.
3. Stir in the frozen cauliflower rice and increase the heat to medium-high. Cook for 5 minutes more, or until the water evaporates.
4. For each portion, use three lettuce leaves. Spoon one-quarter of the filling onto the lettuce leaves, and top with one-quarter of the cheese. Roll up the lettuce to close the wrap. Repeat with the remaining lettuce leaves and filling.

Nutrition:
Calories: 290
Fat: 15.1g
Protein: 31.1g
Carbohydrates: 7.1g
Fiber: 3.1g
Sugar: 4.0g
Sodium: 265mg

212. Zucchini Carbonara

Preparation Time: 10 minutes **Cooking Time:** 25 minutes **Servings:** 4

Ingredients:
- 6 slices bacon, cut into pieces
- 1 red onion, finely chopped
- 3 zucchinis, cut into noodles
- 1 cup peas
- ½ teaspoon sea salt
- 3 garlic cloves, minced
- 3 large eggs, beaten
- 1 tablespoon heavy cream
- Pinch red pepper flakes
- ½ cup grated Parmesan cheese

Directions:
1. In a skillet with medium-high heat, cook the bacon, about 5 minutes. With a slotted spoon, set the bacon to a plate.
2. Attach the onion to the bacon fat in the pan and cook, stirring, until soft, 3 to 5 minutes. Attach the zucchini, peas, and salt. Cook, stirring, until the zucchini softens, about 3 minutes. Attach the garlic and cook, stirring constantly, for 5 minutes.
3. In a small bowl, whisk together the eggs, cream, and red pepper flakes. Add to the vegetables.
4. Detach the pan from the stove top and stir for 3 minutes, allowing the heat of the pan to cook the eggs without setting them.
5. Return the bacon to the pan and stir to mix.
6. Serve topped with Parmesan cheese, if desired.

Nutrition:
Calories: 327
Fat: 24.1g
Protein: 14.1g
Carbohydrates: 14.9g
Fiber: 3.9g
Sugar: 11.0g
Sodium: 556mg

213. Steak and Broccoli Bowls

Preparation Time: 10 minutes **Cooking Time:** 15 minutes **Servings:** 4

Ingredients:
- 2 tablespoons extra-virgin olive oil
- 1 pound (454 g) sirloin steak, cut into ¼-inch-thick strips
- 2 cups broccoli florets
- 1 garlic clove, minced
- 1 teaspoon peeled and grated fresh ginger
- 2 tablespoons reduced-sodium soy sauce
- ¼ cup beef broth
- ½ teaspoon Chinese hot mustard
- Pinch red pepper flakes

Directions:
1. In a skillet with medium-high heat, heat the olive oil until it shimmers. Add the beef. Cook, stirring, until it browns, 3 to 5 minutes. With a slotted spoon, detach the beef from the oil and set it aside on a plate.
2. Add the broccoli to the oil. Cook, stirring, until it is crisp-tender, about 4 minutes.
3. Add the garlic and ginger and cook, stirring constantly, for 30 seconds.
4. Set the beef to the pan, along with any juices that have collected.
5. In a small bowl, whisk together the soy sauce, broth, mustard, and red pepper flakes.
6. Attach the soy sauce mixture to the skillet and cook, stirring, until everything warms through, about 3 minutes.

Nutrition:
Calories: 230
Fat: 11.1g
Protein: 27.1g
Carbohydrates: 4.9g
Fiber: 1.0g
Sugar: 3.0g
Sodium: 376mg

214. Cauliflower and Beef Fajita

Preparation Time: 10 minutes **Cooking Time:** 15 minutes **Servings:** 4

Ingredients:
- 4 tablespoons extra-virgin olive oil, divided
- 1 head cauliflower, riced

- 1 pound (454 g) sirloin steak, cut into ¼-inch-thick strips
- 1 red bell pepper, seeded and sliced
- 1 onion, thinly sliced

Directions:
1. In a skillet with medium-high, heat 2 tablespoons of olive oil until it shimmers. Attach the cauliflower. Cook and stir, until it softens, about 3 minutes. Keep aside.
2. Wipe out the skillet with a paper towel. Attach the remaining 2 tbsp. of oil to the skillet, and warmth it on medium-high until it shimmers. Attach the steak and cook, stirring occasionally, until it browns, about 3 minutes. Use a slotted spoon to discharge the steak from the oil in the pan and set aside.

- 2 garlic cloves, minced
- Juice of 2 limes
- 1 teaspoon chili powder

3. Attach the bell pepper and onion to the pan. Cook and stir occasionally.
4. Attach the garlic and cook, stirring constantly, for 30 seconds.
5. Set the beef along with any juices that have collected and the cauliflower to the pan. Add the lime juice and chili powder. Cook and stir, until everything is warmed through, 2 to 3 minutes.

Nutrition:
Calories: 311
Fat: 18.1g
Protein: 27.1g
Carbohydrates: 13.1g
Fiber: 2.9g
Sugar: 10.0g
Sodium: 94mg

215. Lamb Kofta with Cucumber Salad

Preparation Time: 10 minutes **Cooking Time:** 15 minutes **Servings:** 4

Ingredients:
- ¼ cup red wine vinegar
- Pinch red pepper flakes
- 1 teaspoon sea salt, divided
- 2 cucumbers, peeled and chopped
- ½ red onion, finely chopped
- 1 pound (454 g) ground lamb
- 2 teaspoons ground coriander
- 1 teaspoon ground cumin
- 3 garlic cloves, minced
- 1 tablespoon fresh mint, chopped

Directions:
1. Preheat the oven to 375F (190C). Set a rimmed baking sheet with parchment paper.
2. In a medium bowl, whisk together the vinegar, red pepper flakes, and ½ teaspoon of salt. Attach the cucumbers and onion and toss to combine. Set aside.
3. In a large bowl, mix the lamb, coriander, cumin, garlic, mint, and remaining ½ teaspoon of salt. Shape the mixture into 1-inch meatballs and set them on the prepared baking sheet.
4. Bake until the lamb reaches 140F (60C) internally, about 15 minutes.
5. Serve with the salad on the side.

Nutrition:
Calories: 346
Fat: 27.1g
Protein: 20.1g
Carbohydrates: 6.9g
Fiber: 1.1g
Sugar: 5.0g
Sodium: 363mg

216. Mustard Pork Chops

Preparation Time: 5 minutes **Cooking Time:** 25 minutes **Servings:** 4

Ingredients:
- ¼ cup Dijon mustard
- 1 tablespoon pure maple syrup
- 2 tablespoons rice vinegar
- 4 bone-in, thin-cut pork chops

Directions:
1. Preheat the oven to 400F (205C).
2. In a small saucepan, combine the mustard, maple syrup, and rice vinegar. Stir to mix and bring to a simmer over medium heat. Cook until just slightly thickened.
3. In a baking dish, place the pork chops and spoon the sauce over them, flipping to coat.
4. Bake, uncovered, for 18 to 22 minutes until the juices run clear.

Nutrition:
Calories: 258
Fat: 7.1g
Protein: 39.1g
Carbohydrates: 6.9g
Fiber: 0g
Sugar: 4.0g
Sodium: 465mg

217. Parmesan Golden Pork Chops

Preparation Time: 10 minutes **Cooking Time:** 25 minutes **Servings:** 4

Ingredients:
- Nonstick cooking spray
- 4 bone-in, thin-cut pork chops
- 2 tablespoons butter
- ½ cup grated Parmesan cheese
- 3 garlic cloves, minced
- ¼ teaspoon salt
- ¼ teaspoon dried thyme
- Freshly ground black pepper, to taste

Directions:
1. Preheat the oven to 400F (205C). Set a baking sheet with parchment paper and spray with nonstick cooking spray.
2. Arrange the pork chops on the prepared baking sheet so they do not overlap.
3. In a small bowl, merge the butter, cheese, garlic, salt, thyme, and pepper. Press 2 tablespoons of the cheese mixture onto the top of each pork chop.
4. Bake for 22 minutes until the pork is cooked through and its juices run clear. Set the broiler to high, and then broil for 1 to 2 minutes to brown the tops.

Nutrition:
Calories: 333
Fat: 16.1g
Protein: 44.1g
Carbohydrates: 1.1g
Fiber: 0g
Sugar: 0g
Sodium: 441mg

218. Mango Pork Tenderloin

Preparation Time: 10 minutes **Cooking Time:** 20 minutes **Servings:** 4

Ingredients:
- 1 pound (454 g) boneless pork tenderloin, trimmed of fat
- 1 teaspoon chopped fresh rosemary
- 1 teaspoon chopped fresh thyme
- ¼ teaspoon salt, divided
- ¼ teaspoon freshly ground black pepper, divided
- 1 teaspoon extra-virgin olive oil
- 1 tablespoon honey
- 2 tablespoons white wine vinegar
- 2 tablespoons dry cooking wine
- 1 tablespoon minced fresh ginger
- 1 cup diced mango

Directions:
1. Preheat the oven to 400F (205C).
2. Season the tenderloin with the rosemary, thyme, ⅛ teaspoon of salt, and ⅛ teaspoon of pepper.
3. Warmth the olive oil in an oven-safe skillet over medium-high heat and sear the tenderloin until browned on all sides.
4. Bring the skillet to the oven and roast for 12 to 15 minutes until the pork is cooked through. Set to a cutting board to rest for 5 minutes.
5. In a small bowl, combine the honey, vinegar, cooking wine, and ginger. Into the same skillet, pour the honey mixture and simmer for 1 minute. Add the mango and toss to coat. Set to a blender and purée until smooth. Season with the remaining ⅛ teaspoon of salt and ⅛ teaspoon of pepper.
6. Divide the pork and serve with the mango sauce.

Nutrition:
Calories: 183
Fat: 4.1g
Protein: 24.1g
Carbohydrates: 11.9g
Fiber: 1.1g
Sugar: 10.0g
Sodium: 241mg

219. Steak Sandwich

Preparation Time: 10 minutes **Cooking Time:** 10 minutes **Servings:** 4

Ingredients:
- 2 tablespoons balsamic vinegar
- 2 teaspoons freshly squeezed lemon juice
- 1 teaspoon fresh parsley, chopped
- 2 teaspoons fresh oregano, chopped
- 2 teaspoons garlic, minced
- 2 tablespoons olive oil
- 1 pound (454 g) flank steak, trimmed of fat
- 4 whole-wheat pitas
- 1 tomato, chopped
- 1 ounce (28 g) low-sodium feta cheese
- 2 cups lettuce, shredded
- 1 red onion, thinly sliced

Directions:
1. Combine the balsamic vinegar, lemon juice, parsley, oregano, garlic, and olive oil in a bowl.
2. Dunk the steak in the bowl to coat well, then wrap the bowl in plastic and refrigerate for at least 1 hour.
3. Preheat the oven to 450F (235C).
4. Remove the bowl from the refrigerator. Discard the marinade and arrange the steak on a baking sheet lined with aluminum foil.
5. Broil in the preheated oven for 10 minutes for medium. Flip the steak to cook.
6. Detach the steak from the oven and allow cooling for 10 minutes. Slice the steak into strips.
7. Assemble the pitas with steak, tomato, feta cheese, lettuce, and onion to make the sandwich, and serve warm.

Nutrition:
Calories: 345
Fat: 15.8g
Protein: 28.1g
Carbohydrates: 21.9g
Fiber: 3.1g
Sodium: 295mg

220. Easy Beef Roast with Green Peppercorn Sauce

Preparation Time: 10 minutes **Cooking Time:** 100 minutes **Servings:** 4

Ingredients:
- 1½ pounds (680 g) top rump beef roast
- Salt and freshly ground black pepper
- 3 teaspoons olive oil, divided
- 3 shallots, diced
- 1 tablespoon green peppercorns
- 2 teaspoons garlic, minced
- 2 tablespoons dry sherry
- 2 tablespoons all-purpose flour
- 1 cup low-sodium beef broth

Directions:
1. Preheat the oven to 300F (150C).
2. On a clean work surface, massage the beef with salt and black pepper.
3. Heat 2 teaspoons olive oil in an oven-safe skillet over medium-high heat until shimmering.
4. Attach the beef to the skillet and cook for 10 minutes until well browned on both sides. Flip the beef to cook.
5. Roast in the warmth oven for 1 hour and 30 minutes or until the beef reaches the desired doneness.
6. Meanwhile, warmth the remaining olive oil in a saucepan over medium-high heat.
7. Add the shallots to the saucepan and sauté for 4 minutes or until translucent.
8. Add the peppercorns and garlic to the pan and sauté for 1 minute until fragrant.
9. Pour the sherry into the pan for deglazing, and then fold in the flour and stir until the mixture has a thick consistency. Cook for an additional minute. Keep stirring during the cooking.

10. Attach the beef broth to the pan and stir until the sauce is thick and smooth, then sprinkle with salt and black pepper.
11. Remove the beef from the oven and serve with the peppercorn sauce on top.

Nutrition:
Calories: 332
Fat: 17.8g
Protein: 36.1g
Carbohydrates: 3.9g
Fiber: 0g
Sugar: 1.1g
Sodium: 205mg

---

221. Coffeed and Herbed Steak
Preparation Time: 10 minutes **Cooking Time:** 10 minutes **Servings:** 4

Ingredients:
- ¼ cup whole coffee beans
- 2 teaspoons fresh rosemary, chopped
- 2 teaspoons fresh thyme, chopped
- 2 teaspoons garlic, minced
- 1 teaspoon freshly ground black pepper
- 2 tablespoons apple cider vinegar
- 2 tablespoons olive oil
- 1 pound (454 g) flank steak, trimmed of fat

Directions:
1. Put the coffee beans, rosemary, thyme, garlic, and black pepper in a food processor. Pulse until well ground and combined.
2. Spill the mixture in a large bowl, pour the vinegar and olive oil in the bowl. Stir to mix well.
3. Dunk the steak in the mixture, then wrap the bowl in plastic and refrigerate to marinate for 2 hours.
4. Preheat the broiler to MEDIUM.
5. Detach the bowl from the refrigerator and discard the marinade.
6. Place the marinated steak on a baking sheet lined with aluminum foil.
7. Broil in the preheated broiler for 10 minutes or until the steak reaches your desired doneness. Flip the steak to cook.

Nutrition:
Calories: 316
Fat: 19.8g
Protein: 31.1g
Carbohydrates: 0g
Fiber: 0g
Sugar: 0g
Sodium: 78mg

---

222. Pork Loin, Carrot, and Gold Tomato Roast
Preparation Time: 5 minutes **Cooking Time:** 40 minutes **Servings:** 4

Ingredients:
- 1 pound (454 g) pork loin
- 2 teaspoons honey
- ½ teaspoon dried rosemary
- ¼ teaspoon freshly ground black pepper
- 1 tablespoon extra-virgin olive oil, divided
- 4 (6-inch) carrots, chopped into ½-inch rounds
- 2 small gold potatoes, chopped into 2-inch cubes

Directions:
1. Preheat the oven to 350F (180C).
2. On a clean work surface, massage the pork with honey, rosemary, black pepper, and ½ tablespoon of olive oil. Brush the carrots and gold potatoes with remaining olive oil.
3. Place the pork, carrots, and potatoes in s single layer on a baking sheet.
4. Roast in the warmth oven for 40 minutes or until the pork is lightly browned and the vegetables are soft.
5. Remove them from the oven. Allow to cool before serving.

Nutrition:
Calories: 346
Fat: 9.9g
Protein: 26.1g
Carbohydrates: 25.9g
Fiber: 4.1g
Sugar: 5.9g
Sodium: 107mg

---

223. Sloppy Joes
Preparation Time: 10 minutes **Cooking Time:** 15 minutes **Servings:** 4

Ingredients:
- 1 tablespoon extra-virgin olive oil
- 1 pound (454 g) 93% lean ground beef
- 1 medium red bell pepper, chopped
- ½ medium yellow onion, chopped
- 2 tablespoons low-sodium Worcestershire sauce
- 1 (15-ounce / 425-g) can low-sodium tomato sauce
- 2 tablespoons low-sodium, sugar-free ketchup
- 4 whole-wheat sandwich thins, cut in half
- 1 cup cabbage, shredded

Directions:
1. Warmth the olive oil in a nonstick skillet over medium heat until shimmering.
2. Add the beef, bell pepper, and onion to the skillet and sauté for 8 minutes or until the beef is cooked.
3. Pour the Worcestershire sauce, tomato sauce, and ketchup in the skillet. Set up the heat to medium-high and simmer for 5 minutes.
4. Assemble the sandwich thin halves with beef mixture and cabbage to make the sloppy Joes, then serve warm.

Nutrition:
Calories: 329
Fat: 8.9g
Protein: 31.2g
Carbohydrates: 35.9g
Fiber: 7.9g
Sugar: 10.9g
Sodium: 271mg

---

224. Lemony Dijon Meat Loaf
Preparation Time: 10 minutes **Cooking Time:** 35 minutes **Servings:** 3-4

Ingredients:
- 2 pounds lean ground beef
- 1 cup almond meal
- 2 eggs
- 1 tablespoon lemon, zest, and juice
- 2 teaspoons Dijon mustard
- Seasoning Salt and black pepper, to taste

Directions:
1. Pour 1-½ cups of water and place trivet inside the instant pot.
2. Mix all the listed ingredients in a mixing bowl. Make a large loaf of the meat mixture.
3. Now place meatloaf over an aluminum foil and wrap the meat in foil.
4. Place foil on the trivet.
5. Secure the lid and set a timer to 35 minutes at high pressure.
6. Once timer beeps, do a natural release for 15 minutes, followed by quick release.
7. Remove the meatloaf from the foil.
8. Set to cutting board and cut into slices after letting it get cold. Serve.

Nutrition:
Calories: 559
Protein: 65.25g
Fat: 30.26g
Carbohydrates: 2.05g

225. Mushroom, Beef, and Cauliflower Rice in Lettuce

Preparation Time: 5 minutes **Cooking Time:** 20 minutes **Servings:** 4

Ingredients:
- 1 tablespoon avocado oil
- 1 cup Portobello mushrooms, chopped
- ½ cup white onion, chopped
- 1 pound (454 g) 93% lean ground beef
- ½ teaspoon garlic powder
- Salt, to taste
- 1 (10-ounce / 284-g) bag frozen cauliflower rice
- ¾ cup Cheddar cheese, shredded
- 12 iceberg lettuce leaves

Directions:
1. Heath the avocado oil in a nonstick skillet over medium heat.
2. Add the mushrooms and onion to the skillet and sauté for 5 minutes until the mushrooms are soft and the onion starts to become translucent.
3. Add the beef, garlic powder, and salt to the skillet and sauté for another 5 minutes to brown the beef.
4. Increase the heat to medium-high, and then add the cauliflower rice and sauté for an additional 5 minutes.
5. Divide the mixture and cheese on all lettuce leaves with a spoon, then roll up the lettuce to seal the wrap and serve warm.

Nutrition:
Calories: 289
Fat: 14.8g
Protein: 31.2g
Carbohydrates: 6.9g
Fiber: 3.1g
Sugar: 3.8
Sodium: 262mg

226. Beef Fajitas

Preparation Time: 6 minutes **Cooking Time:** 19 minutes **Servings:** 4

Ingredients:
- 1 lbs. beef stir-fry strips
- 1 medium red onion
- 1 red bell pepper
- 1 yellow bell pepper
- ½ teaspoon of cumin
- ½ teaspoon of chili powder
- Splash of oil - Salt
- Pepper - Half juice of lime
- Freshly chopped cilantro (also called coriander)
- 1 avocado

Directions:
1. Over medium fire steam a cast-iron pan.
2. Clean and dress bell peppers and cut them to long strips of 0.5cm thick and then Set aside.
3. Clean and cut the red onion into strips. Set aside.
4. Add a little bit of oil once the skillet is heated.
5. Add 2-3 packets of stir-fry strips while the oil is hot. Please ensure the strips wouldn't hit one another. Inside the pan, stir-fry each beef batch thoroughly with salt and pepper. Cook on each side and set aside on a plate and covered to stay warm.
6. Chopped onion as well as ringer peppers to the residual meat juice 76 when all the beef is finished cooking and set aside. Sweetened with chili powder and cumin, then simmer-fry till the preferred consistency is achieved.
7. Move the stir-fry strips of vegetables and beef to just a plate and eat alongside a chopped avocado, a sprinkling of lemon juice, and a spray of fresh cilantro.

Nutrition:
Calories: 245
Fat: 10g
Protein: 33g
Carbohydrates: 6g
Sugars: 2g

227. Beef and Mushroom Barley Soup

Preparation Time: 10 minutes **Cooking Time:** 80 minutes **Servings:** 6

Ingredients:
- 1-pound beef stew meat, cubed
- ¼ teaspoon salt
- ¼ teaspoon freshly ground black pepper
- 1 tablespoon extra-virgin olive oil
- 8 ounces sliced mushrooms
- 1 onion, chopped
- 2 carrots, chopped
- 3 celery stalks, chopped
- 6 garlic cloves, minced
- ½ teaspoon dried thyme
- 4 cups low-sodium beef broth
- 1 cup water
- ½ cup pearl barley

Directions:
1. Season the meat well.
2. In an Instant Pot, heat the oil over high heat. Cook meat on all sides. Remove from the pot and set aside.
3. Attach the mushrooms to the pot and cook for 1 to 2 minutes. Remove the mushrooms and set aside with the meat.

4. Sauté onion, carrots, and celery for 3 to 4 minutes. Add the garlic and continue to cook until fragrant, about 30 seconds longer.
5. Set the meat and mushrooms to the pot, and then add the thyme, beef broth, and water. Change the pressure on high and cook for 15 minutes. Let the pressure release naturally.
6. Open the Instant Pot and add the barley. Continue to cook for 1 hour. Serve.

Nutrition:
Calories: 303
Fat: 7g
Protein: 32g
Carbohydrates: 27g
Sugars: 7g

228. Roasted Beef with Peppercorn Sauce

Preparation Time: 10 minutes
Cooking Time: 90 minutes
Servings: 4

Ingredients:
- 1½ pounds top rump beef roast
- 3 teaspoons extra-virgin olive oil
- 3 shallots, minced
- 2 teaspoons minced garlic
- 1 tablespoon green peppercorns
- 2 tablespoons dry sherry
- 2 tablespoons all-purpose flour
- 1 cup sodium-free beef broth

Directions:
1. Heat the oven to 300F.
2. Season the roast with salt and pepper.
3. Position huge skillet over medium-high heat and add 2 teaspoons of olive oil.
4. Brown the beef on all sides, about 10 minutes in total, and transfer the roast to a baking dish.
5. Roast until desired doneness, about 1½ hours for medium.
6. In a medium saucepan over medium-high heat, set the shallots in the remaining 1 teaspoon of olive oil until translucent, about 4 minutes.
7. Stir in the garlic and peppercorns and cook for another minute. Whisk in the sherry to deglaze the pan.
8. Spill in the flour to form a thick paste, cooking for 1 minute and stirring constantly.
9. Fill in the beef broth and whisk for 4 minutes. Season the sauce.
10. Serve the beef with a generous spoonful of sauce.

Nutrition:
Calories: 200
Fat: 8g
Protein: 30g
Carbohydrates: 1g

229. Italian Pork Chops

Preparation Time: 5 minutes
Cooking Time: 45 minutes
Servings: 4

Ingredients:
- 4 pork chops, boneless
- 3 garlic cloves, minced
- 1 tsp. dried rosemary, crushed
- ¼ tsp. pepper
- ¼ tsp. sea salt

Directions:
1. Prepare the oven to 425 F/ 218 C.
2. Line baking tray with cooking spray and season pork chops with pepper and salt.
3. Combine garlic and rosemary and rub all over pork chops.
4. Place pork chops in a prepared baking tray.
5. Roast pork chops in preheated oven for 10 minutes.
6. Set temperature to 180 C and roast for 25 minutes.
7. Serve and enjoy

Nutrition:
Calories: 44
Protein: 0.39g
Fat: 0.07g
Carbohydrates: 12.18g

230. Pork Rind Nachos

Preparation Time: 6 minutes
Cooking Time: 5 minutes
Servings: 2

Ingredients:
- 2 tbsp. of pork rinds
- ¼ cup shredded cooked chicken
- ½ cup shredded Monterey jack cheese
- ¼ cup sliced pickled jalapeños
- ¼ cup guacamole
- ¼ cup full-fat sour cream

Directions:
1. Put pork rinds in a 6 "round baking pan. Fill with grilled chicken and Monterey cheese jack. Place the pan in the basket with the air fryer.
2. Set the temperature to 370F and set the timer for 5 minutes or until the cheese has been melted.
3. Eat right away with jalapeños, guacamole, and sour cream.

Nutrition:
Calories: 320
Fat: 4g
Protein: 23g
Carbohydrates: 48g
Sugar: 1.1g
Fiber: 3g

231. Jamaican Jerk Pork

Preparation Time: 10 minutes
Cooking Time: 20 minutes
Servings: 4

Ingredients:
- Pork, cut into three-inch pieces
- Jerk paste: ¼ cup

Directions:
1. Rub jerk paste all over the pork pieces.
2. Let it marinate for four hours, at least, in the refrigerator. Or for more time.
3. Let the air fryer preheat to 390 F. spray with olive oil
4. Before putting in the air fryer, let the meat sit for 20 minutes at room temperature.
5. Cook for 20 minutes at 390F in the air fryer, flip halfway through.

6. Take out from the air fryer let it rest for ten minutes before slicing.
7. Serve with micro greens.

Nutrition:
Calories: 144
Fat: 4
Carbohydrates: 1.1g
Fiber: 0.6g
Sugar: 0.1g

232. Pork Souvlakia with Tzatziki Sauce
Preparation Time: 20 minutes **Cooking Time:** 12 minutes **Servings:** 4

Ingredients:
- ¼ cup lemon juice
- 1 tablespoon dried oregano
- ¼ teaspoon salt

Tzatziki Sauce:
- ½ cup plain Greek yogurt
- 1 large cucumber, peeled, deseeded and grated
- 1 tablespoon fresh lemon juice

Special Equipment:
- 8 bamboo skewers, dipped in water for 30 minutes

- ¼ teaspoon ground black pepper
- 1 pound (454 g) pork tenderloin, cut into 1-inch cubes
- 1 tablespoon olive oil

- 4 cloves garlic, minced or grated
- ¼ teaspoon ground black pepper

Directions:
1. Combine the lemon juice, oregano, salt, and ground black pepper in a large bowl. Stir to mix well.
2. Dunk the pork cubes in the bowl of mixture, then toss to coat well. Wrap the bowl in plastic and refrigerate to marinate for 10 minutes or overnight.
3. Preheat the oven to 450F (235C) or broil. Grease a baking sheet with the olive oil.
4. Remove the bowl from the refrigerator. Run the bamboo skewers through the pork cubes. Set the skewers on the baking sheet, then brush with marinade.
5. Broil the skewers in the preheated oven for 12 minutes or until well browned. Flip skewers at least 3 times during the broiling.
6. Meanwhile, combine the ingredients for the tzatziki sauce in a small bowl.
7. Remove the skewers from the oven and baste with the tzatziki sauce and serve immediately.

Nutrition:
Calories: 332
Fat: 17.8g
Protein: 36.1g
Carbohydrates: 3.9g
Fiber: 0g
Sugar: 1.1g

233. Beef, Tomato, and Pepper Tortillas
Preparation Time: 15 minutes **Cooking Time:** 0 minutes **Servings:** 6

Ingredients:
- 6 whole wheat flour tortillas (10-inch)
- 6 large romaine lettuce leaves
- 12 ounces (340 g) cooked deli roast beef, thinly sliced
- 1 cup diced red bell peppers
- 1 cup diced tomatoes

- 1 tablespoon red wine vinegar
- 1 teaspoon cumin
- ¼ teaspoon freshly ground black pepper
- 1 tablespoon olive oil

Directions:
1. Unfold the tortillas on a clean work surface, then top each tortilla with a lettuce leaf. Divide the roast beef over the leaf.
2. Combine the remaining ingredients in a bowl. Stir to mix well. Pour the mixture over the beef.
3. Fold the tortillas over the fillings, and then roll them up. Serve immediately.

Nutrition:
Calories: 355
Fat: 27.1g
Protein: 19.8g
Carbs: 5.9g
Fiber: 1.0g
Sugar: 4.0g

234. Spiced Leg of Lamb
Preparation Time: 15 minutes **Cooking Time:** 1 hour 40 minutes **Servings:** 6

Ingredients:
- ⅔ cup fat-free plain Greek yogurt
- 1 tablespoon homemade tomato puree
- 1 tablespoon fresh lemon juice
- 3-4 garlic cloves, minced
- 2 tablespoons fresh rosemary, chopped
- 2 teaspoons ground coriander

- ½ teaspoon ground cumin
- 1 teaspoon ground cinnamon
- 1 teaspoon red pepper flakes, crushed
- ¼ teaspoon sweet paprika
- Sea salt and freshly ground black pepper
- (4½ pound) bone-in leg of lamb

Directions:
1. In a large bowl, add yogurt, tomato puree, lemon juice, garlic, rosemary, and spices and mix until well combined.
2. Add leg of lamb and coat with marinade generously. Cover and refrigerate to marinate for about 8-10 hours, flipping occasionally.
3. Remove the marinated leg of lamb from refrigerator and keep in room temperature for about 25-30 minutes before roasting.
4. Set the oven to 425F. Line a large roasting pan with a greased foil piece.
5. Arrange the leg of lamb into prepared roasting pan. Roast for 20 minutes.
6. Remove the roasting pan from oven and change the side of leg of lamb.
7. Now, reduce the temperature of oven to 325 F.

8. Roast for 40 minutes. Now loosely cover the roasting pan with a large piece of foil. Roast for 40 minutes more. Detach from oven and place onto a cutting board for about 10-15 minutes before slicing.
9. With a sharp knife cut the leg of lamb in desired sized slices and serve.

Nutrition:
Calories 478
Fat 15.5g
Carbohydrates 3.3 g
Sugar 1.3 g
Fiber 0.9
Protein 72.3 g

---

235. Baked Lamb and Spinach

Preparation Time: 15 minutes **Cooking Time:** 2 hours 55 minutes **Servings:** 6

Ingredients:
- 2 tablespoons olive oil
- 2 pounds lamb necks, trimmed and cut into 2-inch pieces crosswise
- Salt, as required
- 2 medium onions, chopped
- 3 tablespoons fresh ginger, minced
- 4 garlic cloves, minced
- 2 tablespoons ground coriander
- 1 tablespoon ground cumin
- 1 teaspoon ground turmeric
- ¼ cup fat-free plain Greek yogurt
- ½ cup tomatoes, chopped
- 2 cups boiling water
- 30 ounces frozen spinach, thawed and squeezed
- 1½ tablespoons garam masala
- 1 tablespoon fresh lemon juice Ground black pepper, as required

Directions:
1. Preheat the oven to 300 F.
2. Dutch oven, warmth the oil over medium-high heat and stir fry the lamb necks with a little salt for about 4-5 minutes or until browned completely.
3. With a slotted spoon, transfer the lamb onto a plate and now, reduce the heat to medium.
4. In the same pan, attach the onion and sauté for about 10 minutes.
5. Add the ginger, garlic and spices and sauté for about 1 minute.
6. Add the yogurt and tomatoes and cook for about 3-4 minutes.
7. Blend the mixture until smooth. Add the lamb, boiling water and salt and bring to a boil. Cover the pan and transfer into the oven.
8. Bake for about 2½ hours. Now, remove the pan from oven and place over medium heat. Stir in spinach and garam masala and cook for about 3-5 minutes. Stir in lemon juice, salt and black pepper and remove from heat.
9. Serve hot.

Nutrition:
Calories: 333
Fat: 16.1g
Protein: 44.1g
Carbohydrates: 1.1g
Fiber: 0g
Sugar: 0g

---

236. Beef with Barley and Veggies

Preparation Time: 15 minutes **Cooking Time:** 1 hour 5 minutes **Servings:** 2

Ingredients:
- ¾ cup filtered water
- ¼ cup pearl barley
- 2 teaspoons olive oil
- 7 ounces lean ground beef
- 1 cup fresh mushrooms, sliced
- ¾ cup onion, chopped
- 2 cups frozen green beans
- ¼ cup low-sodium beef broth
- 2 tablespoon fresh parsley, chopped

Directions:
1. In a pan, add water, barley and pinch of salt and bring to a boil over medium heat.
2. Now, set the heat to low and parboil, covered for about 30-40 minutes or until all the liquid is absorbed.
3. Remove from heat and set aside.
4. In a skillet, warmth oil over medium-high heat and cook beef for about 8-10 minutes.
5. Add the mushroom and onion and cook for about 6-7 minutes.
6. Add the green beans and cook for about 2-3 minutes. Stir in cooked barley and broth and cook for about 3-5 minutes more.
7. Stir in the parsley and serve hot.

Nutrition:
Calories: 200
Fat: 8g
Protein: 30g
Carbohydrates: 1g
Sugars: 1g
Fiber: 0g

---

237. Beef with Broccoli

Preparation Time: 10 minutes **Cooking Time:** 14 minutes **Servings:** 4

Ingredients:
- 2 tablespoons olive oil, divided
- 2 garlic cloves, minced
- 1 pound beef sirloin steak, trimmed and sliced into thin strips
- ¼ cup low-sodium chicken broth
- 2 teaspoons fresh ginger, grated
- 1 tablespoon ground flax seeds
- ½ teaspoon red pepper flakes, crushed
- Salt and ground black pepper, as required
- 1 large carrot, peeled and sliced thinly
- 2 cups broccoli florets
- 1 medium scallion, sliced thinly

Directions:
1. In a large skillet, warmth 1 tablespoon of oil over medium-high heat and sauté the garlic for about 1 minute.
2. Add the beef and cook for about 4-5 minutes or until browned. With a slotted spoon, transfer the beef into a bowl.
3. Remove the excess liquid from skillet. In a bowl, add the broth, ginger, flax seeds, red pepper flakes, salt and black pepper.
4. In the same skillet, warmth remaining oil over medium heat.
5. Add the carrot, broccoli and ginger mixture and cook for about 3-4 minutes or until desired doneness. Stir in beef and scallion and cook for about 3-4 minutes.

Nutrition:
Calories: 140　　　Protein: 18g　　　Sugars: 1g
Fat: 7g　　　Carbohydrates: 3g　　　Fiber: 1g

238. Barbecue Beef Brisket

Preparation Time: 25 minutes　　**Cooking Time:** 10 hours　　**Servings:** 10

Ingredients:
- 4 lb. beef brisket (boneless), trimmed and sliced
- 1 bay leaf
- 2 onions, sliced into rings
- ½ teaspoon dried thyme, crushed
- ¼ cup chili sauce
- 1 clove garlic, minced
- Salt and pepper to taste
- 2 tablespoons light brown sugar
- 2 tablespoons cornstarch
- 2 tablespoons cold water

Directions:
1. Put the meat in a slow cooker. Add the bay leaf and onion. In a bowl, mix the thyme, chili sauce, salt, pepper.
2. Pour the sauce over the meat. Mix well. Seal the pot and cook on low heat for 10 hours.
3. Discard the bay leaf. Pour cooking liquid in a pan.
4. Add the mixed water and cornstarch.
5. Simmer until the sauce has thickened.
6. Pour the sauce over the meat.

Nutrition:
Calories: 258　　　Carbohydrates: 6.9g　　　Sodium: 465mg
Fat: 7.1g　　　Fiber: 0g
Protein: 39.1g　　　Sugar: 1.0g

239. Lamb and Chickpeas

Preparation Time: 30 minutes　　**Cooking Time:** 30 minutes　　**Servings:** 4

Ingredients:
- 3 lb. lamb leg (boneless), trimmed and sliced into small pieces
- 2 tablespoons olive oil
- 1 teaspoon ground coriander
- Salt and pepper to taste
- ½ teaspoon ground cumin
- ¼ teaspoon red pepper, crushed
- ¼ cup fresh mint, chopped
- 2 teaspoons lemon zest
- 2 cloves garlic, minced
- 30 oz. unsalted chickpeas, rinsed and drained
- 1 cup tomatoes, chopped
- cup English cucumber, chopped
- ¼ cup fresh parsley, snipped
- 1 tablespoon red wine vinegar

Directions:
1. Preheat your oven to 375 F.
2. Place the lamb on a baking dish.
3. Toss in half of the following: oil, cumin and coriander.
4. Season with red pepper, salt and pepper.
5. Mix well. Roast for 20 minutes. In a bowl, merge the rest of the ingredients with the remaining seasonings.
6. Add salt and pepper. Serve lamb with chickpea mixture.

Nutrition:
Calories: 144　　　Fiber: 0.6g　　　Sodium: 215mg
Fat: 4　　　Sugar: 0.1g
Carbohydrates: 1.1g　　　Protein: 24.4g

240. Classic Stroganoff

Preparation Time: 15 minutes　　**Cooking Time:** 20 minutes　　**Servings:** 4

Ingredients:
- 5 ounces (142 g) cooked egg noodles
- 2 teaspoons olive oil
- 1 pound (454 g) beef tenderloin tips, boneless, sliced into 2-inch strips
- 1½ cups white button mushrooms, sliced
- ½ cup onion, minced
- 1 tablespoon all-purpose flour
- ½ cup dry white wine
- 1 (14.5-ounce / 411-g) can fat-free, low-sodium beef broth
- 1 teaspoon Dijon mustard
- ½ cup fat-free sour cream
- ¼ teaspoon salt
- ¼ teaspoon black pepper

Directions:
1. Put the cooked egg noodles on a large plate.
2. Warmth the olive oil in a skillet until shimmering.
3. Add the beef and sauté for 3 minutes or until lightly browned. Detach the beef from the skillet and set on the plate with noodles.
4. Add the mushrooms and onion to the skillet and sauté for 5 minutes or until tender and the onion browns.
5. Attach the flour and cook for a minute. Add the white wine and cook for 2 more minutes.
6. Add the beef broth and Dijon mustard. Bring to a boil. Keep stirring. Set the heat to low and parboil for another 5 minutes.
7. Add the beef back to the skillet and simmer for an additional 3 minutes. Attach the remaining ingredients and simmer for 1 minute.
8. Pour them over the egg noodles and beef and serve immediately.

Nutrition:
Calories: 275　　　Carbs: 29.0g　　　Sodium: 250mg
Fat: 7.0g　　　Fiber: 4.0g
Protein: 23.0g　　　Sugar: 3.0g

241. Ritzy Beef Stew

Preparation Time: 20 minutes **Cooking Time:** 2 hours **Servings:** 6

Ingredients:
- 2 tablespoons all-purpose flour
- 1 tablespoon Italian seasoning
- 2 pounds (907 g) top round, cut into ¾-inch cubes
- 2 tablespoons olive oil
- 4 cups low-sodium chicken broth, divided
- 1½ pounds (680 g) cremini mushrooms, rinsed, stems removed, and quartered
- 1 large onion, coarsely chopped
- 3 cloves garlic, minced
- 3 medium carrots, peeled and cut into ½-inch pieces
- 1 cup frozen peas
- 1 tablespoon fresh thyme, minced
- 1 tablespoon red wine vinegar
- ½ teaspoon freshly ground black pepper

Directions:
1. Combine the flour and Italian seasoning in a large bowl. Dredge the beef cubes in the bowl to coat well.
2. Warmth the olive oil in a pot over medium heat until shimmering.
3. Add the beef to the single layer in the pot and cook for 2 to 4 minutes until golden brown on all sides. Flip the beef cubes frequently.
4. Detach the beef from the pot and set aside, then add ¼ cup of chicken broth to the pot.
5. Add the mushrooms and sauté for 4 minutes or until soft. Remove the mushrooms from the pot and set aside.
6. Pour ¼ cup of chicken broth in the pot. Add the onions and garlic to the pot and sauté for 4 minutes or until translucent.
7. Put the beef back to the pot and pour in the remaining broth. Bring to a boil.
8. Reduce the heat to low and cover. Simmer for 45 minutes. Stir periodically.
9. Add the carrots, mushroom, peas, and thyme to the pot and simmer for 45 more minutes or until the vegetables are soft.
10. Open the lid, drizzle with red wine vinegar and season with black pepper. Stir and serve in a large bowl.

Nutrition:
Calories: 25 Carbs: 24.0g Sodium: 290mg
Fat: 7.0g Fiber: 3.0g
Protein: 25.0g Sugar: 2.5g

242. Slow Cooked Beef and Vegetables Roast

Preparation Time: 15 minutes **Cooking Time:** 4 hours **Servings:** 2

Ingredients:
- 1 tablespoon olive oil
- 2 medium celery stalks, halved lengthwise and cut into 3-inch pieces
- 4 medium carrots, scrubbed, halved lengthwise, and cut into 3-inch pieces
- 1 medium onion, cut in eighths
- 1¼ pounds (567 g) lean chuck roast, boneless, trimmed of fat
- 2 teaspoons Worcestershire sauce
- 1 tablespoon balsamic vinegar
- 2 tablespoons water
- 1 tablespoon onion soup mix
- ½ teaspoon ground black pepper

Directions:
1. Grease a slow cooker with olive oil.
2. Put the celery, carrots, and onion in the slow cooker, then add the beef.
3. Top them with Worcestershire sauce, balsamic vinegar, and water, then sprinkle with onion soup mix and black pepper.
4. Secure and cook on high for 4 hours.
5. Allow to cool for 20 minutes, then serve them on a large plate.

Nutrition:
Calories: 250 Protein: 33.0g Fiber: 3.0g Sugar: 6.0g
Fat: 6.0g Carbs: 15.0g Sodium: 510mg

243. Easy Lime Lamb Cutlets

Preparation Time: 4 hours 20 minutes **Cooking Time:** 8 minutes **Servings:** 4

Ingredients:
- ¼ cup freshly squeezed lime juice
- 2 tablespoons lime zest
- 2 tablespoons chopped fresh parsley
- Sea salt and freshly ground black pepper
- 1 tablespoon extra-virgin olive oil
- 12 lamb cutlets (about 1½ pounds / 680 g in total)

Directions:
1. Combine the lime juice and zest, parsley, salt, black pepper, and olive oil in a large bowl. Stir to mix well.
2. Dunk the lamb cutlets in the bowl of the lime mixture, then toss to coat well. Set the bowl in plastic and refrigerate to marinate for at least 4 hours.
3. Preheat the oven to 450F (235C) or broil. Line a baking sheet with aluminum foil.
4. Detach the bowl from the refrigerator and let sit for 10 minutes, then discard the marinade. Arrange the lamb cutlets on the baking sheet.
5. Broil the lamb in the preheated oven for 8 minutes or until it reaches your desired doneness. Flip the cutlets with tongs to make sure they are cooked evenly.
6. Serve immediately.

Nutrition:
Calories: 297 Carbs: 1.0g Sugar: 0g
Protein: 31.0g Fiber: 0g Sodium: 100mg

244. Sumptuous Lamb and Pomegranate Salad

Preparation Time: 8 hours 30 minutes **Cooking Time:** 30 minutes **Servings:** 8

Ingredients:
- 1½ cups pomegranate juice
- 4 tablespoons olive oil, divided

- 1 tablespoon ground cinnamon
- 1 teaspoon cumin
- 1 tablespoon ground ginger
- 3 cloves garlic, minced
- Salt and freshly ground black pepper
- 1 (4-pound / 1.8-kg) lamb leg, deboned, butterflied, and fat trimmed
- 2 tablespoons pomegranate balsamic vinegar
- 2 teaspoons Dijon mustard
- ½ cup pomegranate seeds
- 5 cups baby kale
- 4 cups fresh green beans, blanched
- ¼ cup toasted walnut halves
- 2 fennel bulbs, thinly sliced
- 2 tablespoons Gorgonzola cheese

Directions:
1. Mix the pomegranate juice, 1 tablespoon of olive oil, cinnamon, cumin, ginger, garlic, salt, and black pepper in a large bowl. Stir to mix well.
2. Dunk the lamb leg in the mixture, press to coat well. Set the bowl in plastic and refrigerate to marinate for at least 8 hours.
3. Remove the bowl from the refrigerate and let sit for 20 minutes. Pat the lamb dry with paper towels.
4. Preheat the grill to high heat.
5. Brush the grill grates with 1 tablespoon of olive oil, then arrange the lamb on the grill grates.
6. Grill for 30 minutes until the internal temperature of the lamb reaches at least 145F (63C). Flip the lamb halfway through the cooking time.
7. Remove the lamb from the grill and wrap with aluminum foil. Let stand for 15 minutes.
8. Meanwhile, Combine the vinegar, mustard, salt, black pepper, and remaining olive oil in a separate large bowl. Stir to mix well.
9. Add the remaining ingredients and lamb leg to the bowl and toss to combine well. Serve immediately.

Nutrition:
Calories: 380
Fat: 21.0g
Protein: 32.0g
Carbs: 16.0g
Fiber: 5.0g
Sugar: 3g
Sodium: 240mg

245. Easy Pot Roast and Vegetables

Preparation Time: 20 minutes **Cooking Time:** 35 minutes **Servings:** 6

Ingredients:
- 3-4 pound chuck roast, trimmed of fat and cut into serving-sized chunks
- 4 medium potatoes, cubed, unpeeled
- 4 medium carrots, sliced, or 1 pound baby carrots
- 2 celery ribs, sliced thin
- 1 envelope dry onion soup mix
- 3 cups water

Directions:
1. Place the pot roast chunks and vegetables into the Instant Pot along with the potatoes, carrots and celery.
2. Merge together the onion soup mix and water and pour over the contents of the Instant Pot.
3. Bring the Instant Pot to Manual mode for 35 minutes. Let pressure release naturally when cook time is up.

Nutrition:
Calorie: 325
Fat: 8g
Protein: 35g
Carbs: 26g
Sugars: 6g
Fiber: 4g
Sodium: 560mg

246. Couscous and Sweet Potatoes with Pork

Preparation Time: 20 minutes **Cooking Time:** 10 minutes **Servings:** 5

Ingredients:
- 1¼ cups uncooked couscous
- 1 lb. pork tenderloin, thinly cut
- 1 medium sweet potato, peeled, set into julienne strips
- 1 cup chunky-style salsa
- ½ cup water
- 2 tbsp. honey
- ¼ cup chopped fresh cilantro

Directions:
1. Cook couscous as directed on package.
2. While couscous is cooking, set 12-inch skillet with cooking spray. Cook pork in skillet over medium heat, stirring occasionally.
3. Set sweet potato, salsa, water and honey into pork. Heat to boiling; set heat to medium.
4. Cover and cook, stirring occasionally. Sprinkle with cilantro. Serve pork mixture over couscous.

Nutrition:
Calorie: 320
Fat: 4g
Protein: 23g
Carbs: 48g
Sugars: 1.1g
Fiber: 3g
Sodium: 420mg

247. Easy Beef Curry

Preparation Time: 15 minutes **Cooking Time:** 10 minutes **Servings:** 6

Ingredients:
- 1 tablespoon extra-virgin olive oil
- 1 small onion, thinly sliced
- 2 teaspoons minced fresh ginger
- 3 garlic cloves, minced
- 2 teaspoons ground coriander
- 1 teaspoon ground cumin
- 1 jalapeño or serrano pepper, split lengthwise but not all the way through
- ¼ teaspoon ground turmeric
- ¼ teaspoon salt
- 1 pound grass-fed sirloin tip steak, top round steak, or top sirloin steak, cut into bite-size pieces

- 2 tablespoons chopped fresh cilantro

Directions:
1. In a large skillet, warmth the oil over medium high.
2. Attach the onion and cook for 3 to 5 minutes until browned and softened. Add the ginger and garlic, stirring continuously until fragrant, about 30 seconds.
3. In a small bowl, merge the coriander, cumin, jalapeño, turmeric, and salt. Attach the spice mixture to the skillet and stir continuously for 1 minute. Set the skillet with about ¼ cup of water.
4. Add the beef and stir continuously for about 5 minutes until well-browned yet still medium rare. Remove the jalapeño. Serve topped with the cilantro.

Nutrition:
Calorie: 140
Fat: 7g
Protein: 18g
Carbs: 3g
Sugars: 1g
Fiber: 1g
Sodium: 141mg

248. Bunless Sloppy Joes

Preparation Time: 15 minutes **Cooking Time:** 40 minutes **Servings:** 6

Ingredients:
- 6 small sweet potatoes
- 1 pound (454 g) lean ground beef
- 1 onion, finely chopped
- 1 carrot, finely chopped
- ¼ cup finely chopped mushrooms
- ¼ cup chopped red bell pepper
- 3 garlic cloves, minced
- 2 teaspoons Worcestershire sauce
- 1 tablespoon white wine vinegar
- 1 (15-ounce / 425-g) can low-sodium tomato sauce
- 2 tablespoons tomato paste

Directions:
1. Preheat the oven to 400F (205C).
2. Set the sweet potatoes in a single layer in a baking dish. Bake for 25 to 40 minutes, depending on the size, until they are soft and cooked through.
3. In a skillet, cook the beef until it's browned, breaking it apart into small pieces as you stir.
4. Add the onion, carrot, mushrooms, bell pepper, and garlic, and sauté briefly for 1 minute.
5. Stir in the Worcestershire sauce, vinegar, tomato sauce, and tomato paste. Set to a simmer, reduce the heat, and cook for 5 minutes for the flavors to meld.
6. Set ½ cup of the meat mixture on top of each baked potato and serve.

Nutrition:
Calories: 372
Fat: 19g
Protein: 16g
Carbs: 34g
Sugars: 1.3g
Fiber: 6g
Sodium: 161mg

249. Beef Curry

Preparation Time: 15 minutes **Cooking Time:** 10 minutes **Servings:** 6

Ingredients:
- 1 tablespoon extra-virgin olive oil
- 1 small onion, thinly sliced
- 2 teaspoons minced fresh ginger
- 3 garlic cloves, minced
- 2 teaspoons ground coriander
- 1 teaspoon ground cumin
- 1 jalapeño or serrano pepper, split lengthwise but not all the way through
- ¼ teaspoon ground turmeric
- ¼ teaspoon salt
- 1 pound (454 g) grass-fed sirloin tip steak, top round steak, or top sirloin steak, cut into bite-size pieces
- 2 tablespoons chopped fresh cilantro

Directions:
1. In a skillet, warmth the oil over medium high.
2. Attach the onion and cook for 3 to 5 minutes until browned and softened. Add the ginger and garlic, stirring continuously until fragrant, about 30 seconds.
3. In a small bowl, merge the coriander, cumin, jalapeño, turmeric, and salt. Attach the spice mixture to the skillet and stir
4. Continuously for 1 minute. Set the skillet with about ¼ cup of water.
5. Add the beef and stir continuously for about 5 minutes until well-browned yet still medium rare. Remove the jalapeño. Serve topped with the cilantro.

Nutrition:
Calories: 140
Fat: 7g
Protein: 18g
Carbs: 3g
Sugars: 1g
Fiber: 1g
Sodium: 141mg

250. Asian Grilled Beef Salad

Preparation Time: 15 minutes **Cooking Time:** 15 minutes **Servings:** 4

Ingredients:
Dressing:
- ¼ cup freshly squeezed lime juice
- 1 tbsp. low-sodium tamari or gluten-free soy sauce
- 1 tablespoon extra-virgin olive oil

Salad:
- 1 pound (454 g) grass-fed flank steak
- ¼ teaspoon salt
- 1 garlic clove, minced
- 1 teaspoon honey
- ¼ teaspoon red pepper flakes
- Pinch freshly ground black pepper
- 6 cups chopped leaf lettuce

- 1 cucumber, halved lengthwise and thinly cut into half moons
- ½ small red onion, sliced
- 1 carrot, cut into ribbons
- ¼ cup chopped fresh cilantro

Directions:
1. Make the Dressing
2. In a small bowl, set together the lime juice, tamari, olive oil, garlic, honey, and red pepper flakes. Set aside.
3. Make the Salad
4. Set the beef on both sides with the salt and pepper.
5. Heat a skillet over high heat until hot. Cook the beef for 3 to 6 minutes per side, depending on preferred doneness. Set aside, tented with aluminum foil, for 10 minutes.
6. In a large bowl, set the lettuce, cucumber, onion, carrot, and cilantro.
7. Slice the beef thinly against the grain and transfer to the salad bowl.
8. Drizzle with the dressing and toss. Serve.

Nutrition:
Calories: 231
Fat: 10g
Protein: 26g
Carbs: 10g
Sugars: 4g
Fiber: 2g
Sodium: 349mg

251. Mustard Glazed Pork Chop

Preparation Time: 5 minutes **Cooking Time:** 25 minutes **Servings:** 4

Ingredients:
- ¼ cup Dijon mustard
- 1 tablespoon pure maple syrup
- 2 tablespoons rice vinegar
- 4 bone-in, thin-cut pork chops

Directions:
1. Preheat the oven to 400F (205C).
2. In a small saucepan, combine the mustard, maple syrup, and rice vinegar. Stir to mix and bring to a simmer over medium heat. Cook until just slightly thickened.
3. In a baking dish, place the pork chops and spoon the sauce over them, flipping to coat.
4. Bake, uncovered, for 18 to 22 minutes until the juices run clear.

Nutrition:
Calories: 257
Fat: 7g
Protein: 39g
Carbs: 7g
Sugars: 4g
Fiber: 0g
Sodium: 466mg

252. Parmesan-Crusted Pork Chops

Preparation Time: 10 minutes **Cooking Time:** 25 minutes **Servings:** 4

Ingredients:
- Nonstick cooking spray
- 4 bone-in, thin-cut pork chops
- 2 tablespoons butter
- ½ cup grated Parmesan cheese
- 3 garlic cloves, minced
- ¼ teaspoon salt
- ¼ teaspoon dried thyme
- Freshly ground black pepper, to taste

Directions:
1. Preheat the oven to 400F (205C). Set a baking sheet with parchment paper and spray with nonstick cooking spray.
2. Arrange the pork chops on the prepared baking sheet so they do not overlap.
3. In a small bowl, merge the butter, cheese, garlic, salt, thyme, and pepper. Press 2 tablespoons of the cheese mixture onto the top of each pork chop.
4. Bake until the pork is cooked through and its juices run clear. Set the broiler to high, then broil for 1 to 2 minutes to brown the tops.

Nutrition:
Calories: 332
Fat: 16g
Protein: 44g
Carbs: 1g
Sugars: 0g
Fiber: 0g
Sodium: 440mg

253. Pork Tenderloin Roast with Mango Glaze

Preparation Time: 10 minutes **Cooking Time:** 20 minutes **Servings:** 4

Ingredients:
- 1 pound (454 g) boneless pork tenderloin, trimmed of fat
- 1 teaspoon chopped fresh rosemary
- 1 teaspoon chopped fresh thyme
- ¼ tsp. salt
- ¼ tsp. freshly ground black pepper
- 1 teaspoon extra-virgin olive oil
- 1 tablespoon honey
- 2 tablespoons white wine vinegar
- 2 tablespoons dry cooking wine
- 1 tablespoon minced fresh ginger
- 1 cup diced mango

Directions:
1. Preheat the oven to 400F (205C).
2. Season the tenderloin with the rosemary, thyme, ⅛ teaspoon of salt, and ⅛ teaspoon of pepper.
3. Warmth the olive oil in an oven-safe skillet over medium-high heat and sear the tenderloin until browned on all sides.
4. Set the skillet to the oven and roast for 12 to 15 minutes until the pork is cooked through. Bring to a cutting board to rest for 5 minutes.
5. In a small bowl, merge the honey, vinegar, cooking wine, and ginger. Into the same skillet, pour the honey mixture and simmer for 1 minute. Add the mango and toss to coat. Transfer to a

blender and purée until smooth. Season with the remaining ⅛ teaspoon of salt and ⅛ teaspoon of pepper.

Nutrition:
Calories: 182
Fat: 4g
Protein: 24g
Carbs: 12g
Sugars: 10g
Fiber: 1g

6. Serve with the mango sauce.

Sodium: 240mg

---

254. Curried Pork and Vegetable Skewers

Preparation Time: 15 minutes **Cooking Time:** 15 minutes **Servings:** 4

Ingredients:
- ¼ cup plain nonfat Greek yogurt
- 2 tablespoons curry powder
- 1 teaspoon garlic powder
- 1 teaspoon ground turmeric
- Zest and juice of 1 lime
- ¼ teaspoon salt
- Pinch freshly ground black pepper
- 1 pound (454 g) boneless pork tenderloin, cut into bite-size pieces
- 1 red bell pepper, seeded and set into 2-inch squares
- 1 green bell pepper, seeded and set into 2-inch squares
- 1 red onion, quartered and split into segments

Directions:
1. In a large bowl, merge the yogurt, curry powder, garlic powder, turmeric, lime zest, lime juice, salt, and pepper.
2. Add the pieces of pork tenderloin to the bowl and stir to coat. Refrigerate for at least 1 hour or if 6 hours.
3. Preheat a grill or broiler to medium.
4. Thread the pork pieces, bell peppers, and onions onto skewers.
5. Grill or broil for 15 minutes, flipping every 3 or 4 minutes, until the pork is cooked through.
6. Serve.

Nutrition:
Calories: 175
Fat: 3g
Protein: 27g
Carbs: 10g
Sugars: 4g
Fiber: 3g

Sodium: 188mg

---

255. Lamb Burgers with Mushrooms and Cheese

Preparation Time: 15 minutes **Cooking Time:** 15 minutes **Servings:** 4

Ingredients:
- 8 ounces (227 g) grass-fed ground lamb
- 8 ounces (227 g) brown mushrooms, finely chopped
- ¼ teaspoon salt
- ¼ teaspoon freshly ground black pepper
- ¼ cup crumbled goat cheese
- 1 tablespoon minced fresh basil

Directions:
1. In a large mixing bowl, merge the lamb, mushrooms, salt, and pepper, and mix well.
2. In a small bowl, mix the goat cheese and basil.
3. Form the lamb mixture into 4 patties, reserving about ½ cup of the mixture in the bowl. In each patty, make an indentation in the center and fill with 1 tablespoon of the goat cheese mixture.

Use the reserved meat mixture to close the burgers. Press the meat firmly to hold together.

4. Heat the barbecue or a large skillet over medium-high heat. Add the burgers and cook for 5 to 7 minutes on each side, until cooked through. Serve.

Nutrition:
Calories: 173
Fat: 13g
Protein: 11g
Carbs: 3g
Sugars: 1g
Fiber: 0g

Sodium: 154mg

---

256. Cherry-Glazed Lamb Chops

Preparation Time: 10 minutes **Cooking Time:** 20 minutes **Servings:** 4

Ingredients:
- 4 (4-ounce / 113-g) lamb chops
- 1½ teaspoons chopped fresh rosemary
- ¼ teaspoon salt
- ¼ teaspoon freshly ground black pepper
- 1 cup frozen cherries, thawed
- ¼ cup dry red wine
- 2 tablespoons orange juice
- 1 teaspoon extra-virgin olive oil

Directions:
1. Set the lamb chops with the rosemary, salt, and pepper.
2. In a small saucepan over medium-low heat, combine the cherries, red wine, and orange juice, and simmer, stirring regularly, until the sauce thickens, 8 to 10 minutes.
3. Heat a large skillet over medium-high heat. When the pan is warmth, add the olive oil to lightly coat the bottom.
4. Cook the lamb chops on each side until well-browned yet medium rare.
5. Serve, topped with the cherry glaze.

Nutrition:
Calories: 356
Fat: 27g
Protein: 20g
Carbs: 6g
Sugars: 4g
Fiber: 1g

Sodium: 199mg

---

257. Lamb and Vegetable Stew

Preparation Time: 10 minutes **Cooking Time:** 3-6 hours **Servings:** 6

Ingredients:
- 1 pound (454 g) boneless lamb stew meat
- 1 pound (454 g) turnips, peeled and chopped
- 1 fennel bulb, trimmed and thinly sliced
- 10 ounces (283 g) mushrooms, sliced

- 1 onion, diced
- 3 garlic cloves, minced
- 2 cups low-sodium chicken broth
- 2 tablespoons tomato paste
- ¼ cup dry red wine (optional)
- 1 teaspoon chopped fresh thyme
- ½ teaspoon salt
- ¼ teaspoon freshly ground black pepper
- Chopped fresh parsley, for garnish

Directions:
1. In a slow cooker, combine the lamb, turnips, fennel, mushrooms, onion, garlic, chicken broth, tomato paste, red wine (if using), thyme, salt, and pepper.
2. Secure and cook on high for 3 hours or on low for 6 hours. When the meat is tender and falling apart, garnish with parsley and serve.
3. If you don't have a slow cooker, in a large pot, heat 2 teaspoons of olive oil over medium heat, and set the lamb on all sides. Remove from the pot and set aside. Add the turnips, fennel, mushrooms, onion, and garlic to the pot, and cook until the vegetables begin to soften. Add the chicken broth, tomato paste, red wine (if using), thyme, salt, pepper, and browned lamb.
4. Set to a boil, then set the heat to low. Simmer for 1½ to 2 hours until the meat is tender. Garnish with parsley and serve.

Nutrition:
Calories: 303　　Carbs: 27g　　Sodium: 310mg
Fat: 7g　　Sugars: 7g
Protein: 32g　　Fiber: 4g

258. Beef and Butternut Squash Stew

Preparation Time: 15 minutes　　**Cooking Time:** 38 minutes　　**Servings:** 8

Ingredients:
- 1½ tbsp. smoked paprika
- 2 tsp. ground cinnamon
- 1½ tsp. kosher salt
- 1 tsp. ground ginger
- 1 tsp. red pepper flakes
- ½ tsp. freshly ground black pepper
- 2 lb. (907 g) beef shoulder roast, cut into 1-inch cubes
- 2 tbsp. avocado oil, divided
- 1 cup low-sodium beef or vegetable broth
- 1 medium red onion, et into wedges
- 8 garlic cloves, minced
- 1 (28-ounce / 794-g) carton or can no-salt-added diced tomatoes
- 2 lb. (907 g) butternut squash, peeled and cut into 1-inch pieces
- Chopped fresh cilantro or parsley, for serving

Directions:
1. In a zip-top bag or medium bowl, merge the paprika, cinnamon, salt, ginger, red pepper, and black pepper. Add the beef and toss to coat.
2. Bring the electric pressure cooker to the Sauté setting. When the pot is warmth, pour in 1 tablespoon of avocado oil.
3. Attach half of the beef to the pot and cook, stirring occasionally, until the beef is no longer pink. Bring it to a plate, then add the remaining 1 tablespoon of avocado oil and brown the remaining beef. Transfer to the plate. Hit Cancel.
4. Set in the broth and scrape up any brown bits from the bottom of the pot. Set the beef to the pot and add the onion, garlic, tomatoes and their juices, and squash. Stir well.
5. Close and lock lid of pressure cooker. Set the valve to sealing.
6. Cook on high pressure for 30 minutes.
7. When cooking is done, hit Cancel. Let the pressure to release naturally for 10 minutes, then quick release any remaining pressure.
8. Unlock and remove lid.
9. Spoon into serving bowls, sprinkle with cilantro or parsley, and serve.

Nutrition:
Calories: 268　　Carbs: 26g　　Sodium: 3887mg
Fat: 10g　　Sugars: 7g
Protein: 25g　　Fiber: 7g

259. Corned Beef and Cabbage Soup

Preparation Time: 15 minutes　　**Cooking Time:** 26 minutes　　**Servings:** 4

Ingredients:
- 2 tablespoons avocado oil
- 1 small onion, chopped
- 3 celery stalks, chopped
- 3 medium carrots, chopped
- ¼ teaspoon allspice
- 4 cups chicken bone broth, vegetable broth, low-sodium store-bought beef broth, or water
- 4 cups sliced green cabbage (about ⅓ medium head)
- ¾ cup pearled barley
- 4 ounces (113 g) cooked corned beef, cut into thin strips or chunks
- Freshly ground black pepper, to taste

Directions:
1. Bring the electric pressure cooker to the Sauté setting. When the pot is warmth, pour in the avocado oil.
2. Merge the onion, celery, and carrots for 3 to 5 minutes or until the vegetables begin to soften. Stir in the allspice. Hit Cancel.
3. Stir in the broth, cabbage, and barley.
4. Secure the lid of the pressure cooker. Set the valve to sealing.
5. Cook on high pressure for 20 minutes.
6. When done, let the pressure to free naturally for 10 minutes, then quick release any remaining pressure. Hit Cancel.
7. Once the pin drops, unlock and detach the lid.
8. Stir in the corned beef, season with pepper, and replace the lid. Let the soup sit for about 5 minutes to let the corned beef warm up.
9. Spoon into serving bowls and serve.

Nutrition:
Calories: 321
Fat: 13g
Protein: 11g
Carbs: 42g
Sugars: 0g
Fiber: 11g
Sodium: 412mg

260. Rosemary-garlic Lamb Racks

Preparation Time: 30 minutes **Cooking Time:** 25 minutes **Servings:** 4

Ingredients:
- 4 tablespoons extra-virgin olive oil
- 2 tablespoons finely chopped fresh rosemary
- 2 teaspoons minced garlic Pinch sea salt
- 2 (1-pound) racks
- French-cut lamb chops (8 bones each)

Directions:
1. In a small bowl, spill together the olive oil, rosemary, garlic, and salt. Set the racks in a sealable freezer bag and pour the olive oil mixture into the bag.
2. Press the meat through the bag so it is coated with the marinade. Press the air out of the bag and secure it. Set to marinate the lamb racks in the refrigerator for 1 to 2 hours. Preheat the oven to 450F. Set a large skillet over medium-high heat.
3. Take the lamb racks out of the bag and sear them in the skillet on all sides, about 5 minutes in total.
4. Arrange the racks upright in the skillet, with the bones interlaced, and roast them until they reach your desired doneness, about 20 minutes for medium-rare or until the internal temperature reaches 125F.
5. Let the lamb rest and then cut the racks into chops. Serve 4 chops per person.

Nutrition:
Calories: 346
Fat: 9.9g
Protein: 26.1g
Carbohydrates: 25.9g
Fiber: 4.1

Poultry

261. Turkey Chili

Preparation Time: 15 minutes　　**Cooking Time:** 30 minutes　　**Servings:** 6

Ingredients:
- 1 tablespoon extra-virgin olive oil
- 1 pound lean ground turkey
- 1 large onion, diced
- 3 garlic cloves, minced
- 1 red bell pepper, seeded and diced
- 1 cup chopped celery
- 2 tablespoons chili powder
- 1 tablespoon ground cumin
- 1 (28-ounce) can reduced-salt diced tomatoes
- 1 can low-sodium kidney beans, drained and washed
- 2 cups low-sodium chicken broth
- ½ teaspoon salt
- Shredded cheddar cheese, for serving (optional)

Directions:
1. In a large pot, warmth the oil over medium heat. Attach the turkey, onion, and garlic, and cook, stirring regularly, until the turkey is cooked through.
2. Add the bell pepper, celery, chili powder, and cumin. Stir well and cook for 1 minute.
3. Add the tomatoes with their liquid, kidney beans, and chicken broth. Bring to a boil, set the heat to low, and simmer for 20 minutes.
4. Season with the salt and serve topped with cheese (if using).

Nutrition:
Calories: 276
Fat: 10g
Protein: 23g
Carbohydrates: 27g
Sugars: 7g
Fiber: 8g
Sodium: 556mg

262. Barbecue Turkey Burger Sliders

Preparation Time: 15 minutes　　**Cooking Time:** 15 minutes　　**Servings:** 4

Ingredients:

For the Sauce
- ½ cup Low-Carb No-Cook Tomato Ketchup (here)
- 2 tablespoons apple cider vinegar

- 1 tablespoon pure maple syrup
- ½ teaspoon freshly ground black pepper
- ½ teaspoon onion powder

For the Burgers
- 8 ounces lean ground turkey
- 1 celery stalk, finely chopped
- 1 scallion, white and green parts, finely hashed

Directions:

To Make the Sauce
1. In a small saucepan, merge the ketchup, vinegar, maple syrup, black pepper, onion powder, lemon juice, Worcestershire sauce, and white pepper, and bring to a simmer over medium heat.

To Make the Burgers
1. In a mixing bowl, combine the turkey, celery, and scallion, and stir well to combine. Form the turkey mixture into 4 small patties.
2. In a grill pan or a cast iron pan over medium-high heat, brown the burgers for about 3 minutes on each side. Using a pastry brush, glaze the tops of the burgers with the barbecue sauce, then

Nutrition:
Calories: 213
Fat: 7g
Protein: 15g
Carbohydrates: 26g
Sugars: 11g
Fiber: 4g

- Juice of ½ lemon
- ½ teaspoon Worcestershire sauce
- Freshly ground white pepper

- 4 whole-wheat dinner rolls, split
- 4 lettuce leaves
- 4 tomato slices

2. Simmer for about 5 minutes until the sauce is thickened. Set aside.

flip, and spread sauce on the opposite side. Cook until the juices run clear.
3. Open the dinner rolls and place one burger in each. Top with lettuce and tomato and serve.

Sodium: 276mg

263. Turkey and Quinoa Caprese Casserole

Preparation Time: 10 minutes **Cooking Time:** 35 minutes **Servings:** 8

Ingredients:
- ⅔ cup quinoa
- 1⅓ cups water
- Nonstick cooking spray
- 2 teaspoons extra-virgin olive oil
- 1 pound lean ground turkey
- ¼ cup chopped red onion
- ½ teaspoon salt

- 1 (15-ounce can) fire-roasted tomatoes, drained
- 4 cups spinach leaves, finely sliced
- 3 garlic cloves, minced
- ¼ cup sliced fresh basil
- ¼ cup chicken or vegetable broth
- 2 large ripe tomatoes, sliced
- 4 ounces mozzarella cheese, thinly sliced

Directions:
1. In a small pot, merge the quinoa and water. Set to a boil, reduce the heat, cover, and simmer for 10 minutes. Turn off the heat, and let the quinoa sit for 5 minutes to absorb any remaining water.
2. Preheat the oven to 400F. Set a baking dish with nonstick cooking spray.
3. In a large skillet, warmth the oil over medium heat. Add the turkey, onion, and salt. Cook until the turkey is cooked through and crumbled.
4. Add the tomatoes, spinach, garlic, and basil. Stir in the broth and cooked quinoa. Set the mixture to the prepared baking dish. Arrange the tomato and cheese slices on top.
5. Bake for 15 minutes. Serve.

Nutrition:
Calories: 218
Fat: 9g
Protein: 18g
Carbohydrates: 1.7g
Sugars: 3g
Fiber: 3g
Sodium: 340mg

264. Turkey Divan Casserole

Preparation Time: 10 minutes **Cooking Time:** 50 minutes **Servings:** 6

Ingredients:
- Nonstick cooking spray
- 3 teaspoons extra-virgin olive oil, divided
- 1 pound turkey cutlets
- Pinch salt
- ¼ teaspoon freshly ground black pepper, divided
- ¼ cup chopped onion
- 2 garlic cloves, minced

- 2 tablespoons whole-wheat flour
- 1 cup unsweetened plain almond milk
- 1 cup low-sodium chicken broth
- ½ cup shredded Swiss cheese, divided
- ½ teaspoon dried thyme
- 4 cups chopped broccoli
- ¼ cup coarsely ground almonds

Directions:
1. Preheat the oven to 375F. Set a baking dish with nonstick cooking spray.
2. In a skillet, heat 1 teaspoon of oil over medium heat. Flavor the turkey with the salt and ⅛ teaspoon of pepper. Sauté the turkey cutlets for 5 to 7 minutes on each side until cooked through. Set to a cutting board, cool briefly, and cut into bite-size pieces.
3. In the same pan, warmth the remaining 2 teaspoons of oil over medium-high heat. Sauté the onion for 3 minutes until it begins to soften. Attach the garlic and continue cooking for another minute.
4. Stir in the flour and mix well. Whisk in the almond milk, broth, and remaining ⅛ teaspoon of pepper, and continue whisking until smooth. Add ¼ cup of cheese and the thyme and continue stirring until the cheese is melted.
5. In the prepared baking dish, arrange the broccoli on the bottom. Cover with half the sauce. Set the turkey pieces on top of the

broccoli, and cover with the remaining sauce. Sprinkle with the remaining ¼ cup of cheese and the ground almonds.

6. Bake for 35 minutes.

Nutrition:

Calories: 207
Fat: 8g
Protein: 25g

Carbohydrates: 9g
Sugars: 2g
Fiber: 3g

Sodium: 128mg

265. Spiced Chicken Breast

Preparation Time: 5 minutes **Cooking Time:** 12 minutes **Servings:** 1

Ingredients:
- ½ tablespoon avocado oil
- ½ teaspoon ground cumin
- ⅛ teaspoon smoked paprika
- Pinch of cayenne pepper
- Salt and ground black pepper, as required
- 1 (4-ounce) boneless, skinless chicken breast

Directions:
1. Preheat the grill to medium-high heat. Grease the grill grate.
2. In a small bowl, attach the oil, spices, salt and black pepper and mix well. Rub the chicken breast with oil mixture evenly.
3. Place the chicken breast onto the grill and cook for about 4-6 minutes per side.
4. Serve hot.

Nutrition:

Calories: 144
Fat: 4
Carbohydrates: 1.1g

Fiber: 0.6g
Sugar: 0.1g
Protein: 24.4g

Sodium: 215mg

266. Seasoned Chicken Breast

Preparation Time: 10 minutes **Cooking Time:** 14 minutes **Servings:** 1

Ingredients:
- 1 tablespoon balsamic vinegar
- ½ tablespoon olive oil
- ¼ teaspoon lemon-pepper seasoning
- 1 (6-ounce) boneless, skinless chicken breast half, pounded slightly

Directions:
1. In a glass bowl, place the vinegar, oil and seasoning and mix well. Add the chicken breast and coat with the mixture generously. Refrigerate to marinate for about 25-30 minutes.
2. Preheat the grill to medium heat. Grease the grill grate.
3. Remove the chicken breast from bowl and discard the remaining marinade.
4. Place the chicken breast onto the grill and cover with the lid. Cook for about 5-7 minutes per side.
5. Serve immediately.

Nutrition:

Calories: 258
Fat: 10.5g
Carbohydrates: 0.5g

Fiber: 0.1g
Sugar: 0.1g
Protein: 36.1g

Sodium: 88mg

267. Bruschetta Chicken

Preparation Time: 10 minutes **Cooking Time:** 40 minutes **Servings:** 1

Ingredients:
- 1 skinless chicken breast
- Salt and ground black pepper, as required
- 1 small tomato, chopped
- ½ tablespoon fresh basil, chopped
- ¼ of garlic clove, minced
- ¼ teaspoon balsamic vinegar
- ¼ teaspoon olive oil

Directions:
1. Preheat your oven to 375F. Grease a baking dish.
2. Flavor the chicken breast with salt and black pepper evenly.
3. Arrange the chicken breast into the prepared baking dish. Seal the baking dish and bake for approximately 35-40 minutes or until chicken is done completely.
4. Meanwhile, in a bowl, add the tomatoes, basil, garlic, vinegar, oil and salt mix. Refrigerate until using.
5. Remove the baking dish of chicken from oven and transfer the chicken breast onto serving plates. Top with tomato mixture and serve.

Nutrition:

Calories: 297
Fat: 10.5g
Carbohydrates: 3.8g

Fiber: 1.1g
Sugar: 2.3g
Protein: 40.6g

Sodium: 275mg

268. Chicken with Caper Sauce

Preparation Time: 10 minutes **Cooking Time:** 15 minutes **Servings:** 1

Ingredients:
- 2-3 tablespoons almond flour
- Salt, as required
- 1 (5-ounce) skinless, boneless chicken breast half
- ½ tablespoon olive oil
- 2-3 tablespoons low-sodium chicken broth
- 2 teaspoons fresh lemon juice
- 1 tablespoon capers, drained

Directions:
1. In a shallow bowl, merge together the flour and salt. Add the chicken breast and oat with flour mixture evenly. Then, shake off the excess flour.
2. In a small skillet, warmth the oil over medium-high heat and cook the chicken breast. With a slotted spoon, transfer the

chicken breast onto a plate and with a piece of foil, cover them to keep warm.
3. In the same skillet, attach the broth and bring to a boil, scraping up the browned bits from the bottom of the pan. Add the lemon juice and cook for about 2-3 minutes or until reduced by half.

4. Remove from the heat and stir in the capers.
5. Place the caper sauce over the chicken breast and serve.

Nutrition:
Calories: 333
Fat: 17.5g
Carbohydrates: 2.3g
Fiber: 1.6g
Sugar: 0.8g
Protein: 31.6g
Sodium: 265mg

---

269. Yogurt and Parmesan Chicken Bake

Preparation Time: 10 minutes **Cooking Time:** 45 minutes **Servings:** 1

Ingredients:
- 2 tablespoons fat-free plain Greek yogurt
- 1 tablespoon low-fat Parmesan cheese, grated
- Salt and ground black pepper, as required
- 1 (4-ounce) boneless, skinless chicken breast

Directions:
1. Warmth your oven to 375 F. Line baking sheet with a greased piece of foil.
2. In a bowl, add the yogurt, cheese, garlic powder and black pepper and mix well. Add the chicken breast and coat with the yogurt mixture evenly.
3. Arrange the chicken breast onto the prepared baking sheet. Bake for approximately 45 minutes.
4. Serve hot.

Nutrition:
Calories: 156
Fat: 3.5g
Carbohydrates: 2.2g
Fiber: 0g
Sugar: 0g
Protein: 26.3g
Sodium: 285mg

---

270. Pesto Chicken Bake

Preparation Time: 10 minutes **Cooking Time:** 42 minutes **Servings:** 1

Ingredients:
- 1 (4-ounce) boneless, skinless chicken breast half
- 1 tablespoon basil pesto
- 1 tablespoon part-skim mozzarella cheese, shredded

Directions:
1. Preheat your oven to 400F. Line baking sheet with a greased piece of foil.
2. In a bowl, add the chicken breast and pesto and mix until well combined.
3. Arrange the chicken breast onto the prepared baking sheet in a single layer. Bake for approximately 35 minutes.
4. Remove from the oven and top the chicken breast with the cheese. Bake for approximately 5-7 minutes or until cheese melts completely.
5. Serve hot.

Nutrition:
Calories: 210
Fat: 7.9g
Carbohydrates: 1.1g
Fiber: 0g
Sugar: 0g
Protein: 32.1g
Sodium: 225mg

---

271. Chicken and Broccoli Bake

Preparation Time: 10 minutes **Cooking Time:** 45 minutes **Servings:** 1

Ingredients:
- 1 (5-ounce) skinless, boneless chicken thigh
- 3 ounces broccoli florets
- 1 garlic clove, minced
- 1 tablespoon extra-virgin olive oil
- ¼ teaspoon dried oregano, crushed
- ¼ teaspoon dried rosemary, crushed
- Salt and ground black pepper, as required

Directions:
1. Preheat your oven to 375F. Grease a small baking dish.
2. In a bowl, attach all the ingredients and toss to coat well.
3. Set the broccoli florets in the bottom of prepared baking dish and top with chicken breast.
4. Bake for approximately 45 minutes.
5. Serve hot.

Nutrition:
Calories: 333
Fat: 17.5g
Carbohydrates: 7.1g
Fiber: 2.6g
Sugar: 1.5g
Protein: 34.3g
Sodium: 235mg

---

272. Chicken and Veggies Bake

Preparation Time: 10 minutes **Cooking Time:** 45 minutes **Servings:** 1

Ingredients:
- 1 (5-ounce) boneless, skinless chicken thigh
- ¼ teaspoon dried oregano, crushed
- Salt and ground black pepper, as required
- 2 teaspoons olive oil, divided
- 2 fresh mushrooms, sliced
- 1 tablespoon yellow onion, chopped
- 1 small garlic clove, minced
- ¼ cup fresh spinach, chopped
- 1 tablespoon sun-dried tomatoes, sliced
- 1 tablespoon low-fat cheddar cheese, grated

Directions:
1. Preheat your oven to 375F.
2. Season the chicken thigh with the oregano, salt and black pepper evenly.
3. In a small oven-proof skillet, heat 1 teaspoon of oil over medium-high heat and cook the chicken thigh for about 2-3 minutes per side or until browned completely. With a slotted spoon, transfer the chicken thigh onto a plate.
4. In the same skillet, warmth the remaining oil over medium heat and sauté the mushrooms, onions and garlic for about 5-7 minutes.
5. Spill the spinach and sun-dried tomatoes and remove from the heat.
6. Sprinkle with cheese and transfer the skillet into the oven. Bake for 20-30 minutes until desired doneness of chicken.
7. Remove from the oven and set aside for about 5 minutes before serving.

Nutrition:
Calories: 300
Fat: 14.5g
Carbohydrates: 5.1g
Fiber: 1.9g
Sugar: 2g
Protein: 31.8g
Sodium: 265mg

273. Chicken with Olives
Preparation Time: 10 minutes **Cooking Time:** 30 minutes **Servings:** 1

Ingredients:
- 1 boneless, skinless chicken breast
- ¼ tablespoon garlic, minced
- ¼ teaspoon dried oregano, divided
- Salt and ground black pepper, as required
- ¼ cup low-sodium chicken broth
- ½ tablespoon fresh lemon juice
- ¼ cup onion, chopped finely
- ¼ cup tomato, chopped
- 1 tablespoon green olives, pitted and sliced
- 1 teaspoon fresh parsley leaves, chopped

Directions:
1. With a knife, make 3 slits on both sides of each chicken breast. Massage both sides of each breast with garlic, inserting some into the slits. Season the chicken with ½ of the oregano, salt and black pepper evenly.
2. In a small cast iron skillet, heat the oil over medium-high heat and cook for about 5 minutes per side. Stir in the broth, lemon juice and remaining oregano and bring to a gentle boil.
3. Set the heat to medium and cook, covered tightly for about 10-15 minutes, flipping the chicken breast once halfway through.
4. Uncover and place the onions, tomatoes and olives on top. Cook, covered tightly for about 3-5 minutes.
5. Stir in the parsley and serve hot.

Nutrition:
Calories: 201
Fat: 4.5g
Carbohydrates: 6.4g
Fiber: 1.6g
Sugar: 2.6g
Protein: 31.6g
Sodium: 265mg

274. Chicken with Bell Peppers
Preparation Time: 10 minutes **Cooking Time:** 26 minutes **Servings:** 1

Ingredients:
- ½ tablespoon extra-virgin olive oil
- ½ of small onion, chopped
- 1 garlic clove, minced
- ¼ teaspoon fresh ginger, minced
- 1 (4-ounce) skinless, boneless chicken breast, cubed
- 1 small tomato, seeded and chopped
- 1 small bell pepper, seeded and chopped
- ¼ tablespoon fresh lemon juice
- Salt and ground black pepper, as required

Directions:
1. In a skillet, warmth the oil over medium heat and sauté the onion for about 4-5 minutes. Attach the garlic and ginger and sauté for about 1 minute.
2. Add the chicken and cook for about 10 minutes or until browned from all sides. Add the tomato and bell pepper and cook for about 5-7 minutes or until vegetables become tender. Add the lemon juice, salt and black pepper and cook for about 2-3 minutes.
3. Serve hot.

Nutrition:
Calories: 252
Fat: 10.5g
Carbohydrates: 9.1g
Fiber: 3.2g
Sugar: 4.3g
Protein: 27.4g
Sodium: 205mg

275. Chicken with Bok Choy
Preparation Time: 10 minutes **Cooking Time:** 12 minutes **Servings:** 1

Ingredients:
- ½ tablespoon olive oil
- ¼ of onion, sliced thinly
- ¼ teaspoons fresh ginger, grated finely
- 1 small garlic clove, minced
- 2 tablespoons low-sodium chicken broth
- 2 tablespoons fresh orange juice
- ¼ pound cooked chicken, chopped
- ⅓ pound bok choy leaves
- Ground black pepper, as required

Directions:
1. In a small skillet, warmth oil over medium heat and sauté onion for about 3-4 minutes. Add ginger and garlic and sauté for about 1 minute. Add orange zest, broth and orange juice and stir to combine. Add the bok choy and cook for about 1-2 minutes.

2. Add the chicken meat and cook for about 3 minutes. Stir in the black pepper and detach from the heat.

3. Serve hot.

Nutrition:
Calories: 280
Fat: 9.5g
Carbohydrates: 8.1g
Fiber: 2.3g
Sugar: 4.3g
Protein: 35.6g
Sodium: 180mg

---

276. Chicken with Cabbage

Preparation Time: 10 minutes **Cooking Time:** 15 minutes **Servings:** 1

Ingredients:
- ¾ tablespoon olive oil, divided
- ½ tablespoon apple cider vinegar
- Salt and ground black pepper, as required
- 1 (4-ounce) skinless, boneless chicken breast, sliced thinly
- 1 tablespoon onion, chopped
- ¼ of head cabbage, sliced thinly
- 2 tablespoons water

Directions:
1. In a bowl, mix ¼ tablespoon of oil, vinegar, salt, black pepper, Add the chicken and coat with mixture generously. Set aside for about 5 minutes.
2. Warmth a small non-stick skillet over medium-high heat and stir fry the chicken slices for about 3-4 minutes or until golden brown. Transfer the chicken onto a plate.
3. In the same skillet, melt the remaining oil over medium heat and cook the onion and cabbage for about 4-5 minutes. Attach the chicken and water and cook for about 5-6 minutes or until desired doneness.
4. Serve hot.

Nutrition:
Calories: 22
Fat: 14.5g
Carbohydrates: 9.1g
Fiber: 3.6g
Sugar: 4.3g
Protein: 27.6g
Sodium: 225mg

---

277. Chicken with Mushrooms

Preparation Time: 10 minutes **Cooking Time:** 18 minutes **Servings:** 1

Ingredients:
- ½ tablespoon olive oil, divided
- 1 (4-ounce) boneless, skinless chicken breast, divided into small pieces
- Salt and ground black pepper, as required
- ⅓ cup fresh mushrooms, sliced
- ¼ cup low-sodium chicken broth

Directions:
1. In a skillet, heat 1 tbsp. of oil over medium-high heat and stir fry the chicken pieces, salt, and black pepper for about 4-5 minutes or until golden-brown. With a slotted spoon, set the chicken pieces onto a plate.
2. In the same skillet, heat the remaining oil over medium heat and sauté the onion, ginger for about 1 minute. Attach the mushrooms and cook for about 6-7 minutes, stirring frequently. Add the cooked chicken and coconut milk and stir fry for about 3-4 minutes. Attach in the salt and black pepper and remove from the heat.
3. Serve hot.

Nutrition:
Calories: 198
Fat: 9.5g
Carbohydrates: 1g
Fiber: 0.2g
Sugar: 0.4g
Protein: 25.1g
Sodium: 235mg

---

278. Chicken with Broccoli and Mushroom

Preparation Time: 10 minutes **Cooking Time:** 25 minutes **Servings:** 1

Ingredients:
- ½ tablespoon extra-virgin olive oil
- ¼ pound skinless, boneless chicken breast, cubed
- ¼ of small onion, chopped
- 1 garlic clove, minced
- ¼ cup fresh mushrooms, sliced
- ¼ cup small broccoli florets
- 2-3 tablespoons water
- Salt and ground black pepper, as required

Directions:
1. Warmth the oil over medium heat and cook the chicken cubes for about 4-5 minutes. With a slotted spoon, transfer the chicken cubes onto a plate.
2. In the same wok, attach the onion and sauté for about 4-5 minutes. Attach the mushrooms and cook for about 4-5 minutes. Stir in the cooked chicken, broccoli and water and cook, covered for about 8-10 minutes, stirring occasionally.
3. Stir in salt and black pepper and remove from heat.
4. Serve hot.

Nutrition:
Calories: 285
Fat: 17.5g
Carbohydrates: 4g
Fiber: 1.2g
Sugar: 1.5g
Protein: 25.6g
Sodium: 205mg

---

279. Chicken with Zucchini Noodles

Preparation Time: 10 minutes **Cooking Time:** 13 minutes **Servings:** 1

Ingredients:
- 1 small zucchinis, spiralized with Blade C
- Salt, as required
- ¼ teaspoon garlic, minced
- ¼ teaspoon fresh ginger, minced

- 1 (4-ounce) skinless, boneless chicken breast, cubed
- 1 tablespoon fresh orange juice, divided
- ¼ tablespoon fresh lime juice

Directions:
1. Arrange a strainer over sink. Place the zucchini noodles in a strainer and sprinkle with a pinch of salt. Let the excess moisture release for about 10 minutes. Squeeze the moisture from zucchini and pat dry with paper towels.
2. In a non-stick skillet, warmth oil over medium heat and sauté ginger and garlic for about 1 minute. Stir in chicken and cook for about 4-5 minutes.

- 1-2 drops liquid stevia
- ½ teaspoon fresh lime zest, grated finely

3. Add in the remaining ingredients and cook for about 4-5 minutes, stirring occasionally.
4. Attach in zucchini noodles and toss to coat well. Cook for about 1-2 minutes.
5. Serve hot.

Nutrition:
Calories: 171
Fat: 4.3g
Carbohydrates: 6.3g
Fiber: 1.5g
Sugar: 3.3g
Protein: 26g
Sodium: 205mg

280. Chicken with Yellow Squash

Preparation Time: 10 minutes **Cooking Time:** 18 minutes **Servings:** 1

Ingredients:
- ½ tablespoon olive oil, divided
- ¼ pound skinless, boneless chicken breast, divided into bite sized pieces
- Salt and ground black pepper, as required
- 1 garlic clove, minced
- ¼ pound yellow squash, sliced
- ¼ tablespoon fresh lemon juice
- ¼ tablespoon fresh parsley, minced

Directions:
1. In a small skillet, warmth ½ tablespoon of oil over medium heat and stir fry chicken for about 6-8 minutes or until golden brown from all sides. Transfer the chicken onto a plate.
2. In the same skillet, warmth remaining oil over medium heat and sauté garlic for about 1 minute. Add squash slices and cook for about 5-6 minutes. Stir in chicken and cook for about 2 minutes.
3. Stir in lemon juice, zest and parsley and remove from heat.
4. Serve hot.

Nutrition:
Calories: 226
Fat: 11g
Carbohydrates: 4.9g
Fiber: 1.4g
Sugar: 2.1g
Protein: 26.9g
Sodium: 206mg

281. Chicken in Veggie Sauce

Preparation Time: 15 minutes **Cooking Time:** 30 minutes **Servings:** 1

Ingredients:
- ½ tablespoon olive oil
- 1 (4-ounce) skinless chicken breast, cut into bite-sized pieces
- ¼ of onion, minced
- 1 small garlic clove, crushed
- ½ of small bell peppers, seeded and chopped finely
- ½ of small carrot, peeled and chopped finely
- ½ of small zucchini, chopped finely
- ¼ cup tomatoes, chopped finely
- 2-3 tablespoons unsweetened coconut milk
- ⅛ teaspoon ground turmeric
- Salt and ground black pepper, as required

Directions:
1. In a small skillet, heat ¼ tablespoon of the olive oil over medium-high heat and cook the chicken pieces for bout 6-8 minutes. With a slotted spoon, transfer the cooked chicken onto a plate.
2. In the same skillet, warmth the remaining olive oil over medium heat and sauté the onion and garlic for about 1-2 minutes. Add the bell pepper, carrot and zucchini and cook for about 10 minutes, stirring frequently. Attach the tomatoes and cook for about 1-2 minutes, stirring frequently. Stir in the coconut milk, salt and black pepper and bring to a boil. Cook for about 10 minutes, stirring occasionally.
3. Detach from the heat and set aside to cool slightly. In a blender, add the veggie mixture and pulse until smooth.
4. Return the sauce to the skillet with chicken over medium heat and cook for about 2-3 minutes or until heated through.
5. Serve hot.

Nutrition:
Calories: 328
Fat: 13.5g
Carbohydrates: 1.1g
Fiber: 3.2g
Sugar: 4.3g
Protein: 34.6g
Sodium: 125mg

282. Chicken with Cranberries

Preparation Time: 10 minutes **Cooking Time:** 22 minutes **Servings:** 1

Ingredients:
- ½ tablespoon olive oil
- 1 (4-ounce) skinless, boneless chicken thigh
- Salt and ground black pepper, as required
- 1 tablespoon onion, chopped finely
- ¼ teaspoon fresh ginger, minced
- 1 bay leaf
- ¼ cup low-sodium chicken broth
- 1 teaspoon fresh lemon juice
- 3 tablespoons fresh cranberries
- 1 teaspoon Erythritol

Directions:
1. In a small skillet, heat oil over medium heat and cook the chicken thigh with salt and black pepper for about 4-5 minutes per side. With a slotted spoon, transfer the chicken thigh into a large bowl and cover with a piece of foil to keep it warm.
2. In the same skillet, add onion over medium heat and sauté for about 2-3 minutes. Add bay leaf and broth in skillet and bring to a boil, stirring occasionally to loosen the brown bits of skillet.
3. Stir in cranberries and cook or about 5 minutes. Stir in Erythritol, salt and black pepper and cook for about 1-2 minutes.
4. Pour cranberry mixture over chicken and serve.

Nutrition:
Calories: 212
Fat: 10.5g
Carbohydrates: 1.6g
Fiber: 0.3g
Sugar: 0.6g
Protein: 26g
Sodium: 215mg

283. Chicken Kabobs

Preparation Time: 10 minutes **Cooking Time:** 7 minutes **Servings:** 1

Ingredients:
- 1 tablespoon low-fat Parmesan cheese, grated
- ½ tablespoon olive oil
- ¼ cup fresh basil leaves, chopped
- Salt and ground black pepper, as required
- ⅓ pound boneless, skinless chicken breast, cut into 1-inch cubes

Directions:
1. In a food processor, add the cheese, oil, garlic, basil, salt, and black pepper, and pulse until it blends.
2. Set the basil mixture into a large bowl. Add the chicken cubes and mix well. Seal the bowl and refrigerate to marinate for at least 4-5 hours.
3. Preheat the grill to medium-high heat. Generously, grease the grill grate.
4. Thread the chicken cubes onto pre-soaked wooden skewers. Grill for about 3-4 minutes. Flip and cook.
5. Serve hot.

Nutrition:
Calories: 247
Fat: 10.5g
Carbohydrates: 0.2g
Fiber: 0.1g
Sugar: 0g
Protein: 33.2g
Sodium: 295mg

284. Chicken and Grape Kabobs

Preparation Time: 10 minutes **Cooking Time:** 15 minutes **Servings:** 1

Ingredients:
- ½ tablespoon extra-virgin olive oil, divided
- 1 garlic clove, minced
- ¼ tablespoon fresh rosemary, minced
- ¼ tablespoon fresh oregano, minced
- Pinch of red pepper flakes, crushed
- ¼ pound boneless, skinless chicken breast, divided into ¾-inch cubes
- ⅓ cup green seedless grapes, rinsed
- Salt, as required
- ¼ tablespoon fresh lemon juice

Directions:
1. In a small bowl, add half of oil, garlic, fresh herbs, lemon zest and red pepper flakes and beat until well combined.
2. Thread the chicken cubes and grapes onto 12 metal skewers. In a large baking dish, arrange the skewers. Place the marinade and mix well. Refrigerate to marinate for about 4-24 hours.
3. Preheat the grill to medium-high heat. Grease the grill grate.
4. Remove skewers from baking dish and shake off the excess marinade. Now, sprinkle the skewers with the salt.
5. Grill the skewers for about 3-5 minutes per side or until chicken is done completely.
6. Remove from the grill and transfer the skewers onto a serving platter.
7. Drizzle with lemon juice and remaining oil and serve.

Nutrition:
Calories: 222
Fat: 9.5g
Carbohydrates: 7.7g
Fiber: 1.3g
Sugar: 4.3g
Protein: 24.6g
Sodium: 215mg

285. Chicken and Zucchini Kabobs

Preparation Time: 10 minutes **Cooking Time:** 20 minutes **Servings:** 1

Ingredients:
- 1 tablespoon fresh lemon juice
- 1 tablespoon olive oil
- 1 small garlic clove, minced
- Pinch of dried thyme, crushed
- Pinch of dried oregano, crushed
- ¼ teaspoon ground cumin
- Salt and ground black pepper, as required
- ¼ pound skinless, boneless chicken breast, cubed into ½-inch size
- ½ of zucchini, sliced

Directions:
1. In a bowl, add the vinegar, lemon juice, oil, garlic, dried herbs, cumin, salt and black pepper and mix until well combined. Add the chicken cubes and coat with mixture generously. Refrigerate, covered to marinate for about 2-4 hours.
2. Preheat the outdoor grill to medium-high heat. Grease the grill grate.
3. Detach the chicken from the bowl and discard the excess marinade.
4. Thread the chicken and zucchini onto pre-soaked wooden skewers respectively.
5. Grill the skewers cook for about 10 minutes, flipping occasionally or until desired doneness.
6. Serve hot.

Nutrition:
Calories: 284
Fat: 17.5g
Carbohydrates: 4g
Fiber: 1.3g
Sugar: 2g
Protein: 26.7g
Sodium: 206mg

286. Chicken and Broccoli Kabobs

Preparation Time: 10 minutes **Cooking Time:** 20 minutes **Servings:** 1

Ingredients:
- ¼ pound skinless, boneless chicken breast, cubed
- 1 tablespoon olive oil, divided
- ¼ teaspoon dried marjoram, crushed
- 1 small garlic clove, minced
- ½ tablespoon sugar-free tomato paste
- ½ cup broccoli florets
- Salt and ground black pepper, as required

Directions:
1. In a bowl, add the chicken, ¼ tablespoon of oil, marjoram, garlic, tomato paste, broccoli and black pepper and mix well. Seal the bowl and set aside at room temperature for about 10-15 minutes.
2. Thread the chicken and broccoli onto pre-soaked wooden skewers.
3. In a large grill pan, heat remaining oil over medium heat and cook chicken skewers and cook for about 9-10 minutes per side or until desired doneness.
4. Serve hot.

Nutrition:
Calories: 289
Fat: 17.5g
Carbohydrates: 5.6g
Fiber: 1.6g
Sugar: 1.8g
Protein: 27.1g
Sodium: 219mg

287. Chicken and Veggie Kabobs

Preparation Time: 10 minutes **Cooking Time:** 8 minutes **Servings:** 1

Ingredients:
- ½ tablespoon olive oil
- ¼ tablespoon fresh lemon juice
- ½ of garlic clove, minced
- ¼ tablespoon fresh basil leaves, minced
- Salt and ground black pepper, as required
- ¼ pound boneless, skinless chicken breast, divided into 1-inch cubes
- ¼ of bell pepper, seeded and cubed
- 4 cherry tomatoes

Directions:
1. In a bowl, attach the oil, lemon juice, garlic, basil, salt, and black pepper and mix well. Add the chicken cubes and mix well. Seal the bowl and refrigerate to marinate for at least 4-5 hours.
2. Preheat the grill to medium-high heat. Generously, grease the grill grate.
3. Thread the chicken, bell pepper cubes and tomatoes onto presoaked wooden skewers.
4. Grill the skewers for about 6-8 minutes, flipping occasionally.
5. Remove from the grill and place onto a platter for about 5 minutes before serving.

Nutrition:
Calories: 203
Fat: 10g
Carbohydrates: 2.9g
Fiber: 0.8g
Sugar: 1.4g
Protein: 24.6g
Sodium: 216mg

288. Chicken and Zucchini Soup

Preparation Time: 10 minutes **Cooking Time:** 30 minutes **Servings:** 1

Ingredients:
- ½ tablespoon olive oil
- 2 tablespoons onion, chopped
- 1 tablespoon celery stalk, chopped
- ½ of garlic clove, minced
- ⅓ cup zucchini, sliced
- 1 cup low-sodium chicken broth
- ½ cups cooked chicken, chopped
- Ground black pepper, as required
- ½ teaspoon fresh lemon juice
- 1 teaspoon fresh cilantro, chopped

Directions:
1. In a saucepan, warmth oil over medium heat and sauté onion and celery for about 8-9 minutes.
2. Attach garlic and sauté for about 1 minute. Add zucchini and broth and bring to a boil over high heat.
3. Set the heat to medium-low and simmer for about 5-10 minutes. Add the cooked chicken and simmer for about 5 minutes.
4. Stir in black pepper, lemon juice and cilantro and remove from heat.
5. Serve hot.

Nutrition:
Calories: 199
Fat: 9.3g
Carbohydrates: 5g
Fiber: 1g
Sugar: 1.7g
Protein: 32.2g
Sodium: 12mg

289. Chicken and Spinach Stew

Preparation Time: 10 minutes **Cooking Time:** 30 minutes **Servings:** 2

Ingredients:
- 1 tablespoon olive oil
- ½ of onion, chopped
- ¼ tablespoon garlic, minced
- ¼ tablespoon fresh ginger, minced
- ¼ teaspoon paprika
- ¼ teaspoon ground cumin

- ⅛ teaspoon ground coriander
- ⅛ teaspoon ground turmeric
- 6 ounces boneless, skinless chicken thigh, trimmed and cut into 1-inch pieces
- 1 tomato, chopped
- ¼ cup low-sodium chicken broth
- Salt and ground black pepper, as required
- 1½ cup fresh spinach, chopped

Directions:
1. In a small heavy-bottomed pan, heat oil over medium heat and sauté the onion for about 3-4 minutes. Add the ginger, garlic, and spices, and sauté for about 1 minute.
2. Add the chicken and cook for about 4-5 minutes. Add the tomatoes, broth, salt, and black pepper, and bring to gentle simmer.
3. Now, adjust the heat to low and simmer, covered for about 10-15 minutes. Spill in the spinach and cook for about 4-5 minutes.
4. Serve hot.

Nutrition:
Calories: 191
Fat: 6.5g
Carbohydrates: 5.9g
Fiber: 1.7g
Sugar: 2.2g
Protein: 26.3g
Sodium: 163mg

290. Chicken and Bell Pepper Stew

Preparation Time: 10 minutes **Cooking Time:** 45 minutes **Servings:** 1

Ingredients:
- ½ tablespoon olive oil, divided
- 1 (4-ounce) boneless, skinless chicken thigh
- ¼ of celery stalk, chopped
- ½ of small bell pepper, seeded and chopped
- 1 tablespoon yellow onion, chopped
- ¼ cup tomato, chopped
- ⅛ teaspoon dried thyme
- ⅛ teaspoon dried oregano
- ¼ teaspoon smoked paprika
- ½ cup low-sodium chicken broth
- ½ tablespoon fresh cilantro, chopped
- Salt and ground black pepper, as required

Directions:
1. In a small heavy-bottomed pan, warmth half of oil over medium-high heat and sear the chicken thigh for about 4-5 minutes or until browned all completely. With a slotted spoon, transfer the chicken thigh onto a plate.
2. In the same pan, warmth the remaining oil over medium heat and cook the bell pepper, celery, onion and red chili for about 4-5 minutes. Add the tomatoes, dried herbs and spices and cook for about 1-2 minutes. Stir in the cooked chicken and broth and bring to a boil.
3. Set the heat to low and parboil for about 25-30 minutes.
4. Stir in the cilantro, salt and black pepper and serve hot.

Nutrition:
Calories: 306
Fat: 15.5g
Carbohydrates: 5.6g
Fiber: 1.8g
Sugar: 2.6g
Protein: 34.8g
Sodium: 285mg

291. Chicken and Tomato Curry

Preparation Time: 10 minutes **Cooking Time:** 30 minutes **Servings:** 1

Ingredients:
- ½ tablespoon olive oil
- ¼ of onion, chopped
- ¼ teaspoon ginger paste
- ¼ teaspoon garlic paste
- 1 tomato, chopped finely
- ¼ teaspoon ground cumin
- ¼ teaspoon ground coriander
- ¼ teaspoons red chili powder
- Pinch of ground turmeric
- Salt and ground black pepper, as required
- ¼ pound boneless, skinless chicken breast, divide into cubes
- ½ cup water, divided
- ¼ tablespoon fresh cilantro, chopped

Directions:
1. In a non-stick saucepan, heat oil over medium heat and sauté onion for about 3-4 minutes. Add ginger and garlic and sauté for about 1 minute. Add tomato and spices and stir to blend.
2. Set the heat to medium-low and cook for about 5-10 minutes, stirring occasionally.
3. Add the chicken and water and cook for about 10-15 minutes, stirring occasionally.
4. Serve hot with the topping of cilantro.

Nutrition:
Calories: 219
Fat: 10.3g
Carbohydrates: 6.3g
Fiber: 1.7g
Sugar: 2.9g
Protein: 25.2g
Sodium: 228mg

292. Chicken and Cauliflower Curry

Preparation Time: 10 minutes **Cooking Time:** 20 minutes **Servings:** 1

Ingredients:
- ½ tablespoon olive oil
- ½ teaspoon curry powder
- ¼ pound skinless, boneless chicken thigh, cut into bite-sized pieces
- Salt and ground black pepper, as required
- 3 ounces cauliflower, cut into small pieces
- 2 ounces unsweetened coconut milk
- 1 teaspoon fresh parsley, chopped

Directions:
1. In a non-stick skillet, warmth the oil over medium heat and sauté the garlic and curry powder for about 1 minute.
2. Attach the chicken, salt and black pepper and cook for about 5-6 minutes, stirring frequently. With a slotted spoon, transfer the chicken onto a plate.
3. In the skillet, add the cauliflower and cook for about 2-3 minutes. Add the coconut milk and simmer for about 5-7 minutes. Stir in the cooked chicken, salt and black pepper and cook for about 2-3 minutes.
4. Serve hot with the garnishing of parsley.

Nutrition:
Calories: 237
Fat: 12g
Carbohydrates: 5.6g
Fiber: 2.7g
Sugar: 2.1g
Protein: 27.2g
Sodium: 167mg

293. Chicken and Broccoli Curry
Preparation Time: 10 minutes **Cooking Time:** 13 minutes **Servings:** 1

Ingredients:
- 2-3 ounces unsweetened coconut milk
- ¼ teaspoon fresh ginger, grated
- ½ teaspoon curry powder
- 1 tablespoon olive oil, divided
- 1 (4-ounce) skinless, boneless chicken breast, sliced thinly
- ¼ of small onion, chopped
- ½ cup broccoli florets

Directions:
1. In a bowl, add the coconut milk, ginger and curry powder and mix well. Keep aside.
2. In a small skillet, warmth ½ tablespoon of oil over medium-high heat and stir fry the chicken slices for about 3-4 minutes or until golden brown. Transfer the chicken slices onto a plate.
3. In the same skillet, warmth the remaining oil over medium-high heat and sauté the onion for about 2 minutes. Add the broccoli and stir fry for about 3 minutes. Add the cooked chicken and coconut mixture and stir fry for about 3-4 minutes.
4. Serve hot.

Nutrition:
Calories: 300
Fat: 17.5g
Carbohydrates: 6g
Fiber: 2.2g
Sugar: 1.6g
Protein: 26.9g
Sodium: 157mg

294. Chicken and Spinach Curry
Preparation Time: 10 minutes **Cooking Time:** 15 minutes **Servings:** 1

Ingredients:
- ½ tablespoon olive oil
- 1 tablespoon onion, chopped
- ½ garlic clove, minced
- ¼ teaspoon fresh ginger, minced
- ¼ tablespoon curry powder
- ¼ pound skinless, boneless chicken breast, divide into bite-sized pieces
- Salt and ground black pepper, as required
- 2 ounces unsweetened coconut milk
- 4-5 ounces fresh spinach, chopped

Directions:
1. In a skillet, warmth the oil over medium heat and sauté the onion for about 3-4 minutes.
2. Attach the garlic, ginger and curry powder and sauté for about 1 minute.
3. Add the chicken, salt and black pepper and cook for about 3-4 minutes, stirring frequently.
4. Attach the coconut milk and bring to a boil.
5. Stir in the spinach and cook for about 3-4 minutes.
6. Serve hot.

Nutrition:
Calories: 155
Fat: 7.5g
Carbohydrates: 5.1g
Fiber: 0.6g
Sugar: 3.3g
Protein: 15.6g
Sodium: 165mg

295. Chicken and Sweet Potato Curry
Preparation Time: 10 minutes **Cooking Time:** 35 minutes **Servings:** 1

Ingredients:
- 1 tablespoon olive oil, divided
- ¼ pound skinless, boneless chicken breast, divide into chunks
- Salt and ground black pepper, as required
- ¼ of small onion, chopped
- 1 small garlic clove, minced
- 1 teaspoon curry powder
- ½ of medium sweet potato, peeled and cubed
- ¼ cup low-sodium chicken broth
- ¼ cup unsweetened coconut milk

Directions:
1. In a small skillet, warmth ½ tablespoon of oil over medium heat and cook chicken and with salt and black pepper for about 4-6 minutes. With a slotted spoon, transfer the chicken onto a plate.
2. In the same skillet, warmth remaining oil over medium heat and sauté onion for about 5-7 minutes. Add garlic, ground ginger and curry powder and sauté for about 1-2 minutes. Stir in chicken, sweet potato, broth and coconut milk and simmer, covered for about 15-20 minutes.
3. Stir in salt and black pepper and serve hot.

Nutrition:
Calories: 251
Fat: 12.5g
Carbohydrates: 6.9g
Fiber: 3.5g
Sugar: 1g
Protein: 29g
Sodium: 287mg

296. Green Chicken and Veggies Curry

Preparation Time: 10 minutes **Cooking Time:** 30 minutes **Servings:** 1

Ingredients:
- ½ tablespoon olive oil
- ¼ tablespoon green curry paste
- ¼ pound skinless, boneless chicken breast, cubed
- 2-3 tablespoons unsweetened coconut milk
- ¼ cup low-sodium chicken broth
- ¼ cup fresh green beans, ends trimmed and cut into pieces
- ¼ cup asparagus spears, ends removed and cut into pieces
- Salt and ground black pepper, as required
- 1 teaspoon fresh basil leaves, chopped

Directions:
1. In a wok, heat the oil over medium heat and sauté the curry paste for about 1-2 minutes. Add the chicken and cook for about 8-10 minutes. Now, add in the coconut milk and broth and bring to a boil.
2. Adjust the heat low and cook for about 8-10 minutes. Add the asparagus, green beans, salt and black pepper and cook for about 4-5 minutes or until desired doneness.
3. Garnish with basil and serve hot.

Nutrition:
Calories: 315 Fiber: 1.8g Sodium: 215mg
Fat: 13.8g Sugar: 1g
Carbohydrates: 4.8g Protein: 27.3g

297. Ground Chicken and Tofu Soup

Preparation Time: 10 minutes **Cooking Time:** 15 minutes **Servings:** 1

Ingredients:
- 1 teaspoons olive oil
- 3 ounces lean ground chicken
- 3 ounces firm tofu, pressed, drained and cubed
- ¾ cup low-sodium chicken broth
- Pinch of freshly ground white pepper
- 1 scallion, chopped

Directions:
1. In a small skillet, warmth olive oil over medium-high heat and cook chicken for about 8-10 minutes. Transfer the chicken into a bowl.
2. In the same skillet, add tofu and cook for about 2-3 minutes or until browned from all sides.
3. In a small saucepan, add broth over medium-low heat and bring to a gentle boil. Reduce the heat to low. Stir in cooked chicken, tofu and black pepper and simmer for about 4-5 minutes.
4. Stir in the scallion and immediately remove from heat.
5. Serve hot.

Nutrition:
Calories: 228 Fiber: 1.2g Sodium: 159mg
Fat: 12.8g Sugar: 0.9g
Carbohydrates: 3.4g Protein: 26g

298. Gingered Ground Chicken

Preparation Time: 10 minutes **Cooking Time:** 15 minutes **Servings:** 1

Ingredients:
- ½ tablespoon avocado oil
- ½ of small onion, chopped finely
- ½ teaspoon fresh ginger, minced
- 1 small garlic clove, minced
- ⅓ pound lean ground chicken
- 1 small tomato, chopped finely
- Salt and ground black pepper, as required
- 1 teaspoon fresh parsley, chopped

Directions:
1. In a small skillet, warmth the oil over medium heat and sauté the onion, ginger, and garlic for about 4-5 minutes. Add the ground chicken, salt, and black pepper, and cook over medium-high heat for about 4-5 minutes, breaking up the meat into smaller strips with a wooden spoon.
2. Add the tomato and cook for about 4-5 minutes, stirring frequently.
3. Stir in salt and black pepper and remove from the heat.
4. Serve hot with the garnishing of parsley.

Nutrition:
Calories: 243 Fiber: 2.3g Sodium: 299mg
Fat: 9.2g Sugar: 3.9g
Carbohydrates: 6.9g Protein: 32.1g

299. Chicken Meatballs Curry

Preparation Time: 10 minutes **Cooking Time:** 25 minutes **Servings:** 1

Ingredients:
For Meatballs
- ¼ pound lean ground chicken
- ¼ tablespoon onion paste
- ¼ teaspoons fresh ginger paste
- ¼ teaspoons garlic paste
- ¼ of green chili, chopped finely

For Curry
- ½ tablespoon extra-virgin olive oil
- ⅛ teaspoon cumin seeds
- 1 (¼-inch) cinnamon stick
- ¼ tablespoon fresh cilantro leaves, chopped
- ¼ teaspoon ground cumin
- ⅛ teaspoon red chili powder
- ⅛ teaspoon ground turmeric
- Salt, as required
- ¼ of onion, chopped
- ¼ teaspoons fresh ginger, minced
- ¼ teaspoons garlic, minced

- 1 small tomato, chopped finely
- ¼ teaspoons ground coriander
- ¼ teaspoon garam masala powder
- ⅛ teaspoon red chili powder

Directions:
1. For meatballs: in a bowl, attach all ingredients and mix until well combined. Make small equal-sized meatballs from mixture.
2. In a small deep skillet, heat oil over medium heat and cook meatballs for about 3-5 minutes or until browned from all sides. With a slotted spoon, transfer the meatballs into a bowl.
3. In the same skillet, add cumin seeds and cinnamon stick and sauté for about 1 minute. Add onions and sauté for about 4-5

- ⅛ teaspoon ground turmeric
- Salt, as required
- ⅓ cup water
- 1 teaspoon fresh cilantro, chopped

minutes. Add ginger and garlic paste and sauté for about 1 minute. Add tomato and spices and cook for about 2-3 minutes, crushing with the back of spoon.
4. Add water and meatballs and bring to a boil. Reduce the heat to low and simmer for about 10 minutes.
5. Serve hot with the garnishing of cilantro.

Nutrition:
Calories: 247
Fat: 12.5g
Carbohydrates: 7.1g
Fiber: 2.2g
Sugar: 3.7g
Protein: 24.4g
Sodium: 296mg

300. Spicy Chicken Burger
Preparation Time: 10 minutes **Cooking Time:** 10 minutes **Servings:** 1
Ingredients:
- 1 (¼-inch) piece fresh ginger, grated
- ¼ pound lean ground turkey
- ¼ of medium onion, grated
- ½ of garlic clove, minced
- ½ teaspoon fresh mint leaves, chopped finely
- ¼ teaspoon ground coriander
- ¼ teaspoon ground cumin
- ⅛ teaspoon ground allspice
- ⅛ teaspoon ground cinnamon
- Salt and ground black pepper, as required

Directions:
1. Preheat the broiler of oven. Lightly, grease a broiler pan.
2. In a bowl, squeeze the juice of ginger. Add remaining ingredients and mix until well combined.
3. Shape the mixture into a patty.
4. Arrange the patty onto the prepared broiler pan and broil for about 5 minutes per side.
5. Serve hot.

Nutrition:
Calories: 175
Fat: 8.3g
Carbohydrates: 2.8g
Fiber: 0.7g
Sugar: 0.8g
Protein: 22.7g
Sodium: 244mg

301. Turkey and Veggie Salad
Preparation Time: 10 minutes **Cooking Time:** 13 minutes **Servings:** 1
Ingredients:
- ¼ pound cooked turkey meat, chopped
- ¼ of English cucumber, chopped
- ¼ cup green cabbage, shredded
- 1 teaspoon fresh mint leaves, chopped
- ¼ tablespoon olive oil
- ¼ tablespoon fresh lime juice
- Salt and ground black pepper, as required

Directions:
1. In a salad bowl, attach all ingredients and toss to coat well.
2. Serve immediately.

Nutrition:
Calories: 240
Fat: 9.3g |
Carbohydrates: 4g
Fiber: 1g
Sugar: 1.8g
Protein: 34g
Sodium: 240mg

302. Turkey Lettuce Wraps
Preparation Time: 10 minutes **Cooking Time:** 20 minutes **Servings:** 1
Ingredients:
- ½ tablespoon olive oil
- 2 tablespoons of onion, chopped
- 3 ounces lean ground turkey
- ¼ cup fresh mushrooms, chopped
- ⅛ teaspoon cayenne pepper
- ⅛ teaspoon ground cumin
- 2 large romaine lettuce leaves
- ¼ teaspoon fresh cilantro leaves, chopped

Directions:
1. In a skillet, warmth oil over medium heat and sauté onion for about 4-5 minutes. Add turkey and cook, stirring occasionally for about 6-8 minutes. Add mushroom, ginger, tamari, cayenne pepper and cumin and cook for about 5-7 minutes. Remove from heat and set aside.
2. Arrange the lettuce leaves onto serving plates. Place turkey mixture over each lettuce leaf evenly.
3. Top with cilantro evenly and serve.

Nutrition:
Calories: 196
Fat: 13.3g
Carbohydrates: 3g
Fiber: 0.8g
Sugar: 1.3g
Protein: 17.6g
Sodium: 70mg

303. Seasoned Turkey Legs

Preparation Time: 10 minutes **Cooking Time:** 1 hour 40 minutes **Servings:** 1

Ingredients:
- 1 bone-in, skinless turkey leg
- ½ tablespoon olive oil
- ¼ teaspoon dried thyme
- ¼ teaspoon poultry seasoning
- Salt and ground black pepper, as required
- ¼ cup low-sodium chicken broth

Directions:
1. Preheat your oven to 350 F.
2. Place the oil, thyme, poultry seasoning, salt, and black pepper in a small bowl and mix well. Rub the turkey leg with oil mixture.
3. Arrange turkey leg into a small roasting pan. Pour the broth into the roasting pan around the turkey leg. Roast for 1 hour and 40 minutes.
4. Remove the roasting pan from oven and with a piece of foil, cover it. Set aside for 10 minutes before serving.

Nutrition:
Calories: 429
Fat: 18.5g
Carbohydrates: 0.7g
Fiber: 0.1g
Sugar: 0g
Protein: 51.6g
Sodium: 173mg

---

304. Turkey with Mushrooms

Preparation Time: 10 minutes **Cooking Time:** 7 minutes **Servings:** 1

Ingredients:
- ½ tablespoon olive oil
- 1 garlic clove, crushed
- ¼ pound boneless, skinless turkey breast, cut into 2-inch strips
- ½ cup fresh mushrooms, sliced
- ¼ cup low-sodium chicken broth
- 1 tablespoon sugar-free tomato paste
- Salt and ground white pepper, as required

Directions:
1. In a non-stick skillet, warmth the oil over medium heat and sauté the garlic for about 1 minute. Add the turkey slices and cook for about 4-6 minutes. With a slotted spoon, transfer the turkey slices onto a plate.
2. In the skillet, attach the mushrooms and cook for about 2-3 minutes, stirring continuously. Add the broth, tomato paste, salt and black pepper and cook for about 3-5 minutes, stirring occasionally.
3. Stir in the cooked turkey slices and cook for about 2-3 minutes.
4. Serve hot.

Nutrition:
Calories: 219
Fat: 7.7g
Carbohydrates: 5.4g
Fiber: 1.1g
Sugar: 2.6g
Protein: 30.5g
Sodium: 246mg

---

305. Ground Turkey in Tomato Sauce

Preparation Time: 10 minutes **Cooking Time:** 22 minutes **Servings:** 1

Ingredients:
- ½ tablespoon extra-virgin olive oil
- ¼ of onion, chopped
- ¼ pound lean ground turkey
- ½ of garlic clove, minced
- ¼ teaspoon dried oregano
- ¼ cup sugar-free tomato sauce
- 1 teaspoon fresh parsley, chopped

Directions:
1. In a small skillet, warmth the oil over medium heat and sauté the onion for about 5 minutes. Add the ground turkey, garlic, oregano and red pepper flakes and cook for about 6-7 minutes.
2. Stir in the tomato sauce and parboil for about 8-10 minutes.
3. Serve hot with the garnishing of parsley.

Nutrition:
Calories: 252
Fat: 14.5g
Carbohydrates: 5.16g
Fiber: 1.6g
Sugar: 3.3g
Protein: 23.6g
Sodium: 309mg

---

306. Ground Turkey with Asparagus

Preparation Time: 10 minutes **Cooking Time:** 18 minutes **Servings:** 1

Ingredients:
- ¼ pound lean ground turkey
- ½ tablespoon olive oil
- ¼ of small onion, chopped
- 1 garlic clove, minced
- ½ cup asparagus, trimmed and divide into 1-inch pieces
- 2-3 tablespoons water
- ⅛ teaspoon red pepper flakes, crushed
- Salt and ground black pepper, as required

Directions:
1. Warmth a non-stick skillet over medium-high heat and cook turkey for about 5-7 minutes or until browned. With a slotted spoon transfer the turkey into a bowl and discard the grease from skillet.
2. In the same skillet, warmth oil over medium heat and sauté onion and garlic for about 5 minutes. Stir in the asparagus, water and cooked turkey and cook for about 4-5 minutes. Stir in salt and black pepper and remove from the heat.
3. Serve hot.

Nutrition:
Calories: 248
Fat: 14.5g
Carbohydrates: 5.1g

Fiber: 1.8g
Sugar: 2.1g
Protein: 24.2g
Sodium: 245mg

307. Ground Turkey with Pumpkin

Preparation Time: 10 minutes **Cooking Time:** 30 minutes **Servings:** 1

Ingredients:
- ½ tablespoon extra-virgin olive oil
- ¼ of small onion, chopped
- 1 garlic clove, chopped finely
- ¼ pound lean ground turkey
- 1 small tomato, chopped finely
- 3 ounces sugar-free pumpkin puree
- ¼ teaspoon ground cumin
- ⅛ teaspoon ground turmeric
- Salt and ground black pepper, as required
- ¼ cup water

Directions:
1. In a saucepan, warmth oil over medium-low heat and sauté the onion and garlic for about 5 minutes. Add turkey and cook for about 4-5 minutes. Add tomato and cook for about 2-3 minutes. Stir pumpkin puree, spices and water and bring to a boil over high heat.
2. Reduce the heat to medium-low heat and simmer, covered for about 10-15 minutes, stirring occasionally.
3. Serve hot.

Nutrition:
Calories: 281
Fat: 13.5g
Carbohydrates: 10.1g
Fiber: 4.6g
Sugar: 4.3g
Protein: 24.3g
Sodium: 252mg

308. Turkey Stuffed Zucchini

Preparation Time: 10 minutes **Cooking Time:** 30 minutes **Servings:** 1

Ingredients:
- ½ zucchini
- 2 ounces lean ground turkey
- 1 tablespoon white onion, chopped
- 1 ounce fresh mushrooms, sliced
- ¼ of tomato, chopped
- ½ tablespoon whole-wheat breadcrumbs
- Ground black pepper, as required
- 1½ tablespoon part-skim mozzarella cheese, shredded and divided

Directions:
1. Preheat your oven to 350F.
2. With a small spoon, set out the pulp from the zucchini half, leaving ¼-inch shells. Transfer the zucchini pulp into a large bowl and set aside.
3. Arrange the zucchini shell into an ungreased microwave-safe baking dish. Seal the baking dish and microwave on High for about 3 minutes. Drain the water from baking dish and set aside.
4. Warmth a non-stick skillet over medium heat and cook the ground turkey and onion for about 6-7 minutes until meat is no longer pink. Drain the grease from the skillet. Remove from the heat.
5. In the bowl of zucchini pulp, add the cooked turkey, mushrooms, tomato, egg, tomato sauce, black pepper and ½ tablespoon of the cheese and mix until well combined.
6. Place the turkey mixture into the zucchini shell and sprinkle with the remaining cheese. Bake for 20 minutes until top becomes golden brown.
7. Serve hot.

Nutrition:
Calories: 285
Fat: 14.4g
Carbohydrates: 15.1g
Fiber: 3.3g
Sugar: 3g
Protein: 27g
Sodium: 295mg

309. Turkey Meatballs Kabobs

Preparation Time: 10 minutes **Cooking Time:** 14 minutes **Servings:** 1

Ingredients:
- ¼ of yellow onion, chopped roughly
- 2 tablespoons lemongrass, chopped roughly
- ½ of garlic clove, chopped roughly
- ⅓ pound lean ground turkey
- ½ teaspoon olive oil
- ¼ tablespoon arrowroot starch
- Pinch of powdered stevia
- Salt and ground black pepper, as required

Directions:
1. Preheat the grill to medium-high heat. Grease the grill grate.
2. In a mini food processor, add the onion, lemongrass and garlic and pulse until chopped finely.
3. Transfer the onion mixture into a large bowl. Add the remaining ingredients and mix until well combined. Make 12 equal-sized balls from meat mixture.
4. Thread the balls onto the presoaked wooden skewers.
5. Grill the skewers for about 6-7 minutes per side.
6. Serve hot.

Nutrition:
Calories: 256
Fat: 13.2g
Carbohydrates: 4.8g
Fiber: 0.7g
Sugar: 1.2g
Protein: 30.1g
Sodium: 271mg

310. Turkey, Apple and Veggies Burgers

Preparation Time: 10 minutes **Cooking Time:** 12 minutes **Servings:** 1

Ingredients:
- 3 ounces lean ground turkey
- ¼ of small apple, peeled, cored and grated

- 1 tablespoon red onion, minced
- ½ of small garlic clove, minced
- ¼ tablespoon fresh ginger, minced
- ½ tablespoon fresh cilantro, chopped
- ¼ teaspoon ground cumin
- Salt and ground black pepper, as required
- ½ teaspoon olive oil

Directions:
1. Preheat the grill to medium heat. Grease the grill grate.
2. In a bowl, attach all the ingredients except for oil and mix until well combined. Shape the mixture into a patty. Brush the patty with olive oil evenly.
3. Place the patty onto the grill and cook for about 5-6 minutes per side.
4. Serve hot.

Nutrition:
Calories: 169
Fat: 8.6g
Carbohydrates: 6.7g
Fiber: 1.4g
Sugar: 3.6g
Protein: 17.1g
Sodium: 222mg

---

311. Turkey and Pumpkin Meatloaf
Preparation Time: 15 minutes **Cooking Time:** 1 hour 25 minutes **Servings:** 5

Ingredients:
- 1 pound lean ground turkey
- 1 tablespoon olive oil
- ½ of onion, chopped finely
- 2 carrots, peeled and grated
- 3 celery stalks, chopped finely
- 3 tablespoons dried parsley
- 1½ teaspoon ground sage
- ¾ teaspoon ground cinnamon
- ½ teaspoon ground nutmeg
- Salt and ground black pepper, as required
- 2 eggs
- ¾ cup almond meal
- ¼ cup sugar-free pumpkin puree

Directions:
1. Warmth your oven to 375 F. Grease a loaf pan.
2. In a skillet, heat the oil over medium-high heat and sauté the onion for about 5 minutes. Add the carrot, celery, parsley, sage, spices, salt and black pepper and cook for about 4-5 minutes. Detach from heat and set aside to cool.
3. In a large bowl, add the turkey, eggs, almond meal, pumpkin puree and vegetable mixture and mix until well combined.
4. Place the turkey mixture into the prepared loaf pan evenly. Bake for approximately 1¼ hours.
5. Detach from the oven and let the meatloaf rest for 8-10 minutes before serving. Cut into desired sized slices and serve.

Nutrition:
Calories: 285
Fat: 17.5g
Carbohydrates: 5.5g
Fiber: 3.5g
Sugar: 3g
Protein: 23.7g
Sodium: 152mg

---

312. Duck Breast
Preparation Time: 10 minutes **Cooking Time:** 16 minutes **Servings:** 21

Ingredients:
- 1 small shallot, sliced thinly
- 1 teaspoon fresh ginger, minced
- ¼ tablespoon fresh thyme, chopped
- Salt and ground black pepper, as required
- 1 (12-ounce) duck breast

Directions:
1. In a bowl, place the shallot, ginger, thyme, salt, and black pepper, and mix well. Add the duck breast and coat with marinade evenly. Refrigerate to marinate for about 2–12 hours.
2. Preheat the grill to medium-high heat. Grease the grill grate.
3. Place the duck breast onto the grill, skin-side down, and cook for about 6-8 minutes per side.
4. Serve hot.

Nutrition:
Calories: 229
Fat: 6.9g
Carbohydrates: 2g
Fiber: 0.2g
Sugar: 0g
Protein: 37.7g
Sodium: 79mg

---

313. Spiced Quail
Preparation Time: 10 minutes **Cooking Time:** 31 minutes **Servings:** 1

Ingredients:
- 1 tablespoon olive oil, divided
- ⅛ teaspoon ground cumin
- Pinch of ground coriander
- Salt and ground black pepper, as required
- Pinch of cayenne pepper
- 1 (5¼-ounce) whole quail
- 2 lemon slices

Directions:
1. Place ¼ tablespoon of olive oil, cumin, coriander, salt and black pepper in a large baking dish and mix well. Place quail and coat with oil mixture generously.
2. Place 1 lemons slice in the cavity of each quail. With a kitchen twine, tie the legs.
3. Warmth the remaining olive oil in a large ovenproof wok over high heat. Place the quail and cook for about 2-4 minutes per side or until golden brown.
4. Now, arrange the quail in wok, breast-side facing up. Place 1 lemon slice over each quail and sprinkle with cayenne pepper. Transfer the wok into oven and Roast for approximately 10-15 minutes.

5. Remove from the oven and place each quail onto a plate for about 10 minutes before serving.

Nutrition:
Calories: 412
Fat: 17.5g
Carbohydrates: 0.3g
Fiber: 0.1g
Sugar: 0g
Protein: 52.6g
Sodium: 156mg

314. White chicken chili
Preparation Time: 10 minutes **Cooking Time:** 31 minutes **Servings:** 8

Ingredients:
- 1 can (ten ounces) white chunk chicken
- 2 cans (fifteen ounces each) low-sodium white beans, drained
- 1 can low-sodium diced tomatoes
- Low-sodium chicken broth (4 cups)
- 1 medium onion, chopped
- ½ medium green pepper, chopped
- 1 medium red pepper, chopped
- 2 garlic cloves, minced
- 2 teaspoons chili powder
- 1 tsp. Ground cumin
- 1 teaspoon dried oregano
- Cayenne pepper, to taste
- 8 tablespoons shredded reduced-fat Monterey Jack cheese
- 2 tablespoons chopped fresh cilantro

Directions:
1. Combine the chicken, beans, tomatoes, and chicken broth in a large soup pot. Simmer, covered, over medium heat.
2. In the meantime, grease a nonstick frying pan. Sauté the onions, peppers, and garlic for 3 to 5 minutes, or until the vegetables are tender.
3. In a soup saucepan, combine the onion and pepper mixture. Add the chili powder, cumin, oregano, and cayenne pepper to taste. Cook and stir occasionally for about ten minutes, or until all the vegetables are tender.
4. Ladle into warmed bowls. Drizzle each serving with 1 tablespoon cheese and garnish with cilantro.

Nutrition:
Calories: 212
Sodium: 241mg
Fat: 4g
Cholesterol: 27mg
Carbohydrate: 25g
Protein: 19g

315. Ritzy Jerked Chicken Breasts
Preparation Time: 4 hours 10 minutes **Cooking Time:** 15 minutes **Servings:** 4

Ingredients:
- 2 habanero chili peppers, halved lengthwise, seeded
- ½ sweet onion, cut into chunks
- 1 tablespoon minced garlic
- 1 tablespoon ground allspice
- 2 teaspoons chopped fresh thyme
- ¼ cup freshly squeezed lime juice
- ½ teaspoon ground nutmeg
- ¼ teaspoon ground cinnamon
- 1 teaspoon freshly ground black pepper
- 2 tablespoons extra-virgin olive oil
- 4 (5-ounce / 142-g) boneless, skinless chicken breasts
- 2 cups fresh arugula
- 1 cup halved cherry tomatoes

Directions:
1. Combine the habaneros, onion, garlic, allspice, thyme, lime juice, nutmeg, cinnamon, black pepper, and olive oil in a blender. Pulse to blender well.
2. Transfer the mixture into a large bowl or two medium bowls, then dunk the chicken in the bowl and press to coat well.
3. Set the bowl in the refrigerator and marinate for at least 4 hours.
4. Preheat the oven to 400F (205C).
5. Remove the bowl from the refrigerator, then discard the marinade.
6. Arrange the chicken on a baking sheet, then roast in the preheated oven for 15 minutes or until golden brown and lightly charred. Bend the chicken halfway through the cooking time.
7. Remove the baking sheet from the oven and let sit for 5 minutes. Transfer the chicken on a large plate and serve with arugula and cherry tomatoes.

Nutrition:
Calories: 226
Fat: 9.0g
Protein: 33.0g
Carbs: 3.0g
Fiber: 0g
Sugar: 1g
Sodium: 92mg

316. Roasted Chicken with Root Vegetables
Preparation Time: 20 minutes **Cooking Time:** 41 minutes **Servings:** 6

Ingredients:
- 1 teaspoon minced fresh rosemary
- 1 teaspoon minced fresh thyme
- 1 teaspoon salt
- 1 teaspoon ground black pepper
- 2 tablespoons olive oil, divided
- 6 (6-ounce / 170-g) boneless, skinless chicken breast halves
- 2 medium fennel bulbs, chopped
- 4 medium peeled carrots, chopped
- 3 peeled medium radishes, chopped
- 3 tablespoons honey
- ½ cup white wine
- 2 cups chicken stock
- 3 bay leaves

Directions:
1. Preheat the oven to 375F (190C).
2. Mix the rosemary, thyme, salt, and black pepper in a small bowl.
3. Heat 1 tbsp. of olive oil in a nonstick skillet over medium-high heat until shimmering.
4. On a clean work surface, massage the chicken breasts with half of the seasoning mixture.

5. Place the chicken in the skillet and cook for 6 minutes or until lightly browned on both sides. Detach the chicken from the skillet and set aside.
6. Mix the fennel bulbs, carrots, and radishes in a microwave-safe bowl, then sprinkle with remaining seasoning mixture and drizzle with honey, white wine, and remaining olive oil. Toss to combine well.
7. Cover the bowl and microwave the root vegetables for 10 minutes or until soft.
8. Arrange the root vegetables and chicken in a baking sheet, then pour in the chicken stock and honey mixture remains in the bowl. Top them with bay leaves.
9. Set the sheet in the preheated oven and roast for 25 minutes.
10. Remove the sheet from the oven and transfer the chicken and vegetables on a large plate. Discard the bay leaves, then allow to cool for a few minutes before serving.

Nutrition:
Calories: 364
Fat: 10.2g
Protein: 41.8g
Carbs: 12g
Fiber: 3.8g
Sugar: 1.5g
Sodium: 650mg

317. Roasted Vegetable and Chicken Tortillas

Preparation Time: 10 minutes **Cooking Time:** 20 minutes **Servings:** 4

Ingredients:
- 1 red bell pepper, seeded and set into 1-inch-wide strips
- ½ small eggplant, cut into ¼-inch-thick slices
- ½ small red onion, sliced
- 1 medium zucchini, cut lengthwise into strips
- 1 tablespoon extra-virgin olive oil
- Salt and ground black pepper, to taste
- 4 whole-wheat tortilla wraps
- 2 (8-ounce / 227-g) cooked chicken breasts, sliced

Directions:
1. Preheat the oven to 400F (205C). Line a baking sheet with aluminum foil.
2. Combine the bell pepper, eggplant, red onion, zucchini, and olive oil in a large bowl. Toss to coat well.
3. Pour the vegetables into the baking sheet, then sprinkle with salt and pepper.
4. Roast in the warmth oven for 20 minutes or until tender and charred.
5. Unfold the tortillas on a clean work surface, then divide the vegetables and chicken slices on the tortillas.
6. Wrap and serve immediately.

Nutrition:
Calories: 483
Fat: 25.0g
Protein: 20.0g
Carbs: 4.5g
Fiber: 3.0g
Sugar: 4.0g
Sodium: 730mg

318. Chicken with Carrot, and Kale

Preparation Time: 15 minutes **Cooking Time:** 27 minutes **Servings:** 2

Ingredients:
- ½ cup couscous
- 1 cup water, divided
- ⅓ cup basil pesto
- 3 teaspoons olive oil, divided
- 3 (2-ounce / 57-g) whole carrots, rinsed, thinly sliced
- Salt and ground black pepper, to taste
- 1 (about 6-ounce / 170-g) bunch kale, rinsed, stems removed, chopped
- 2 cloves garlic, minced
- 2 tablespoons dried currants
- 1 tablespoon red wine vinegar
- 2 (6-ounce / 170-g) boneless, skinless chicken breasts, rinsed
- 1 tablespoon Italian seasoning

Directions:
1. Pour the couscous and ¾ cup of water in a pot. Bring to a boil on high heat. Reduce the heat to low. Simmer for 7 minutes or until most of the water has been absorbed. Fluffy with a fork and mix in the basil pesto.
2. Warmth 1 tsp. of olive oil in a skillet.
3. Attach the carrots, then sprinkle with salt and pepper. Sauté for 3 minutes or until tender.
4. Attach the kale and garlic and sauté for 2 minutes or until the kale is lightly wilted.
5. Add the currents and remaining water and sauté for 3 minutes or until most of the water is cooked off.
6. Set off the heat, then mix in the red wine vinegar. Transfer them in a large bowl and cover to keep warm.
7. On a clean work surface, massage the chicken with Italian seasoning, salt, and pepper.
8. Clean the skillet and heat 2 teaspoons of olive oil over medium-high heat until shimmering.
9. Add the chicken and sear for 12 minutes or until well browned. Flip the chicken halfway through the cooking time.
10. Bring the chicken to a large plate, then spread with vegetables and couscous. Slice to serve.

Nutrition:
Calories: 461
Fat: 14.2g
Protein: 57.0g
Carbs: 26.1g
Fiber: 6.5g
Sugar: 1.5g
Sodium: 1210mg

319. Turkey Meatball and Vegetable Kabobs

Preparation Time: 15 minutes **Cooking Time:** 20 minutes **Servings:** 6

Ingredients:
- 20 ounces (567 g) lean ground turkey (93% fat-free)
- 2 egg whites
- 2 tablespoons grated Parmesan cheese
- 2 cloves garlic, minced
- ½ teaspoon salt, or to taste
- ¼ teaspoon ground black pepper
- 1 tablespoon olive oil

- 8 ounces (227 g) fresh cremini mushrooms, cut in half to make 12 pieces
- 24 cherry tomatoes

Special Equipment:
- 12 bamboo skewers, dip in water for at least 30 minutes

- 1 medium onion, cut into 12 pieces
- ¼ cup balsamic vinegar

Directions:
1. Mix the ground turkey, egg whites, Parmesan, garlic, salt, and pepper in a large bowl. Stir to combine well.
2. Set the mixture into 12 meatballs and place on a baking sheet. Refrigerate for at least 30 minutes.
3. Preheat the oven to 375F (190C). Grease another baking sheet with 1 tbsp. of olive oil.
4. Remove the meatballs from the refrigerator. Run the bamboo skewers through 2 meatballs, 1 mushroom, 2 cherry tomatoes, and 1 onion piece alternatively.
5. Arrange the kabobs on the greased baking sheet and brush with balsamic vinegar.
6. Grill in the preheated oven for 20 minutes or until an instant-read thermometer inserted in the middle of the meatballs reads at least 165F (74C). Flip the kabobs halfway through the cooking time.
7. Allow the kabobs to cool for 10 minutes, then serve warm.

Nutrition:
Calories: 200　　Carbs: 7.0g　　Sodium: 120mg
Fat: 8.0g　　Fiber: 1.0g
Protein: 22.0g　　Sugar: 4.0g

320. Shredded Buffalo Chicken

Preparation Time: 10 minutes　　**Cooking Time:** 20 minutes　　**Servings:** 8

Ingredients:
- 2 tbsp. avocado oil
- ½ cup finely minced onion
- 1 celery stalk, finely minced
- 1 large carrot, minced
- ⅓ cup mild hot sauce
- ½ tbsp. apple cider vinegar
- ¼ tsp. garlic powder
- 2 bone-in, skin-on chicken breasts

Directions:
1. Bring the electric pressure cooker to the Sauté setting. When the pot is warmth, spill in the avocado oil.
2. Stir the onion, celery, and carrot for 3 to 5 minutes until the onion begins to soften. Choose Cancel.
3. Set in the hot sauce, vinegar, and garlic powder. Bring the chicken breasts in the sauce, meat-side down.
4. Secure the lid of the pressure cooker. Set the valve to sealing.
5. Cook on high pressure.
6. When cooking is done, hit Cancel and quick free the pressure.
7. Using tongs, set the chicken breasts to a cutting board. Detach the skin, shred the chicken and return it to the pot. Let the chicken dip in the sauce for at least 5 minutes.
8. Serve immediately.

Nutrition:
Calories: 139　　Carbs: 2g　　Sodium: 295mg
Fat: 9g　　Sugars: 1g
Protein: 12g　　Fiber: 1g

321. Herbed Whole Turkey Breast

Preparation Time: 10 minutes　　**Cooking Time:** 30 minutes　　**Servings:** 12

Ingredients:
- 3 tbsp. extra-virgin olive oil
- 1½ tbsp. herbs de Provence or poultry seasoning
- 2 tsp. minced garlic
- 1 tsp. lemon zest
- 1 tbsp. kosher salt
- 1½ tsp. ground black pepper
- 1 bone-in, skin-on whole turkey breast, rinsed and patted dry

Directions:
1. In a small bowl, set together the olive oil, herbs de Provence, garlic, lemon zest, salt, and pepper.
2. Massage the outside of the turkey and under the skin with the olive oil mixture.
3. Spill 1 cup of water into the electric pressure cooker and insert a wire rack or trivet.
4. Set the turkey on the rack, skin-side up.
5. Secure the lid of the pressure cooker.
6. Cook on high pressure for 30 minutes.
7. When the cooking is complete, hit Cancel. Let the pressure to release naturally for 20 minutes, then quick free any remaining pressure.
8. Once the pin drops, unlock and detach the lid.
9. Carefully set the turkey to a cutting board. Detach the skin, slice, and serve.

Nutrition:
Calories: 146　　Carbs: 0g　　Sodium: 413mg
Fat: 9g　　Sugars: 0g
Protein: 16g　　Fiber: 0g

322. Garlic Galore Rotisserie Chicken

Preparation Time: 5 minutes　　**Cooking Time:** 3 minutes　　**Servings:** 4

Ingredients:
- 3 pounds whole chicken
- 2 tbsp. olive oil, divided
- Salt and Pepper, to season
- 20 to 30 cloves fresh garlic
- 1 cup low-sodium chicken stock, broth
- 2 tbsp. garlic powder

- 2 tsp. onion powder
- ½ tsp. basil
- ½ tsp. cumin
- ½ tsp. chili powder

Directions:
1. Massage chicken with one tablespoon of the olive oil and sprinkle with salt and pepper.
2. Bring the garlic cloves inside the chicken. Use butcher's twine to secure the legs.
3. Set the Sauté button on the Instant Pot, then add the rest of the olive oil to the inner pot.
4. When the pot is hot, set the chicken inside.
5. Detach the chicken and set aside. Set the trivet at the bottom of the inner pot and pour in the chicken stock.
6. Merge together the remaining seasonings and rub them all over the entire chicken.
7. Set the chicken back inside the inner pot, breast-side up, on top of the trivet and secure the lid to the sealing position.
8. Choose the Manual button and use the "+/-" button to set it for 25 minutes.
9. When the timer beeps, let the pressure to release naturally for 15 minutes.
10. Let the chicken rest before serving.

Nutrition:
Calories: 33
Fat: 23g
Protein: 24g
Carbs: 9g
Sugars: 0g
Fiber: 1g
Sodium: 110mg

323. Buttery Lemon Chicken

Preparation Time: 15 minutes **Cooking Time:** 7 minutes **Servings:** 4

Ingredients:
- 2 tbsp. margarine
- 1 medium onion, chopped
- 4 cloves garlic, minced
- ½ tsp. paprika
- ½ tsp. pepper
- 1 tsp. dried parsley, or 1 tbsp. minced fresh parsley
- 2 lb. (907 g) boneless chicken breasts or thighs
- ½ cup low-sodium chicken broth
- ⅓ cup lemon juice
- 1 teaspoon salt
- 1 to 2 tablespoons cornstarch
- 1 tablespoon water

Directions:
1. Set the Instant Pot to Sauté. When it is hot, attach margarine to the inner pot and melt.
2. Attach the onion, garlic, paprika, pepper, and parsley to melted margarine and sauté until onion starts to soften. Set onion to side of pot.
3. With the Instant Pot still at Sauté, attach the chicken and sear on each side.
4. Mix broth, lemon juice, and salt together. Spill over chicken and stir to merge.
5. Put on lid and set Instant Pot, set vent to sealing, and press Poultry. Set cook time for 7 minutes.
6. Detach chicken, leaving sauce in pot. Merge the cornstarch in water and add to sauce.

Nutrition:
Calories: 350
Fat: 12g
Protein: 52g
Carbs: 6g
Sugars: 1g
Fiber: 0g
Sodium: 658mg

324. Chicken in Wine

Preparation Time: 10 minutes **Cooking Time:** 12 minutes **Servings:** 6

Ingredients:
- 2 lb. Chicken breasts, trimmed of skin and fat
- 1 can 98% fat-free, reduced-sodium cream of mushroom soup
- 1 can onion soup
- 1 cup dry white wine

Directions:
1. Set the chicken into the Instant Pot.
2. Merge soups and wine. Spill over chicken.
3. Secure the lid. Cook on Manual mode.
4. When cook time is done, let the pressure release naturally for 5 minutes and then release the rest manually.

Nutrition:
Calories: 225
Fat: 5g
Protein: 35g
Carbs: 7g
Sugars: 3g
Fiber: 1g
Sodium: 645mg

325. Greek Chicken

Preparation Time: 25 minutes **Cooking Time:** 20 minutes **Servings:** 6

Ingredients:
- 4 potatoes
- 2 lb. (907 g) chicken pieces, trimmed of skin and fat
- 2 large onions
- 1 whole bulb garlic, cloves minced
- 3 tsp. dried oregano
- ¾ tsp. salt
- ½ tsp. pepper
- 1 tbsp. olive oil
- 1 cup water

Directions:
1. Set potatoes, chicken, onions, and garlic into the inner pot of the Instant Pot, then sprinkle with seasonings. Set with oil and water.
2. Cook for 20 minutes.
3. When cook time is done, let the pressure release naturally for 5 minutes, then release the rest manually.

Nutrition:
Calories: 278　　Carbs: 29g　　Sodium: 358mg
Fat: 6g　　Sugars: 9g
Protein: 27g　　Fiber: 4g

326. Chicken Casablanca
Preparation Time: 20 minutes　　**Cooking Time:** 12 minutes　　**Servings:** 8

Ingredients:
- 2 large onions, minced
- 1 tsp. ground ginger
- 3 garlic cloves, minced
- 2 tbsp. canola oil, divided
- 3 lb. (1.4 kg) skinless chicken pieces
- 3 large carrots, diced
- 2 large potatoes, unpeeled, diced
- ½ tsp. ground cumin
- ½ teaspoon salt
- ½ tsp. pepper
- ¼ tsp. cinnamon
- 2 tablespoons raisins
- 1 (14½-ounce / 411-g) can chopped tomatoes
- 3 small zucchinis, sliced
- 1 (15-ounce / 425-g) can garbanzo beans, drained
- 2 tbsp. chopped parsley

Directions:
1. Process and cook the onions, ginger, and garlic in 1 tbsp. of the oil, stirring constantly. Detach onions, ginger, and garlic and set aside.
2. Brown the chicken pieces with the remaining oil, then add the cooked onions, ginger and garlic back in as well as all the remaining ingredients, except the parsley.
3. Secure the lid and make sure vent is in the sealing position. Cook on Manual mode
4. When cook time is done, let the pressure release naturally for 5 minutes and then release the rest of the pressure manually.

Nutrition:
Calories: 39　　Carbs: 40g　　Sodium: 390mg
Fat: 10g　　Sugars: 10g
Protein: 36g　　Fiber: 8g

327. Mexican Turkey Tenderloin
Preparation Time: 5 minutes　　**Cooking Time:** 8 minutes　　**Servings:** 6

Ingredients:
- 1 cup bottled salsa
- 1 tsp. chili powder
- ½ tsp. ground cumin
- ¼ tsp. dried oregano
- 1½ lb. unseasoned turkey tenderloin or boneless turkey breast, cut into 6 pieces
- Freshly ground black pepper
- ½ cup shredded Monterey cheese or Mexican cheese blend

Directions:
1. In a small bowl or measuring cup, merge the salsa, chili powder, cumin, and oregano. Spill half of the mixture into the electric pressure cooker.
2. Set the turkey into the sauce. Set some pepper onto each piece of turkey. Spill the remaining salsa mixture on top.
3. Secure and lock the lid of the pressure cooker.
4. Cook on high pressure.
5. When the cooking is done, hit Cancel. Let the pressure to release naturally for 10 minutes, then quick release any remaining pressure.
6. Once the pin drops, unlock and detach the lid.
7. Whisk the cheese on top and put the lid back on for a few minutes to let the cheese melt.
8. Serve immediately.

Nutrition:
Calories: 168　　Carbs: 3g　　Sodium: 559mg
Fat: 5g　　Sugars: 2g
Protein: 28g　　Fiber: 1g

328. Chicken Zoodle Soup
Preparation Time: 15 minutes　　**Cooking Time:** 35 minutes　　**Servings:** 2

Ingredients:
- 1lb chopped cooked chicken
- 1lb spiralized zucchini
- 1 cup low sodium chicken soup
- 1 cup diced vegetables

Directions:
1. Merge all the ingredients except the zucchini in your Instant Pot.
2. Cook on Stew for 35 minutes.
3. Release the pressure naturally.
4. Stir in the zucchini and allow to heat thoroughly.

Nutrition:
Calories: 250　　Sugar: 0g　　Protein: 40g
Carbs: 5g　　Fat: 10g

329. Turkey and Spaghetti Squash
Preparation Time: 15 minutes　　**Cooking Time:** 35 minutes　　**Servings:** 2

Ingredients:
- 1lb minced turkey
- 1 cup chicken broth
- 1tbsp mixed Italian herbs
- ½ spaghetti squash, to fit the Instant Pot

Directions:
1. Mix the herbs into the turkey.
2. Pack the turkey into the squash.
3. Pour the broth in your Instant Pot.
4. Put the squash into the Instant Pot.

5. Cook on Stew for 35 minutes.
6. Release the pressure naturally.

Nutrition:
Calories: 260　　Sugar: 0g　　Protein: 41g
Carbs: 5g　　Fat: 5g

7. Shred the squash and mix the "spaghetti" with the turkey.

330. Thai Green Turkey Curry
Preparation Time: 15 minutes　　**Cooking Time:** 20 minutes　　**Servings:** 2

Ingredients:
- 0.5lb chopped cooked turkey
- 0.5 cup minced scallions and greens
- 0.5 cup chopped tomato
- 3tbsp Thai green curry paste
- 1tbsp oil or ghee

Directions:
1. Bring the Instant Pot to sauté and attach the oil and curry paste.
2. When mixed, add the remaining ingredients and seal.
3. Cook on Stew for 20 minutes.
4. Release the pressure naturally.

Nutrition:
Calories: 350　　Sugar: 5g　　Protein: 43g
Carbs: 16g　　Fat: 15g

331. Duck in Orange Sauce
Preparation Time: 15 minutes　　**Cooking Time:** 35 minutes　　**Servings:** 2

Ingredients:
- 1lb diced duck breast
- 1lb stir fry vegetables
- 1 cup low sodium broth
- 1 cup orange juice
- 2tbsp marmalade

Directions:
1. Mix all the ingredients in your Instant Pot.
2. Cook on Stew for 35 minutes.
3. Release the pressure naturally.

Nutrition:
Calories: 315　　Sugar: 3g　　Protein: 37g
Carbs: 13g　　Fat: 16g

332. Lemon Cilantro Chicken
Preparation Time: 15 minutes　　**Cooking Time:** 35 minutes　　**Servings:** 2

Ingredients:
- 1lb diced chicken breast
- 1lb chopped vegetables
- 1 cup chicken broth
- juice of half a lemon
- 2tbsp dry cilantro

Directions:
1. Mix all the ingredients in your Instant Pot.
2. Cook on Stew for 35 minutes.
3. Release the pressure naturally.

Nutrition:
Calories: 280　　Sugar: 0g　　Protein: 45g
Carbs: 4g　　Fat: 12g

333. Chicken Liver Curry
Preparation Time: 15 minutes　　**Cooking Time:** 35 minutes　　**Servings:** 2

Ingredients:
- 1lb diced chicken breast
- 0.5lb diced chicken liver
- 1lb chopped vegetables
- 1 cup broth
- 3tbsp curry paste

Directions:
1. Mix all the ingredients in your Instant Pot.
2. Cook on Stew for 35 minutes.
3. Release the pressure naturally.

Nutrition:
Calories: 350　　Sugar: 2g　　Protein: 52g
Carbs: 10g　　Fat: 17g

334. Balsamic Turkey Breast
Preparation Time: 15 minutes　　**Cooking Time:** 35 minutes　　**Servings:** 2

Ingredients:
- 1lb diced turkey breast
- 1lb chopped vegetables
- 1 cup chicken soup
- 2tbsp balsamic reduction

Directions:
1. Mix all the ingredients in your Instant Pot.
2. Cook on Stew for 35 minutes.
3. Release the pressure naturally.

Nutrition:
Calories: 295
Carbs: 5g
Sugar: 2g
Fat: 14g
Protein: 46g

335. Almond crusted chicken

Preparation Time: 10 minutes **Cooking Time:** 25 minutes **Servings:** 1

Ingredients:
- ¾ cup Ground almonds
- ½ cup All-purpose flour
- 1 tsp. Dry thyme
- 1 tsp. Onion powder
- 1 tsp. Garlic powder
- ½ tsp. Salt
- ½ tsp. Pepper
- ½ tsp. Skim milk
- 4 boneless, skinless, chicken breast (Four ounces each)
- 1 tbsp. Olive

Directions:
1. Preheat the oven to 400 F. Use cooking spray to slightly coat a baking sheet.
2. Toss the ground almonds, flour, thyme, onion powder, garlic powder, salt, and pepper together in a medium mixing bowl.
3. In a medium-sized mixing bowl, pour the milk. Place each chicken breast on a baking sheet after coating it in the almond mixture, then in the milk, and redo again in the almond mixture.
4. Warmth the olive oil in a nonstick sauté pan over medium-high heat. Place the chicken breasts in the pan once it is heated and turn the heat down to medium.
5. Sear the chicken breasts on 1 side till golden brown, then flip and sear for 1 minute on the other side.
6. Return the chicken to the oiled baking sheet and bake for ten minutes, or until the internal temperature reaches 165 F.

Nutrition:
Calories: 250
Carbohydrate: 9g
Cholesterol: 83mg
Protein: 28g
Fat: 11g

Fish and Seafood

336. Salmon Cakes

Preparation Time: 9 minutes **Cooking Time:** 7 minutes **Servings:** 2

Ingredients:
- 8 oz. fresh salmon fillet
- 1 egg
- ⅛ salt
- ¼ garlic powder
- 1 Sliced lemon

Directions:
1. In the bowl, chop the salmon, attach the egg and spices.
2. Form tiny cakes.
3. Let the air fryer preheat to 390F. Set the air fryer bowl of sliced lemons-place cakes on top.
4. Cook them for 7 minutes.

Nutrition:
Calories: 194
Fat: 9g
Carbohydrates: 1g
Proteins: 25g

337. Coconut Shrimp

Preparation Time: 9 minutes **Cooking Time:** 8-10 minutes **Servings:** 4

Ingredients:
- ½ cup pork rinds: ½ cup
- 4 cups jumbo shrimp: 4 cups.
- ½ cup coconut flakes,
- 2 eggs

Dipping sauce:
- 3 tbsp. mayonnaise
- ½ cup coconut flour
- 1 tbsp. olive oil
- Freshly ground black pepper and kosher
- ½ cup sour cream

- ¼ tsp. coconut extract or to taste
- 3 tbsp. coconut cream
- ¼ tsp. pineapple flavoring as much to taste.
- 3 tbsp. coconut flakes preferably unsweetened (optional)

Directions:

Sauce:
1. Merge all the ingredients into a tiny bowl for the dipping sauce (Pineapple flavor). Stir well and put in the fridge until ready to serve.

Shrimps:
1. Spill all eggs in a deep bowl and in a small shallow bowl; attach the hashed pork rinds, coconut flakes, coconut flour, sea salt and ground black pepper.
2. Set the shrimp one by one in the mixed eggs for dipping, then in the coconut flour blend. Set them on a clean plate or put them on your air fryer's basket.
3. Set the shrimp battered in a single layer on your air fryer basket. Drizzle the shrimp with oil and cook for 8 to 10 minutes at 360F, flipping them through halfway.
4. Enjoy hot with dipping sauce.

Nutrition:
Calories: 340
Proteins: 25g
Carbohydrates: 9g
Fat: 16g

338. Crispy Fish Sticks

Preparation Time: 9 minutes **Cooking Time:** 10 minutes **Servings:** 4

Ingredients:
- 1 lb. whitefish such as cod
- ¼ cup mayonnaise
- 2 tbsp. Dijon mustard
- 2 tbsp. water
- 1 ½ cup pork rind
- ¾ tsp. Cajun seasoning
- Kosher salt and pepper to taste
- Cooking spray

Directions:
1. Set with non-stick cooking spray to the air fryer rack.
2. Set the fish dry and cut into sticks about 1 inch by 2 inches' broad
3. Spill together the mayonnaise, mustard, and water in a tiny small dish. Merge the pork rinds and Cajun seasoning into another small container.
4. Operating for one slice of fish at a time, sink to cover in the mayonnaise mix, and then tap off the excess. Dips into the mixture of pork rind, then flip to cover. Set on the rack of an air fryer.
5. Set at 400F to air fry for 5 minutes, then turn the fish with tongs and bake for another 5 minutes. Serve.

Nutrition:
Calories: 263
Fat: 16 g
Carbohydrates: 1 g
Proteins: 26.4 g

339. Honey-Glazed Salmon

Preparation Time: 11 minutes **Cooking Time:** 16 minutes **Servings:** 2

Ingredients:
- 6 tsp. gluten-free soy sauce
- 2 pcs. Salmon fillets
- 3 tsp. sweet rice wine
- 1 tsp. water
- 6 tbsp. honey

Directions:
1. In a bowl, merge sweet rice wine, soy sauce, honey, and water.
2. Set half of it aside.
3. Marinate the fish and keep it rest for 2 hours.
4. Let the air fryer preheat to 180C.
5. Cook the fish, flip halfway through, and cook for another 5 minutes.
6. Set the salmon with marinade mixture after 3 or 4 minutes.
7. The half of marinade pours in a saucepan, reduce to half, and serve with a sauce.

Nutrition:
Calories: 254
Fat: 12g
Carbohydrates: 9.9g
Proteins: 20g

340. Basil-Parmesan Crusted Salmon

Preparation Time: 5 minutes **Cooking Time:** 7 minutes **Servings:** 4

Ingredients:
- 3 tbsp. grated Parmesan
- 4 skinless salmon fillets
- ¼ tsp. salt
- Freshly ground black pepper
- 3 tbsp. low-fat mayonnaise
- ¼ cup basil leaves, chopped
- ½ lemon
- Olive oil for spraying

Directions:
1. Let the air fryer preheat to 400F. Spray the basket with olive oil.
2. With salt, pepper, and lemon juice, seasons the salmon.
3. In a bowl, merge 2 tablespoons of Parmesan cheese with mayonnaise and basil leaves.
4. Attach this mix and more parmesan on top of salmon and cook for 7 minutes or until fully cooked.
5. Serve hot.

Nutrition:
Calories: 289
Fat: 18.5g
Carbohydrates: 1.5g
Proteins: 30g

341. Cajun Shrimp

Preparation Time: 9 minutes **Cooking Time:** 3 minutes **Servings:** 4

Ingredients:
- 24 extra-jumbo shrimp, peeled,
- 2 tbsp. olive oil
- 1 tbsp. Cajun seasoning
- 1 zucchini, thick slices (half-moons)
- ¼ cup cooked turkey
- 2 yellow squash, sliced half-moons
- ¼ tsp. kosher salt

Directions:
1. In a bowl, merge the shrimp with Cajun seasoning.
2. In another bowl, attach zucchini, turkey, salt, squash, and coat with oil.
3. Let the air fryer preheat to 400F.
4. Set the shrimp and vegetable mix to the fryer basket and cook for 3 minutes.
5. Serve hot.

Nutrition:
Calories: 284
Fat: 14g
Carbohydrates: 8g
Proteins: 31g

342. Crispy Air Fryer Fish

Preparation Time: 11 minutes **Cooking Time:** 18 minutes **Servings:** 4

Ingredients:
- 2 tsp. old bay
- 4-6, cut in half, whiting fish fillets
- ¼ cup fine cornmeal
- ¼ cup flour
- 1 tsp. paprika
- ½ tsp. garlic powder
- 1 ½ tsp. salt
- ½ freshly ground black pepper

Directions:
1. In a Ziploc bag, attach all ingredients and coat the fish fillets with it.
2. Set oil on the basket of the air fryer and put the fish in it.
3. Cook for ten minutes at 400F. Flip fish and coat with oil spray and cook for another 7 minutes.
4. Serve with salad green.

Nutrition:
Calories: 254
Fat: 12.7g
Carbohydrates: 8.2g
Proteins: 17.5g

343. Air Fryer Lemon Cod

Preparation Time: 5 minutes **Cooking Time:** 10 minutes **Servings:** 1

Ingredients:
- 1 cod fillet
- 1 tbsp. chopped dried parsley
- Kosher salt and pepper to taste
- 1 tbsp. garlic powder
- 1 lemon

Directions:
1. In a bowl, merge all ingredients and coat the fish fillet with spices.
2. Slice the lemon and set it at the bottom of the air fryer basket.
3. Put spiced fish on top. Cover the fish with lemon slices.
4. Cook for 10 minutes at 375F, the internal temperature of fish should be 145F.
5. Serve.

Nutrition:
Calories: 101
Fat: 1g
Carbohydrates: 10g
Proteins: 16g

344. Salmon Fillets

Preparation Time: 5 minutes **Cooking Time:** 15 minutes **Servings:** 2

Ingredients:
- ¼ cup low-fat Greek yogurt
- 2 salmon fillets
- 1 tbsp. fresh dill (chopped)
- 1 lemon juice
- ½ garlic powder
- Kosher salt and pepper

Directions:
1. Set the lemon into slices and lay it at the bottom of the air fryer basket.
2. Flavor the salmon with kosher salt and pepper. Set salmon on top of lemons.
3. Let it cook at 330F for 15 minutes.
4. In the meantime, merge garlic powder, lemon juice, salt, pepper with yogurt and dill.
5. Serve the fish with sauce.

Nutrition:
Calories: 194
Fat: 7g
Carbohydrates: 6g
Proteins: 25g

345. Fish and Chips

Preparation Time: 11 minutes **Cooking Time:** 35 minutes **Servings:** 4

Ingredients:
- 4 cups any fish fillet
- ¼ cup flour
- 1 cup whole-wheat breadcrumbs
- 1 egg
- 2 tbsp. oil
- 2 potatoes
- 1 tsp. salt

Directions:
1. Cut the potatoes in fries. Then coat with oil and salt.
2. Cook for 20 minutes at 400F, toss the fries halfway through.
3. In the meantime, coat fish in flour, then in the whisked egg, and finally in breadcrumbs mix.
4. Set the fish in the air fryer and let it cook at 330F for 15 minutes.
5. Flip it halfway through, if needed.
6. Serve with tartar sauce and salad green.

Nutrition:
Calories: 409
Fat: 11g
Carbohydrates: 44g
Proteins: 30g

346. Grilled Salmon with Lemon

Preparation Time: 9 minutes **Cooking Time:** 8 minutes **Servings:** 4

Ingredients:
- 2 tbsp. olive oil
- 2 salmon fillets
- ⅓ cup lemon juice
- ⅓ cup water
- ⅓ cup gluten-free light soy sauce
- ⅓ cup honey
- Scallion slices to garnish
- Freshly ground black pepper, garlic powder, kosher salt to taste

Directions:
1. Season salmon with pepper and salt.
2. In a bowl, mix honey, soy sauce, lemon juice, water, oil. Add salmon to this marinade and let it rest for at least 2 hours.
3. Let the air fryer preheat at 180C.
4. Place fish in the air fryer and cook for 8 minutes.
5. Move to a dish and top with scallion slices.

Nutrition:
Calories: 211
Fat: 9g
Carbohydrates: 4.9g
Proteins: 15g

347. Fish Nuggets

Preparation Time: 15 minutes **Cooking Time:** 12 minutes **Servings:** 4

Ingredients:
- 2 cups (skinless) fish fillets in cubes
- 1 egg beaten
- 5 tbsp. flour
- 5 tbsp. water
- Kosher salt and pepper to taste
- ½ cup breadcrumbs mix
- ¼ cup whole-wheat breadcrumbs
- Oil for spraying

Directions:
1. Season the fish cubes with kosher salt and pepper.
2. In a bowl, add flour and gradually add water, mixing as you add.
3. Then mix in the egg. Keep mixing but do not over mix.
4. Coat the cubes in batter, then in the breadcrumb mix. Coat well.
5. Set the cubes in a baking tray and spray with oil.
6. Let the air fryer preheat to 200C.
7. Place cubes in the air fryer and cook for 12 minutes or until well cooked and golden brown.
8. Serve with salad greens.

Nutrition:
Calories: 184
Fat: 3g
Carbohydrates: 10g
Proteins: 19g

348. Garlic Rosemary Grilled Prawns

Preparation Time: 5 minutes **Cooking Time:** 11 minutes **Servings:** 2

Ingredients:
- ½ tbsp. melted butter
- 8 green capsicum slices
- 8 prawns
- ⅛ cup rosemary leaves
- Kosher salt and freshly ground black pepper
- 3-4 cloves minced garlic

Directions:
1. In a bowl, merge all the ingredients and marinate the prawns in it for at least 60 minutes or more.
2. Add 2 prawns and 2 slices of capsicum on each skewer.
3. Let the air fryer preheat to 180C.
4. Cook for 5 to 6 minutes. Then change the temperature to 200C and cook for another 5 minutes.
5. Serve with lemon wedges.

Nutrition:
Calories: 194
Fat: 10g
Carbohydrates: 12g
Proteins: 26g

349. Cajun Catfish

Preparation Time: 5 minutes **Cooking Time:** 15 minutes **Servings:** 4

Ingredients:
- 4 (8 oz.) catfish fillets
- What you'll need from store cupboard:
- 2 tbsp. olive oil
- 2 tsp. garlic salt
- 2 tsp. thyme
- 2 tsp. paprika
- ½ tsp. cayenne pepper
- ½ tsp. red hot sauce
- ¼ tsp. black pepper
- Nonstick cooking spray

Directions:
1. Heat oven to 450F. Set a 9x13-inch baking dish with cooking spray.
2. In a small bowl whisk together everything but catfish. Brush both sides of fillets, using all the spice mix.
3. Bake 10-13 minutes or until fish flakes easily with a fork. Serve.

Nutrition:
Calories: 366
Carbohydrates: 0g
Protein: 35g
Fat: 24g
Sugar: 0g
Fiber: 0g

350. Cajun Flounder and Tomatoes

Preparation Time: 10 minutes **Cooking Time:** 15 minutes **Servings:** 4

Ingredients:
- 4 flounder fillets
- 2 ½ cups tomatoes, diced
- ¾ cup onion, diced
- ¾ cup green bell pepper, diced

What you'll need from store cupboard:
- 2 cloves garlic, diced fine
- 1tbsp. Cajun seasoning
- 1tsp. olive oil

Directions:
1. Warmth oil in a large skillet over med-high heat. Add onion and garlic and cook 2 minutes, or until soft.
2. Add tomatoes, peppers and spices, and cook 2-3 minutes until tomatoes soften.
3. Lay fish over top. Seal reduce heat to medium and cook, 5-8 minutes, or until fish flakes easily with a fork.
4. Set fish to serving plates and top with sauce.

Nutrition:
Calories: 194
Carbohydrates: 6g
Protein: 32g
Fat: 3g
Sugar: 5g
Fiber: 2g

351. Cajun Shrimp and Roasted Vegetables

Preparation Time: 5 minutes **Cooking Time:** 15 minutes **Servings:** 4

Ingredients:
- 1lb. large shrimp, peeled and deveined
- 2 zucchinis, sliced
- 2 yellow squashes, sliced
- ½ bunch asparagus, cut into thirds
- 2 red bell peppers, cut into chunks

What you'll need from store cupboard:
- 2 tbsp. olive oil
- 2 tbsp. Cajun Seasoning
- Salt and pepper, to taste

Directions:
1. Heat oven to 400F.
2. Merge shrimp and vegetables in a large bowl. Add oil and seasoning and toss to coat.
3. Spread evenly in a large baking sheet and bake 15-20 minutes, or until vegetables are tender.
4. Serve.

Nutrition:
Calories: 251
Carbohydrates: 1.3g
Protein: 30g
Fat: 9g
Sugar: 6g
Fiber: 4g

352. Cilantro Lime Grilled Shrimp

Preparation Time: 5 minutes **Cooking Time:** 5 minutes **Servings:** 6

Ingredients:
- ½ lbs. large shrimp raw, peeled, deveined with tails on
- Juice and zest of 1 lime
- 2 tbsp. fresh cilantro chopped
- ¼ cup olive oil
- 2 cloves garlic, diced fine
- 1tsp. smoked paprika
- ¼ tsp. cumin
- ½ teaspoon salt
- ¼ tsp. cayenne pepper

Directions:
1. Set the shrimp in a large Ziploc bag.
2. Mix remaining Ingredients in a small bowl and pour over shrimp. Let marinate 20-30 minutes.
3. Heat up the grill and cook the shrimp 2-3 minutes, per side, just until they turn pick. Be careful not to overcook them. Serve garnished with cilantro.

Nutrition:
Calories: 317
Carbohydrates: 4g
Protein: 39g
Fat: 15g
Sugar: 0g
Fiber: 0g

353. Crab Frittata

Preparation Time: 10 minutes **Cooking Time:** 50 minutes **Servings:** 4

Ingredients:
- 4 eggs
- 2 cups lump crabmeat
- 1cup half-n-half
- cup green onions, diced
- 1 cup reduced fat parmesan cheese, grated
- ½tsp. salt
- ½tsp. pepper
- 1tsp. smoked paprika
- 1tsp. Italian seasoning
- Nonstick cooking spray

Directions:
1. Heat oven to 35F. Spray an 8-inch spring form pan, or pie plate with cooking spray.
2. In a large bowl, whisk together the eggs and half-n-half. Add seasonings and parmesan cheese, stir to mix.
3. Stir in the onions and crab meat. Spill into prepared pan and bake 35-40 minutes, or eggs are set and top is lightly browned.
4. Let and then slice and serve warm or at room temperature.

Nutrition:
- Calories: 276
- Carbohydrates: 5g
- Protein: 25g
- Fat: 17g
- Sugar: 1g
- Fiber: 1g

354. Crunchy Lemon Shrimp

Preparation Time: 5 minutes **Cooking Time:** 10 minutes **Servings:** 4

Ingredients:
- 1lb. raw shrimp, peeled and deveined
- 2 tbsp. Italian parsley, roughly chopped
- 2 tbsp. lemon juice, divided
- ⅔ cup panko breadcrumbs
- 2½ tbsp. olive oil, divided
- Salt and pepper, to taste

Directions:
1. Heat oven to 400F.
2. Set the shrimp evenly in a baking dish and sprinkle with salt and pepper.
3. Drizzle on 1 tbsp. lemon juice and 1 tbsp. of olive oil. Set aside.
4. In a medium bowl, combine parsley, remaining lemon juice, breadcrumbs, remaining olive oil, and ¼ tsp. each of salt and pepper. Set the panko mixture evenly on top of the shrimp.
5. Bake 8-10 minutes or until shrimp are cooked through and the panko is golden brown.

Nutrition:
- Calories: 283
- Carbohydrates: 1.5g
- Protein: 28g
- Fat: 12g
- Sugar: 1g
- Fiber: 1g

355. Grilled Tuna Steaks

Preparation Time: 5 minutes **Cooking Time:** 10 minutes **Servings:** 6

Ingredients:
- 6 6 oz. tuna steaks
- 3 tbsp. fresh basil, diced
- 4 ½tsp. olive oil
- ¾ tsp. salt
- ¼ tsp. pepper
- Nonstick cooking spray

Directions:
1. Heat grill to medium heat. Spray rack with cooking spray.
2. Drizzle both sides of the tuna with oil. Sprinkle with basil, salt and pepper.
3. Place on grill and cook 5 minutes per side, tuna should be slightly pink in the center.
4. Serve.

Nutrition:
- Calories: 343
- Carbohydrates: 0g
- Protein: 51g
- Fat: 14g
- Sugar: 0g
- Fiber: 0g

356. Red Clam Sauce and Pasta

Preparation Time: 10 minutes **Cooking Time:** 3 hours **Servings:** 4

Ingredients:
- 1 onion, diced
- ¼ cup fresh parsley, diced
- 2 6 ½ oz. cans clams, chopped, undrained
- 14 ½ oz. tomatoes, diced, undrained
- 6 oz. tomato paste
- 2 cloves garlic, diced
- 1 bay leaf
- 1 tbsp. sunflower oil
- 1 tsp. Splenda
- 1 tsp. basil
- ½ tsp. thyme
- ½ Homemade Pasta, cook and drain

Directions:
1. Warmth oil in a small skillet over med-high heat. Add onion and cook until tender,
2. Add garlic and cook 1 minute more. Transfer to crock pot.
3. Add remaining Ingredients, except pasta, cover and cook on low 3-4 hours.
4. Detach bay leaf and serve over cooked pasta.

Nutrition:
- Calories: 223
- Carbohydrates: 3.2g
- Protein: 12g
- Fat: 6g
- Sugar: 15g
- Fiber: 5g

357. Salmon Milano

Preparation Time: 10 minutes **Cooking Time:** 20 minutes **Servings:** 6

Ingredients:
- 2 ½ lb. salmon filet
- 2 tomatoes, sliced
- ½ cup margarine
- ½ cup basil pesto

Directions:
1. Heat the oven to 400F. Line a 9x15-inch baking sheet with foil, making sure it covers the sides. Place another large piece of foil onto the baking sheet and place the salmon filet on top of it.
2. Place the pesto and margarine in blender or food processor and pulse until smooth. Spread evenly over salmon.
3. Place tomato slices on top.
4. Wrap the foil around the salmon, tenting around the top to prevent foil from touching the salmon as much as possible.
5. Bake 15-25 minutes, or salmon flakes easily with a fork. Serve.

Nutrition:
- Calories: 444
- Carbohydrates: 2g
- Protein: 55g
- Fat: 24g
- Sugar: 1g
- Fiber: 0g

358. Shrimp and Artichoke Skillet

Preparation Time: 5 minutes **Cooking Time:** 10 minutes **Servings:** 4

Ingredients:
- ½ cups shrimp, peel and devein
- 2 shallots, diced
- 1tbsp. margarine
- What you'll need from store cupboard
- 2 12 oz. jars artichoke hearts, drain and rinse
- 2 cups white wine
- 2 cloves garlic, diced fine

Directions:
1. Melt margarine in a large skillet over med-high heat. Add shallot and garlic and cook until they start to brown, stirring frequently.
2. Add artichokes and cook 5 minutes. Reduce heat and add wine. Cook 3 minutes, stirring occasionally.
3. Attach the shrimp and cook just until they turn pink.
4. Serve.

Nutrition:
Calories: 487 Protein: 64g Sugar: 3g
Carbohydrates: 2.6g Fat: 5 Fiber: 9g

359. Tuna Carbonara

Preparation Time: 5 minutes **Cooking Time:** 25 minutes **Servings:** 4

Ingredients:
- ½ lb. tuna fillet, cut in pieces
- 2 eggs
- 4 tbsp. fresh parsley, diced
- ½ Homemade Pasta, cook and drain,
- ½ cup reduced fat parmesan cheese
- 2 cloves garlic, peeled
- 2 tbsp. extra virgin olive oil
- Salt and pepper, to taste

Directions:
1. In a bowl, whisk the eggs, parmesan and a dash of pepper.
2. Heat the oil in a large skillet over med-high heat.
3. Add garlic and cook until browned. Add the tuna and cook 2-3 minutes, or until tuna is almost cooked through. Discard the garlic.
4. Add the pasta and reduce heat. Stir in egg mixture and cook, stirring constantly, 2 minutes. If the sauce is too thick, thin with water, a little bit at a time, until it has a creamy texture.
5. Salt and pepper to flavor and serve garnished with parsley.

Nutrition:
Calories: 409 Protein: 25g Sugar: 3g
Carbohydrates: 7g Fat: 30g Fiber: 1g

360. Mediterranean Fish Fillets

Preparation Time: 10 minutes **Cooking Time:** 3 minutes **Servings:** 4

Ingredients:
- 4 cod fillets
- 1lb. grape tomatoes, halved
- 1cup olives, pitted and sliced
- 2 tbsp. capers
- 1 tsp. dried thyme
- 2 tbsp. olive oil
- 1tsp. garlic, minced
- Pepper and Salt
- 1 cup water

Directions:
1. Spill 1 cup water into the instant pot then place steamer rack in the pot.
2. Spray heat-safe baking dish with cooking spray.
3. Add half grape tomatoes into the dish and season with pepper and salt.
4. Arrange fish fillets on top of cherry tomatoes. Drizzle with oil and season with garlic, thyme, capers, pepper, and salt.
5. Spread olives and remaining grape tomatoes on top of fish fillets.
6. Place dish on top of steamer rack in the pot.
7. Seal pot with a lid and select manual and cook on high for 3 minutes.
8. Once done, release pressure using quick release. Remove lid.
9. Serve and enjoy.

Nutrition:
Calories: 212 Sugar: 3 g Cholesterol: 55 mg
Fat: 11.9 g Protein: 21.4 g

361. Lemony Salmon

Preparation Time: 10 minutes **Cooking Time:** 3 Minutes **Servings:** 3

Ingredients:
- 1pound salmon fillet, cut into 3 pieces
- 3 teaspoons fresh dill, chopped
- 5 tablespoons fresh lemon juice, divided
- Salt and ground black pepper, as required

Directions:
1. Arrange a steamer trivet in Instant Pot and pour ¼ cup of lemon juice.
2. Flavor the salmon with salt and black pepper evenly.
3. Place the salmon pieces on top of trivet, skin side down and drizzle with remaining lemon juice.
4. Now, sprinkle the salmon pieces with dill evenly.
5. Seal the lid and place the pressure valve to "Seal" position.
6. Press "Steam" and use the default time of 3 minutes.
7. Press "Cancel" and allow a "Natural" release.
8. Open the lid and serve hot.

Nutrition:
Calories: 20 Carbohydrates: 1.1g Proteins: 29.7g
Fat: 9.6g Sugar: 0.5g Sodium: 74mg

362. Shrimp with Green Beans

Preparation Time: 10 minutes **Cooking Time:** 2 Minutes **Servings:** 4

Ingredients:
- ¾ pound fresh green beans, trimmed
- 1 pound medium frozen shrimp, peeled and deveined
- 2 tablespoons fresh lemon juice
- 2 tablespoons olive oil
- Salt and ground black pepper, as required

Directions:
1. Arrange a steamer trivet in the Instant Pot and pour cup of water.
2. Arrange the green beans on top of trivet in a single layer and top with shrimp.
3. Drizzle with oil and lemon juice.
4. Sprinkle with salt and black pepper.
5. Seal the lid and place the pressure valve to "Seal" position.
6. Press "Steam" and just use the default time of 2 minutes.
7. Press "Cancel" and allow a "Natural" release.
8. Open the lid and serve.

Nutrition:
Calories: 223 Carbohydrates: 7.9g Proteins: 27.4g
Fat: 1g Sugar: 1.4g Sodium: 322mg

363. Crab Curry

Preparation Time: 10 minutes **Cooking Time:** 20 minutes **Servings:** 2

Ingredients:
- 0.5lb chopped crab
- 1 thinly sliced red onion
- 0.5 cup chopped tomato
- 3 tbsp curry paste
- 1 tbsp oil or ghee

Directions:
1. Set the Instant Pot to sauté and attach the onion, oil, and curry paste.
2. When the onion is soft, add the remaining ingredients and seal.
3. Cook on Stew for 20 minutes.
4. Release the pressure naturally.

Nutrition:
Calories: 2 Sugar: 4 Protein: 24
Carbohydrates: 11 Fat: 10

364. Mixed Chowder

Preparation Time: 10 minutes **Cooking Time:** 35 minutes **Servings:** 2

Ingredients:
- 1lb fish stew mix
- 2 cups white sauce
- 3tbsp old bay seasoning

Directions:
1. Mix all the ingredients in your Instant Pot.
2. Cook on Stew for 35 minutes.
3. Release the pressure naturally.

Nutrition:
Calories: 320 Sugar: 2g Protein: 4g
Carbohydrates: 9g Fat: 16g

365. Mussels in Tomato Sauce

Preparation Time: 10 minutes **Cooking Time:** 3 minutes **Servings:** 4

Ingredients:
- 2 tomatoes, seeded and chopped finely
- 2 pounds mussels, scrubbed and de-bearded
- 1 cup low-sodium chicken broth
- 1 tablespoon fresh lemon juice
- 2 garlic cloves, minced

Directions:
1. In the pot of Instant Pot, place tomatoes, garlic, wine and bay leaf and stir to combine.
2. Arrange the mussels on top.
3. Seal the lid and place the pressure valve to "Seal" position.
4. Press "Manual" and cook under "High Pressure" for about 3 minutes.
5. Press "Cancel" and carefully allow a "Quick" release.
6. Open the lid and serve hot.

Nutrition:
Calories: 213 Carbohydrates: 11g Proteins: 28.2g
Fats: 25.2g Sugar: 1g Sodium: 670mg

366. Citrus Salmon

Preparation Time: 10 minutes **Cooking Time:** 7 minutes **Servings:** 4

Ingredients:
- 4 (4-ounce) salmon fillets
- cup low-sodium chicken broth
- 1 teaspoon fresh ginger, minced
- 2 teaspoons fresh orange zest, grated finely
- 3 tablespoons fresh orange juice
- 1 tablespoon olive oil
- Ground black pepper, as required

Directions:
1. In Instant Pot, add all ingredients and mix.
2. Seal the lid and place the pressure valve to "Seal" position.
3. Press "Manual" and cook under "High Pressure" for about 7 minutes.

4. Press "Cancel" and allow a "Natural" release.

5. Open the lid and serve the salmon fillets with the topping of cooking sauce.

Nutrition:
Calories: 190
Fat: 10.5g
Carbohydrates: 1.8g
Sugar: 1g
Protein: 22g
Sodium: 68mg

367. Herbed Salmon
Preparation Time: 10 minutes **Cooking Time:** 3 minutes **Servings:** 4

Ingredients:
- 4 (4-ounce) salmon fillets
- ¼ cup olive oil
- 2 tablespoons fresh lemon juice
- 1 garlic clove, minced
- ¼ teaspoon dried oregano
- Salt and ground black pepper, as required
- 4 fresh rosemary sprigs
- 4 lemon slices

Directions:
1. For dressing: in a large bowl, add oil, lemon juice, garlic, oregano, salt and black pepper and beat until well co combined.
2. Arrange a steamer trivet in the Instant Pot and pour 1½ cups of water in Instant Pot.
3. Set the salmon fillets on top of trivet in a single layer and top with dressing.
4. Arrange 1 rosemary sprig and 1 lemon slice over each fillet. Close the lid and place the pressure valve to "Seal" position.
5. Press "Steam" and just use the default time of 3 minutes.
6. Press "Cancel" and carefully allow a "Quick" release.
7. Open the lid and serve hot.

Nutrition:
Calories: 262
Fat: 17g
Carbohydrates: 0.7g
Sugar: 0.2g
Proteins: 22.1g
Sodium: 91mg

368. Salmon in Green Sauce
Preparation Time: 10 minutes **Cooking Time:** 12 minutes **Servings:** 4

Ingredients:
- 4 (6-ounce) salmon fillets
- 1 avocado, peeled, pitted and chopped
- ½ cup fresh basil, chopped
- 3 garlic cloves, chopped
- 1 tablespoon fresh lemon zest, grated finely

Directions:
1. Grease a large piece of foil.
2. In a large bowl, attach all ingredients except salmon and water and with a fork, mash completely.
3. Place fillets in the center of foil and top with avocado mixture evenly.
4. Fold the foil around fillets to seal them.
5. Arrange a steamer trivet in the Instant Pot and pour ½ cup of water.
6. Place the foil packet on top of trivet.
7. Close the lid and place the pressure valve to "Seal" position.
8. Press "Manual" and cook under "High Pressure" for about minutes.
9. Meanwhile, preheat the oven to broiler.
10. Press "Cancel" and allow a "Natural" release.
11. Open the lid and transfer the salmon fillets onto a broiler pan.
12. Broil for about 3-4 minutes.
13. Serve warm.

Nutrition:
Calories: 333
Fat: 20.3g
Carbohydrates: 5.5g
Sugar: 0.4g
Proteins: 34.2g
Sodium: 79mg

369. Braised Shrimp
Preparation Time: 10 minutes **Cooking Time:** 4 minutes **Servings:** 4

Ingredients:
- pound frozen large shrimp, peeled and deveined
- 2 shallots, chopped
- ¾ cup low-sodium chicken broth
- 2 tablespoons fresh lemon juice
- 2 tablespoons olive oil
- 1 tablespoon garlic, crushed
- Ground black pepper, as required

Directions:
1. In the Instant Pot, place oil and press "Sauté". Now add the shallots and cook for about 2 minutes.
2. Add the garlic and cook for about 1 minute.
3. Press "Cancel" and stir in the shrimp, broth, lemon juice and black pepper.
4. Close the lid and place the pressure valve to "Seal" position.
5. Press "Manual" and cook under "High Pressure" for about 1 minute.
6. Press "Cancel" and carefully allow a "Quick" release.
7. Open the lid and serve hot.

Nutrition:
Calories: 209
Fat: 9g
Carbohydrates: 4.3g
Sugar: 0.2g
Proteins: 26.6g
Sodium: 293mg

370. Shrimp Coconut Curry
Preparation Time: 10 minutes **Cooking Time:** 20 minutes **Servings:** 2

Ingredients:
- 0.5lb cooked shrimp
- 1 thinly sliced onion
- 1 cup coconut yogurt
- 3tbsp curry paste
- 1tbsp oil or ghee

Directions:
1. Set the Instant Pot to sauté and attach the onion, oil, and curry paste.
2. When the onion is soft, add the remaining ingredients and seal.
3. Cook on Stew for 20 minutes.
4. Release the pressure naturally.

Nutrition:
Calories: 380
Carbohydrates: 1g
Sugar: 4g
Fat: 22g
Protein: 40g

371. Trout Bake
Preparation Time: 10 minutes **Cooking Time:** 35 minutes **Servings:** 2

Ingredients:
- 1lb trout fillets, boneless
- 1lb chopped winter vegetables
- 1 cup low sodium fish broth
- 1 tbsp mixed herbs
- sea salt as desired

Directions:
1. Mix all the ingredients except the broth in a foil pouch.
2. Place the pouch in the steamer basket your Instant Pot.
3. Pour the broth into the Instant Pot.
4. Cook on Steam for 35 minutes.
5. Release the pressure naturally.

Nutrition:
Calories: 310
Carbohydrates: 14g
Sugar: 2g
Fat: 12g
Protein: 40g

372. Sardine Curry
Preparation Time: 10 minutes **Cooking Time:** 35 minutes **Servings:** 2

Ingredients:
- 5 tons of sardines in tomato
- 1lb chopped vegetables
- 1 cup low sodium fish broth
- 3 tbsp curry paste

Directions:
1. Mix all the ingredients in your Instant Pot.
2. Cook on Stew for 35 minutes.
3. Release the pressure naturally.

Nutrition:
Calories: 320
Carbohydrates: 8g
Sugar: 2g
Fat: 16g
Protein: 20g

373. Swordfish Steak
Preparation Time: 10 minutes **Cooking Time:** 35 minutes **Servings:** 2

Ingredients:
- 1lb swordfish steak, whole
- 1lb chopped Mediterranean vegetables
- 1 cup low sodium fish broth
- 2 tbsp soy sauce

Directions:
1. Mix all the ingredients except the broth in a foil pouch.
2. Place the pouch in the steamer basket for your Instant Pot.
3. Pour the broth into the Instant Pot. Lower the steamer basket into the Instant Pot.
4. Cook on Steam for 35 minutes.
5. Release the pressure naturally.

Nutrition:
Calories: 270
Carbohydrates: 5g
Sugar: 1g
Fat: 10g
Protein: 48.1g

374. Lemon Sole
Preparation Time: 10 minutes **Cooking Time:** 5 minutes **Servings:** 2

Ingredients:
- 1lb sole fillets, boned and skinned
- cup low sodium fish broth
- 2 shredded sweet onions
- juice of half a lemon
- 2 tbsp dried cilantro

Directions:
1. Mix all the ingredients in your Instant Pot.
2. Cook on Stew for 5 minutes.
3. Release the pressure naturally.

Nutrition:
Calories: 230
Carbohydrates: 6g
Sugar: 1g
Fat: 6g
Protein: 46g

375. Tuna Sweet corn Casserole
Preparation Time: 10 minutes **Cooking Time:** 35 minutes **Servings:** 2

Ingredients:
- 3 small tins of tuna
- 0.5lb sweet corn kernels
- 1lb chopped vegetables
- 1 cup low sodium vegetable broth
- 2 tbsp spicy seasoning

Directions:
1. Mix all the ingredients in your Instant Pot.
2. Cook on Stew for 35 minutes.
3. Release the pressure naturally.

Nutrition:
Calories: 300
Carbohydrates: 6g
Sugar: 1g
Fat: 9g
Protein: 21g

376. Lemon Pepper Salmon

Preparation Time: 10 minutes **Cooking Time:** 10 minutes **Servings:** 4

Ingredients:
- 3 tbsps. ghee or avocado oil
- lb. skin-on salmon filet
- julienned red bell pepper
- julienned green zucchini
- 1 julienned carrot
- ¾ cup water
- A few sprigs of parsley, tarragon, dill, basil or a combination
- ½ sliced lemon
- ½ tsp. black pepper
- ¼ tsp. sea salt

Directions:
1. Add the water and the herbs into the bottom of the Instant Pot and put in a wire steamer rack making sure the handles extend upwards.
2. Place the salmon filet onto the wire rack, with the skin side facing down.
3. Drizzle the salmon with ghee, season with black pepper and salt, and top with the lemon slices.
4. Close and seal the Instant Pot, making sure the vent is turned to "Sealing".
5. Select the "Steam" setting and cook for 3 minutes.
6. While the salmon cooks, julienne the vegetables, and set aside.
7. Once done, release the pressure immediately, and then press the "Keep Warm/Cancel" button.
8. Uncover and wearing oven mitts, carefully remove the steamer rack with the salmon.
9. Remove the herbs and discard them.
10. Add the vegetables to the pot and put the lid back on.
11. Select the "Sauté" function and cook for 1-2 minutes.
12. Serve the vegetables with salmon and add the remaining fat to the pot.
13. Spill a little of the sauce over the fish and vegetables if desired.

Nutrition:
Calories: 296
Carbohydrates: 8g
Fat: 15 g
Protein: 31g

377. Almond Crusted Baked Chili Mahi Mahi

Preparation Time: 20 minutes **Cooking Time:** 15 minutes **Servings:** 4

Ingredients:
- 4 mahi mahi fillets 1 lime
- 2 teaspoons olive oil
- Salt and pepper to taste
- ½ cup almonds
- ¼ teaspoon paprika
- ¼ teaspoon onion powder
- ¾ teaspoon chili powder
- ½ cup red bell pepper, chopped
- ¼ cup onion, chopped
- ¼ cup fresh cilantro, chopped

Directions:
1. Warmth your oven to 325 F. Line your baking pan with parchment paper. Squeeze juice from the lime.
2. Grate zest from the peel. Put juice and zest in a bowl. Add the oil, salt and pepper. In another bowl, add the almonds, paprika, onion powder and chili powder.
3. Put the almond mixture in a food processor. Pulse until powdery.
4. Dip each fillet in the oil mixture.
5. Dredge with the almond and chili mixture.
6. Arrange on a single layer in the oven. Bake for 12 to 15 minutes until fully cooked.
7. Serve with red bell pepper, onion and cilantro.

Nutrition:
Calories: 322
Fat: 12 g
Cholesterol: 83 mg
Sodium: 328 mg
Carbohydrates: 28 g
Sugars: 10 g
Protein: 28 g

378. Salmon and Asparagus

Preparation Time: 15 minutes **Cooking Time:** 10 minutes **Servings:** 2

Ingredients:
- 2 salmon fillets
- 8 spears asparagus, trimmed
- 2 tablespoons balsamic vinegar
- 1 teaspoon olive oil
- 1 teaspoon dried dill
- Salt and pepper to taste

Directions:
1. Preheat your oven to 325F.
2. Dry salmon with paper towels.
3. Arrange the asparagus around the salmon fillets on a baking pan. In a bowl, mix the rest of the ingredients.
4. Pour mixture over the salmon and vegetables.
5. Bake for 10 minutes.

Nutrition:
Calories: 328
Fat: 15 g
Cholesterol: 67 mg
Sodium: 365 mg
Carbohydrates: 6 g
Sugars: 5 g
Protein: 28 g

379. Halibut with Spicy Apricot Sauce

Preparation Time: 15 minutes **Cooking Time:** 17 minutes **Servings:** 4

Ingredients:
- 4 fresh apricots, pitted
- ⅓ cup apricot preserves
- ½ cup apricot nectar
- ½ teaspoon dried oregano
- 3 tablespoons scallion, sliced
- 1 teaspoon hot pepper sauce Salt to taste
- 4 halibut steaks
- tablespoon olive oil

Directions:
1. Put the apricots, preserves, nectar, oregano, scallion, hot pepper sauce and salt in a saucepan.
2. Set to a boil and then simmer for 8 minutes. Set aside.
3. Brush the halibut steaks with olive oil.
4. Grill for 7 to 9 minutes.
5. Brush one tablespoon of the sauce on both sides of the fish.
6. Serve with the reserved sauce.

Nutrition:
Calories: 304
Fat: 8 g
Cholesterol: 73 mg
Sodium: 260 mg
Carbohydrates: 27 g
Sugar: 16 g
Protein: 29 g

380. Popcorn Shrimp

Preparation Time: 15 minutes **Cooking Time:** 8 minutes **Servings:** 4

Ingredients:
- Cooking spray
- ½ cup all-purpose flour
- 2 eggs, beaten
- 2 tablespoons water
- ½ cups panko breadcrumbs
- 1 tablespoon garlic powder
- 1 tablespoon ground cumin
- 1 lb. shrimp, peeled and deveined
- ½ cup ketchup
- 2 tablespoons fresh cilantro, chopped
- 2 tablespoons lime juice Salt to taste

Directions:
1. Set the air fryer basket with cooking spray
2. Put the flour in a dish. In the second dish, beat the eggs and water.
3. In the third dish, mix the breadcrumbs, garlic powder and cumin.
4. Ladle each shrimp in each of the three dishes, first in the dish with flour, then the egg and then breadcrumb mixture.
5. Set the shrimp in the air fryer basket.
6. Cook at 360 F for 8 minutes, flipping once halfway through.
7. Combine the rest of the ingredients as dipping sauce for the shrimp.

Nutrition:
Calories: 297
Fat: 4 g
Cholesterol: 276 mg
Sodium: 291 mg
Carbohydrates: 35 g
Sugar: 9 g
Protein: 29 g

381. Shrimp Lemon Kebab

Preparation Time: 10 minutes **Cooking Time:** 5 minutes **Servings:** 4

Ingredients:
- ½ lb. shrimp, peeled and deveined but with tails intact
- ⅓ cup olive oil
- ¼ cup lemon juice
- 2 teaspoons lemon zest
- 1 tablespoon fresh parsley, chopped
- 8 cherry tomatoes, quartered
- 2 scallions, sliced

Directions:
1. Mix the olive oil, lemon juice, lemon zest and parsley in a bowl.
2. Marinate the shrimp in this mixture for 15 minutes.
3. Thread each shrimp into the skewers.
4. Grill for 4 to 5 minutes, turning once halfway through.
5. Serve with tomatoes and scallions.

Nutrition:
Calories: 271
Fat: 12 g
Cholesterol: 259 mg
Sodium: 255 mg
Carbohydrates: 4 g
Sugars: 1 g
Protein: 25

382. Grilled Herbed Salmon with Raspberry Sauce and Cucumber Dill Dip

Preparation Time: 15 minutes **Cooking Time:** 30 minutes **Servings:** 4

Ingredients:
- 3 salmon fillets
- 1 tablespoon olive oil
- Salt and pepper to taste
- 1 teaspoon fresh sage, chopped
- 1 tablespoon fresh parsley, chopped
- 2 tablespoons Apple juice
- 1 cup raspberries
- 1 teaspoon Worcestershire sauce
- cup cucumber, chopped
- 2 tablespoons light mayonnaise
- ½ teaspoon dried dill

Directions:
1. Coat the salmon fillets with oil. Season with salt, pepper, sage and parsley.
2. Cover the salmon with foil.
3. Grill for 20 minutes or until fish is flaky.
4. While waiting, mix the apple juice, raspberries and Worcestershire sauce.

5. Pour the mixture into a saucepan over medium heat. Bring to a boil and then simmer for 8 minutes.

6. In another bowl, mix the rest of the ingredients.
7. Serve salmon with raspberry sauce and cucumber dip.

Nutrition:
Calories: 256
Fat: 15 g
Cholesterol: 68 mg
Sodium: 176 mg
Carbohydrates: 6 g
Sugar: 5 g
Protein: 23 g

---

383. Tarragon Scallops

Preparation Time: 10 minutes **Cooking Time:** 15 minutes **Servings:** 4

Ingredients:
- 2cup water
- 1lb. asparagus spears, trimmed
- 2 lemons 1
- ¼ lb. scallops
- Salt and pepper to taste
- 1 tablespoon olive oil
- 1tablespoon fresh tarragon, chopped

Directions:
1. Pour water into a pot. Bring to a boil. Add asparagus spears. Cover and cook for 5 minutes.
2. Drain and transfer to a plate. Slice one lemon into wedges.
3. Squeeze juice and shred zest from the remaining lemon.
4. Season the scallops with salt and pepper.
5. Put a pan over medium heat.
6. Add oil to the pan.
7. Cook the scallops until golden brown.
8. Transfer to the same plate, putting scallops beside the asparagus.
9. Add lemon zest, juice and tarragon to the pan. Cook for 1 minute.
10. Drizzle tarragon sauce over the scallops and asparagus.

Nutrition:
Calories: 253
Fat: 12 g
Cholesterol: 47 mg
Sodium: 436 mg
Carbohydrates: 14 g
Sugars: 3 g
Protein: 27 g

---

384. Garlic Shrimp and Spinach

Preparation Time: 10 minutes **Cooking Time:** 10 minutes **Servings:** 4

Ingredients:
- 3 tablespoons olive oil, divided
- 6 clove garlic, sliced and divided
- 1 lb. spinach Salt to taste
- 1 tablespoons lemon juice
- 1lb. shrimp, peeled and deveined
- ¼ teaspoon red pepper, crushed
- 1tablespoon parsley, chopped
- 1teaspoon lemon zest

Directions:
1. Pour 1 tablespoon olive oil in a pot over medium heat.
2. Cook the garlic for 1 minute.
3. Add the spinach and season with salt.
4. Cook for 3 minutes. Stir in lemon juice.
5. Transfer to a bowl. Pour the remaining oil.
6. Add the shrimp. Season with salt and add red pepper.
7. Cook for 5 minutes.
8. Sprinkle parsley and lemon zest over the shrimp before serving

Nutrition:
Calories: 226
Fat: 12 g
Cholesterol: 183 mg
Sodium: 444 mg
Carbohydrates: 6 g
Sugar: 1 g
Protein: 26 g

---

385. Herring and Veggies Soup

Preparation Time: 15 minutes **Cooking Time:** 25 minutes **Servings:** 5

Ingredients:
- 2 tablespoons olive oil
- 1shallot, chopped
- 2 small garlic cloves, minced
- 1jalapeño pepper, chopped
- 1head cabbage, chopped
- 1 small red bell pepper, seeded and hashed finely
- 1 small yellow bell pepper, seeded and hashed finely
- 5 cups low-sodium chicken broth
- 2 (4-ounce) boneless herring fillets, cubed
- ¼ cup fresh cilantro, minced
- 2 tablespoons fresh lemon juice
- Ground black pepper, as required
- 2 scallions, chopped

Directions:
1. In a large soup pan, warmth the oil over medium heat and sauté shallot and garlic for 2-3 minutes.
2. Add the cabbage and bell peppers and sauté for about 3-4 minutes.
3. Attach the broth and bring to a boil over high heat.
4. Now, reduce the heat to medium-low and simmer for about 10 minutes.
5. Add the herring cubes and cook for about 5-6 minutes.
6. Stir in the cilantro, lemon juice, salt and black pepper and cook for about 1-2 minutes.
7. Serve hot with the topping of scallion.

Nutrition:
Calories: 215
Fat: 11.2g
Cholesterol: 35 mg
Carbohydrates: 14.7 g
Sugar: 7 g
Fiber: 4.5 g
Sodium: 152 mg

386. Salmon Soup

Preparation Time: 15 minutes **Cooking Time:** 20 minutes **Servings:** 4

Ingredients:
- 1 tablespoon olive oil
- 1 yellow onion, chopped
- 1 garlic clove, minced
- 4 cups low-sodium chicken broth
- 1 pound boneless salmon, cubed
- 2 tablespoon fresh cilantro, chopped
- 1 Ground black pepper, as required
- 1 tablespoon fresh lime juice

Directions:
1. In a large pan warmth, the oil over medium heat and sauté the onion for about 5 minutes.
2. Attach the garlic and sauté for about 1 minute.
3. Stir in the broth and bring to a boil over high heat. Now, set the heat to low and parboil for about 10 minutes.
4. Add the salmon, and soy sauce and cook for about 3-4 minutes. Stir in black pepper, lime juice, and cilantro and serve hot.

Nutrition:
Calories: 208
Fat: 10.5 g
Cholesterol: 50 mg
Carbohydrates 3.9 g
Sugar: 1.2 g
Fiber: 0.6 g
Sodium: 121 mg

387. Salmon Curry

Preparation Time: 15 minutes **Cooking Time:** 30 minutes **Servings:** 6

Ingredients:
- 6 (4-ounce) salmon fillets
- 1 teaspoon ground turmeric, divided
- Salt, as required
- 3 tablespoon olive oil, divided
- 1 yellow onion, chopped finely
- 1 teaspoon garlic paste
- 1 teaspoon fresh ginger paste
- 3-4 green chilies, halved
- ½ teaspoon red chili powder
- ½ teaspoon ground cumin
- ½ teaspoon ground cinnamon
- ¾ cup fat-free plain Greek yogurt, whipped
- ¾ cup filtered water
- 3 tablespoon fresh cilantro, chopped

Directions:
1. Season each salmon fillet with ½ teaspoon of the turmeric and salt.
2. In a large skillet, melt 1 tablespoon of the butter over medium heat and cook the salmon fillets per side.
3. Transfer the salmon onto a plate. In the same skillet, dissolve the remaining butter over medium heat and sauté the onion for about 4-5 minutes.
4. Add the garlic paste, ginger paste, green chilies, remaining turmeric and spices and sauté for about 1 minute.
5. Now, reduce the heat to medium-low. Slowly, add the yogurt and water, stirring continuously until smooth.
6. Cover the skillet and simmer for about 10-15 minutes or until desired doneness of the sauce.
7. Carefully, add the salmon fillets and simmer for about 5 minutes. Serve hot with the garnishing of cilantro.

Nutrition:
Calories: 242
Fat: 14.3 g
Cholesterol: 51 mg
Carbohydrates: 4.1 g
Sugar: 2 g
Fiber: 0.8 g
Sodium: 98 mg

388. Salmon with Bell Peppers

Preparation Time: 15 minutes **Cooking Time:** 20 minutes **Servings:** 6

Ingredients:
- 6 (3-ounce) salmon fillets Pinch of salt
- ½ Ground black pepper, as required
- 1 yellow bell pepper, seeded and cubed
- 1 red bell pepper, seeded and cubed,
- 4 plum tomatoes, cubed
- 1 small onion, sliced thinly
- ½ cup fresh parsley, chopped
- ¼ cup olive oil
- 2 tablespoons fresh lemon juice

Directions:
1. Preheat the oven to 400F. Flavor each salmon fillet with salt and black pepper lightly. In a bowl, mix the bell peppers, tomato and onion.
2. Arrange 6 foil pieces onto a smooth surface. Place 1 salmon fillet over each foil paper and sprinkle with salt and black pepper.
3. Place veggie mixture over each fillet evenly and top with parsley and capers evenly.
4. Drizzle with oil and lemon juice. Fold each foil around salmon mixture to seal it. Arrange the foil packets onto a large baking sheet in a single layer.
5. Bake for about 20 minutes. Serve hot.

Nutrition:
Calories: 220
Fat: 14 g
Cholesterol: 38 mg
Carbohydrates: 7.7 g
Sugar: 4.8 g
Fiber: 2 g
Sodium: 74 mg

389. Shrimp Salad

Preparation Time: 20 minutes **Cooking Time:** 4 minutes **Servings:** 6

Ingredients:
For Salad:
- 1 pound shrimp, peeled and deveined
- Salt and ground black pepper, as required
- 1 teaspoon olive oil
- 1½ cups carrots, peeled and julienned

- 1½ cups red cabbage, shredded
- ½ cup cucumber, julienned
- 5 cups fresh baby arugula
- ¼ cup fresh basil, chopped

For Dressing:
- 2 tablespoons natural almond butter
- garlic clove, crushed
- ½ tablespoon fresh cilantro, chopped
- 1 tablespoon fresh lime juice
- 1 tablespoon unsweetened applesauce

- ¼ cup fresh cilantro, chopped
- 4 cups lettuce, torn
- ¼ cup almonds, chopped

- 2 teaspoons balsamic vinegar
- ½ teaspoon cayenne pepper
- Salt, as required
- tablespoon water ⅓ cup olive oil

Directions:
1. Slowly, add the oil, beating continuously until smooth.

For salad:
1. In a bowl, add shrimp, salt, black pepper and oil and toss to coat well. Heat a skillet over medium-high heat and cook the shrimp for about 2 minutes per side.

For dressing:
1. In a bowl, attach all ingredients except oil and beat until well combined.

2. Detach from the heat and set aside to cool. In a large bowl, add the shrimp, vegetables and mix well.

2. Place the dressing over shrimp mixture and gently, toss to coat well. Serve immediately.

Nutrition:
Calories: 274
Fat: 17.7 g
Cholesterol: 159 mg
Carbohydrates: 10 g
Sugar: 3.8 g
Fiber: 2.9 g
Sodium: 242 mg

---

390. Shrimp and Veggies Curry

Preparation Time: 20 minutes **Cooking Time:** 20 minutes **Servings:** 6

Ingredients:
- 2 teaspoons olive oil
- 1½ medium white onions, sliced
- 2 medium green bell peppers, seeded and hashed
- 3 medium carrots, peeled and sliced thinly
- 3 garlic cloves, chopped finely
- 1 tablespoon fresh ginger, chopped finely

- 2½ teaspoons curry powder
- 1½ pounds shrimp, peeled and deveined
- 1 cup filtered water
- 2 tablespoons fresh lime juice
- Salt and ground black pepper, as required
- 2 tablespoons fresh cilantro, chopped

Directions:
1. In a large skillet, warmth oil over medium-high heat and sauté the onion for about 4-5 minutes.
2. Add the bell peppers and carrot and sauté for about 3-4 minutes. Add the garlic, ginger and curry powder and sauté for about 1 minute.
3. Attach the shrimp and sauté for about 1 minute. Stir in the water and cook for about 4-6 minutes, stirring occasionally.
4. Spill in lime juice and remove from heat. Serve hot with the garnishing of cilantro.

Nutrition:
Calories: 193
Fat: 3.8g
Cholesterol: 239mg
Carbohydrates: 12g
Sugar: 4.7g
Fiber: 2.3g
Sodium 328mg

Veggies

391. Baked Zucchini Recipe from Mexico

Preparation Time: 10 minutes   **Cooking Time:** 30 minutes   **Servings:** 4

Ingredients:

- 1 tablespoon olive oil
- 1-½ pounds' zucchini, cubed
- ½ cup chopped onion
- ½ teaspoon garlic salt
- ½ teaspoon paprika
- ½ teaspoon dried oregano
- ½ teaspoon cayenne pepper
- ½ cup cooked long-grain rice
- ½ cup cooked pinto beans
- 1-¼ cups salsa

- ¾ cup shredded Cheddar cheese

Directions:
1. Set the baking pan of air fryer with olive oil. Add onions and zucchini and for 10 minutes, cook on 360F. Halfway through cooking time, stir.
2. Season with cayenne, oregano, paprika, and garlic salt. Mix well.
3. Stir in salsa, beans, and rice. Cook for 5 minutes.
4. Stir in cheddar cheese and mix well.
5. Cover pan with foil.
6. Cook for 15 minutes at 390F until bubbly.
7. Serve and enjoy.

Nutrition:
Calories: 263
Carbohydrates: 24.6g
Protein: 12.5g
Fat: 12.7g

392. Banana Pepper Stuffed with Tofu 'n Spices

Preparation Time: 5 minutes **Cooking Time:** 10 minutes **Servings:** 8

Ingredients:
- ½ teaspoon red chili powder
- ½ teaspoon turmeric powder
- 1 onion, finely chopped
- 1 package firm tofu, crumbled
- 1 teaspoon coriander powder
- 3 tablespoons coconut oil
- 8 banana peppers, top end sliced and seeded
- Salt to taste

Directions:
1. Preheat the air fryer for 5 minutes.
2. In a mixing bowl, combine the tofu, onion, coconut oil, turmeric powder, red chili powder, coriander power, and salt. Mix until well-combined.
3. Scoop the tofu mixture into the hollows of the banana peppers.
4. Place the stuffed peppers in the air fryer.
5. Close and cook for 10 minutes at 3250F.

Nutrition:
Calories: 72
Carbohydrates: 4.1g
Protein: 1.2g
Fat: 5.6

393. Baked Potato Topped with Cream cheese 'n Olives

Preparation Time: 15 minutes **Cooking Time:** 40 minutes **Servings:** 1

Ingredients:
- ¼ teaspoon onion powder
- 1 medium russet potato, scrubbed and peeled
- 1 tablespoon chives, chopped
- 1 tablespoon Kalamata olives
- 1 teaspoon olive oil
- ⅛ teaspoon salt
- a dollop of vegan butter
- a dollop of vegan cream cheese

Directions:
1. Place inside the air fryer basket and cook for 40 minutes. Be sure to turn the potatoes once halfway.
2. Set the potatoes in a bowl and pour in olive oil, onion powder, salt, and vegan butter.
3. Preheat the air fryer to 400F.
4. Serve the potatoes with vegan cream cheese, Kalamata olives, chives, and other vegan toppings that you want.

Nutrition:
Calories: 504
Carbohydrates: 68.34g
Protein: 9.31g
Fat: 21.53g

394. Brussels sprouts with Balsamic Oil

Preparation Time: 5 minutes **Cooking Time:** 15 minutes **Servings:** 4

Ingredients:
- ¼ teaspoon salt
- 1 tablespoon balsamic vinegar
- 2 cups Brussels sprouts, halved
- 2 tablespoons olive oil

Directions:
1. Preheat the air fryer for 5 minutes.
2. Mix all ingredients in a bowl until the zucchini fries are well coated.
3. Place in the air fryer basket.
4. Close and cook for 15 minutes for 350F.

Nutrition:
Calories: 82
Carbohydrates: 4.6g
Protein: 1.5g
Fat: 6.8g

395. Bell Pepper-Corn Wrapped in Tortilla

Preparation Time: 5 minutes **Cooking Time:** 15 minutes **Servings:** 4

Ingredients:
- 1 small red bell pepper, chopped
- 1 small yellow onion, diced
- 1 tablespoon water
- 2 cobs grilled corn kernels
- 4 large tortillas
- 4 pieces' commercial vegan nuggets, chopped
- mixed greens for garnish

Directions:
1. Preheat the air fryer to 400F.
2. In a skillet heated over medium heat, water sauté the vegan nuggets together with the onions, bell peppers, and corn kernels. Set aside.
3. Place filling inside the corn tortillas.
4. Fold the tortillas and place inside the air fryer and cook for 15 minutes until the tortilla wraps are crispy.
5. Serve with mix greens on top.

Nutrition:
Calories: 548
Carbohydrates: 43.54g
Protein: 46.73g
Fat: 20.76g

396. Black Bean Burger with Garlic-Chipotle

Preparation Time: 10 minutes **Cooking Time:** 20 minutes **Servings:** 3

Ingredients:
- ½ cup corn kernels
- ½ teaspoon chipotle powder
- ½ teaspoon garlic powder
- ¾ cup salsa
- 1 ¼ teaspoon chili powder
- 1 ½ cup rolled oats
- 1 can black beans, rinsed and drained
- 1 tablespoon soy sauce

Directions:
1. In a mixing bowl, merge all Ingredients and mix using your hands.
2. Form small patties using your hands and set aside.
3. Brush patties with oil if desired.
4. Place the grill pan in the air fryer and place the patties on the grill pan accessory.
5. Seal the lid and cook for 20 minutes on each side at 330F.

Nutrition:
Calories: 395
Carbohydrates: 52.2g
Protein: 24.3g
Fat: 5.8g

397. Vegan Edamame Quinoa Collard Wraps

Preparation Time: 5 minutes **Cooking Time:** 15 minutes **Servings:** 4

Ingredients:
For the wrap:
- 2 to 3 Collard leaves.
- ¼ cup Grated carrot
- ¼ cup Sliced cucumber

For the dressing:
- Fresh ginger root; 3 tablespoons; peeled and chopped
- Cooked chickpeas; 1 cup
- Clove of garlic; 1
- Rice vinegar; 4 tablespoons
- Low sodium tamari/coconut aminos; 2 tablespoons
- ¼ thin strips red bell pepper.
- ¼ thin strips orange bell pepper.
- ⅓ cup cooked quinoa.
- ⅓ cup Shelled defrosted edamame
- Lime juice; 2 tablespoons
- Water; ¼ cup
- Few pinches of chili flakes
- Stevia; 1 pack

Directions:
1. For the dressing, merge all the ingredients and purée in a food processor until smooth.
2. Load into a little jar or tub and set aside.
3. Place the collar leaves on a flat surface, covering one another to create a tighter tie.
4. Take one tablespoon of ginger dressing and blend it up with the prepared quinoa.
5. Spoon the prepared quinoa onto the leaves and shape a simple horizontal line at the closest end.
6. Supplement the edamame with all the veggie fillings left over.
7. Drizzle around one tablespoon of the ginger dressing on top, then fold the cover's sides inwards.
8. Pullover the fillings, the side of the cover closest to you, then turn the whole body away to seal it up.

Nutrition:
Calories: 295
Sugar: 3 g
Sodium: 200 mg
Fat: 13 g

398. Baked Eggplant with Marinara

Preparation Time: 20 minutes **Cooking Time:** 45 minutes **Servings:** 3

Ingredients:
- 1 clove garlic, sliced
- 1 large eggplants
- 1 tablespoon olive oil
- 1 tablespoon olive oil
- ½ pinch salt, or as needed
- ¼ cup and 2 tbsp. dry breadcrumbs
- ¼ cup and 2 tablespoons ricotta cheese
- ¼ cup grated Parmesan cheese
- ¼ cup grated Parmesan cheese
- ¼ cup water, plus as needed
- ¼ teaspoon red pepper flakes
- 1-½ cups prepared marinara sauce
- 1-½ teaspoons olive oil
- 2 tablespoons shredded pepper jack cheese
- salt and freshly ground black pepper

Directions:
1. Cut the eggplant crosswise into 5 pieces. Peel a pumpkin, grate it and cut it into two cubes.
2. Lightly turn skillet with 1 Tbsp. olive oil. Heat the oil at 390F for 5 minutes. Add half of the aubergines and cook 2 minutes on each side. Transfer to a plate.
3. Add 1 tbsp. of olive oil and add garlic. Cook for one minute. Add the chopped aubergines. Season with pepper flakes and salt. Cook for 4 minutes. Lower the heat to 330F and continue cooking the eggplants until soft, about 8 more minutes.
4. Stir in water and marinara sauce. Cook for 7 minutes until heated through. Stirring every now and then. Transfer to a bowl.
5. In a bowl, whisk well pepper, salt, pepper jack cheese, Parmesan cheese, and ricotta. Evenly spread cheeses over eggplant strips and then fold in half.
6. Lay folded eggplant in baking pan. Pour marinara sauce on top.
7. In a small bowl whisk well olive oil, and breadcrumbs. Sprinkle all over sauce.
8. Cook for 15 minutes at 390F until tops are lightly browned.
9. Serve and enjoy.

Nutrition:
Calories: 405
Carbohydrates: 41.1g
Protein: 12.7g
Fat: 21.4g

399. Crispy-Topped Baked Vegetables

Preparation Time: 10 minutes
Cooking Time: 40 minutes
Servings: 4

Ingredients:
- 2 tbsp. olive oil
- 1 onion, chopped
- 1 celery stalk, chopped
- 2 carrots, grated
- ½-pound turnips, sliced
- 1 cup vegetable broth
- 1 tsp. turmeric
- Sea salt and black pepper, to taste
- ½ tsp. liquid smoke
- 1 cup Parmesan cheese, shredded
- 2 tbsp. fresh chives, chopped

Directions:
1. Set oven to 360F and grease a baking dish with olive oil.
2. Set a skillet with medium heat and warm olive oil.
3. Sweat the onion until soft, and place in the turnips, carrots, and celery; and cook for 4 minutes.
4. Remove the vegetable mixture to the baking dish.
5. Combine vegetable broth with turmeric, pepper, liquid smoke, and salt.
6. Spread this mixture over the vegetables.
7. Sprinkle with Parmesan cheese and bake for about 30 minutes.
8. Garnish with chives to serve.

Nutrition:
Calories: 242
Fats: 16.3 g
Carbohydrates: 8.6 g
Protein: 16.3 g

400. Creamy Spinach and Mushroom Lasagna

Preparation Time: 60 minutes
Cooking Time: 20 minutes
Servings: 6

Ingredients:
- 10 lasagna noodles
- 1 package whole milk ricotta
- 2 packages of frozen chopped spinach.

For the Sauce:
- ¼ cup of butter (unsalted)
- 2 cloves garlic
- 1 pound of thinly sliced cremini mushroom
- 1 diced onion
- ¼ cup flour
- 4 cups mozzarella cheese (divided and shredded)
- ¾ cup grated fresh Parmesan
- 3 tablespoons chopped fresh parsley leaves (optional)
- 4 cups milk, kept at room temperature
- 1 teaspoon basil (dried)
- Pinch of nutmeg
- Salt and freshly ground black pepper

Directions:
1. Preheat oven to 352F.
2. To make the sauce, over a medium heat, melt your butter. Add garlic, mushrooms, and onion. Cook and stir at intervals until it becomes tender at about 3-4 minutes.
3. Whisk in flour until lightly browned, it takes about 1 minute for it to become brown.
4. Next, whisk in the milk gradually, and cook, constantly whisking, about 2-3 minutes till it becomes thickened. Stir in basil, oregano, and nutmeg, season with salt and pepper for taste.
5. Then set aside.
6. In another set of pot of boiling salted water, cook lasagna noodles according to the package instructions.
7. Spread one cup mushroom sauce onto the bottom of a baking dish; top it with four lasagna noodles, ½ of the spinach, one cup mozzarella cheese, and ¼ cup Parmesan.
8. Repeat this process with remaining noodles, mushroom sauce, and cheeses.
9. Place into oven and bake for 35-45 minutes, or until it starts bubbling. Then boil for 2-3 minutes until it becomes brown and translucent.
10. Let cool for 15 minutes.
11. Serve it with garnished parsley (optional)

Nutrition:
Calories: 488.3
Fats: 19.3 g
Cholesterol: 88.4 mg
Sodium: 451.9 mg
Carbohydrates: 51.0 g
Protein: 25.0 g

401. Zucchini Parmesan Chips

Preparation Time: 5 minutes
Cooking Time: 8 minutes
Servings: 10

Ingredients:
- ½ tsp. paprika
- ½ C. grated parmesan cheese
- ½ C. Italian breadcrumbs
- 1 lightly beaten egg
- 1 thinly sliced zucchinis

Directions:
1. Use a very sharp knife or mandolin slicer to slice zucchini as thinly as you can. Pat off extra moisture.
2. Beat egg with a pinch of pepper and salt and a bit of water.
3. Combine paprika, cheese, and breadcrumbs in a bowl.
4. Dip slices of zucchini into the egg mixture and then into breadcrumb mixture. Press gently to coat.
5. With olive oil cooking spray, mist coated zucchini slices. Place into your air fryer in a single layer.
6. Cook 8 minutes at 350F.
7. Sprinkle with salt and serve with salsa.

Nutrition:
Calories: 211
Fat: 16g
Protein: 8g
Sugar: 0g

402. Roasted Squash Puree

Preparation Time: 20 minutes **Cooking Time:** 6 to 7 hours **Servings:** 8

Ingredients:
- 1 (3-pound) butternut squash, skinned, seeded, and cut into 1-inch pieces
- 3 (1-pound) acorn squash, peeled, seeded, and cut into 1-inch pieces
- 2 onions, chopped
- 3 garlic cloves, minced
- 2 tablespoons olive oil
- 1 teaspoon dried marjoram leaves
- ½ teaspoon salt
- ⅛ teaspoon freshly ground black pepper

Directions:
1. In a 6-quart slow cooker, mix all the ingredients.
2. Seal and cook on low for 6 to 7 hours, or until the squash is tender when pierced with a fork.
3. Smash the squash right in the slow cooker.

Nutrition:
Calories: 175
Carbohydrates: 38 g
Sugar: 1 g
Fiber: 3 g
Fat: 4 g
Saturated Fat: 1 g
Protein: 3 g
Sodium: 149 mg

403. Roasted Root Vegetables

Preparation Time: 20 minutes **Cooking Time:** 6 to 8 hours **Servings:** 8

Ingredients:
- 6 carrots, cut into 1-inch chunks
- 2 yellow onions, cut into 8 wedges
- 2 sweet potatoes, skinned and cut into chunks
- 6 Yukon Gold skinned, cut into chunks
- 8 whole garlic cloves, peeled
- 4 parsnips, peeled and cut into chunks
- 3 tablespoons olive oil
- 1 teaspoon dried thyme leaves
- ½ teaspoon salt
- ⅛ teaspoon freshly ground black pepper

Directions:
1. In a 6-quart slow cooker, mix all the ingredients.
2. Seal and cook on low for 6 to 8 hours, or until the vegetables are tender.
3. Serve and enjoy!

Nutrition:
Calories: 214
Carbohydrates: 40 g
Sugar: 7 g
Fiber: 6 g
Fat: 5 g
Saturated Fat: 1 g
Protein: 4 g
Sodium: 201 mg

404. Hummus

Preparation Time: 10 minutes **Cooking Time:** 10 minutes **Servings:** 32

Ingredients:
- 4 cups of cooked garbanzo beans
- 1 cup of water
- 1½ tablespoons of lemon juice
- 2 teaspoons of ground cumin
- 1½ teaspoon of ground coriander.
- 1 teaspoon of finely chopped garlic
- ½ teaspoon of salt
- ¼ teaspoon of fresh ground pepper
- Paprika for garnish

Directions:
1. On a food processor, place together the garbanzo beans, lemon juice, water, garlic, salt, and pepper and process it until it becomes smooth and creamy.
2. To achieve your desired consistency, add more water.
3. Then spoon out the hummus in a serving bowl
4. Sprinkle your paprika and serve.

Nutrition:
Protein: 0.7 g
Carbohydrates: 2.5 g
Sugars: 0 g
Fat: 1.7 g

405. Thai Roasted Veggies

Preparation Time: 20 minutes **Cooking Time:** 6 to 8 hours **Servings:** 8

Ingredients:
- 4 large carrots, peeled and cut into chunks
- 2 onions, peeled and sliced
- 6 garlic cloves, peeled and sliced
- 2 parsnips, peeled and sliced
- 2 jalapeño peppers, minced
- ½ cup Roasted Vegetable Broth
- ⅓ cup canned coconut milk
- 3 tablespoons lime juice
- 2 tablespoons grated fresh ginger root
- 2 teaspoons curry powder

Directions:
1. In a 6-quart slow cooker, mix the carrots, onions, garlic, parsnips, and jalapeño peppers.
2. In a small bowl, mix the vegetable broth, coconut milk, lime juice, ginger root, and curry powder until well blended. Pour this mixture into the slow cooker.

3. Seal and cook on low for 6 to 8 hours, do it until the vegetables are tender when pierced with a fork.

Nutrition:
Calories: 69
Carbohydrates: 13 g
Sugar: 6 g
Fiber: 3 g
Fat: 3g
Saturated Fat: 3g
Protein: 1g
Sodium: 95mg

406. Cheesy Cauliflower Fritters

Preparation Time: 5 minutes
Cooking Time: 14 minutes
Servings: 8

Ingredients:
- ½ Cup chopped parsley
- 1 Cup Italian breadcrumbs
- ⅓ Cup shredded mozzarella cheese
- ⅓ Cup shredded sharp cheddar cheese
- 1 egg
- 1 minced garlic cloves
- 1 chopped scallions
- 1 head of cauliflower

Directions:
1. Cut cauliflower up into florets. Wash well and pat dry. Place into a food processor and pulse 20-30 seconds till it looks like rice.
2. Place cauliflower rice in a bowl and mix with pepper, salt, egg, cheeses, breadcrumbs, garlic, and scallions.
3. With hands, form 15 patties of the mixture. Add more breadcrumbs if needed.
4. With olive oil, spritz patties, and place into your air fryer in a single layer.
5. Cook 14 minutes at 390F, flipping after 7 minutes.

Nutrition:
Calories: 209
Fat: 17g
Protein: 6g
Sugar: 0.5g

407. Crispy Jalapeno Coins

Preparation Time: 10 minutes
Cooking Time: 10 minutes
Servings: 8 to 10

Ingredients:
- 1 egg
- 2-3 tbsp. coconut flour
- 1 sliced and seeded jalapeno
- Pinch of garlic powder
- Pinch of onion powder
- Pinch of Cajun seasoning (optional)
- Pinch of pepper and salt

Directions:
1. Ensure your air fryer is preheated to 400F.
2. Mix all dry ingredients.
3. Pat jalapeno slices dry. Dip coins into egg wash and then into dry mixture. Toss to coat thoroughly.
4. 4Add coated jalapeno slices to air fryer in a singular layer. Spray with olive oil.
5. Cook just till crispy.

Nutrition:
Calories: 128
Fat: 8g
Protein: 7g
Sugar: 0g

408. Jicama Fries

Preparation Time: 10 minutes
Cooking Time: 20 minutes
Servings: 8

Ingredients:
- 1 tbsp. dried thyme
- ¾ Cup arrowroot flour
- ½ large Jicama
- 3 eggs

Directions:
1. Sliced jicama into fries.
2. Whisk eggs together and pour over fries. Toss to coat.
3. Mix a pinch of salt, thyme, and arrowroot flour together. Toss egg-coated jicama into dry mixture, tossing to coat well.
4. Set the air fryer basket with olive oil and add fries. Cook 20 minutes on CHIPS setting. Toss halfway into the cooking process.

Nutrition:
Calories: 211
Fat: 19g
Protein: 9g
Sugar: 1g

409. Air Fryer Brussels sprouts

Preparation Time: 5 minutes
Cooking Time: 10 minutes
Servings: 5

Ingredients:
- ¼ tsp. salt
- 1 tbsp. balsamic vinegar
- 1 tbsp. olive oil
- 1 Cup Brussels sprouts

Directions:
1. Cut Brussels sprouts in half lengthwise. Toss with salt, vinegar, and olive oil till coated thoroughly.
2. Add coated sprouts to air fryer, cooking 8-10 minutes at 400 F. Shake after 5 minutes of cooking.
3. Brussels sprouts are ready to devour when brown and crisp!

Nutrition:
Calories: 118
Fat: 9g
Protein: 11g
Sugar: 1g

410. Spaghetti Squash Tots

Preparation Time: 5 minutes **Cooking Time:** 15 minutes **Servings:** 8 to 10

Ingredients:
- ¼ tsp. pepper
- ½ tsp. salt
- 1 thinly sliced scallion
- 1 spaghetti squash

Directions:
1. Rinse and cut the squash in half lengthwise. Scrape out the seeds.
2. With a fork, remove spaghetti meat by strands and throw out skins.
3. In a clean towel, toss in squash and wring out as much moisture as possible. Place in a bowl and with a knife slice through meat a few times to cut up smaller.
4. Add pepper, salt, and scallions to squash and mix well.
5. Create "tot" shapes with your hands and place in air fryer. Spray with olive oil.
6. Cook 15 minutes at 350 F until golden and crispy!

Nutrition:
Calories: 231
Fat: 18g
Protein: 5g
Sugar: 0g

411. Cinnamon Butternut Squash Fries

Preparation Time: 10 minutes **Cooking Time:** 10 minutes **Servings:** 2

Ingredients:
- 1 pinch of salt
- 1 tbsp. Stevia
- ½ tsp. nutmeg
- 1 tsp. cinnamon
- 1 tbsp. coconut oil
- 1 ounces pre-cut butternut squash fries

Directions:
1. In a plastic bag, pour in all ingredients. Coat fries with other components till coated and Stevia is dissolved.
2. Spread coated fries into a single layer in the air fryer. Cook 10 minutes at 390 F until crispy.

Nutrition:
Calories: 175
Fat: 8g
Protein: 1g
Sugar: 5g

412. Carrot and Zucchini Muffins

Preparation Time: 5 minutes **Cooking Time:** 14 minutes **Servings:** 4

Ingredients:
- 2 tablespoons butter, melted
- ¼ cup carrots, shredded
- ½ cup zucchini, shredded
- 1 ½ cups almond flour
- 1 tablespoon liquid Stevia
- teaspoons baking powder
- Pinch of salt
- 2 eggs
- 1 tablespoon yogurt
- 1 cup milk

Directions:
1. Preheat your air fryer to 350F.
2. Beat the eggs, yogurt, milk, salt, pepper, baking soda, and
3. Stevia.
4. Whisk in the flour gradually.
5. Add zucchini and carrots.
6. Grease muffin tins with butter and pour muffin batter into tins. Cook for 14-minutes and serve.

Nutrition:
Calories: 224
Total Fats: 12.3g
Carbohydrates: 11.2g
Protein: 14.2g

413. Curried Cauliflower Florets

Preparation Time: 5 minutes **Cooking Time:** 10 minutes **Servings:** 4

Ingredients:
- ¼ cup sultanas or golden raisins
- ¼ teaspoon salt
- 1 tablespoon curry powder
- 1 head cauliflower, broken into small florets
- ¼ cup pine nuts
- ½ cup olive oil

Directions:
1. In a cup of boiling water, soak your sultanas to plump. Preheat your air fryer to 350 F.
2. Add oil and pine nuts to air fryer and toast for a minute or so.
3. In a bowl toss the cauliflower and curry powder as well as salt, then add the mix to air fryer mixing well.
4. Cook for 10-minutes. Drain the sultanas, toss with cauliflower, and serve.

Nutrition:
Calories: 275,
Total Fat: 11.3g
Carbohydrates: 8.6g
Protein: 9.5g

414. Oat and Chia Porridge

Preparation Time: 5 minutes **Cooking Time:** 5 minutes **Servings:** 4

Ingredients:
- 2 tablespoons peanut butter
- 2 teaspoons liquid Stevia
- 1 tablespoon butter, melted
- 2 cups milk

- 2 cups oats
- 1 cup chia seeds

Directions:
1. Preheat your air fryer to 390F.
2. Whisk the peanut butter, butter, milk and Stevia in a bowl.
3. Stir in the oats and chia seeds.
4. Pour the mixture into an oven-proof bowl and place in the air fryer and cook for 5-minutes.

Nutrition:
Calories: 228
Total Fats: 11.4g
Carbohydrates: 10.2g
Protein: 14.5g

415. Feta and Mushroom Frittata

Preparation Time: 15 minutes **Cooking Time:** 30 minutes **Servings:** 4

Ingredients:
- 1 red onion, thinly sliced
- 2 cups button mushrooms, thinly sliced
- Salt to taste
- 2 tablespoons feta cheese, crumbled
- 3 medium eggs
- Non-stick cooking spray
- 1½ tablespoons olive oil

Directions:
1. Set the onion and mushrooms in olive oil over medium heat until the vegetables are tender.
2. Remove the vegetables from pan and drain on a paper towel-lined plate.
3. In a mixing bowl, whisk eggs and salt. Coat all sides of baking dish with cooking spray.
4. Preheat your air fryer to 325F. Pour the beaten eggs into prepared baking dish and scatter the sautéed vegetables and crumble feta on top. Bake in the air fryer for 30-minutes. Allow to cool slightly and serve!

Nutrition:
Calories: 226
Fat: 9.3g
Carbohydrates: 8.7g
Protein: 12.6g

416. Butter Glazed Carrots

Preparation Time: 20 minutes **Cooking Time:** 15 minutes **Servings:** 4

Ingredients:
- Baby carrots-2 cups
- Stevia-1 tbsps.
- Butter; melted-½ tbsps.
- Salt and black pepper- a pinch

Directions:
1. Take a baking dish suitable to fit in your air fryer.
2. Toss carrots with stevia, butter, salt and black peppers in that baking dish.
3. Place this dish in the air fryer basket and seal the fryer.
4. Cook the carrots for 10 minutes at 350 F on Air fryer mode.

Nutrition:
Calories: 151
Fat: 2
Fiber: 4
Carbohydrates: 14
Protein: 4

417. Spinach with Tomatoes

Preparation Time: 10 minutes **Cooking Time:** 10 minutes **Servings:** 1

Ingredients:
- ½ tablespoon olive oil
- ¼ of small onion, chopped
- 1 small tomato, chopped
- 1 tablespoon fresh basil, chopped
- 1 cup fresh spinach, chopped
- Salt and ground black pepper, as required

Directions:
1. In a skillet, warmth oil over medium-high heat and sauté onion for about 5 minutes. Add tomato and cook for about 1-2 minutes.
2. Stir in basil, spinach, salt and black pepper and cook for about 2-3 minutes.
3. Serve hot.

Nutrition:
Calories: 91
Fat: 7.3g
Carbohydrates: 6.3g
Fiber: 2.2g
Sugar: 3.3g
Protein: 1.9g
Sodium: 184mg

418. Lemony Kale

Preparation Time: 10 minutes **Cooking Time:** 20 minutes **Servings:** 1

Ingredients:
- ¼ tablespoon extra-virgin olive oil
- ¼ of lemon, seeded sliced thinly
- ¼ of onion, chopped
- 1 small garlic clove, minced
- 5 ounces fresh kale, tough ribs removed and chopped
- ½ of scallion, chopped
- Salt and ground black pepper, as required

Directions:
1. In a small skillet, heat oil over medium heat and cook the lemon slices for about 5 minutes. With a slotted spoon, remove the lemon slices.
2. In the same skillet, add the onion and garlic and sauté for about 5 minutes. Add the kale, scallions, agave nectar, salt, and black pepper and cook for about 8-10 minutes, stirring occasionally.
3. Serve hot.

Nutrition:

Calories: 115
Fat: 4.4g
Sugar: 1.4g
Carbohydrates: 15.1g
Fiber: 4g
Protein: 5.2g
Sodium: 212mg

419. Kale with Cranberries and Pine Nuts
Preparation Time: 10 minutes **Cooking Time:** 14 minutes **Servings:** 1

Ingredients:
- ⅓ pound fresh kale, tough ribs removed and chopped
- ½ tablespoon extra-virgin olive oil
- ½ teaspoon garlic, minced
- 1 tablespoon dried unsweetened cranberries
- Salt and ground black pepper, as required
- 1 tablespoon pine nuts

Directions:
1. Set a salted water to boil and cook the kale for about 3-4 minutes. In a colander, drain the kale and immediately transfer into an ice bath. Drain the kale and set aside.
2. In a skillet, warmth the oil over medium heat and sauté the garlic for about 1 minute. Add kale, cranberries, salt and black pepper and cook for about 4-6 minutes, tossing frequently with tongs.
3. Stir in the pine nuts and serve hot.

Nutrition:
Calories: 199
Fat: 13.8g
Carbohydrates: 15.1g
Fiber: 3.9g
Sugar: 1.1g
Protein: 6.2g
Sodium: 213mg

420. Broccoli with Bell Pepper
Preparation Time: 10 minutes **Cooking Time:** 10 minutes **Servings:** 1

Ingredients:
- ½ tablespoon olive oil
- 1 garlic clove, minced
- ¼ of white onion, sliced
- ¼ cup small broccoli florets
- ½ of bell pepper, seeded and sliced
- 1-2 tablespoons low-sodium vegetable broth
- Salt and ground black pepper, as required

Directions:
1. In a small skillet, heat the oil over medium heat and sauté the garlic for about 1 minute. Add the onion, broccoli and bell pepper and stir fry for about 5 minutes.
2. Add the broth and stir fry for about 4 minutes more.
3. Serve hot.

Nutrition:
Calories: 96
Fat: 7.2g
Carbohydrates: 7.9g
Fiber: 2.3g
Sugar: 3g
Protein: 1.8g
Sodium: 160mg

421. Kale with Carrot
Preparation Time: 10 minutes **Cooking Time:** 15 minutes **Servings:** 1

Ingredients:
- ½ tablespoon extra-virgin olive oil
- ¼ of small onion, chopped
- 1 small garlic clove, minced
- 3 ounces fresh kale, tough ribs removed and chopped
- 2 ounces carrot, peeled and shredded
- ¼ tablespoon fresh lemon juice
- Salt and ground black pepper, as required

Directions:
1. Warmth the oil over medium heat and sauté the onion or about 4-5 minutes. Stir in the garlic and sauté for about 1 minute. Attach the kale and cook for about 3-4 minutes. Stir in the carrot, lemon juice, salt and black pepper and cook for about 4-5 minutes.
2. Serve hot.

Nutrition:
Calories: 124
Fat: 7.4g
Carbohydrates: 12g
Fiber: 3.1g
Sugar: 3.3g
Protein: 2.6g
Sodium: 205mg

422. Bok Choy and Mushroom Stir-Fry
Preparation Time: 10 minutes **Cooking Time:** 10 minutes **Servings:** 1

Ingredients:
- 3 ounces baby bok choy
- 1 teaspoon extra-virgin olive oil
- ¼ teaspoon fresh ginger, minced
- 1 garlic clove, chopped
- 3 ounces fresh mushrooms, sliced
- 2 tablespoons low-sodium vegetable broth
- ½ tablespoon low-sodium soy sauce
- Ground black pepper, as required

Directions:
1. Trim bases of bok choy and separate outer leaves from stalks, leaving the smallest inner leaves attached.
2. In a cast-iron wok, heat the oil over medium-high heat and sauté the ginger and garlic for about 1 minute. Stir in the mushrooms and cook for about 4-5 minutes, stirring frequently. Stir in the bok choy leaves and stalks and cook for about 1 minute, tossing with tongs.
3. Stir in the broth, soy sauce and black pepper and cook for about 2-3 minutes, tossing occasionally.
4. Serve hot.

Nutrition:
Calories: 40
Fat: 2.5g
Carbohydrates: 3.3g
Fiber: 0.9g
Sugar: 1.5g
Protein: 2.5g
Sodium: 245mg

---

423. Mushroom with Brussels Sprout

Preparation Time: 10 minutes **Cooking Time:** 25 minutes **Servings:** 1

Ingredients:
- ¼ tablespoon olive oil
- ¼ of small yellow onion, chopped
- ½ teaspoon fresh thyme, chopped
- 1 small garlic clove, minced
- 3 ounces fresh button mushroom, sliced
- 3 ounces Brussels sprouts, trimmed and halved
- Salt and ground black pepper, as required

Directions:
1. In a small skillet, warmth the oil over medium heat and sauté the onion for about 3-4 minutes. Add the thyme and garlic and sauté for about 1 minute. Add the mushrooms and cook for about 15 minutes or until caramelized. Attach the Brussels sprouts and cook for about 3-5 minutes.
2. Spill in the salt and black pepper and remove from the heat. Serve hot.

Nutrition:
Calories: 47
Fat: 2g
Carbohydrates: 6.3g
Fiber: 2.3g
Sugar: 2g
Protein: 2.9g
Sodium: 91mg

---

424. Bell Peppers and Zucchini Stir Fry

Preparation Time: 10 minutes **Cooking Time:** 15 minutes **Servings:** 1

Ingredients:
- ½ tablespoon olive oil
- ¼ of onion, chopped
- 1 small garlic clove, minced
- 1 bell pepper, seeded and cubed
- ¼ cup zucchini, sliced
- Salt and ground black pepper, as required

Directions:
1. In a non-stick skillet, warmth the oil over medium heat and sauté the onion and garlic for about 4-5 minutes. Add the vegetables and stir fry for about 4-5 minutes. Add the water and stir fry for about 3-4 minutes more.
2. Serve hot.

Nutrition:
Calories: 90
Fat: 7.1g
Carbohydrates: 7g
Fiber: 2.2g
Sugar: 3.3g
Protein: 1.3g
Sodium: 161mg

---

425. Stir Fried Veggie Noodles

Preparation Time: 10 minutes **Cooking Time:** 13 minutes **Servings:** 1

Ingredients:
- ½ tablespoon olive oil
- 1 tablespoon onion, chopped
- 1 garlic clove, minced
- ¼ of jalapeño pepper, seeded and chopped
- ¼ of small carrot, peeled and spiralized with Blade C
- ¼ of small zucchini, spiralized with Blade C
- ¼ of small yellow squash, spiralized
- ½ tablespoon fresh lemon juice
- Salt and ground black pepper, as required

Directions:
1. In a non-stick skillet, warmth oil over medium heat and sauté onion for about 4-5 minutes. Add garlic and jalapeño pepper and sauté for about 1 minute. Add carrot and cook for about 2-3 minutes. Add squash and zucchini and sauté for about 3-4 minutes.
2. Stir in lime juice, salt and black pepper and remove from heat.
3. Serve hot.

Nutrition:
Calories: 86
Fat: 7.2g
Carbohydrates: 5.5g
Fiber: 1.4g
Sugar: 2.3g
Protein: 1.2g
Sodium: 160mg

---

426. Ratatouille

Preparation Time: 10 minutes **Cooking Time:** 45 minutes **Servings:** 1

Ingredients:
- 1½ ounces sugar-free tomato paste
- 1 tablespoon olive oil, divided
- ¼ of small onion, chopped
- ¼ tablespoon garlic, minced
- Salt and ground black pepper, as required
- 1½-2 tablespoons water
- ¼ of zucchini, sliced into thin circles
- ¼ of yellow squash, sliced into circles thinly
- ¼ of eggplant, sliced into circles thinly
- ½ of small bell pepper, seeded and sliced into circles thinly
- ¼ tablespoon fresh thyme leaves, minced
- ¼ tablespoon fresh lemon juice

Directions:
1. Preheat your oven to 375 F.
2. In a bowl, add the tomato paste, ½ tablespoon of oil, onion, garlic, salt and black pepper and blend nicely.
3. Set the tomato paste mixture evenly in the bottom of a baking dish. Arrange alternating vegetable slices, starting at the outer edge of the baking dish and working concentrically towards the center.
4. Drizzle the vegetables with the remaining oil and sprinkle with salt and black pepper, followed by the thyme. Arrange a piece of parchment paper over the vegetables.
5. Bake for approximately 45 minutes.
6. Serve hot.

Nutrition:
Calories: 205
Fat: 12.5g
Carbohydrates: 15.1g
Fiber: 6.6g
Sugar: 5.3g
Protein: 3.9g
Sodium: 235mg

427. Yellow Squash and Bell Pepper Bake
Preparation Time: 20 minutes **Cooking Time:** 20 minutes **Servings:** 4

Ingredients:
- ½ of yellow squash, chopped
- 1 small bell pepper, seeded and cubed
- ¼ of onion, cubed
- ¼ tablespoon olive oil
- ¼ teaspoon cayenne powder
- Salt, as required

Directions:
1. Warmth your oven to 375 F. Lightly grease a small baking dish.
2. In a bowl, add all the ingredients and mix well.
3. Set the vegetable mixture into the prepared baking dish. Bake for approximately 15-20 minutes.
4. Serve hot.

Nutrition:
Calories: 73
Fat: 3.9g
Carbohydrates: 9.5g
Fiber: 3.1g
Sugar: 4.3g
Protein: 2.2g
Sodium: 168mg

428. Curried Veggies Bake
Preparation Time: 20 minutes **Cooking Time:** 20 minutes **Servings:** 1

Ingredients:
- ¼ of small zucchini, chopped
- ¼ of small summer squash, chopped
- ¼ of eggplant, cubed
- 1 small bell pepper, seeded and cubed
- ¼ of onion, sliced thinly
- 2-3 drops liquid stevia
- ½ tablespoon olive oil
- ½ teaspoon curry powder
- Salt and ground black pepper, as required

Directions:
1. Warmth your oven to 375 F. Lightly grease a small baking dish.
2. In a glass bowl, add all ingredients and mix well.
3. Place the vegetables mixture into prepared baking dish and spread in an even layer. Bake for approximately 15-20 minutes.
4. Serve hot.

Nutrition:
Calories: 127
Fat: 7.5g
Carbohydrates: 15.1g
Fiber: 5.6g
Sugar: 5.3g
Protein: 2.9g
Sodium: 165mg

429. Veggie Casserole
Preparation Time: 10 minutes **Cooking Time:** 55 minutes **Servings:** 2

Ingredients:
- ½ tablespoon olive oil, divided
- ½ of small yellow onion, chopped and divided
- 1 small garlic clove, minced and divided
- ½ of large carrot, peeled and chopped
- ½ of sweet potato, peeled and chopped
- ⅓ cup fresh mushrooms, chopped
- ¼ tablespoon fresh rosemary, chopped
- ⅓ cup low-sodium vegetable broth
- Salt and ground black pepper, as required

Directions:
1. Preheat your oven to 375F.
2. In a skillet, heat ¼ tablespoon of oil over medium heat and sauté half of onion and garlic for about 4-5 minutes. Attach carrot and sweet potato and sauté for about 4-5 minutes. Transfer the carrot mixture into a small casserole dish evenly.
3. In another skillet, warmth the remaining oil over medium heat and sauté remaining onion, garlic, mushrooms and rosemary for about 4-5 minutes.
4. Pour broth and bring to a boil. Stir in salt and black pepper and remove from heat and
5. Place the mushroom mixture over vegetables mixture evenly. Bake for 30-40 minutes or until top becomes golden brown. Serve hot.

Nutrition:
Calories: 76
Fat: 3.7g
Carbohydrates: 10.1g
Fiber: 2.1g
Sugar: 3.3g
Protein: 1.6g
Sodium: 113mg

430. Mushrooms Curry

Preparation Time: 10 minutes **Cooking Time:** 25 minutes **Servings:** 1

Ingredients:
- ¼ cup plum tomatoes, chopped
- ¼ tablespoon olive oil
- ¼ of small onion, chopped finely
- 1 teaspoon curry powder
- ¾ cup fresh button mushrooms, sliced
- 2-3 tablespoons unsweetened coconut milk
- Salt and ground black pepper, as required

Directions:
1. In a mini food processor, attach the tomatoes and pulse until a smooth paste form.
2. In a saucepan, warmth the oil over medium heat and sauté the onion for about 5-6 minutes. Attach the tomato paste and curry powder and cook for about 5 minutes.
3. Stir in the mushrooms, water and coconut milk and bring to a boil. Cook for about 10-12 minutes, stirring occasionally. Season with the salt and remove from the heat.
4. Serve hot.

Nutrition:
Calories: 71
Fat: 4.8g
Carbohydrates: 6.6g
Fiber: 2.3g
Sugar: 2.9g
Protein: 2.5g
Sodium: 162mg

431. Veggies and Walnut Loaf

Preparation Time: 10 minutes **Cooking Time:** 1 hour 10 minutes **Servings:** 4

Ingredients:
- ½ tablespoon olive oil
- 1 yellow onion, chopped
- 1 garlic clove, minced
- ½ teaspoon dried rosemary, crushed
- ½ cup walnuts, chopped
- 1 large carrot, peeled and chopped
- ½ of celery stalk, chopped
- ½ of bell pepper, seeds removed and chopped
- ½ cup fresh button mushrooms, chopped
- 3 small eggs
- ½ cup plus 2 tbsp. almond flour
- Salt and ground black pepper, as required

Directions:
1. Preheat your oven to 350F. Line a loaf pan with a lightly greased parchment paper.
2. In a wok, heat the olive oil over medium heat and sauté the onion for about 4-5 minutes. Add the garlic and rosemary and sauté for about 1 minute. Add the walnuts and vegetables and cook for about 3-4 minutes. Remove the wok of vegetable from heat and transfer the mixture into a large bowl. Set aside to cool slightly.
3. In another mixing bowl, add the eggs, flour, sea salt, and black pepper, and beat until well combined. Add the egg mixture into the bowl with vegetable mixture and mix until well combined.
4. Place the mixture into the prepared loaf pan evenly. Bake for approximately 56–60 minutes or until the top of loaves becomes golden-brown.
5. Remove the loaf pan from oven and set aside to cool slightly. Carefully, invert the loaf onto a platter. Cut into desired sized slices and serve.

Nutrition:
Calories: 195
Fat: 12.5g
Carbohydrates: 9.1g
Fiber: 3.2g
Sugar: 3.3g
Protein: 5g
Sodium: 95mg

432. Veggie Stuffed Bell Peppers

Preparation Time: 10 minutes **Cooking Time:** 25 minutes **Servings:** 1

Ingredients:
- 2 ounces shiitake mushrooms
- 3 tablespoons celery stalk
- ½ of garlic clove, peeled
- 2 tablespoons walnuts, chopped
- ½ tablespoon olive oil
- Salt and ground black pepper, as required
- 1 small bell pepper, halved and seeded

Directions:
1. Preheat oven to 400F. Grease a small baking sheet.
2. Remove stem and seeds from bell pepper.
3. In a mini food processor, add mushrooms, celery, garlic, walnuts, oil, salt and pepper and pulse until chopped finely.
4. Stuff the bell pepper halves with mushroom mixture.
5. Arrange the bell pepper halves onto the prepared baking sheet. Bake for approximately 20-25 minutes.
6. Serve warm.

Nutrition:
Calories: 134
Fat: 7.6g
Carbohydrates: 12g
Fiber: 3.1g
Sugar: 3.3g
Protein: 2.3g
Sodium: 265mg

433. Veggie Kabobs

Preparation Time: 10 minutes **Cooking Time:** 10 minutes **Servings:** 1

Ingredients:
For Marinade
- ½ of garlic clove, minced
- ½ teaspoon fresh basil, minced
- ½ teaspoon fresh oregano, minced
- ¼ teaspoon cayenne pepper
- Salt and ground black pepper, as required
- ½ tablespoon fresh lemon juice
- ½ tablespoon olive oil

For Veggies
- ½ of zucchinis, cut into thick slices
- 2 large button mushrooms, quartered
- ½ of bell pepper, seeded and cubed

Directions:
1. For marinade: in a glass bowl, add all the ingredients and mix until well combined. Attach the vegetables and toss to coat well. Cover and refrigerate to marinate for at least 6-8 hours.
2. Preheat the grill to medium-high heat. Generously, grease the grill grate.
3. Remove the vegetables from the bowl and thread onto pre-soaked wooden skewers.
4. Place the skewers onto the grill and cook for about 8-10 minutes or until done completely, flipping occasionally.
5. Serve hot.

Nutrition:
Calories: 106
Fat: 7.5g
Carbohydrates: 9.1g
Fiber: 3.2g
Sugar: 4.3g
Protein: 3.3g
Sodium: 165mg

434. Sweet Potato and Spinach Stew

Preparation Time: 10 minutes **Cooking Time:** 40 minutes **Servings:** 1

Ingredients:
- ½ tablespoon olive oil
- ¼ of onion, chopped
- ¼ of sweet potato, peeled and cubed into ½-inch size
- ¼ teaspoon fresh ginger, minced
- 1 garlic clove, minced
- ¼ teaspoon ground cumin
- Pinch of red pepper flakes, crushed
- 1 small tomato, chopped finely
- ¾ cup low-sodium vegetable broth
- 1 cup fresh spinach, chopped
- Salt and ground black pepper, as required

Directions:
1. In a small heavy-bottomed pan, heat oil over medium heat and sauté onion for about 4-6 minutes. Add sweet potato and cook for about 5-8 minutes. Add ginger, garlic and spices and sauté for about 1 minute. Add tomato and cook for about 2-3 minutes.
2. Add broth and bring to a boil. Set the heat to low and parboil, covered for about 15 minutes. Stir in spinach and simmer for about 5 minutes. Season with required salt and black pepper and remove from heat.
3. Serve hot.

Nutrition:
Calories: 144
Fat: 7.5g
Carbohydrates: 15.1g
Fiber: 3.6g
Sugar: 5g
Protein: 4.5g
Sodium: 250mg

435. Cabbage and Carrot Stew

Preparation Time: 10 minutes **Cooking Time:** 20 minutes **Servings:** 1

Ingredients:
- ½ tablespoon olive oil
- ¼ of small onion, chopped
- 1 small garlic clove, minced
- ¼ teaspoon fresh ginger, minced
- ¼ teaspoon ground turmeric
- ¼ teaspoon ground coriander
- Salt and ground black pepper, as required
- ½ cup water
- ¼ cup cabbage, shredded
- 1 small carrot, peeled and sliced

Directions:
1. In a small saucepan, warmth the oil over medium heat and sauté the onion for about 2-3 minutes. Stir in the ginger, garlic, spices, salt and black pepper and sauté for about 1 minute.
2. Add the water and vegetables and bring to a boil. Simmer, covered for about 10-15 minutes, stirring occasionally.
3. Serve hot.

Nutrition:
Calories: 100
Fat: 7.1g
Carbohydrates: 9g
Fiber: 2.3g
Sugar: 3.8g
Protein: 1.1g
Sodium: 185mg

436. Tofu Lettuce Wraps

Preparation Time: 10 minutes **Cooking Time:** 6 minutes **Servings:** 1

Ingredients:
- ¼ tablespoon olive oil
- 2 ounces extra-firm tofu, drained, pressed and cut into cubes
- ¼ teaspoon curry powder
- Salt, as required
- 2 lettuce leaves
- ¼ of small carrot, peeled and julienned
- 2 tablespoons radishes, sliced
- 1 teaspoon peanuts, chopped
- 1 teaspoon fresh cilantro, chopped
- 1 teaspoon fresh lime juice

Directions:
1. In a small skillet, warmth the oil over medium heat and cook the tofu, curry powder and a little salt for about 5-6 minutes or until golden brown, stirring frequently. Remove from the heat and set aside to cool slightly.
2. Set the lettuce leaves onto a serving plate. Divide the tofu, carrot, radish and peanuts over each leaf evenly.
3. Set with lime juice and serve with the garnishing of cilantro.

Nutrition:
Calories: 104
Fat: 7.9g
Carbohydrates: 3.8g
Fiber: 1.2g
Sugar: 1.4g
Protein: 6.5g
Sodium: 165mg

437. Tofu and Veggie Burger

Preparation Time: 10 minutes **Cooking Time:** 8 minutes **Servings:** 1

Ingredients:
- ¼ cup firm tofu, pressed and drained
- ¼ of carrot, peeled and grated
- ½ of garlic clove, chopped finely
- ½ tablespoon fresh parsley, chopped
- ½ tablespoon leek, chopped
- ½ tablespoon onion, chopped
- ½ tablespoon arrowroot flour
- 1 teaspoon low-sodium soy sauce
- ½ teaspoon nutritional yeast flakes
- ¼ teaspoon paprika
- ¼ teaspoon curry powder
- ¼ teaspoon mustard
- ¼ tablespoon olive oil

Directions:
1. Place the tofu in a bowl and with a fork, mash it. Add the remaining ingredients except for oil and mix until well combined. Shape the mixture into a patty.
2. Warmth oil in a small non-stick frying pan over medium heat and cook the patties for about 4 minutes per side.
3. Serve hot.

Nutrition:
Calories: 105
Fat: 6.4g
Carbohydrates: 6.4g
Fiber: 2.1g
Sugar: 1.9g
Protein: 6.6g
Sodium: 315mg

438. Tofu with Kale

Preparation Time: 10 minutes **Cooking Time:** 14 minutes **Servings:** 1

Ingredients:
- ½ tablespoon extra-virgin olive oil
- 3 ounces tofu, drained, pressed and cut into 1-inch cubes
- ¼ tablespoon low-sodium soy sauce
- 2 tablespoons water
- ¾ cup fresh baby kale

Directions:
1. In a cast-iron sauté pan, warmth the olive oil over medium heat and cook the tofu cubes for about 8-10 minutes or until golden from all sides.
2. Add the remaining ingredients and cook for about 3-4 minutes.

Nutrition:
Calories: 146
Fat: 10.5g
Carbohydrates: 6g
Fiber: 1.4g
Sugar: 0.8g
Protein: 8.6g
Sodium: 250mg

439. Tofu with Broccoli

Preparation Time: 10 minutes **Cooking Time:** 18 minutes **Servings:** 1

Ingredients:
- 3 ounces firm tofu, drained, pressed and cut into 1-inch slices
- 1 tablespoon arrowroot starch, divided
- ¾ tablespoon olive oil
- ¼ teaspoon fresh ginger, grated
- ¼ of onion, sliced thinly
- 1 tablespoon low-sodium soy sauce
- ½ tablespoon balsamic vinegar
- ¼ teaspoon sesame oil
- 2 drops liquid stevia
- 2 tablespoons water
- ¼ cup broccoli florets

Directions:
1. In a shallow bowl, place ½ tablespoon of arrowroot starch and tofu cubes and toss to coat.
2. In a cast iron skillet, warmth the olive oil over medium heat and cook the tofu cubes for about 8-10 minutes or until golden from all sides. With a slotted spoon, transfer the tofu cubes onto a plate. Set aside.
3. Meanwhile, in a pan of water, arrange a steamer basket and bring to a boil. Reduce the heat to medium-low. Set the broccoli florets in the steamer basket and steam, covered for about 5-6 minutes.
4. Drain the broccoli and set aside.
5. In the same skillet, attach the ginger and sauté for about 1 minute. Add the onions and sauté for about 2-3 minutes. Add the soy sauce, vinegar, sesame oil and stevia and bring to a gentle simmer.
6. In a bowl, dissolve the remaining cornstarch in water. Slowly, add the arrowroot starch mixture into the sauce, stirring continuously.
7. Stir in the cooked tofu and broccoli cook for about 1-2 minutes.
8. Serve hot.

Nutrition:
Calories: 233
Fat: 17.1g
Carbohydrates: 13g
Fiber: 2.2g
Sugar: 3g
Protein: 8.9g
Sodium: 465mg

440. Tofu with Brussels Sprout

Preparation Time: 10 minutes **Cooking Time:** 15 minutes **Servings:** 1

Ingredients:
- ¾ tablespoon olive oil, divided
- 3 ounces extra-firm tofu, drained, pressed and cut into slices
- 1 garlic clove, chopped
- 1 tablespoon pecans, toasted and chopped
- 1-2 drops liquid stevia
- 1 teaspoon fresh cilantro, chopped
- ¼ pound Brussels sprouts, trimmed and cut into wide ribbons

Directions:
1. In a skillet, heat ½ tablespoon of the oil over medium heat and sauté the tofu and for about 6-7 minutes or until golden brown. Add the garlic and pecans and sauté for about 1-2 minutes. Spill in the cilantro and remove from heat. Transfer tofu into a plate and set aside.
2. In the same skillet, warmth the remaining oil over medium-high heat and cook the Brussels sprouts for about 5 minutes. Stir in the tofu and remove from the heat.
3. Serve hot.

Nutrition:
Calories: 270 Fiber: 4.6g Sodium: 35mg
Fat: 13.5g Sugar: 3.1g
Carbohydrates: 13g Protein: 13.2g

441. Tofu with Peas

Preparation Time: 10 minutes **Cooking Time:** 20 minutes **Servings:** 1

Ingredients:
- ¾ tablespoon olive oil, divided
- 3 ounces extra-firm tofu, drained, pressed and cubed
- 2 tablespoons onion, chopped
- ¼ teaspoon fresh ginger, minced
- 1 small garlic clove, minced
- ½ of small tomato, chopped finely
- ¼ cup frozen peas, thawed
- 1 tablespoon low-sodium soy sauce

Directions:
1. In a cast-iron skillet, heat ½ tablespoon of oil over medium-high heat and cook the tofu for about 4-5 minutes or until browned completely, stirring occasionally. Transfer the tofu into a bowl.
2. In the same skillet, warmth the remaining oil over medium heat and sauté the onion for about 3-4 minutes. Attach the ginger and garlic and sauté for about 1 minute.
3. Add the tomato and cook for about 4-5 minutes, crushing with the back of spoon. Stir in all three peas and cook for about 2-3 minutes. Spill in the soy sauce and tofu and cook for about 1-2 minutes.
4. Serve hot.

Nutrition:
Calories: 226 Fiber: 3.6g Sodium: 465mg
Fat: 13.5g Sugar: 4.3g
Carbohydrates: 12g Protein: 12.3g

442. Tofu and Spinach Soup

Preparation Time: 10 minutes **Cooking Time:** 35 minutes **Servings:** 1

Ingredients:
- ½ tablespoon olive oil
- 1 tablespoon onion, sliced thinly
- 1 garlic clove, sliced
- 1 cup low-sodium vegetable broth
- 1 (1-inch piece) lemongrass, sliced and smashed
- 3 ounces fresh baby spinach
- 2 ounces firm tofu, pressed, drained, and cut into ½-inch cubes
- ¼ tablespoon fresh cilantro, chopped
- ½ tablespoon fresh lime juice

Directions:
1. In a heavy-bottomed saucepan, warmth the oil over medium-low heat and cook the onions, garlic, and a little salt for about 15 minutes, stirring occasionally. Stir in the broth and lemongrass and cover the pan.
2. Set the heat and bring to a boil. Remove from the heat and set aside, covered for about 15 minutes. Uncover the pan and discard lemongrass.
3. In the pan, add the spinach, tofu, cilantro, and lime juice, and stir to combine. Place the pan over medium heat and cook for about 3-4 minutes or until spinach is wilted, stirring occasionally.
4. Stir in the salt and remove from the heat. Serve hot.

Nutrition:
Calories: 143 Fiber: 2.6g Sodium: 145mg
Fat: 9.5g Sugar: 1.2g
Carbohydrates: 7.1g Protein: 9.4g

443. Tofu and Bell Pepper Stew

Preparation Time: 10 minutes **Cooking Time:** 15 minutes **Servings:** 1

Ingredients:
- ¼ tablespoon garlic
- ½ of jalapeño pepper, seeded and chopped
- 1 ounce roasted red peppers, rinsed, drained and chopped
- ½ cup low-sodium vegetable broth
- ½ of small bell pepper, seeded and sliced thinly
- 3 ounces extra-firm tofu, drained and cubed
- 2 ounces frozen baby spinach, thawed

Directions:
1. Add the garlic, jalapeño pepper and roasted red peppers in a food processor and pulse until smooth.
2. In a saucepan, add the puree, broth and water over medium-high heat and cook until boiling. Add the bell peppers and tofu and stir to combine.
3. Reduce the heat to medium and cook for about 5 minutes. Spill in the spinach and cook for about 5 minutes.
4. Serve hot.

Nutrition:
Calories: 118
Fat: 5.4g
Carbohydrates: 8.8g
Fiber: 2.6g
Sugar: 3.1g
Protein: 11.6g
Sodium: 150mg

---

444. Tofu and Veggies Curry

Preparation Time: 10 minutes **Cooking Time:** 3- minutes **Servings:** 1

Ingredients:
- ½ tablespoon olive oil
- ½ of small yellow onion, chopped
- ¼ teaspoon fresh ginger, minced
- 1 small garlic clove, minced
- ¼ tablespoon curry powder
- Salt and ground black pepper, as required
- 2-3 tablespoons fresh mushrooms, sliced
- 2-3 tablespoons carrots, peeled and sliced
- 2 tablespoons unsweetened coconut milk
- ¼ cup low-sodium vegetable broth
- 3 ounces firm tofu, drained, pressed and cut into ½-inch cubes
- ¼ cup fresh spinach, tough ribs removed and chopped
- ¼ tablespoon fresh lime juice
- 1 teaspoon fresh parsley, chopped

Directions:
1. In a small Dutch oven, warmth the oil over medium heat and sauté the onion, ginger and garlic for about 5 minutes. Spill in the curry powder, salt and black pepper and cook for about 2 minutes, stirring occasionally. Attach the mushrooms and carrot and cook for about 4-5 minutes.
2. Stir in the coconut milk and broth and brown sugar and bring to a boil. Add the tofu and spinach and simmer for about 12-15 minutes, stirring occasionally.
3. Stir in the lime juice and parsley and remove from the heat.
4. Serve hot.

Nutrition:
Calories: 224
Fat: 17.5g
Carbohydrates: 10g
Fiber: 3.4g
Sugar: 3.3g
Protein: 9.4g
Sodium: 51mg

---

445. Potatoes with Parsley

Preparation Time: 10 minutes **Cooking Time:** 5 minutes **Servings:** 4

Ingredients:
- 3 tablespoons margarine, divided
- 2 pounds medium red potatoes (about 2 ounces each), halved lengthwise
- 1 clove garlic, minced
- ½ teaspoon salt
- ½ cup low-sodium chicken broth
- 2 tablespoons chopped fresh parsley

Directions:
1. Place 1 tablespoon margarine in the inner pot of the Instant Pot and select Sauté.
2. After margarine is melted, add potatoes, garlic, and salt, stirring well.
3. Sauté 4 minutes, stirring frequently.
4. Add chicken broth and stir well.
5. Seal lids make sure vent is on sealing, then select Manual for 5 minutes on high pressure.
6. When cooking time is done, manually release the pressure.
7. Strain potatoes toss with remaining 2 tablespoons margarine and chopped parsley and serve immediately.

Nutrition:
Calorie: 237
Fat: 9g
Protein: 5g
Carbs: 37g
Sugars: 3g
Fiber: 4g
Sodium: 389mg

---

446. Peas with Mushrooms and Thyme

Preparation Time: 10 minutes **Cooking Time:** 10 minutes **Servings:** 6

Ingredients:
- 2 tsp. olive, canola or soybean oil
- 1 medium onion, diced
- 1 cup sliced fresh mushrooms
- 1 bag frozen sweet peas
- ¼ tsp. coarse (kosher or sea) salt
- ⅛ tsp. white pepper
- 1 tsp. chopped fresh or ¼ tsp. dried thyme leaves

Directions:
1. In 10-inch skillet, warmth oil over medium heat. Attach onion and mushrooms; cook 3 minutes, stirring occasionally. Stir in peas. Cook 3 to 5 minutes until vegetables are tender.
2. Set with salt, pepper and thyme. Serve immediately.

Nutrition:
Calorie: 80
Fat: 1.5g
Protein: 4g
Carbs: 11g
Sugars: 4g
Fiber: 2g
Sodium: 150mg

447. Sautéed Mixed Vegetables

Preparation Time: 20 minutes **Cooking Time:** 8 minutes **Servings:** 4

Ingredients:
- 2 teaspoons extra-virgin olive oil
- 2 carrots, peeled and sliced
- 4 cups broccoli florets
- 4 cups cauliflower florets
- 1 red bell pepper slice into long strips
- 1 cup green beans, trimmed
- Sea salt
- Freshly ground black pepper

Directions:
1. Set a skillet over medium heat and attach the olive oil.
2. Sauté the carrots, broccoli, and cauliflower until tender-crisp, about 6 minutes.
3. Add the bell pepper and green beans, and sauté 2 minutes more.
4. Season with salt and pepper and serve.

Nutrition:
Calories: 106
Fat: 3g
Cholesterol: 0mg
Sodium: 142mg
Carbohydrates: 18g
Sugar: 1.7g
Fiber: 7g.
Protein: 6g

448. Zucchini Noodles with Lime-Basil Pesto

Preparation Time: 20 minutes **Cooking Time:** 0 minutes **Servings:** 4

Ingredients:
- 2 cups packed fresh basil leaves
- ½ cup pine nuts
- 2 teaspoons minced garlic
- Zest and juice of 1 lime
- Pinch sea salt
- Pinch freshly ground black pepper
- ¼ cup extra-virgin olive oil
- 4 green or yellow zucchini, rinsed, dried, and julienned or spiralized
- 1 tomato, diced

Directions:
1. Place the basil, pine nuts, garlic, lime zest, lime juice, salt, and pepper in a food processor or a blender and pulse until very finely chopped.
2. While the machine is running, add the olive oil in a thin stream until a thick paste form.
3. In a large bowl, merge the zucchini noodles and tomato. Add the pesto by the tablespoonful until you have the desired flavor. Serve the zucchini pasta immediately.

Nutrition:
Calories: 261
Fat: 23g
Cholesterol: 0mg
Sodium: 80mg
Carbohydrates: 10g
Sugar: 5g
Fiber: 3g
Protein: 5g

449. Spaghetti Squash with Sun-Dried Tomatoes

Preparation Time: 20 minutes **Cooking Time:** 1 hour 15 minutes **Servings:** 4

Ingredients:
- 1 spaghetti squash, halved and seeded
- 3 teaspoons extra-virgin olive oil, divided
- ¼ sweet onion, chopped
- 1 teaspoon minced garlic
- 2 cups fresh spinach
- ¼ cup chopped sun-dried tomatoes
- ¼ cup roasted sunflower seeds
- ½ lemon Juice
- Sea salt and ground black pepper

Directions:
1. Warmth the oven to 350F. Set a baking sheet with parchment paper.
2. Bring the squash on the baking sheet and garnish the cut edges with 2 teaspoons of olive oil.
3. Bake the squash until it is crisp and separates into strands with a fork, about 1 hour.
4. Let the squash cool then use a fork to scrape out the strands from both halves of the squash. Cover the squash strands and set them aside.
5. Set a skillet over medium-high heat and attach the remaining 1 teaspoon of olive oil. Sauté the onion and garlic.
6. Whisk in the spinach and sun-dried tomatoes, and sauté until the spinach is wilted, about 4 minutes.
7. Detach the skillet from the heat and stir in the squash strands, sunflower seeds, and lemon juice.
8. Set with salt and pepper and serve warm.

Nutrition:
Calories: 103
Fat: 6g
Cholesterol: 0mg
Sodium: 163mg
Carbohydrates: 13g
Sugar: 2g
Fiber: 1g
Protein: 3g

450. Sun-Dried Tomato Brussels Sprouts

Preparation Time: 15 minutes **Cooking Time:** 20 minutes **Servings:** 4

Ingredients:
- 1 pound Brussels sprouts, trimmed and halved
- 1 tablespoon extra-virgin olive oil
- Sea salt
- Freshly ground black pepper
- ½ cup sun-dried tomatoes, chopped
- 2 tablespoons freshly squeezed lemon juice
- 1 teaspoon lemon zest

Directions:
1. Preheat the oven to 400F. Set a large baking sheet with aluminum foil.
2. In a large bowl, toss the Brussels sprouts with oil and season with salt and pepper.
3. Spread the Brussels sprouts on the baking sheet in a single layer.
4. Roast the sprouts until they are caramelized, about 20 minutes.
5. Transfer the sprouts to a serving bowl. Mix in the sun-dried tomatoes, lemon juice, and lemon zest.
6. Stir to combine and serve.

Nutrition:
Calories: 110
Fat: 6g
Cholesterol: 0mg
Sodium: 105mg
Carbohydrates: 14g
Sugar: 3g
Fiber: 5g
Protein: 5g

451. Pico de Gallo Navy Beans

Preparation Time: 20 minutes **Cooking Time:** 0 minutes **Servings:** 4

Ingredients:
- 2½ cups cooked navy beans
- 1 tomato, diced
- ½ red bell pepper, minced and seeded
- ¼ jalapeño pepper, chopped
- 1 scallion, white and green parts, chopped
- 1 teaspoon minced garlic
- 1 teaspoon ground cumin
- ½ teaspoon ground coriander
- ½ cup low-sodium feta cheese

Directions:
1. Put the beans, tomato, bell pepper, jalapeño, scallion, garlic, cumin, and coriander in a medium bowl and stir until well mixed.
2. Top with the feta cheese and serve.

Nutrition:
Calories: 224
Fat: 4g
Cholesterol: 13mg
Sodium: 164mg
Carbohydrates: 34g
Sugar: 2g
Fiber: 13g
Protein: 14g

452. Fennel and Chickpeas

Preparation Time: 10 minutes **Cooking Time:** 20 minutes **Servings:** 6

Ingredients:
- 1 tablespoon extra-virgin olive oil
- 1 small fennel bulb, trimmed and cut into ¼-inch-thick slices
- 1 sweet onion, thinly sliced
- 1 (15½-ounce) can sodium-free chickpeas, rinsed and drained
- 1 cup low-sodium chicken broth
- 2 tsp. fresh thyme
- ¼ tsp. sea salt
- ¼ tsp. freshly ground black pepper
- 1 tbsp. butter

Directions:
1. Set a saucepan over medium-high heat and attach the oil.
2. Sauté the fennel and onion until tender and lightly browned, about 10 minutes.
3. Add the chickpeas, broth, thyme, salt, and pepper.
4. Secure and cook, stirring occasionally, until the liquid has reduced by about half.
5. Detach the pan from the heat and stir in the butter.
6. Serve hot.

Nutrition:
Calories: 215
Fat: 5g
Cholesterol: 5mg
Sodium: 253mg
Carbohydrates: 32g
Sugar: 2g
Fiber: 15g
Protein: 12g

453. Italian Roasted Vegetables

Preparation Time: 15 minutes **Cooking Time:** 20 minutes **Servings:** 4

Ingredients:
- 2 tablespoons extra-virgin olive oil
- 2 teaspoons chopped fresh oregano
- 1 teaspoon chopped fresh basil
- 1 teaspoon minced garlic
- ½ pound whole cremini mushrooms
- 2 cups cauliflower florets
- 1 zucchini, cut into 1-inch chunks
- 2 cups cherry tomatoes
- Sea salt
- Freshly ground black pepper

Directions:
1. Preheat the oven to 400F. Line a baking sheet with aluminum foil.
2. In a bowl, merge together the oil, oregano, basil, and garlic.
3. Add the mushrooms, cauliflower, zucchini, and cherry tomatoes and toss to coat.
4. Set the vegetables to the baking sheet and roast until they are tender and lightly browned, about 20 minutes.
5. Season with salt and pepper and serve.

Nutrition:
Calories: 115
Fat: 8g
Cholesterol: 0mg
Sodium: 86mg
Carbohydrates: 11g
Sugar: 3.5g
Fiber: 4g
Protein: 4g

454. Roasted Eggplant with Goat Cheese

Preparation Time: 15 minutes **Cooking Time:** 20 minutes **Servings:** 4

Ingredients:
- 1 pound eggplant, cut into 1-inch chunks
- 2 tablespoons extra-virgin olive oil

- Sea salt
- Freshly ground black pepper
- 2 tablespoons balsamic vinegar
- 2 ounces goat cheese, crumbled
- 2 teaspoons chopped fresh basil

Directions:
1. Preheat the oven to 400F. Line a baking sheet with aluminum foil.
2. In a bowl, merge the eggplant with the oil.
3. Season generously with salt and pepper.
4. Scatter the eggplant on the baking sheet and roast, turning once, until the eggplant is caramelized and tender, about 20 minutes.
5. Set the eggplant to a serving bowl and toss with the vinegar.
6. Top with the goat cheese and basil and serve immediately.

Nutrition:
Calories: 154
Fat: 12g
Cholesterol: 15mg
Sodium: 110mg
Carbohydrates: 7g
Sugar: 4g
Fiber: 4g
Protein: 5g

455. Roasted Cinnamon Celery Root

Preparation Time: 10 minutes **Cooking Time:** 20 minutes **Servings:** 4

Ingredients:
- 2 celery roots (about 1 pound total), peeled and diced
- 1 teaspoon extra-virgin olive oil
- 1 teaspoon butter, melted
- ½ teaspoon ground cinnamon
- Sea salt
- Freshly ground black pepper

Directions:
1. Preheat the oven to 350F. Line a baking sheet with aluminum foil.
2. In a large bowl, set the celery roots with the oil.
3. Set the roots to the baking sheet and roast until very tender, about 20 minutes.
4. Detach them from the oven and transfer to a bowl.
5. Add the butter and cinnamon to the bowl and use a potato masher to mash the roots until fluffy.
6. Season with salt and pepper. Serve warm.

Nutrition:
Calories: 117
Fat: 3g
Cholesterol: 3mg
Sodium: 299mg
Carbohydrates: 22g
Sugar: 2.4g
Fiber: 4g
Protein: 4g

456. Roasted Beets, Carrots, and Parsnips

Preparation Time: 10 minutes **Cooking Time:** 30 minutes **Servings:** 4

Ingredients:
- 1 pound beets, peeled and quartered
- ½ pound carrots, peeled and set into chunks
- ½ pound parsnips, peeled and cut into chunks
- 1 tablespoon extra-virgin olive oil
- 1 teaspoon apple cider vinegar
- Sea salt
- Freshly ground black pepper

Directions:
1. Preheat the oven to 375F. Line a baking tray with aluminum foil.
2. In a large bowl, set the beets, carrots, and parsnips with the oil and vinegar until everything is well coated. Spread them out on the baking sheet.
3. Fry until the vegetables are tender and lightly caramelized, about 30 minutes.
4. Transfer the vegetables to a serving bowl, season with salt and pepper, and serve warm.

Nutrition:
Calories: 148
Fat: 4g
Cholesterol: 0mg
Sodium: 196mg
Carbohydrates: 27g
Sugar: 15g
Fiber: 6g
Protein: 3g

457. Vegetable Medley

Preparation Time: 20 minutes **Cooking Time:** 2 minutes **Servings:** 8

Ingredients:
- 2 medium parsnips
- 4 medium carrots
- 1 turnip, about 4½ inches diameter
- 1 cup water
- 1 teaspoon salt
- 3 tablespoons stevia
- 2 tablespoons canola or olive oil
- ½ teaspoon salt

Directions:
1. Wash and peel vegetables. Cut in 1-inch pieces.
2. Set the cup of water and 1 tsp. salt into the inner pot with the vegetables.
3. Secure the lid and choose Manual and set for 2 minutes.
4. When done, take off the pressure manually and choose Cancel. Spill the water from the inner pot.
5. Choose Sauté and stir in stevia, oil, and salt. Cook until stevia is dissolved. Serve.

Nutrition:
Calories: 63
Fat: 2g
Protein: 1g
Carbs: 12g
Sugars: 1.1g
Fiber: 2g
Sodium: 327mg

458. Best Brown Rice

Preparation Time: 5 minutes **Cooking Time:** 22 minutes **Servings:** 6-12

Ingredients:
- 2 cups brown rice
- 2½ cups water

Directions:
1. Wash brown rice in a fine-mesh strainer.
2. Attach rice and water to the inner pot of the Instant Pot and secure the lid
3. Choose Manual and select 22 minutes and cook on high pressure.
4. When cooking time is done, Cancel and manually release any remaining pressure.

Nutrition:
Calories: 114
Fat: 1g
Protein: 2g
Carbs: 23g
Sugars: 0g
Fiber: 1g
Sodium: 3mg

459. Vegetable Curry

Preparation Time: 25 minutes **Cooking Time:** 3 minutes **Servings:** 10

Ingredients:
- 1 package baby carrots
- 3 medium potatoes, unpeeled, cubed
- 1lb. fresh or frozen green beans, set in 2-inch pieces
- 1 medium green pepper, minced
- 1 medium onion, minced
- 1 to 2 cloves garlic, minced
- 1 can garbanzo beans, drained
- 1 (28-ounce) can crushed tomatoes
- 3 tsp. curry powder
- 1½ teaspoons chicken bouillon granules
- 1¾ cups boiling water
- 3 tbsp. minute tapioca

Directions:
1. Merge the carrots, potatoes, green beans, pepper, onion, garlic, garbanzo beans, minced tomatoes, and curry powder in the Instant Pot.
2. Set bouillon in boiling water, then spill in tapioca. Spill over the contents of the Instant Pot and stir.
3. Secure the lid and choose Manual and set for 3 minutes.
4. When done, manually release the pressure.

Nutrition:
Calories: 166
Fat: 1g
Protein: 6g
Carbs: 35g
Sugars: 1.4g
Fiber: 8g
Sodium: 436mg

460. Parmesan Cauliflower Mash

Preparation Time: 7 minutes **Cooking Time:** 5 minutes **Servings:** 4

Ingredients:
- 1 head cauliflower, cored and divide into large florets
- ½ tsp. kosher salt
- ½ tsp. garlic pepper
- 2 tbsp. plain Greek yogurt
- ¾ cup freshly grated Parmesan cheese
- 1 tbsp. unsalted butter or ghee (optional)
- Chopped fresh chives

Directions:
1. Spill 1 cup of water into the electric pressure cooker and insert a steamer basket or wire rack.
2. Set the cauliflower in the basket.
3. Secure and lock the lid of the pressure cooker. Set the valve to sealing.
4. Cook on high pressure for 5 minutes.
5. When the cooking is done, hit Cancel and quick free the pressure.
6. Once the pin drops, unlock and detach the lid.
7. Detach the cauliflower from the pot and pour out the water. Return the cauliflower to the pot and attach the salt, garlic pepper, yogurt, and cheese. Use a blender or potato masher to press the cauliflower in the pot.
8. Set into a serving bowl, and garnish with butter (if using) and chives.

Nutrition:
Calories: 141
Fat: 6g
Protein: 12g
Carbs: 12g
Sugars: 1g
Fiber: 4g
Sodium: 592mg

461. Lemony Brussels Sprouts with Poppy Seeds

Preparation Time: 10 minutes **Cooking Time:** 2 minutes **Servings:** 4

Ingredients:
- 1lb. (454 g) Brussels sprouts
- 2 tbsp. avocado oil
- 1 cup vegetable or chicken bone broth
- 1 tbsp. minced garlic
- ½ tsp. kosher salt
- Freshly ground black pepper, to taste
- ½ medium lemon
- ½ tablespoon poppy seeds

Directions:
1. Set the Brussels sprouts by cutting off the stem ends and detaching any loose outer leaves. Cut each in half lengthwise.
2. Bring the electric pressure cooker to the Sauté setting. When the pot is warmth, pour in 1 tablespoon of the avocado oil.
3. Attach half of the Brussels sprouts to the pot, cut-side down, and let them brown for 3 to 5 minutes without disturbing. Set to a bowl and add the remaining tablespoon of avocado oil and the remaining Brussels sprouts to the pot. Choose Cancel and return all the Brussels sprouts to the pot.
4. Attach the broth, garlic, salt, and a few grinds of pepper. Set to distribute the seasonings.
5. Secure the lid of the pressure cooker. Set the valve to sealing.
6. Cook on high pressure for 2 minutes.
7. While the Brussels sprouts are processing, zest the lemon, then cut it into quarters.
8. When the cooking is done, hit Cancel and quick free the pressure.
9. Once the pin drops, unlock and detach the lid.
10. Using a slotted spoon, set the Brussels sprouts to a serving bowl. Set with the lemon zest, a squeeze of lemon juice, and the poppy seeds. Serve immediately.

Nutrition:
Calories: 125　　Carbs: 13g　　Sodium: 504mg
Fat: 8g　　Sugars: 3g
Protein: 4g　　Fiber: 5g

462. Corn on the Cob

Preparation Time: 10 minutes　　**Cooking Time:** 5 minutes　　**Servings:** 12

Ingredients:
- 6 ears corn

Directions:
1. Detach the husks and silk from the corn. Cut or break each ear in half.
2. Spill 1 cup of water into the bottom of the electric pressure cooker. Insert a wire rack or trivet.
3. Set the corn upright on the rack, cut-side down. Secure the lid of the pressure cooker.
4. Cook on high pressure for 5 minutes.
5. When the cooking is done, choose Cancel and quick free the pressure.
6. Once the pin drops, unlock and detach the lid.
7. Use tongs to detach the corn from the pot. Season as desired and serve immediately.

Nutrition:
Calories: 62　　Carbs: 14g　　Sodium: 11mg
Fat: 1g　　Sugars: 5g
Protein: 2g　　Fiber: 1g

463. Parmesan-Topped Acorn Squash

Preparation Time: 10 minutes　　**Cooking Time:** 20 minutes　　**Servings:** 4

Ingredients:
- 1 acorn squash (454 g)
- 1 tbsp. extra-virgin olive oil
- 1 tsp. dried sage leaves, crumbled
- ¼ tsp. freshly grated nutmeg
- ⅛ tsp. kosher salt
- ⅛ tsp. freshly ground black pepper
- 2 tbsp. freshly grated Parmesan cheese

Directions:
1. Set the acorn squash in half lengthwise and remove the seeds. Set each half in half for a total of 4 wedges.
2. In a small bowl, merge the olive oil, sage, nutmeg, salt, and pepper. Garnish the cut sides of the squash with the olive oil.
3. Spill 1 cup of water into the electric pressure cooker and insert a wire rack or trivet.
4. Ser the squash on the trivet in a single layer, skin-side down.
5. Secure the lid of the pressure cooker.
6. Cook on high pressure for 20 minutes.
7. When the cooking is done, choose Cancel and quick release the pressure.
8. Once the pin drops, unlock and detach the lid.
9. Carefully detach the squash from the pot, sprinkle with the Parmesan, and serve.

Nutrition:
Calories: 85　　Carbs: 12g　　Sodium: 282mg
Fat: 4g　　Sugars: 0g
Protein: 2g　　Fiber: 2g

464. Wild Rice Salad with Cranberries and Almonds

Preparation Time: 10 minutes　　**Cooking Time:** 25 minutes　　**Servings:** 8

Ingredients:

Rice:
- 2 cups wild rice blend, washed
- 1 tsp. kosher salt
- 2½ cups vegetable or chicken bone broth

Dressing:
- ¼ cup extra-virgin olive oil
- ¼ cup white wine vinegar
- 1½ tsp. grated orange zest
- ¼ cup Juice of orange
- 1 teaspoon honey or pure maple syrup

Salad:
- ¾ cup unsweetened dried cranberries
- ½ cup sliced almonds, toasted
- Freshly ground black pepper, to taste

Directions:

Make the Rice
1. In the electric pressure cooker, merge the rice, salt, and broth. Secure the lid and cook on high pressure for 25 minutes.
2. When the cooking is done, choose Cancel and allow the pressure to release naturally for 15 minutes, then quick release any remaining pressure.
3. Once the pin drops, unlock and detach the lid. Let the rice cool briefly, then set it with a fork.

Make the Dressing
4. In a jar with a screw-top lid, merge the olive oil, vinegar, zest, juice, and honey. Shake to merged.

Make the Salad:
5. In a large bowl, merge the rice, cranberries, and almonds.
6. Attach the dressing and season with pepper. Serve warm or refrigerate.

Nutrition:
Calories: 126
Fat: 5g
Protein: 3g
Carbs: 18g
Sugars: 2g
Fiber: 2g
Sodium: 120mg

465. Tempeh in Tomato Sauce

Preparation Time: 10 minutes **Cooking Time:** 60 minutes **Servings:** 1

Ingredients:
- 1 tablespoon olive oil, divided
- 4 ounces tempeh, cut into ½-inch slices horizontally
- ¼ of small onion, chopped
- 1 garlic clove, minced
- ⅛ teaspoon dried oregano, crushed
- ⅛ teaspoon dried thyme, crushed
- ¼ teaspoon red chili powder
- 1 large tomato, chopped finely
- ¼ teaspoon balsamic vinegar
- 2 drops liquid stevia
- Pinch of salt

Directions:
1. Preheat your oven to 350 F.
2. In a small non-stick skillet, warmth ½ tablespoon of oil over medium-high heat and cook tempeh slices for about 5 minutes per side. Transfer the cooked tempeh slices into a paper towel lined plate.
3. In another non-stick skillet, warmth remaining oil over medium-low heat and sauté onion, garlic, herbs and chili powder for about 4-5 minutes. Add tomato and cook for about 2-3 minute. Stir in vinegar, stevia and salt and remove from the heat and top with tomato mixture. With a piece of foil, cover the casserole dish. Bake for approximately 1 hour.
4. Serve hot.

Nutrition:
Calories: 308
Fat: 17.5g
Carbohydrates: 15g
Sugar: 3.1g
Protein: 22.2g

Snacks

466. Chicken and Mushrooms

Preparation Time: 10 minutes **Cooking Time:** 15 minutes **Servings:** 6

Ingredients:
- 2 chicken breasts
- 1 cup of sliced white champignons
- 1 cup of sliced green chilies
- ½ cup scallions hacked
- 1 teaspoon of chopped garlic
- 1 cup of low-fat cheddar shredded cheese (1-1.5 lb. grams fat / ounce)
- 1 tablespoon of olive oil
- 1 tablespoon of butter

Directions:
1. Fry the chicken breasts with olive oil.
2. When needed, salt and pepper.
3. Grill breasts of chicken in a plate with grill.
4. For every serving, weigh 4 ounces of chicken. (Make two servings, save leftovers for another meal).
5. In a butter pan, stir in mushrooms, green peppers, scallions, and garlic until smooth, and a little dark.
6. Place the chicken in a baking platter.
7. Cover with mushroom combination.
8. Top on ham.
9. Place the cheese in a 350 oven until it melts.

Nutrition:
Carbohydrates: 2 g
Protein: 23 g
Fat: 11 g
Cholesterol: 112 mg
Sodium: 198 mg
Potassium: 261 mg

467. Cheeseburger Pie

Preparation Time: 20 minutes **Cooking Time:** 90 minutes **Servings:** 4

Ingredients:
- 1 large spaghetti squash
- 1 lb. lean ground beef
- ¼ cup diced onion
- 2 eggs
- ⅓ cup low-fat, plain Greek yogurt
- 2 tbsp. tomato sauce
- ½ tsp. Worcestershire sauce
- ⅔ cup reduced-fat, shredded cheddar cheese
- 2 oz. dill pickle slices
- Cooking spray

Directions:
1. Preheat oven to 400F. Slice spaghetti squash in half lengthwise; dismiss pulp and seeds.
2. Spray insides with cooking spray.
3. Place squash halves cut-side-down onto a foil-lined baking sheet and bake for 30 minutes.
4. Once cooked, let cool to before scraping squash flesh with a fork to remove spaghetti-like strands; set aside.
5. Push squash strands in the bottom and up sides of the greased pie pan, creating an even layer.
6. Meanwhile, set up pie filling.
7. With a medium-sized skillet, cook beef and onion over medium heat 8 to 10 minutes, sometimes stirring, until meat is brown.
8. Drain and remove from heat.
9. In a medium-sized bowl, whisk together eggs, tomato paste, Greek yogurt, and Worcestershire sauce. Spill in ground beef mixture.
10. Set pie filling over squash crust.
11. Drizzle meat filling with cheese, and then top with dill pickle slices.
12. Bake for 40 minutes.

Nutrition:
Calories: 409
Fat: 24.49 g
Carbohydrates: 15.06 g
Protein: 30.69 g

468. Salmon Feta and Pesto Wrap

Preparation Time: 15 minutes **Cooking Time:** 10 minutes **Servings:** 4

Ingredients:
- 8 ounces (250 g) smoked salmon fillet, thinly sliced
- 1 cup (150 g) feta cheese
- 8 (15 g) Romaine lettuce leaves
- 4 (6-inch) pita bread
- ¼ cup (60 g) basil pesto sauce

Directions:
1. Place 1 pita bread on a plate. Top with lettuce, salmon, feta cheese, and pesto sauce. Fold or roll to enclose filling. Repeat procedure for the remaining ingredients.
2. Serve and enjoy.

Nutrition:
Calories: 379
Fat 17.7 g
Carbohydrates: 36.6 g
Protein: 18.4 g
Sodium: 554 mg

469. Salmon Cream Cheese and Onion on Bagel

Preparation Time: 15 minutes **Cooking Time:** 10 minutes **Servings:** 4

Ingredients:
- 8 ounces (250 g) smoked salmon fillet, thinly sliced
- ½ cup (125 g) cream cheese
- 1 medium (110 g) onion, thinly sliced
- 4 bagels (about 80g each), split
- 2 tablespoons (7 g) fresh parsley, chopped
- Freshly ground black pepper, to taste

Directions:
1. Spread the cream cheese on each bottom's half of bagels. Top with salmon and onion, season with pepper, sprinkle with parsley and then cover with bagel tops.
2. Serve and enjoy.

Nutrition:
Calories: 309
Fat 14.1 g
Carbohydrates 32.0 g
Protein 14.7 g
Sodium 571 mg

470. Melon Cucumber Salad

Preparation Time: 2 minutes **Cooking Time:** 3 minutes **Servings:** 5

Ingredients:
- ¼ cup of finely hashed sweet onion like Vidalia
- ⅓ cup of white balsamic vinegar see note
- 2 garlic cloves finely minced
- kosher salt
- freshly ground black pepper
- 1 lime
- 1 medium melon honeydew, cantaloupe, Crenshaw, canary, etc., cut into rounds with a melon baller
- 1 12-inch English or hothouse cucumber, sliced
- 2 tablespoons of extra virgin olive oil

Directions:
1. Peel the lime and then squeeze it.
2. In a bowl, mix the melon balls, onion, cucumber, and lime zest.

Making the dressing:
1. Add the garlic cloves, lime juice, salt, and pepper.
2. Whisk until well combined. Continue whisking and spill in the olive oil in a steady stream.
3. Spill the dressing over the melon mixture and stir to coat.
4. Let stand; refrigerate until ready to serve.

Nutrition:
Calories: 88.4
Fat: 7.6 g
Carbohydrates: 3.9 g
Protein: 2.5 g

471. Greek Baklava

Preparation Time: 20 minutes **Cooking Time:** 20 minutes **Servings:** 18

Ingredients:

- 1 (16 oz.) package phyllo dough
- 1 lb. chopped nuts
- 1 cup butter
- 1 teaspoon ground cinnamon
- 1 cup water
- 1 teaspoon. vanilla extract
- ½ cup honey

Directions:

1. Preheat the oven to 175C or 350F. Set butter on the sides and bottom of a 9-in by 13-in pan.
2. Chop the nuts then mix with cinnamon; set it aside. Unfurl the phyllo dough then halve the whole stack to fit the pan. Use a damp cloth to cover the phyllo to prevent drying as you proceed. Put two phyllo sheets in the pan then butter well. Repeat to make eight layered phyllo sheets. Scatter 2-3 tablespoons. nut mixture over the sheets then places two more phyllo sheets on top, butter then sprinkle with nuts. Layer as you go. The final layer should be six to eight phyllo sheets deep.
3. Make square or diamond shapes with a sharp knife up to the bottom of pan. You can slice into four long rows for diagonal shapes. Bake until crisp and golden for 50 minutes.
4. Meanwhile, boil water and melts to make the sauce; mix in honey and vanilla. Let it simmer for 20 minutes.
5. Take off the baklava out of the oven then drizzle with sauce right away; cool. Serve the baklava in cupcake papers. You can also freeze them without cover. The baklava will turn soggy when wrapped.

Nutrition:
Calories: 393
Carbohydrates: 37.5 g
Cholesterol: 27 mg
Total Fat: 25.9 g
Protein: 6.1 g
Sodium: 196 mg

472. Glazed Bananas in Phyllo Nut Cups

Preparation Time: 30 minutes **Cooking Time:** 45 minutes **Servings:** 6 servings.

Ingredients:

- ¾ cup shelled pistachios
- 1 teaspoon. ground cinnamon

Sauce:

- ¾ cup butter, cubed
- 3 medium firm bananas, sliced
- 4 sheets phyllo dough, (14 inches x 9 inches)
- ¼ cup butter, melted
- ¼ teaspoon. ground cinnamon
- 3 to 4 cups vanilla ice cream

Directions:

1. Finely chop pistachios in a food processor; move to a bowl then mix in cinnamon. Slice each phyllo sheet to 6 four-inch squares, get rid of the trimmings. Pile the squares then use plastic wrap to cover.
2. Slather melted butter on each square one at a time then scatter a heaping tablespoonful of pistachio mixture. Pile 3 squares; flip each at an angle to misalign the corners. Force each stack on the sides and bottom of an oiled eight-oz. custard cup. Bake for 15-20 minutes in a 350F oven until golden; cool for 5 minutes. Set to a wire rack to completely cool.
3. Melt and boil butter in a saucepan to make the sauce, lower heat. Mix in cinnamon and bananas gently, heat completely. Put ice cream in the phyllo cups until full then put banana sauce on top. Serve right away.

Nutrition:
Calories: 735
Carbohydrates: 82 g
Cholesterol: 111 mg
Fat: 45 g
Fiber: 3 g
Protein: 7 g
Sodium: 468 mg

473. Salmon Apple Salad Sandwich

Preparation Time: 15 minutes **Cooking Time:** 10 minutes **Servings:** 4

Ingredients:

- 4 ounces (125 g) canned pink salmon, drained and flaked
- 1 medium (180 g) red apple, cored and diced
- 1 celery stalk (about 60 g), chopped
- 1 shallot (about 40 g), finely chopped
- ⅓ cup (85 g) light mayonnaise
- 8 slices whole grain bread (about 30 g each), toasted
- 8 (15 g) Romaine lettuce leaves
- Salt and freshly ground black pepper

Directions:

1. Combine the salmon, apple, celery, shallot, and mayonnaise in a mixing bowl. Season with salt and pepper.
2. Place 1 slices bread on a plate, top with lettuce and salmon salad, and then covers with another slice of bread. Repeat procedure for the remaining ingredients.
3. Serve and enjoy.

Nutrition:
Calories: 315
Fat: 11.3 g
Carbohydrates: 40.4 g
Protein: 15.1 g
Sodium: 469 mg

474. Smoked Salmon and Cheese on Rye Bread

Preparation Time: 15 minutes **Cooking Time:** 10 minutes **Servings:** 4

Ingredients:

- 8 ounces (250 g) smoked salmon, thinly sliced
- ⅓ cup (85 g) mayonnaise
- 2 tablespoons (30 ml) lemon juice
- 1 tablespoon (15 g) Dijon mustard
- 1 teaspoon (3 g) garlic, minced
- 4 slices cheddar cheese (about 2 oz. or 30 g each)
- 8 slices rye bread (about 2 oz. or 30 g each)
- 8 (15 g) Romaine lettuce leaves

- Salt and freshly ground black pepper

Directions:
1. Mix the mayonnaise, lemon juice, mustard, and garlic in a small bowl. Flavor with salt and pepper and keep aside.
2. Spread dressing on 4 bread slices. Top with lettuce, salmon, and cheese. Cover with remaining rye bread slices.
3. Serve and enjoy.

Nutrition:
Calories: 365
Fat: 16.6 g
Carbohydrates: 31.6 g
Protein: 18.8 g
Sodium: 951 mg

475. Pan-Fried Trout

Preparation Time: 15 minutes **Cooking Time:** 10 minutes **Servings:** 4

Ingredients:
- 1 ¼ pounds trout fillets
- ⅓ cup white, or yellow, cornmeal
- ¼ teaspoon anise seeds
- ¼ teaspoon black pepper
- ½ cup minced cilantro, or parsley
- Vegetable cooking spray
- Lemon wedges

Directions:
1. Coat fish with combined cornmeal, spices, and cilantro, pressing it gently into fish. Set large skillet with cooking spray, heat over medium heat until hot.
2. Add fish and cook until fish is tender and flakes with fork, about 5 minutes on each side. Serve with lemon wedges.

Nutrition:
Calories: 207
Carbohydrates: 19 g
Cholesterol: 27 mg
Fat: 16 g
Fiber: 4 g
Protein: 18g

476. Lemon Cream Fruit Dip

Preparation Time: 5 minutes **Cooking Time:** 0 minutes **Servings:** 4

Ingredients:
- 1 cup (200 g) plain nonfat Greek yogurt
- ¼ cup (28 g) coconut flour 1 tbsp (15 ml) pure maple syrup
- ½ tsp. pure vanilla extract
- ½ tsp. pure almond extract
- Zest of 1 medium lemon
- Juice of ½ medium lemon

Directions:
1. In a medium bowl, merge together the yogurt, coconut flour, maple syrup, vanilla, almond extract, lemon zest, and lemon juice. Serve the dip with fruit or crackers.

Nutrition:
Calories: 80
Fat: 1g
Protein: 7g
Carbs: 10g
Sugar: 6g
Fiber: 3g
Sodium: 37mg

477. Greek Salad Kabobs

Preparation Time: 15 minutes **Cooking Time:** 0 minutes **Servings:** 24

Ingredients:
Dip:
- ¾ cup plain fat-free yogurt
- 2 teaspoons honey
- 2 teaspoons chopped fresh dill weed

Kabobs
- 24 cocktail picks or toothpicks
- 24 pitted kalamata olives
- 24 small grape tomatoes
- 2 teaspoons chopped fresh oregano leaves
- ¼ teaspoon salt
- 1 small clove garlic, finely chopped
- 12 slices (½ inch) English (seedless) cucumber, cut in half crosswise

Directions:
1. In small bowl, mix dip ingredients; set aside. 2 On each cocktail pick, thread 1 olive, 1 tomato and 1 half-slice cucumber. Serve kabobs with dip.

Nutrition:
Calories: 15
Fat: 0.5g
Protein: 0g
Carbohydrates: 2g
Sugars: 1g
Fiber: 0g
Sodium: 70mg

478. Green Goddess White Bean Dip

Preparation Time: 1 minute **Cooking Time:** 45 minutes **Servings:** 3

Ingredients:
- 1 cup dried navy, great Northern, or cannellini beans
- 4 cups water
- 2 teaspoons fine sea salt
- 3 tablespoons fresh lemon juice
- 1 tbsp. and ¼ cup extra-virgin olive oil
- ¼ cup firmly packed flat-leaf parsley leaves
- 1 bunch chives, chopped
- Leaves from 2 tarragon sprigs
- Freshly ground black pepper

Directions:
1. Combine the beans, water, and 1 teaspoon of the salt in the Instant Pot and stir to dissolve the salt.
2. Seal the lid and set the Pressure Release to Sealing. Press the Bean/Chili, Pressure Cook, or Manual setting and set the cooking time for 30 minutes at high pressure if using navy or Great Northern beans or 40 minutes at high pressure if using cannellini beans.
3. When the cooking program is done, release the pressure naturally for 15 minutes. Unseal the pot and scoop out and reserve ½ cup of the cooking liquid.
4. In a food processor or blender, merge the beans, ½ cup cooking liquid, lemon juice, ¼ cup of olive oil, ½ tsp. parsley, chives, tarragon, remaining 1 teaspoon salt, and ½ teaspoon pepper. Process or blend on medium speed, stopping to scrape down the sides of the container as needed, for about 1 minute, until the mixture is smooth.
5. Transfer the dip to a serving bowl. Set with the remaining 1 tbsp. olive oil and set with a few grinds of pepper. Serve at room temperature or chilled.

Nutrition:
Calories: 70
Fat: 5g
Protein: 3g
Carbohydrates: 8g
Sugars: 1g
Fiber: 4g
Sodium: 782mg

---

479. Vietnamese Meatball Lollipops with Dipping Sauce

Preparation Time: 30 minutes **Cooking Time:** 10 minutes **Servings:** 12

Ingredients:
Meatballs
- 1¼ lb. lean ground turkey
- ¼ cup chopped water chestnuts, drained
- ¼ cup hashed fresh cilantro
- 1 tbsp. cornstarch

Dipping Sauce
- ¼ cup water
- ¼ cup reduced-sodium soy sauce
- 2 tbsp. packed stevia
- 2 tbsp. chopped fresh chives or green onions
- 2 tbsp. fish sauce
- ½ tsp. pepper
- 3 cloves garlic, finely chopped
- 2 tbsp. lime juice
- 2 cloves garlic, finely chopped
- ½ tsp. crushed red pepper
- About 6-inch bamboo skewers

Directions:
1. Heat oven to 400F. Set cookie sheet with foil; spray with cooking spray (or use nonstick foil).
2. In large bowl, merge all meatball ingredients until well mixed. Form into 1¼-inch meatballs. On cookie sheet, set meatballs 1 inch apart. Bake 20 minutes, turning halfway through baking.
3. Meanwhile, in 1-quart saucepan, warmth all dipping sauce ingredients over low heat until stevia is dissolved; keep aside.
4. Insert bamboo skewers into cooked meatballs; set on serving plate. Serve with dipping sauce.

Nutrition:
Calories: 80
Fat: 2.5g
Protein: 10g
Carbohydrates: 5g
Sugars: 1g
Fiber: 0g
Sodium: 440mg

---

480. Blackberry Baked Brie

Preparation Time: 5 minutes **Cooking Time:** 15 minutes **Servings:** 5

Ingredients:
- 8-ounce round Brie
- 1 cup water
- ¼ cup sugar-free blackberry preserves
- 2 teaspoons chopped fresh mint

Directions:
1. Strip a grid pattern into the top of the rind of the Brie with a knife.
2. In a 7-inch round baking dish, set the Brie, and then seal the baking dish securely with foil.
3. Set the trivet into the inner pot of the Instant Pot, spill in the water.
4. Make a foil sling and form it on top of the trivet. Set the baking dish on top of the trivet and foil sling.
5. Seal the lid to the locked position and turn the vent to sealing.
6. Choose the Manual and set the Instant Pot for 15 minutes on high pressure.
7. When cooking time is up, set off the Instant Pot and do a quick release of the pressure.
8. When the valve has dropped, detach the lid, and then remove the baking dish.
9. Detach the top rind of the Brie and top with the preserves. Set with the fresh mint.

Nutrition:
Calories: 133
Fat: 10g
Protein: 8g
Carbohydrates: 4g
Sugars: 0g
Fiber: 0g
Sodium: 238mg

---

481. Creamy Spinach Dip

Preparation Time: 13 minutes **Cooking Time:** 5 minutes **Servings:** 11

Ingredients:
- 8 ounces low-fat cream cheese
- 1 cup low-fat sour cream
- ½ cup finely chopped onion
- ½ cup no-sodium vegetable broth
- 5 cloves garlic, minced
- ½ teaspoon salt

- ¼ teaspoon black pepper
- 10 ounces frozen spinach
- 12 ounces reduced-fat shredded Monterey Jack cheese
- 12 ounces reduced-fat shredded Parmesan cheese

Directions:
1. Attach cream cheese, sour cream, onion, vegetable broth, garlic, salt, pepper, and spinach to the inner pot of the Instant Pot.
2. Seal the lid, make sure vent is set to sealing, and set to the Bean/Chili setting on high pressure for 5 minutes.
3. When finished, do a manual release.
4. Attach the cheeses and mix well until creamy and well merged.

Nutrition:
Calories: 274
Fat: 18g
Protein: 19g
Carbohydrates: 10g
Sugars: 3g
Fiber: 1g
Sodium: 948mg

---

482. Pesto Veggie Pizza

Preparation Time: 20 minutes **Cooking Time:** 15 minutes **Servings:** 2

Ingredients:
- Olive oil, for greasing the parchment paper
- ¼ head cauliflower, cut into florets
- 3 tablespoons almond flour
- ½ teaspoons olive oil
- 1 egg, beaten
- Minced garlic
- Pinch sea salt
- ¼ cup Simple Tomato Sauce (here)
- ¼ zucchini, thinly sliced
- ¼ cup baby spinach leaves
- 2 ½ asparagus spears, woody ends trimmed, cut into 3-inch pieces
- Basil pesto

Directions:
1. Preheat the oven to 450F. Put a baking sheet without a rim in the oven.
2. Prepare a piece of parchment paper by lightly brushing with olive oil and set aside.
3. Set a large saucepan filled halfway with water over high heat and bring it to a boil.
4. Set the cauliflower in a food processor, and pulse until very finely chopped, almost flour consistency.
5. Transfer the ground cauliflower to a fine-mesh sieve and put it over the boiling water for about 1 minute, until the cauliflower is cooked.
6. Wring out all the water from the cauliflower using a kitchen towel. Transfer the cauliflower to a large bowl.
7. Stir in the almond flour, oil, egg, garlic, and salt, and mix to create a thick dough. With your hands, press the ingredients together, and transfer the cauliflower mixture to the parchment paper.
8. Press the mixture out into a flat circle, about ½ inch thick. Slide the parchment paper onto the baking sheet in the oven.
9. Bake the crust.
10. Detach the crust from the oven and spread the sauce evenly to the edges of the crust.
11. Arrange the zucchini, spinach, and asparagus on the pizza.
12. Drizzle the pizza with basil pesto and put it back in the oven for about 2 minutes, until the vegetables are tender. Serve.

Nutrition:
Calories: 107
Protein: 5g
Fat: 7g
Carbohydrates: 4g

---

483. Apple Leather

Preparation Time: 10 minutes **Cooking Time:** 8 to 10 hours **Servings:** 24 strips

Ingredients:
- 5 apples, peeled, cored, and sliced
- ¼ cup water
- 1 teaspoon pure vanilla extract
- ¼ teaspoon ground ginger
- ¼ teaspoon ground cloves

Directions:
1. Put the apples, water, vanilla, ginger, and cloves in a large saucepan over medium heat.
2. Set the mixture to a boil, reduce to low heat, and simmer for about 20 minutes, until the apples are very tender.
3. Set the apple mixture to a food processor, and purée until very smooth.
4. Set the oven on the lowest possible setting.
5. Line a baking sheet with parchment paper.
6. Pour the puréed apple mixture onto the baking sheet and spread it out very thinly and evenly.
7. Set the baking sheet, and bake for 8 to 10 hours, until the leather is smooth and no longer sticky.
8. Cut the apple leather with a pizza cutter into 24 strips, and store this treat in a container in a cool, dark place for up to 2 weeks.

Nutrition:
Calories: 41
Protein: 0.1g
Fat: 0.3g
Carbohydrates: 1.2g

---

484. French bread Pizza

Preparation Time: 5 minutes **Cooking Time:** 2-3 hours **Servings:** 2

Ingredients:
- ½ cup asparagus(diced)
- ½ cup Roma tomatoes(diced)
- ½ cup red bell pepper(diced)
- ½ tablespoon minced garlic
- ½ loaf French bread
- ½ cup pizza sauce
- ½ cup low-fat shredded mozzarella cheese

Directions:
1. Heat the oven to 400F. Coat the baking sheet lightly with a cooking spray.
2. Add the asparagus, tomatoes, and pepper in a little dish. Add the garlic and stir gently to coat uniformly.
3. Adjust the French bread to the baking sheet. Apply ¼ cup of the pizza sauce and ¼ of the vegetable paste to each portion of the mixture. Whisk with ¼ cup of mozzarella cheese.
4. Bake until the cheese is finely browned and the vegetables are tender for 8 to 10 minutes. Serve straight away.

Nutrition:
Calories: 265
Fat: 5g
Protein: 15g
Carbohydrates: 2g

485. Candied Pecans

Preparation Time: 5 minutes **Cooking Time:** 11 minutes **Servings:** 6

Ingredients:
- 1 ½ tsp. butter
- 1 ½ cup pecan halves
- 2 ½ tbsp. Splenda, divided
- 1 tsp. cinnamon
- ¼ tsp. ginger
- ⅛ tsp. cardamom
- ⅛ tsp. salt

Directions:
1. In a small bowl, stir together 1 ½ teaspoons Splenda, cinnamon, ginger, cardamom and salt. Set aside.
2. Melt butter in a medium skillet over med-low heat. Add pecans, and two tablespoons Splenda. Reduce heat to low and cook, stirring occasionally, until sweetener dissolves, about 5 to 8 minutes.
3. Attach the spice mixture to the skillet and stir to coat pecans. Spread mixture to parchment paper and let cool for 10-15 minutes. Store in an airtight container. Serving size is ¼ cup.

Nutrition:
Calories 173
Protein 2g
Fat 16g
Carbohydrates: 3.4g

486. Cauliflower Hummus

Preparation Time: 6 minutes **Cooking Time:** 15 minutes **Servings:** 6

Ingredients:
- 3 cup cauliflower florets
- 3 tbsp. fresh lemon juice
- 5 cloves garlic, divided
- 5 tbsp. olive oil, divided
- 2 tbsp. water
- 1 ½ tbsp. Tahini paste
- 1 ¼ tsp. salt, divided
- Smoked paprika and extra olive oil for platter

Directions:
1. In a microwave safe bowl, combine cauliflower, water, 2 tablespoons oil, ½ teaspoon salt, and 3 whole cloves garlic. Microwave on high 15 minutes, or until cauliflower is soft and darkened.
2. Transfer mixture to a food processor or blender and process until almost smooth. Add tahini paste, lemon juice, remaining garlic cloves, remaining oil, and salt. Blend until almost smooth.
3. Set the hummus in a bowl and drizzle lightly with olive oil and a sprinkle or two of paprika. Serve with your favorite raw vegetables.

Nutrition:
Calories 107
Protein 2g
Fat 10g
Carbohydrates: 1g

487. Cheese Crisp Crackers

Preparation Time: 6 minutes **Cooking Time:** 11 minutes **Servings:** 4

Ingredients:
- 4 slices pepper Jack cheese, quartered
- 4 slices Colby Jack cheese, quartered
- 4 slices cheddar cheese, quartered

Directions:
1. Warmth oven to 400 F. Line a cooking sheet with parchment paper.
2. Place cheese in a single layer on prepared pan and bake 10 minutes, or until cheese gets firm.
3. Transfer to paper towel line surface to absorb excess oil. Let cool, cheese will crisp up more as it cools.
4. Store in airtight container, or Ziploc bag. Serve with your favorite dip or salsa.

Nutrition:
Calories 253
Protein 15g
Fat 20g
Carbohydrates: 2.1g

488. Cheesy Onion Dip

Preparation Time: 6 minutes **Cooking Time:** 5 minutes **Servings:** 8

Ingredients:
- 8 oz. low fat cream cheese, soft
- 1 cup onions, grated
- 1 cup low fat Swiss cheese, grated
- 1 cup lite mayonnaise

Directions:
1. Heat oven to broil.
2. Combine all Ingredients in a small casserole dish. Microwave on high, stirring every 30 seconds, until cheese is melted and Ingredients are combined.

3. Set under the broiler until the surface is nicely browned. Serve warm with vegetables for dipping.

Nutrition:
Calories 158
Protein 9g
Fat 11g
Carbohydrates: 3g

489. Cheesy Pita Crisps

Preparation Time: 6 minutes **Cooking Time:** 15 minutes **Servings:** 8

Ingredients:
- ½ cup mozzarella cheese
- ¼ cup margarine, melted
- 4 whole-wheat pita pocket halves
- 3 tbsp. reduced fat parmesan
- ½ tsp. garlic powder
- ½ tsp. onion powder
- ¼ tsp. salt
- ¼ tsp. pepper
- Nonstick cooking spray

Directions:
1. Warmth oven to 400 F. Spray a baking sheet with cooking spray.
2. Cut each pita pocket in half. Cut each half into 2 triangles. Place, rough side up, on prepared pan.
3. In a small bowl, whisk together margarine, parmesan and seasonings.
4. Spread each triangle with margarine mixture. Sprinkle mozzarella over top.
5. Bake 12-15 minutes or until golden brown.

Nutrition:
Calories 131
Protein 4g
Fat 7g
Carbohydrates: 3.1g

490. Cheesy Taco Chips

Preparation Time: 16 minutes **Cooking Time:** 41 minutes **Servings:** 6

Ingredients:
- 1 cup Mexican blend cheese, grated
- 2 large egg whites
- 1 ½ cup crushed pork rinds
- 1 tbsp. taco seasoning
- ¼ tsp. salt

Directions:
1. Warmth oven to 300 F. Set
1. a large baking sheet with parchment paper.
2. In a large bowl, spill egg whites and salt until frothy. Stir in pork rinds, cheese, and seasoning and stir until thoroughly combined.
3. Turn out onto prepared pan. Set another sheet on top and bend out very thin, about 12x12-inches. Remove top sheet of parchment paper, and using a pizza cutter, score dough in 2-inch squares, then score each square in half diagonally.
4. Bake 20 minutes until they start to brown. Turn off oven and let them sit inside the oven until they are firm to the touch, about 10-20 minutes.
5. Detach from oven and cool completely before breaking apart. Eat them as is or with your favorite dip.

Nutrition:
Calories 260
Protein 25g
Fat 17g
Carbohydrates: 9g

491. Chewy Granola Bars

Preparation Time: 11 minutes **Cooking Time:** 35 minutes **Servings:** 36

Ingredients:
- 1 egg, beaten
- ⅔ cup margarine, melted
- 3 ½ cup quick oats
- 1 cup almonds, chopped
- ½ cup honey
- ½ cup sunflower kernels
- ½ cup coconut, unsweetened
- ½ cup dried apples
- ½ cup dried cranberries
- ½ cup Splenda brown sugar
- 1 tsp. vanilla
- ½ tsp. cinnamon
- Nonstick cooking spray

Directions:
1. Warmth oven to 350 F. Spray a large baking sheet with cooking spray.
2. Spread oats and almonds on prepared pan. Bake 12-15 minutes until toasted, stirring every few minutes.
3. In a large bowl, combine egg, margarine, honey, and vanilla. Stir in remaining Ingredients.
4. Stir in oat mixture. Press into baking sheet and bake 13-18 minutes, or until edges are light brown.
5. Cool on a wire rack. Divide into bars and store in an airtight container.

Nutrition:
Calories 119
Protein 2g
Fat 6g
Carbohydrates: 13g

492. Chili Lime Tortilla Chips

Preparation Time: 6 minutes **Cooking Time:** 15 minutes **Servings:** 10

Ingredients:
- 12 6-inch corn tortillas, cut into 8 triangles
- 3 tbsp. lime juice

- 1 tsp. cumin

Directions:
1. Heat oven to 350 F.
2. Set tortilla triangles in a single layer on a large baking sheet.
3. In a small bowl stir together spices.
4. Sprinkle half the lime juice over tortillas, followed by ½ the spice mixture. Bake 7 minutes.

- 1 tsp. chili powder

5. Remove from oven and turn tortillas over. Sprinkle with remaining lime juice and spices. Bake another 8 minutes or until crisp, but not brown.
6. Serve with your favorite salsa, serving size is 10 chips.

Nutrition:
Calories 65
Protein 2g
Fat 1g
Carbohydrates: 2.4g

---

493. Chocolate Chip Blondie's

Preparation Time: 6 minutes **Cooking Time:** 21 minutes **Servings:** 12

Ingredients:
- 1 egg
- ½ cup semi-sweet chocolate chips
- ⅓ cup flour
- ⅓ cup whole wheat flour
- ¼ cup Splenda brown sugar
- ¼ cup sunflower oil
- 2 tbsp. honey
- 1 tsp. vanilla
- ½ tsp. baking powder
- ¼ tsp. salt
- Nonstick cooking spray

Directions:
1. Warmth oven to 350 F. Spray an 8-inch square baking dish with cooking spray.
2. In a small bowl, combine dry Ingredients.
3. In a large bowl, spill together egg, oil, honey, and vanilla. Stir in dry Ingredients just until combined. Stir in chocolate chips.
4. Spread batter in prepared dish. Bake 20-22 minutes or until they pass the toothpick test.
5. Cool on a wire rack then cut into bars.

Nutrition:
Calories 136
Protein 2g
Fat 6g
Carbohydrates: 3.2g

---

494. Cinnamon Apple Chips

Preparation Time: 6 minutes **Cooking Time:** 11 minutes **Servings:** 2

Ingredients:
- 1 medium apple, sliced thin
- ¼ tsp. cinnamon
- ¼ tsp. nutmeg
- Nonstick cooking spray

Directions:
1. Heat oven to 375F. Spray a baking sheet with cooking spray.
2. Set apples in a mixing bowl and add spices. Toss to coat.
3. Arrange apples, in a single layer, on prepared pan. Bake 4 minutes, turn apples over and bake 4 minutes more.
4. Serve immediately or store in airtight container.

Nutrition:
Calories 58
Protein 0.1g
Fat 0.3g
Carbohydrates: 3.9g

---

495. Spicy Bruschetta

Preparation Time: 5 minutes **Cooking Time:** 10 minutes **Servings:** 2

Ingredients:
- 1 baguette roll
- Salt and white pepper
- ½ tomato
- ½ tbsp. acetic balsamic vinegar
- 37.5 g roasted peppers from the jar
- 2 tbsps. oil
- ½ clove of garlic
- 1 red chili
- ½ onion

Directions:
1. Halve the rolls and drizzle with 1 tablespoon of oil.
2. Preheat the oven to 200C and roast the rolls on both sides for 2-3 minutes.
3. Spill boiling water over the tomato and let it steep for a moment. Then peel and core the tomato and dice the pulp.
1. Drain the peppers and cut them into small pieces. Peel and dice the garlic. Peel and chop the onion. Core the chili pepper and divide
4. it into slices.
5. Mix all Ingredients with 3 tablespoons of oil and vinegar. Season the mixture with salt and pepper.
6. Spread the vegetables on the rolls and briefly heat them again in the oven.

Nutrition:
Calories: 205
Fat: 10.4g
Protein: 3.8g
Carbohydrates: 4.2g

---

496. Easy Pizza for Two

Preparation Time: 5 minutes **Cooking Time:** 10 minutes **Servings:** 2

Ingredients:
- ½ cup chunky no-salt-added
- Tomato sauce

- 1 ready-made whole-wheat flatbread (about 10-inch diameter)
- 2 slices of onion, (¼-inch wide)
- 4 sliced red bell pepper (¼-inch wide)
- ½ cup shredded low-fat mozzarella
- 2 tablespoons chopped fresh basil

Directions:
1. Heat the oven to 350F.
2. Coat the baking pan lightly with the cooking oil.
3. Spread the tomato sauce on the flatbread. Cover with tomato, chili pepper, mozzarella, and basil.
4. Place the pizza in a baking pan and cook until the cheese melts and becomes lightly browned approximately five minutes.

Nutrition:
Protein: 8g
Calories: 163
Fat: 5g
Carbohydrates: 3.5g

497. Bean Salad with Balsamic Vinaigrette
Preparation Time: 5 minutes **Cooking Time:** 0 hours **Servings:** 2
Ingredients:
For the Vinaigrette:
- 2 tablespoons balsamic vinegar
- ⅓ cup fresh parsley, chopped
- 4 garlic cloves, finely chopped

For the Salad:
- ⅓ can (15 oz.) low-sodium garbanzo beans, rinsed and drained
- ⅓ can (15 oz.) low-sodium black beans, rinsed and drained
- 1 small red onion, diced
- Ground black pepper, to taste
- ¼ cup Extra-virgin olive oil
- 2 lettuce leaves
- Celery, finely chopped

Directions:
1. In a small pan, mix the balsamic vinegar, the parsley, the garlic, and the pepper to prepare the vinaigrette. Slowly add the olive oil when whisking.
2. In a large pan, combine the beans and the onion.
3. Pour the vinaigrette over the mixture and stir softly, blend thoroughly and coat equally. Cover and refrigerate until ready to serve.
4. Put one lettuce leaf on each plate to serve. Divide the salad between the individual plates and garnish with the minced celery. Serve straight away.

Nutrition:
Calories: 206
Fat: 10g
Protein: 7g
Carbohydrates: 4g

498. Easy Cauliflower Hush Puppies
Preparation Time: 15 minutes **Cooking Time:** 10 minutes **Servings:** 8
Ingredients:
- 1 whole cauliflower, including stalks and florets, roughly chopped
- ¾ cup buttermilk
- ¾ cup low-fat milk
- 1 medium onion, chopped
- 2 medium eggs
- 2 cups yellow cornmeal
- 1½ teaspoons baking powder
- ½ teaspoon salt

Directions:
1. In a blender, combine the cauliflower, buttermilk, milk, and onion and purée. Transfer to a large mixing bowl.
2. Crack the eggs into the purée, and gently fold until mixed.
3. In a medium bowl, whisk the cornmeal, baking powder, and salt together.
4. Gently attach the dry Ingredients to the wet Ingredients and mix until just combined, taking care not to over mix.
5. Working in batches, place ⅓-cup portions of the batter into the basket of an air fryer.
6. Set the air fryer to 390F (199C), close, and cook for 10 minutes. Transfer the hush puppies to a plate. Repeat until no batter remains.
7. Serve warm with greens.

Nutrition:
Calories: 180
Fat: 8.1g
Protein: 4.1g
Carbohydrates: 1.6g

499. Cauliflower Mash
Preparation Time: 7 minutes **Cooking Time:** 20 minutes **Servings:** 2
Ingredients:
- ½ head cauliflower, cored and cut into large florets
- ¼ teaspoon kosher salt
- ¼ teaspoon garlic pepper
- 1 tablespoon plain Greek yogurt
- Freshly grated Parmesan cheese
- ½ tablespoon unsalted butter or ghee (optional)
- Chopped fresh chives

Directions:
1. Pour 1 cup of water into the electric pressure cooker and insert a steamer basket or wire rack.
2. Place the cauliflower in the basket.
3. Secure the pressure cooker lid. Set the valve to sealing.
4. Cook on high pressure for 5 minutes.
5. When it beeps, hit Cancel and quickly release the pressure.
6. Remove the cauliflower from the pot and pour out the water. Return the cauliflower to the pot and add the salt, garlic pepper, yogurt, and cheese. With a blender or potato masher to purée or mash the cauliflower in the pot.

7. Set into a serving bowl, and garnish with butter (if using) and chives.

Nutrition:
Calories: 141
Fat: 6.1g
Protein: 12.1g
Carbohydrates: 1.9g

500. Red Pepper, Goat Cheese, and Arugula Open-Faced Grilled Sandwich

Preparation Time: 5 minutes **Cooking Time:** 15 minutes **Servings:** 2

Ingredients:
- 1 red bell pepper, seeded
- Nonstick cooking spray
- 2 slice whole-wheat thin-sliced bread
- 4 tablespoons crumbled goat cheese
- Pinch dried thyme
- 1 cup arugula

Directions:
1. Preheat the broiler to high heat. Line a baking sheet with parchment paper.
2. Cut the ½ bell pepper lengthwise into two pieces and arrange on the prepared baking sheet with the skin facing up.
3. Broil until the skin is blackened for about 5 to 10 minutes. Transfer to a covered container to steam for 5 minutes, then remove the skin from the pepper using your fingers. Cut the pepper into strips.
4. Heat a small skillet over medium-high heat. Set it with nonstick cooking spray and place the bread in the skillet. Top with the goat cheese and sprinkle with the thyme. Pile the arugula on top, followed by the roasted red pepper strips. Press down with a spatula to hold in place.
5. Cook for 2-3 minutes.

Nutrition:
Calories: 109
Fat: 2g
Protein: 4g
Carbohydrates: 2g

501. Almond Cheesecake Bites

Preparation Time: 5 Minutes **Cooking Time:** 0 Minutes **Servings:** 6

Ingredients:
- ½ cup reduced-fat cream cheese, soft
- ½ cup almonds, ground fine
- ¼ cup almond butter
- 2 Drops Liquid Stevia

Directions:
1. In a large bowl, beat cream cheese, almond butter, and Stevia at high speed until the mixture is smooth and creamy. Cover and chill for 30 minutes.
2. Shape the mixture into 12 balls.
3. Place the ground almonds on a shallow plate. Roll the balls in the nuts completely, covering all sides. Set in an air-tight container in the refrigerator.

Nutrition:
Calories: 68
Protein: 5g
Fat: 5g
Carbohydrates: 4g

502. Almond Coconut Biscotti

Preparation Time: 5 Minutes **Cooking Time:** 51 Minutes **Servings:** 16

Ingredients:
- 1 egg, room temperature
- 1 egg white, room temperature
- ½ cup margarine, melted
- 2 ½ cups flour
- 1 ⅓ cup unsweetened coconut, grated
- ¾ cup almonds, sliced
- ⅔ cups Splenda
- 2 teaspoons baking powder
- 1 teaspoon vanilla
- ½ teaspoon salt

Directions:
1. Heat the oven to 350F. Line a baking sheet with parchment paper.
2. In a large bowl, combine dry ingredients.
3. In a separate mixing bowl, beat the other ingredients together. Add to dry ingredients and mix until thoroughly combined.
4. Divide dough in half. Shape each half into a loaf measuring 8x2 ¾-inches. Set the loaves on a pan 3 inches apart.
5. Bake for 25-30 minutes. Set to cool for 10 minutes.
6. With a serrated knife, cut the loaf diagonally into ½-inch slices. Place the cookies, cut side down, back on the pan, and bake another 20 minutes, or until firm and nicely browned. Store in an air-tight container. The serving size is two cookies.

Nutrition:
Calories: 234
Protein: 5g
Fat: 18g
Carbohydrates: 1g

503. Almond Flour Crackers

Preparation Time: 5 Minutes **Cooking Time:** 15 Minutes **Servings:** 8

Ingredients:
- ½ cup coconut oil, melted
- 1 ½ cups almond flour
- ¼ cup Stevia

Directions:
1. Heat the oven to 350F. Line a cookie sheet with parchment paper.
2. In a mixing bowl, merge all ingredients and mix well.
3. Spread dough onto prepared cookie sheet, ¼-inch thick. Use a paring knife to score into 24 crackers.
4. Bake 10-15 minutes or until golden brown.

5. Separate the cookies and store them in an air-tight container.

Nutrition:
Calories: 281　　　　　　　　　　　　　　　　　　　　　　Fat: 23g
Protein: 4g　　　　　　　　　　　　　　　　　　　　　　　Carbohydrates: 5g

504. Asian Chicken Wings

Preparation Time: 5 Minutes　　**Cooking Time:** 30 Minutes　　**Servings:** 3

Ingredients:
- 24 Chicken wings
- 6 tablespoon soy sauce
- 6 tablespoon Chinese 5 spice
- Salt and pepper
- Non-stick cooking spray

Directions:
1. Heat the oven to 350F. Spray a baking sheet with cooking spray.
2. Combine the soy sauce, 5 spice, salt, and pepper in a large bowl. Add the wings and toss to coat.
3. Pour the wings onto the prepared pan. Bake 15 minutes. Set the chicken over and cook for another 15 minutes until the chicken is cooked through.
4. Serve with your favorite low-carb dipping sauce.

Nutrition:
Calories: 178　　　　　　　　　　　　　　　　　　　　　　Fat: 11g
Protein: 12g　　　　　　　　　　　　　　　　　　　　　　Carbohydrates: 5g

505. Banana Nut Cookies

Preparation Time: 10 Minutes　　**Cooking Time:** 15 Minutes　　**Servings:** 18

Ingredients:
- 1 ½ cup banana, mashed
- 2 cups oats
- 1 cup raisins
- 1 cup walnuts
- ⅓ cup sunflower oil
- 1 teaspoon vanilla
- ½ teaspoon salt

Directions:
1. Heat the oven to 350F.
2. In a large bowl, combine oats, raisins, walnuts, and salt.
3. In a medium bowl, mix banana, oil, and vanilla. Stir into oat mixture until combined. Let rest 15 minutes.
4. Drop by rounded tablespoonful onto two ungreased cookie sheets. Bake 15 minutes, or until they get lightly golden brown. Cool and store in an air-tight container. The serving size is two cookies.

Nutrition:
Calories: 148　　　　　　　　　　　　　　　　　　　　　　Fat: 9g
Protein: 3g　　　　　　　　　　　　　　　　　　　　　　　Carbohydrates: 6g

506. BLT Stuffed Cucumbers

Preparation Time: 15 Minutes　　**Cooking Time:** 15 Minutes　　**Servings:** 4

Ingredients:
- 3 slices bacon, cooked crisp and crumbled
- 1 large cucumber
- ½ cup lettuce, finely diced
- ½ cup baby spinach finely diced
- ¼ cup tomato finely diced
- 1 tablespoon + ½ teaspoon fat-free mayonnaise
- ¼ teaspoon black pepper
- ⅛ teaspoon salt

Directions:
1. Skin the cucumber and slice in half lengthwise. Use a spoon to remove the seeds.
2. In a medium bowl, combine the remaining ingredients and stir well.
3. Spoon the bacon mixture into the cucumber halves. Cut into 2-inch pieces and serve.

Nutrition:
Calories: 95　　　　　　　　　　　　　　　　　　　　　　Fat: 6g
Protein: 6g　　　　　　　　　　　　　　　　　　　　　　Carbohydrates: 6.4g

507. Buffalo Bites

Preparation Time: 6 Minutes 0　　**Cooking Time:** 11 Minutes　　**Servings:** 4

Ingredients:
- 1 egg
- ½ Head of cauliflower, separated into florets
- 1 cup panko breadcrumbs
- 1 cup low-fat ranch dressing
- ½ cup hot sauce
- ½ teaspoon salt
- ½ teaspoon garlic powder
- Black pepper
- Non-stick cooking spray

Directions:
1. Heat the oven to 400F. Spray a baking sheet with cooking spray.
2. Set the egg in a medium bowl and mix in the salt, pepper, and garlic. Place the panko crumbs into a small bowl.
3. Dip the florets first in the egg, then into the panko crumbs-place in a single layer on the prepared pan.
4. Bake 8-10 minutes, stirring halfway through until cauliflower is golden brown and crisp on the outside.
5. In a small bowl, spill the dressing and hot sauce together. Use for dipping.

Nutrition:
Calories: 132
Protein: 6g
Fat: 5g
Carbohydrates: 9g

508. Cinnamon Apple Popcorn
Preparation Time: 31 Minutes **Cooking Time:** 50 Minutes **Servings:** 11

Ingredients:
- 4 tablespoons of margarine, melted
- 10 cups plain popcorn
- 2 cups dried apple rings, unsweetened and chopped
- ½ cup walnuts, chopped
- 2 tablespoons Splenda brown sugar
- 1 teaspoon cinnamon
- ½ teaspoon vanilla

Directions:
1. Heat the oven to 250 F.
2. Place chopped apples in a 9x13-inch baking dish and bake for 20 minutes. Remove from the oven and stir in popcorn and nuts.
3. In a small bowl, whisk together margarine, vanilla, Splenda, and cinnamon. Drizzle evenly over popcorn and toss to coat.
4. Bake 30 minutes, stirring quickly every 10 minutes. If apples start to turn dark brown, remove them immediately.
5. Pout onto waxed paper to cool for at least 30 minutes. Store in an air-tight container.

Nutrition:
Calories: 133
Protein: 3g
Fat: 8g
Carbohydrates: 5.6g

509. Crab and Spinach Dip
Preparation Time: 9 Minutes **Cooking Time:** 2 Hours **Servings:** 10

Ingredients:
- 1 pkg. Frozen chopped spinach, thawed and squeezed nearly dry
- 8 oz. Reduced-fat cream cheese
- 6 ½ oz. Can crabmeat, drained and shredded
- 6 oz. Jar marinated artichoke hearts drained and finely hashed
- ¼ teaspoon hot pepper sauce
- Melba toast or whole-grain crackers (optional)

Directions:
1. Remove any shells or cartilage from the crab.
2. Place all ingredients in a small crockpot. Cover and cook on high 1 ½ - 2 hours, or until heated through and cream cheese is melted. Stir after 1 hour.
3. Serve with Melba toast or whole-grain crackers. The serving size is ¼ cup.

Nutrition:
Calories: 106
Protein: 5g
Fat: 8g
Carbohydrates: 7g

510. Cranberry and Almond Granola Bars
Preparation Time: 14 minutes **Cooking Time:** 21 minutes **Servings:** 12

Ingredients:
- 1 egg
- 1 egg white
- 2 cups low-fat granola
- ¼ cup dried cranberries, sweetened
- ¼ cup almonds, chopped
- 2 tablespoons Splenda
- 1 teaspoon almond extract
- ½ teaspoon cinnamon

Directions:
1. Heat the oven to 350F. Set the bottom and sides of an 8-inch baking dish with parchment paper.
2. In a large bowl, combine dry ingredients, including the cranberries.
3. In a small bowl, spill together egg, egg white, and extract. Pour over dry ingredients and mix until combined.
4. Press the mixture into the prepared pan. Bake 20 minutes or until light brown.
5. Cool in the pan for 5 minutes. Then carefully set the bars from the pan onto a cutting board. Use a sharp knife to cut into 12 bars.
6. Cool completely and set in an air-tight container.

Nutrition:
Calories: 85
Protein: 3g
Fat: 3g
Carbohydrates: 6g

511. Cheesy Broccoli Bites
Preparation Time: 10 minutes **Cooking Time:** 26 minutes **Servings:** 6

Ingredients:
- 2 tablespoons olive oil
- 2 heads broccoli, trimmed
- 1 egg
- ⅓ cup reduced-fat shredded Cheddar cheese
- 1 egg white
- ½ cup onion, chopped
- ⅓ cup breadcrumbs
- ¼ teaspoon salt
- ¼ teaspoon black pepper

Directions:
1. Preheat the oven to 400F (205C). Set a large baking sheet with olive oil.
2. Arrange a colander in a saucepan, and then place the broccoli in the colander. Pour the water in the saucepan to cover the bottom. Bring to a boil, and then reduce the heat to low. Seal and simmer for 6 minutes or until the broccoli is fork-tender. Allow to cool for 10 minutes.
3. Put the broccoli and remaining ingredients in a food processor. Process to combine until lightly chunky. Let sit for 10 minutes.

4. Make the bites: Drop 1 tablespoon of the mixture on the baking sheet. Repeat with the remaining mixture.
5. Bake for 25 minutes until lightly browned. Flip the bites halfway through the cooking time.
6. Serve immediately.

Nutrition:
Calories 119
Protein 2g
Fat 6g
Carbohydrates: 13g

512. Strawberry Smoothie
Preparation Time: 5 Minutes **Cooking Time:** 5 Minutes **Servings:** 1

Ingredients:
- 5 Strawberries, medium
- 6 Ice Cubes 1 cup Soy Milk, unsweetened
- ½ cup Greek Yoghurt, low-fat

Directions:
1. Place strawberries, yogurt, milk, and ice cubes in a blender.
2. Merge them until you get a smooth and luscious smoothie.
3. Set to a serving glass and enjoy it.

Nutrition:
Calories 1671
Carbohydrates 11g
Proteins 16g
Fat 6g
Sodium 161mg

513. Berry Mint Smoothie
Preparation Time: 5 Minutes **Cooking Time:** 5 Minutes **Servings:** 2

Ingredients:
- 1tbsp. Low-carb Sweetener of your choice
- 1 cup Kefir or Low Fat-Yoghurt
- 2 tbsp. Mint
- ¼ cup Orange
- 1cup Mixed Berries

Directions:
1. Set all the ingredients in a high-speed blender and then blend it until smooth.
2. Transfer the smoothie to a serving glass and enjoy it.

Nutrition:
Calories: 137
Carbohydrates: 11g
Proteins: 6g
Fat: 1g
Sodium: 64mg

514. Greenie Smoothie
Preparation Time: 5 Minutes **Cooking Time:** 5 Minutes **Servings:** 2

Ingredients:
- ½ cup Water
- 1tsp. Stevia
- 1Green Apple, ripe
- 1tsp. Stevia
- 1 Green Pear, chopped into chunks
- 1 Lime
- 2 cups Kale, fresh
- ¾ tsp. Cinnamon
- 12 Ice Cubes
- 20 Green Grapes
- ½ cup Mint, fresh

Directions:
1. Pour water, kale, and pear in a high-speed blender and blend them for 2 to 3 minutes until mixed.
2. Stir in all the remaining ingredients into it and blend until it becomes smooth.
3. Transfer the smoothie to serving glass.

Nutrition:
Calories: 123
Carbohydrates: 27g
Proteins: 2g
Fat: 2g
Sodium: 30mg

515. Coconut Spinach Smoothie
Preparation Time: 5 Minutes **Cooking Time:** 5 Minutes **Servings:** 2

Ingredients:
- ¼ cup Coconut Milk
- 2 Ice Cubes
- 2 tbsp. Chia Seeds
- 1 scoop of Protein Powder, preferably vanilla
- 1cup Spin

Directions:
1. Pour coconut milk along with spinach, chia seeds, protein powder, and ice cubes in a high-speed blender.
2. Blend to get a smooth and luscious smoothie.
3. Serve in a glass and enjoy it.

Nutrition:
Calories 251
Carbohydrates 10.9g
Proteins 20.3g
Fat 15.1g.
Sodium: 102mg

516. Oats Coffee Smoothie
Preparation Time: 5 Minutes **Cooking Time:** 5 Minutes **Servings:** 2

Ingredients:
- 1cup Oats, uncooked and grounded
- 2 tbsp. Instant Coffee
- 3 cup Milk, skimmed
- 2 Banana, frozen and sliced into chunks
- 2 tbsp. Flax Seeds, grounded

Directions:
1. Set all the ingredients in a high-speed blender and blend for 2 minutes or until smooth and luscious.
2. Serve and enjoy.

Nutrition:
Calories: 137
Carbohydrates: 11g
Proteins: 6g
Fat: 1g
Sodium: 64mg

517. Veggie Smoothie
Preparation Time: 5 Minutes **Cooking Time:** 5 Minutes **Servings:** 1
Ingredients:
- ¼ of 1 Red Bell Pepper, sliced
- ½ tbsp. Coconut Oil
- 1 cup Almond Milk, unsweetened
- ¼ tsp. Turmeric
- 4 Strawberries, chopped
- Pinch of Cinnamon
- ½ of 1 Banana, preferably frozen

Directions:
1. Combine all the ingredients required to make the smoothie in a high-speed blender.
2. Blend for 3 minutes to get a smooth and silky mixture.
3. Serve and enjoy.

Nutrition:
Calories: 178
Protein: 12g
Fat: 11g
Carbohydrates: 5g

518. Avocado Smoothie
Preparation Time: 10 Minutes **Cooking Time:** 0 Minute **Servings:** 2
Ingredients:
- Avocado, ripe and pit removed
- 2 cups Baby Spinach
- 2 cups Water
- 1 cup Baby Kale
- 1 tbsp. Lemon Juice
- 2 sprigs of Mint
- ½ cup Ice Cubes

Directions:
1. Set all the ingredients needed to make the smoothie in a high-speed blender then blend until smooth.
2. Set to a serving glass and enjoy it.

Nutrition:
Calories 167l
Carbohydrates 11g
Proteins 16g
Fat 6g
Sodium 161mg

519. Orange Carrot Smoothie
Preparation Time: 5 Minutes **Cooking Time:** 0 Minutes **Servings:** 1
Ingredients:
- ½ cups Almond Milk
- ¼ cup Cauliflower, blanched and frozen
- 1 Orange
- 1 tsp. Flax Seed
- ⅓ cup Carrot, grated
- 1 tsp. Vanilla Extract

Directions:
1. Merge all the ingredients in a high-speed blender and blend for 2 minutes or until you get the desired consistency.
2. Set to a serving glass and enjoy it.

Nutrition:
Calories: 216
Carbohydrates: 10g
Proteins: 15g
Fat: 7g
Sodium: 25mg

520. Marinated Green Beans
Preparation Time: 10 minutes **Cooking Time:** 10 minutes **Servings:** 2
Ingredients:
- 2 garlic cloves, pressed
- ½ cup onion, sliced
- 1 teaspoon Dijon mustard
- 1 tablespoon white wine vinegar
- 2 tablespoons olive oil
- 2 cups fresh green beans

Directions:
1. Wash the beans and split them in half after cutting off the ends. Enable them to steam for a few minutes without losing their crunchiness.
2. Drain the water. Toss with the onions in a salad dish. In a pan, combine the remaining ingredients and shake vigorously. Pour the liquid over the beans. You may serve it hot or cold.

Nutrition:
Calories: 372
Fat: 19g
Protein: 16g
Carbs: 34g
Sugars: 1.3g
Fiber: 6g
Sodium: 161mg

521. Marinated Vegetable Salad
Preparation Time: 10 minutes **Cooking Time:** none **Servings:** 8
Ingredients:
- 4 ounces mushrooms, sliced
- ½ cup sliced yellow squash
- ¼ cup thinly sliced red onion
- ¼ cup sliced carrot

- ½ cup cauliflower florets
- 15 cherry tomatoes, halved

Marinade
- ½ teaspoon pressed garlic
- 1 teaspoon dry mustard
- ½ cup red wine vinegar
- 1 teaspoon oregano
- ½ cup broccoli florets
- ½ cup sliced zucchini
- ¼ cup lemon juice
- 1 teaspoon minced onion
- 1 cup olive oil

Directions:
1. In a mixing cup, combine the vegetables. Combine the ingredients for the marinade and spill over the vegetables. Refrigerate for many hours or overnight in the refrigerator.

Nutrition:
Calories: 315
Carbs: 13g
Sugar: 3g
Fat: 16g
Protein: 37g

522. Spinach and Black-Eyed Pea Salad

Preparation Time: 10 minutes **Cooking Time:** 40 minutes **Servings:** 6

Ingredients:
- ½-pound spinach leaves
- 1 cup chopped onion
- 1 tablespoon Dijon mustard
- 14 ounces artichoke hearts
- 4 cups water
- 1 tablespoon Worcestershire sauce
- ½ teaspoon minced garlic
- 4 slices bacon, cooked and crumbled
- ½ pound black-eyed peas

Directions:
1. Sort and wash peas, then combine with the remaining ingredients in a Dutch oven. Bring to a boil, set to low heat, and continue cooking for 40 minutes or until peas are soft. Drain the water.
2. Heat the peas. Drain the artichoke hearts and set aside the juice. Chop the artichoke hearts and toss them in with the black-eyed peas.
3. Toss the peas gently with the reserved artichoke milk, mustard, and Worcestershire sauce. Place spinach leaves on individual salad plates and spoon salad over the top. Serve warm with crumbled bacon on top.

Nutrition:
Calories: 350
Carbs: 10g
Sugar: 2g
Fat: 17g

523. Dried Bean and Cashew Salad

Preparation Time: 10 minutes **Cooking Time:** 10 minutes **Servings:** 6

Ingredients:
- 3 tablespoons balsamic vinegar
- 1 cup black-eyed peas, cooked
- 1 garlic clove, crushed
- ½ cup red bell pepper, seedless and finely chopped
- 1 tablespoon tomato sauce
- ¼ cup green onions, chopped
- 2 tablespoons cashews, roasted
- ¼ teaspoon cumin
- ¼ cup celery, finely chopped
- 6 tablespoons olive oil
- 1 cup dried lima beans, cooked

Directions:
1. Combine the beans, peas, celery, and sweet pepper in a big mixing dish. In a dry frying pan, se the cashew nuts until they are golden brown. Place on paper towels to absorb excess moisture and enable it to cool. Toss the beans with the green onions until they've cooled.
2. Toss together the tomato sauce, ginger, cumin, vinegar, and olive oil. Spill over the beans and toss to combine. Allow for an hour of resting time before serving.

Nutrition:
Calories: 297
Protein: 31.0g
Carbs: 1.0g
Fiber: 0g
Sugar: 0g
Sodium: 100mg

524. Chicken, Bean and Corn Salad

Preparation Time: 10 minutes **Cooking Time:** 10 minutes **Servings:** 4

Ingredients:
- 2 teaspoons olive oil
- 15-ounce kidney beans, rinsed and drained
- 1 tablespoon red wine vinegar
- ½ cup green onion, thinly sliced
- 10 ounces frozen corn, thawed
- 2 tablespoons cilantro, chopped
- 1 cup cooked chicken breast, cut in 1-inch strips

Directions:
1. Combine the chicken and the remaining ingredients in a medium mixing dish. If required, serve on a bed of lettuce.

Nutrition:
Calorie: 140
Fat: 7g
Protein: 18g
Carbs: 3g
Sugars: 1g
Fiber: 1g
Sodium: 141mg

525. Pasta and Kidney Bean Salad

Preparation Time: 10 minutes **Cooking Time:** 10 minutes **Servings:** 6

Ingredients:
- ½ teaspoon paprika
- 2 cups red kidney beans, cooked
- ½ teaspoon chili powder
- 1 cup green bell pepper, diced
- 1 cup mayonnaise
- ⅓ cup green olives, chopped
- 1 cup tomato, chopped
- ½ teaspoon coriander
- 1 cup zucchini, diced
- ¼ teaspoon sage
- 2 cups rotini or other medium-sized pasta

Directions:
1. Cook the pasta. Pour and shower. Apply the remainder of the ingredients to a big mixing cup. Serve at room temperature after carefully mixing.

Nutrition:
Calories: 173
Fat: 13g
Protein: 11g
Carbs: 3g
Sugars: 1g
Fiber: 0g
Sodium: 154mg

526. Pasta and Artichoke Heart Salad

Preparation Time: 10 minutes **Cooking Time:** 10 minutes **Servings:** 4

Ingredients:
- ¼ teaspoon pepper
- ¼ cup red wine vinegar
- 1 cup green bell pepper, chopped
- ½ cup sliced black olives
- ½ cup carrot, coarsely grated
- ½ teaspoon basil
- ¾ pound marinated artichoke hearts
- 2 cups elbow macaroni

Directions:
1. Cook the pasta. Rinse thoroughly with cold spray. Drain the water and place it in a mixing cup.
2. Chop the artichokes into small bits. Toss with spaghetti. Combine the remaining components in a mixing bowl. Enable 2 hours in the refrigerator to chill after thoroughly mixing.

Nutrition:
Calories: 350
Fat: 12g
Protein: 52g
Carbs: 6g
Sugars: 1g
Fiber: 0g
Sodium: 658mg

527. Dilled Cucumbers

Preparation Time: 10 minutes **Cooking Time:** none **Servings:** 10

Ingredients:
- ½ teaspoon freshly ground black pepper
- 1 large onion, sliced
- ½ cup white vinegar
- 1 teaspoon sugar substitute, such as Splenda
- 2 tablespoons fresh dill, chopped
- 2 medium cucumbers, peeled and sliced

Directions:
1. Combine cucumbers, onion, and dill in a medium mixing dish. To dissolve the sugar substitute, stir it into the vinegar.
2. Season with pepper and add to the cucumber mixture. Refrigerate for several hours or overnight after covering.

Nutrition:
Calories: 166
Fat: 1g
Protein: 6g
Carbs: 35g
Sugars: 1.4g
Fiber: 8g

528. Barbecue Coleslaw

Preparation Time: 10 minutes **Cooking Time:** none **Servings:** 6

Ingredients:
- ½ teaspoon liquid smoke
- ½ cup celery, grated
- ¼ teaspoon red pepper flakes
- 1 tablespoon prepared mustard
- 1 and ½ tablespoons Worcestershire sauce
- ¼ cup cider vinegar
- ¾ cup low-sodium catsup
- 2 tbsp. brown sugar substitute, such as Splenda
- 1 cup green bell pepper, grated
- 2 cups cabbage, grated
- ½ cup onion, minced

Directions:
1. Merge all the vegetable ingredients in a large mixing cup. Combine the remaining components in a separate mixing cup.
2. Now mix the two tosses thoroughly and serve chilled.

Nutrition:
Calorie: 325
Fat: 8g
Protein: 35g
Carbs: 26g
Sugars: 6g
Fiber: 4g

529. Oriental Coleslaw

Preparation Time: 10 minutes **Cooking Time:** none **Servings:** 4

Ingredients:
- ⅛ teaspoon red pepper flakes
- 1 teaspoon sesame oil
- 2 teaspoons Reduced Sodium Soy Sauce
- 2 teaspoons sesame seeds, toasted
- 2 teaspoons sugar substitute, such as Splenda
- 3 tablespoons rice wine vinegar
- ¼ cup carrot, coarsely shredded
- ¼ cup green bell pepper, chopped
- 2 cups bok choy, finely shredded

Directions:
1. Toss together the first three components.
2. Combine the remaining components in a dish. Toss the vegetables in the sauce to seal them.

Nutrition:
Calories: 115
Fat: 8g
Cholesterol: 0mg
Sodium: 86mg
Carbohydrates: 11g
Sugar: 3.5g

---

530. Banana Cake

Preparation Time: 10 minutes **Cooking Time:** 40 minutes **Servings:** 24

Ingredients:
- 1 teaspoon vinegar
- 1 teaspoon baking powder
- ¾ cup unsalted butter
- 1 cup mashed bananas
- 1 teaspoon vanilla extract
- 2 eggs
- 2 cups whole wheat pastry flour
- 1 and ½ cups sugar substitute, such as Splenda
- Powdered sugar for dusting (optional)
- ½ cup skim milk

Directions:
1. Merge vinegar and milk in a bowl and set aside for 5 minutes to sour. Combine the butter and sugar in a mixing bowl. Combine the eggs, milk mixture, vanilla, and bananas in a mixing bowl.
2. Blend until completely smooth. Merge the flour and baking powder in a mixing bowl. Mix well with the creamed mixture. Fill an oiled 9 x 13-inch baking sheet halfway with batter. Bake for 35 to 40 minutes at 350F (180C, gas mark 4) until done. If needed, dust with powdered sugar.

Nutrition:
Calories: 231
Fat: 10g
Protein: 26g
Carbs: 10g
Sugars: 4g
Fiber: 2g
Sodium: 349mg

---

531. Chocolate Cake Carrot

Preparation Time: 10 minutes **Cooking Time:** 35 minutes **Servings:** 6

Ingredients:
- 1 tsp. cinnamon
- ¾ cup Splenda
- 1½ cups whole wheat flour
- 1 cup water, boiling
- ½ cup cocoa powder, unsweetened
- ½ cup canola oil
- 1 and ½ teaspoons baking powder
- 1 and ½ cups carrot, grated

Directions:
1. Warmth the oven to 350 degrees Fahrenheit (180 degrees Celsius, or gas mark 4). Combine carrots, starch, and oil in a big mixing cup.
2. Over the mixture, pour water. Combine the remaining components in a small dish. Combine all the ingredients in a large mixing bowl and stir well.
3. Pour into an 8 x 8-inch nonstick or lightly oiled plate.
9.
4. Preheat oven to 350 degrees and bake for 35 minutes.

Nutrition:
Calories: 175
Fat: 3g
Protein: 27g
Carbs: 10g
Sugars: 4g
Fiber: 3g
Sodium: 188mg

---

532. Fruit Slush

Preparation Time: 10 minutes **Cooking Time:** none **Servings:** 6

Ingredients:
- 14 ounces fruit cocktail
- 6 ounces orange juice concentrate undiluted
- 15 ounces crushed pineapple, drained
- 16 ounces lemon-lime carbonated beverage
- ½ cup sugar substitute, such as Splenda
- 2 cups banana, sliced
- 6 ounces lemonade concentrate undiluted

Directions:
1. Hand-mix the products. Put a stop to it.
2. Allow 10 minutes for thawing before serving. To make slush, stir all together.

Nutrition:
Calories: 315
Carbs: 13g
Sugar: 3g
Fat: 16g
Protein: 37g

533. Lemonade

Preparation Time: 10 minutes **Cooking Time:** 10 minutes **Servings:** 20

Ingredients:
- 5 quarts water
- 1 and ½ cups lemon juice
- ½ cup sugar substitute, such as Splenda

Directions:
1. Heat the sugar and lemon juice before the sugar is almost dissolved. Toss in any water. Serve over ice with a stir.

Nutrition:
Calories: 226 Carbs: 3.0g Sodium: 92mg
Fat: 9.0g Fiber: 0g
Protein: 33.0g Sugar: 1g

534. Lime Fizz

Preparation Time: 10 minutes **Cooking Time:** none **Servings:** 1

Ingredients:
- ¼ cup water
- 2 teaspoons sugar substitute, such as Splenda
- 1 cup seltzer water
- 2 tablespoons lime juice

Directions:
1. In a large bottle, combine the juice, artificial sweetener, and water. Stir until the sugar is almost dissolved.
2. Add ice to the mix. Fill the bottle halfway with the seltzer.

Nutrition:
Calories: 25 Carbs: 24.0g Sodium: 290mg
Fat: 7.0g Fiber: 3.0g
Protein: 25.0g Sugar: 2.5g

535. Mocha Spread

Preparation Time: 10 minutes **Cooking Time:** none **Servings:** 12

Ingredients:
- ½ teaspoon vanilla
- ½ teaspoon instant coffee granules
- 1 tablespoon sugar substitute, such as Splenda
- ¼ cup miniature chocolate chips
- 4 ounces cream cheese

Directions:
1. In a food processor or mixer, merge all the ingredients. Cover and phase until they are well combined.

Nutrition:
Calories: 114 Carbs: 23g Sodium: 3mg
Fat: 1g Sugars: 0g
Protein: 2g Fiber: 1g

536. Pineapple Kabobs

Preparation Time: 10 minutes **Cooking Time:** 15 minutes **Servings:** 4

Ingredients:
- 1 teaspoon cinnamon
- 2 tablespoons unsalted butter
- 1 pineapple
- ¼ cup honey

Directions:
1. Combine the sugar, butter, and cinnamon in a mixing bowl.
2. New pineapple should be peeled and sliced into large wedges. 15 minutes over medium fire, basting with sauce. Frequently turn the wheel.

Nutrition:
Calories: 200 Protein: 22.0g Fiber: 1.0g
Fat: 8.0g Carbs: 7.0g Sugar: 4.0g

537. Marbled Cheesecake Muffins

Preparation Time: 10 minutes **Cooking Time:** 45 minutes **Servings:** 4

Ingredients:
For Muffins:
- ½ teaspoon vanilla extract
- 1 teaspoon almond extract
- 1 cup Splenda
- 8 ounces cream cheese, softened
- 16 ounces full-fat ricotta
- 1 and ½ tbsp. unsweetened cocoa powder
- 5 eggs

For Toppings:
- ¼ teaspoon vanilla extract
- 1 tablespoon Splenda
- ½ cup sour cream

Directions:
1. Warmth the oven to 350 degrees Fahrenheit (180 degrees Celsius, or gas mark 4). To produce the muffins, beat the eggs with an electric mixer in a medium mixing cup. To produce the muffins, whisk the eggs together for a few seconds until smooth. In a mixing cup, combine all the muffin ingredients, excluding the chocolate, and beat until smooth.

2. Fill muffin pans with batter until about one-fifth of the batter remains in the bowl (you'll need 12 liners). Toss the remaining butter with the cocoa powder (there is no need to worry about or be exact with the batter leftover in the bowl; this recipe is very forgiving).
3. It can be mixed in. To make a two-toned look, slowly pour a dollop of chocolate batter into the middle of each cupcake. Bake until the surface is puffy and slightly broken, and a toothpick inserted in the middle comes out clean.
4. Let the cupcakes to cool for a few minutes after removing them from the oven. When the cupcakes are baking, combine the topping ingredients combining the products. Set back the cupcakes to the oven for another 5 minutes with a rounded teaspoon of the topping in the middle. Keep calm and refrigerated. These freezes well, so you can always have some on hand.

Nutrition:
Calories: 350
Fat: 12g
Protein: 52g
Carbs: 6g
Sugars: 1g
Fiber: 0g

538. Cheesecake
Preparation Time: 10 minutes **Cooking Time:** 1 hour 10 minutes **Servings:** 10
Ingredients:
- 3 tablespoons heavy cream
- 2 cups Splenda*
Alternative Sweeteners
- 1 teaspoon EZ-Sweetz Travel Size
- 2 teaspoons EZ-Sweetz Family Size
- 5 eggs
- 2 pounds cream cheese, at room temperature
- 2 teaspoons liquid stevia
- 2 cups Stevia in the Raw

Directions:
1. Warmth the oven to 375 degrees Fahrenheit (190 degrees Celsius, or gas mark 5). Using an electric mixer, carefully combine all the ingredients. In a buttered 9-inch springform tray, scatter the batter. Warmth the oven to 350°F and bake the cheesecake for 10 minutes. Reduce the heat to 250F (120C) and continue baking for another hour.
2. Remove the cake and loop a knife along the pan's side at the end of the hour. Return the cake to the hot oven and leave it there until it cools off. Refrigerate overnight before serving.

Nutrition:
Calories: 182
Fat: 4g
Protein: 24g
Carbs: 12g
Sugars: 10g
Fiber: 1g
Sodium: 240mg

539. Cinnamon Nuts
Preparation Time: 10 minutes **Cooking Time:** 10 minutes **Servings:** 4
Ingredients:
- 1 and ½ to 2 tablespoons erythritol
- 1 cup shelled walnuts, pecans, or a combination of the two (I like the combo)
- ½ teaspoon ground cinnamon
- 2 tablespoons butter

Directions:
1. In a heavy skillet over medium heat, dissolve the butter, then add the nuts.
2. Cook, sometimes stirring, for 5 to 6 minutes.
3. Then detach the pan from the heat and quickly scatter the erythritol and cinnamon on top, stirring to evenly spread.

Nutrition:
Calories: 364
Fat: 10.2g
Protein: 41.8g
Carbs: 12g
Fiber: 3.8g
Sugar: 1.5g
Sodium: 650mg

540. Blackberry Smoothie
Preparation Time: 5 Minutes **Cooking Time:** 0 Minutes **Servings:** 1
Ingredients:
- ½ cups Almond Milk
- 1 tbsp. Lemon Juice ½ tsp. Vanilla Extract
- 3 oz. Blackberries, frozen

Directions:
1. Set all the ingredients needed to make the blackberry smoothie in a high-speed blender and blend until you get a smooth mixture.
2. Set to a serving glass and enjoy it.

Nutrition:
Calories: 275
Carbohydrates: 9g
Proteins: 11g
Fat: 17g
Sodium: 73mg

Side Dishes

541. French Lentils

Preparation Time: 5 minutes **Cooking Time:** 25 minutes **Servings:** 10

Ingredients:
- 2 tablespoons olive oil
- 1 medium onion, diced
- 1 medium carrot, peeled and diced
- 2 cloves minced garlic
- 5 ½ cups water
- 2 ¼ cups French lentils, washed and drained
- 1 teaspoon dried thyme
- 2 small bay leaves
- Salt and pepper

Directions:
1. Warmth the oil in a saucepan over medium heat.
2. Attach the onions, carrot, and garlic and sauté for 3 minutes.
3. Stir in the water, lentils, thyme, and bay leaves – season with salt.
4. Set to a boil and cook until tender, about 20 minutes.
5. Drain any excess water and adjust seasoning to taste. Serve hot.

Nutrition:
Calories: 185
Fat: 3.3g
Carbohydrates: 7.9
Protein: 11.4g
Sugar: 1.7g
Fiber: 13.7g
Sodium: 11mg

542. Grain-Free Berry Cobbler

Preparation Time: 5 minutes **Cooking Time:** 25 minutes **Servings:** 10

Ingredients:
- 4 cups fresh mixed berries
- ½ cup ground flaxseed
- ¼ cup almond meal
- ¼ cup unsweetened shredded coconut
- ½ tablespoon baking powder
- 1 teaspoon ground cinnamon
- ¼ teaspoon salt
- Powdered stevia, to taste
- 6 tablespoons coconut oil

Directions:
1. Warmth the oven to 375F and lightly grease a 10-inch cast-iron skillet.
2. Spread the berries on the bottom of the skillet.
3. Spill together the dry ingredients in a mixing bowl.
4. Cut in the coconut oil using a fork to create a crumbled mixture.
5. Set the crumble over the berries and bake for 25 minutes until hot and bubbling.
6. Cool the cobbler for 5 to 10 minutes before serving.

Nutrition:
Calories: 224
Fat: 17.5g
Carbohydrates: 10g
Fiber: 3.4g
Sugar: 3.3g
Protein: 9.4g
Sodium: 51mg

---

543. Coffee-Steamed Carrots

Preparation Time: 10 minutes **Cooking Time:** 3 minutes **Servings:** 4

Ingredients:
- 1 cup brewed coffee
- 1 teaspoon Splenda brown sugar
- ½ teaspoon kosher salt
- Freshly ground black pepper
- 1-pound baby carrots
- Chopped fresh parsley
- 1 teaspoon grated lemon zest

Directions:
1. Pour the coffee into the electric pressure cooker. Stir in the brown sugar, salt, and pepper. Add the carrots.
2. Close the pressure cooker. Set to sealing.
3. Cook on high pressure for minutes.
4. Once complete, click Cancel and quick release the pressure.
5. Once the pin drops, open and remove the lid.
6. Using a slotted spoon, portion carrots to a serving bowl. Topped with the parsley and lemon zest and serve.

Nutrition:
Calories: 205
Fat: 12.5g
Carbohydrates: 15.1g
Fiber: 6.6g
Sugar: 5.3g
Protein: 3.9g
Sodium: 235mg

---

544. Rosemary Potatoes

Preparation Time: 5 minutes **Cooking Time:** 25 minutes **Servings:** 2

Ingredients:
- 1lb red potatoes
- 1 cup vegetable stock
- 2tbsp olive oil
- 2tbsp rosemary sprigs

Directions:
1. Situate potatoes in the steamer basket and add the stock into the Instant Pot.
2. Steam the potatoes in your Instant Pot for 15 minutes.
3. Depressurize and pour away the remaining stock.
4. Set to sauté and add the oil, rosemary, and potatoes.
5. Cook until brown.

Nutrition:
Calories: 209
Fat: 17g
Protein: 6g
Sugar: 0.5g
Carbohydrates: 5g

---

545. Kale and Cabbage Salad with Peanuts

Preparation Time: 15 minutes **Cooking Time:** 0 minutes **Servings:** 6

Ingredients:
- 2 bunches baby kale, thinly sliced

Dressing:
- ¼ cup apple cider vinegar
- Juice of 1 lemon
- 1 teaspoon ground cumin
- ¼ teaspoon smoked paprika
- ½ head green savoy cabbage, cored and thinly sliced
- 1 cup toasted peanuts
- 1 medium red bell pepper, thinly sliced
- 1 garlic clove, thinly sliced

Directions:
1. Toss the kale with cabbage in a large bowl. Set aside.
2. In a separate bowl, spill together the vinegar, lemon juice, cumin, and paprika until completely mixed.
3. Pour the dressing into the bowl of greens and using your hands to massage the greens until thickly coated.
4. Add the peanuts, bell peppers, and garlic to the bowl. Gently toss to combine well.
5. Serve chilled or at room temperature.

Nutrition:
Calories: 297
Fat: 4 g
Cholesterol: 276 mg
Sodium: 291 mg
Carbohydrates: 35 g
Sugar: 9 g
Protein: 29 g

---

546. Chili Lime Salmon

Preparation Time: 6 minutes **Cooking Time:** 10 minutes **Servings:** 2

Ingredients:
For Sauce:
- 1 jalapeno pepper
- 1 tablespoon chopped parsley
- 1 teaspoon minced garlic
- ½ teaspoon cumin
- ½ teaspoon paprika
- ½ teaspoon lime zest
- 1 tablespoon honey
- 1 tablespoon lime juice

- 1 tablespoon olive oil

For Fish:
- 2 salmon fillets, each about 5 ounces
- 1 cup water
- 1 tablespoon water
- ½ teaspoon salt
- ⅛ teaspoon ground black pepper

Directions:
1. Prepare salmon and for this, season salmon with salt and black pepper until evenly coated.
2. Plugin instant pot, insert the inner pot, pour in water, then place steamer basket and place seasoned salmon on it.
3. Seal instant pot with its lid, press the 'steam' button, then press the 'timer' to set the cooking time to 5 minutes and cook on high pressure, for 5 minutes.
4. Transfer all the ingredients for the sauce in a bowl, whisk until combined and set aside until required.
5. When the timer beeps, press 'cancel' button and do quick pressure release until pressure nob drops down.
6. Open the instant pot, then transfer salmon to a serving plate and drizzle generously with prepared sauce.
7. Serve straight away.

Nutrition:
Calories: 224
Fat: 17.5g
Carbohydrates: 10g
Fiber: 3.4g
Sugar: 3.3g
Protein: 9.4g

547. Collard Greens

Preparation Time: 5 minutes **Cooking Time:** 6 hours **Servings:** 12

Ingredients:
- 2 pounds chopped collard greens
- ¾ cup chopped white onion
- 1 teaspoon onion powder
- 1 teaspoon garlic powder
- 1 teaspoon salt
- 2 teaspoons Splenda brown sugar
- ½ teaspoon ground black pepper
- ½ teaspoon red chili powder
- ¼ teaspoon crushed red pepper flakes
- 3 tablespoons apple cider vinegar
- 2 tablespoons olive oil
- 14.5-ounce vegetable broth
- ½ cup water

Directions:
1. Plugin instant pot, insert the inner pot, add onion and collard and then pour in vegetable broth and water.
2. Close instant pot with its lid, seal, press the 'slow cook' button, then press the 'timer' to set the cooking time to 6 hours at high heat setting.
3. When the timer beeps, press 'cancel' button and do natural pressure release until pressure nob drops down.
4. Open the instant pot, add remaining ingredients and stir until mixed.
5. Then press the 'sauté/simmer' button and cook for 3 to minutes or more until collards reach to desired texture.
6. Serve straight away.

Nutrition:
Calories: 228
Fat: 11.4g
Carbohydrates: 10.2g
Protein: 14.5g

548. Mashed Pumpkin

Preparation Time: 9 minutes **Cooking Time:** 15 minutes **Servings:** 2

Ingredients:
- 2 cups chopped pumpkin
- 0.5 cup water
- 2tbsp powdered sugar-free sweetener of choice
- 1tbsp cinnamon

Directions:
1. Place the pumpkin and water in your Instant Pot.
2. Seal and cook on Stew 15 minutes.
3. Remove and mash with the sweetener and cinnamon.

Nutrition:
Calories: 40
Fat: 2.5g
Carbohydrates: 3.3g
Protein: 2.5g

549. Turkey Loaf

Preparation Time: 10 minutes **Cooking Time:** 50 minutes **Servings:** 2

Ingredients:
- ½ lb. 93% lean ground turkey
- ⅓ cup panko breadcrumbs
- ½ cup green onion
- 1 egg
- ½ cup green bell pepper
- 1 tbsp. ketchup
- ¼ cup sauce (Picante)
- ½ tsp. cumin (ground)

Directions:
1. Preheat oven to 350F. Mix lean ground turkey, 3 tbsp Picante sauce, panko breadcrumbs, egg, chopped green onion, chopped green bell pepper and cumin in a bowl (mix well).
2. Put the mixture into a baking sheet; shape into an oval (about 1,5 inches thick). Bake 45 minutes.
3. Mix remaining Picante sauce and the ketchup; apply over loaf. Bake 5 minutes longer. Let stand 5 minutes.

Nutrition:
Calories 136
Protein 2g
Fat 6g
Carbohydrates: 3.2g

550. Mushroom Pasta

Preparation Time: 7 minutes **Cooking Time:** 10 minutes **Servings:** 4

Ingredients:
- 4 oz. whole-grain linguine
- 1 tsp. extra virgin olive oil
- ½ cup light sauce
- 2 tbsp. green onion
- 1 (8-oz) pkg. mushrooms
- 1 clove garlic
- ⅛ tsp. salt
- ⅛ tsp. pepper

Directions:
1. Cook pasta according to package Directions, drain.
2. Fry sliced mushrooms 4 minutes.
3. Stir in fettuccine minced garlic, salt and pepper. Cook 2 minutes.
4. Heat light sauce until heated; top pasta mixture properly with sauce and with finely-chopped green onion.

Nutrition:
Calories: 125
Protein: 20g
Fat: 4g
Carbohydrates: 1.2g

---

551. Garlic Kale Chips

Preparation Time: 6-7 minutes **Cooking Time:** 5 minutes **Servings:** 2

Ingredients:
- 1 tbsp. yeast flakes
- Sea salt to taste
- 4 cups packed kale
- 2 tbsp. olive oil
- 1 tsp. garlic, minced
- ½ cup ranch seasoning pieces

Directions:
1. In a bowl, set the oil, kale, garlic, and ranch seasoning pieces. Attach the yeast and mix well. Set the coated kale into an air fryer basket and cook at 375F for 5 minutes.
2. Shake after 3 minutes and serve.

Nutrition:
Calories: 50
Total Fat: 1.9 g
Carbohydrates: 10 g
Protein: 46 g

---

552. Garlic Salmon Balls

Preparation Time: 6-7 minutes **Cooking Time:** 10 minutes **Servings:** 2

Ingredients:
- 6 oz. tinned salmon
- 1 large egg
- 3 tbsp. olive oil
- 5 tbsp. wheat germ
- ½ tsp. garlic powder
- 1 tbsp. dill, fresh, chopped
- 4 tbsp. spring onion, diced
- 4 tbsp. celery, diced

Directions:
1. Preheat your air fryer to 370F. In a large bowl, merge the salmon, egg, celery, onion, dill, and garlic.
2. Form the mixture into golf ball size balls and twirl them in the wheat germ. In a pan, warm olive oil over medium-low heat. Attach the salmon balls and slowly flatten them. Set them to your air fryer and cook for 10 minutes.

Nutrition:
Calories: 219 Total Fat: 7.7 g
Carbohydrates: 14.8 g Protein: 23.1 g

---

553. Onion Rings

Preparation Time: 7 minutes **Cooking Time:** 10 minutes **Servings:** 3

Ingredients:
- 1 onion, cut into slices, then form into rings
- 1 ½ cup almond flour
- ¾ cup pork rinds
- 1 cup milk
- 1 egg
- 1 tbsp. baking powder
- ½ tsp. salt

Directions:
1. Warmth your air fryer for 10 minutes. In a container, merge the flour, baking powder, and salt.
2. Spill the eggs and the milk, then combines with flour. Gently soak the floured onion rings into the batter to coat them.
3. Set the pork rinds on a plate and dredge the rings in the crumbs. Cook the onion rings in your air fryer for 10 minutes at 360F.

Nutrition:
Calories: 304
Total Fat: 18g
Carbohydrates: 31g
Protein: 38g

---

554. Crispy Eggplant Fries

Preparation Time: 7 minutes **Cooking Time:** 12 minutes **Servings:** 3

Ingredients:
- 2 eggplants
- ¼ cup olive oil
- ¼ cup almond flour
- ½ cup water

Directions:
1. Preheat your air fryer to 390F. Cut the eggplants into ½-inch slices. In a mixing bowl, merge the flour, olive oil, water, and eggplants.
2. Slowly coat the eggplants. Attach eggplants to the air fryer and cook for 12 minutes. Serve with yogurt or tomato sauce.

Nutrition:
Calories: 103
Fat: 7.3 g
Carbohydrates: 12.3 g
Protein: 1.9 g

555. Charred Bell Peppers

Preparation Time: 7 minutes **Cooking Time:** 4 minutes **Servings:** 3

Ingredients:
- 20 bell peppers, sliced and seeded
- 1 tsp. olive oil
- 1 pinch sea salt
- 1 lemon
- Pepper

Directions:
1. Preheat your air fryer to 390F. Set the peppers with oil and salt. Cook the peppers in the air fryer.
2. Set peppers in a bowl, and squeeze lemon juice over the top. Season with salt and pepper.

Nutrition:
Calories: 30
Fat: 0.25 g
Carbohydrates: 6.91 g
Protein: 1.23 g

556. Garlic Tomatoes

Preparation Time: 7 minutes **Cooking Time:** 15 minutes **Servings:** 4

Ingredients:
- 3 tbsp. vinegar
- ½ tsp. thyme, dried
- 4 tomatoes
- 1 tbsp. olive oil
- Salt and black pepper to taste
- 1 garlic clove, minced

Directions:
1. Preheat your air fryer to 390F. Scratch the tomatoes into halves and detach the seeds. Set them in a big bowl and toss them with oil, salt, pepper, garlic, and thyme.
2. Set them into the air fryer and cook for 15 minutes. Drizzle with vinegar and serve.

Nutrition:
Calories: 28.9
Fat: 2.4 g
Carbohydrates: 2.0 g
Protein: 0.4 g

557. Mushroom Stew

Preparation Time: 7 minutes **Cooking Time:** 1 hour 22 minutes **Servings:** 3

Ingredients:
- 1 lb. chicken, cubed, boneless, skinless
- 2 tbsp. canola oil
- 1 lb. fresh mushrooms, sliced
- 1 tbsp. thyme, dried
- ¼ cup water
- 2 tbsp. tomato paste
- 4 garlic cloves, minced
- 1 cup green peppers, sliced
- 3 cups zucchini, diced
- 1 large onion, diced
- 1 tbsp. basil
- 1 tbsp. marjoram
- 1 tbsp. oregano

Directions:
1. Divide the chicken into cubes. Set them in the air fryer basket and pour olive oil over them. Attach mushrooms, zucchini, onion, and green pepper. Merge and add garlic, cook for 2 minutes, then add tomato paste, water, and seasonings.
2. Seal the air fryer and cook the stew for 50 minutes. Set the heat to 340F and cook.
3. Detach from air fryer and transfer into a large pan. Empty in a bit of water and simmer for 10 minutes.

Nutrition:
Calories: 53
Fat: 3.3 g
Carbohydrates: 4.9 g
Protein: 2.3 g

558. Cheese and Onion Nuggets

Preparation Time: 7 minutes **Cooking Time:** 12 minutes **Servings:** 4

Ingredients:
- 7 oz. Edam cheese, grated
- 2 spring onions, diced
- 1 egg, beaten
- 1 tbsp. coconut oil
- 1 tbsp. thyme, dried
- Salt and pepper to taste

Directions:
1. Merge the onion, cheese, coconut oil, salt, pepper, thyme in a bowl. Set 8 small balls and place the cheese in the center.
2. Set in the fridge for about an hour. With a pastry brush, carefully garnish the beaten egg over the nuggets. Cook in the air fryer at 350F.

Nutrition:
Calories: 227
Fat: 17.3 g
Carbohydrates: 4.5 g
Protein: 14.2 g

559. Spiced Nuts

Preparation Time: 7 minutes **Cooking Time:** 25 minutes **Servings:** 3

Ingredients:
- 1 cup almonds
- 1 cup pecan halves

- 1 cup cashews
- 1 egg white, beaten
- ½ tsp. cinnamon, ground
- Pinch cayenne pepper
- ¼ tsp. cloves, ground
- Pinch salt

Directions:
1. Combine the egg white with spices. Preheat your air fryer to 300F.
2. Spill the nuts in the spiced mixture. Cook for 25 minutes, stir throughout cooking time.

Nutrition:
Calories: 88.4
Fat: 7.6 g
Carbohydrates: 3.9 g
Protein: 2.5 g

560. Keto French fries

Preparation Time: 7 minutes **Cooking Time:** 20 minutes **Servings:** 4

Ingredients:
- 1 large rutabaga, peeled, divided into spears about ¼-inch wide
- Salt and pepper to taste
- ½ tsp. paprika
- 2 tbsp. coconut oil

Directions:
1. Preheat your air fryer to 450F. Mix the oil, paprika, salt, and pepper.
2. Spill the oil mixture over the rutabaga fries. Cook for 20 minutes.

Nutrition:
Calories: 113
Fat: 7.2g
Carbohydrates: 12.5g
Protein: 1.9g

561. Fried Garlic Green Tomatoes

Preparation Time: 7 minutes **Cooking Time:** 12 minutes **Servings:** 2

Ingredients:
- 3 green tomatoes, sliced
- ½ cup almond flour
- 2 eggs, beaten
- Salt and pepper to taste
- 1 tsp. garlic, minced

Directions:
1. Flavor the tomatoes with salt, garlic, and pepper. Warmth your air fryer to 400F. Soak the tomatoes first in flour then in the egg mixture.
2. Set the tomato rounds with olive oil and bring them in the air fryer basket. Cook for 8 minutes. Set with zero-carb mayonnaise.

Nutrition:
Calories: 123
Fat: 3.9 g
Carbohydrates: 16 g
Protein: 8.4 g

562. Garlic Cauliflower Tots

Preparation Time: 7 minutes **Cooking Time:** 20 minutes **Servings:** 4

Ingredients:
- 1 crown cauliflower, hashed in a food processor
- ½ cup parmesan cheese, grinded
- Salt and pepper
- ¼ cup almond flour
- 2 eggs
- 1 tsp. garlic, diced

Directions:
1. Merge all the ingredients. Form into tots and spray with olive oil. Preheat your air fryer to 400F.
2. Cook for 10 minutes on each side.

Nutrition:
Calories: 18
Fat: 0.6 g
Carbohydrates: 1.3 g
Protein: 1.8 g

563. Chicken Tikka Masala

Preparation Time: 5 minutes **Cooking Time:** 15 minutes **Servings:** 2

Ingredients:
- ½ lb. chicken breasts
- ¼ cup onion
- 1tsp. extra virgin olive oil
- 1 (14.5-oz) can tomatoes
- 1 tsp. ginger
- 1 tsp. fresh lemon juice
- ⅓ cup plain Greek yogurt (fat-free)
- 1 tbsp. garam masala
- ¼ tsp. salt
- ¼ tsp. pepper

Directions:
1. Flavor chicken cut into 1-inch cubes with 1.5 tsp. garam masala, ⅛ tsp salt and pepper. Cook chicken and diced onion 4 to 5 minutes.
2. Add diced tomatoes, grated ginger, 1.5 tsp. garam masala, ⅛ tsp salt. Cook 8 to 10 minutes. Add lemon juice and yogurt until blended.

Nutrition:
Calories: 205
Fat: 12.5g
Carbohydrates: 15.1g
Fiber: 6.6g
Sugar: 5.3g
Protein: 3.9g
Sodium: 235mg

564. Tomato and Roasted Cod

Preparation Time: 10 minutes **Cooking Time:** 35 minutes **Servings:** 2

Ingredients:
- 2 (4-oz) cod fillets
- 1 cup cherry tomatoes
- ⅔ cup onion
- 2 tsp. orange rind
- 1 tbsp. extra virgin olive oil
- 1 tsp. thyme (dried)
- ¼ tsp. salt, divided
- ¼ tsp. pepper, divided

Directions:
1. Preheat oven to 400F. Mix in half tomatoes, sliced onion, grated orange rind, extra virgin olive oil, dried thyme, and ⅛ salt and pepper. Fry 25 minutes. Remove from oven.
2. Arrange fish on pan, and flavor with remaining ⅛ tsp. each salt and pepper. Put reserved tomato mixture over fish. Bake 10 minutes.

Nutrition:
Calories 253
Protein 15g
Fat 20g
Carbohydrates: 2.1g

565. Ravioli

Preparation Time: 5 minutes **Cooking Time:** 16 minutes **Servings:** 4

Ingredients:
- 8 ounces frozen vegan ravioli, thawed
- 1 teaspoon dried basil
- 1 teaspoon garlic powder
- ⅛ teaspoon ground black pepper
- ¼ teaspoon salt
- 1 teaspoon dried oregano
- 2 teaspoons Nutritional yeast flakes
- ½ cup marinara sauce, unsweetened
- ½ cup panko breadcrumbs
- ¼ cup liquid from chickpeas can

Directions:
1. Place breadcrumbs in a bowl, sprinkle with salt, basil, oregano, and black pepper, add garlic powder and yeast and stir until mixed.
2. Take a bowl and then pour in chickpeas liquid in it.
3. Working on one ravioli at a time, first dip a ravioli in chickpeas liquid and then coat with breadcrumbs mixture.
4. Prepare remaining ravioli in the same manner, then take a fryer basket, grease it well with oil and place ravioli in it in a single layer.
5. Turn on the air fryer, insert fryer basket, sprinkle oil on ravioli, shut with its lid, set the fryer at 390 F, then cook for 6 minutes, turn the ravioli and continue cooking 2 minutes until nicely golden and heated thoroughly.
6. Cook the remaining ravioli in the same manner and serve with marinara sauce.

Nutrition:
Calories: 150
Fat: 3 g
Protein: 5 g
Carbohydrates: 2g

566. Cabbage Wedges

Preparation Time: 10 minutes **Cooking Time:** 29 minutes **Servings:** 6

Ingredients:
- 1 small head of green cabbage
- 6 strips of bacon, thick-cut, pastured
- 1 teaspoon onion powder
- ½ teaspoon ground black pepper
- 1 teaspoon garlic powder
- ¾ teaspoon salt
- ¼ teaspoon red chili flakes
- ½ teaspoon fennel seeds
- 3 tablespoons olive oil

Directions:
1. Turn on the air fryer, insert fryer basket, grease it with olive oil, then shut with its lid, set the fryer at 350 F and warmth for 5 minutes.
2. Open the fryer; attach bacon strips in it, seal with its lid and cook for 10 minutes.
3. Meanwhile, prepare the cabbage and for this, remove the outer leaves of the cabbage and then cut it into eight wedges, keeping the core intact.
4. Prepare the spice mix and for this, set onion powder in a bowl, attach black pepper, garlic powder, salt, red chili, and fennel and stir until mixed.
5. Whisk cabbage wedges with oil and then sprinkle with spice mix until well coated.
6. When air fryer beeps, open its lid, transfer bacon strips to a cutting board and let it rest.
7. Attach the seasoned cabbage wedges into the fryer basket, close with its lid, then cook for 8 minutes at 400 F, flip the cabbage, spray with oil and continue air frying for 6 minutes until nicely golden and cooked.
8. When completed, transfer cabbage wedges to a plate.
9. Slice the bacon, sprinkle it over cabbage and serve.

Nutrition:
Calories: 123
Fat: 11 g
Protein: 4 g
Carbohydrates: 3g

567. Buffalo Cauliflower Wings

Preparation Time: 5 minutes **Cooking Time:** 30 minutes **Servings:** 6

Ingredients:
- 1 tablespoon almond flour
- 1 medium head of cauliflower
- 1 ½ teaspoon salt
- 4 tablespoons hot sauce
- 1 tablespoon olive oil

Directions:
1. Switch on the air fryer, insert fryer basket, grease it with olive oil, then shut with its lid, set the fryer at 400 F and preheat for 5 minutes.
2. Meanwhile, cut cauliflower into bite-size florets and set aside.
3. Place flour in a large bowl, whisk in salt, oil and hot sauce until combined, add cauliflower florets and toss until combined.
4. Open the fryer, add cauliflower florets in it in a single layer, close with its lid and cook for 15 minutes until nicely golden and crispy, shaking halfway through the frying.
5. When air fryer beeps, open its lid, transfer cauliflower florets onto a serving plate and keep warm.
6. Cook the remaining cauliflower florets in the same manner and serve.

Nutrition:
Calories: 48
Fat: 4 g
Protein: 1 g
Carbohydrates: 1.2g

568. Sweet Potato Cauliflower Patties

Preparation Time: 20 minutes **Cooking Time:** 40 minutes **Servings:** 7

Ingredients:
- 1 green onion, chopped
- 1 large sweet potato, peeled
- 1 teaspoon minced garlic
- 1 cup cilantro leaves
- 2 cup cauliflower florets
- ¼ teaspoon ground black pepper
- ¼ teaspoon salt
- ¼ cup sunflower seeds
- ¼ teaspoon cumin
- ¼ cup ground flaxseed
- ½ teaspoon red chili powder
- 2 tablespoons ranch seasoning mix
- 2 tablespoons arrowroot starch

Directions:
1. Cut peeled sweet potato into small pieces, then place them in a food processor and pulse until pieces are broken up.
2. Then add onion, cauliflower florets, and garlic, pulse until combined, add remaining Ingredients and pulse more until incorporated.
3. Tip the mixture in a bowl, shape the mixture into seven 1 ½ inch thick patties, each about ¼ cup, then place them on a baking sheet and freeze for 10 minutes.
4. Switch on the air fryer, insert fryer basket, grease it with olive oil, then shut with its lid, set the fryer at 400F and preheat for 10 minutes.
5. Open the fryer, add patties in it in a single layer, close with its lid and cook for 20 minutes until nicely golden and cooked, flipping the patties halfway through the frying.
6. When air fryer beeps, open its lid, transfer patties onto a serving plate and keep them warm.
7. Cook the remaining patties and serve.

Nutrition:
Calories: 85
Fat: 3 g
Protein: 2.7 g
Carbohydrates: 3.2g

569. Okra

Preparation Time: 10 minutes **Cooking Time:** 10 minutes **Servings:** 4

Ingredients:
- 1 cup almond flour
- 8 ounces fresh okra
- ½ teaspoon sea salt
- 1 cup milk, reduced-fat
- 1 egg, pastured

Directions:
1. Beat the egg in a bowl, pour in the milk and whisk until blended.
2. Cut the stem from each okra, then cut it into ½-inch pieces, add them into egg and stir until well coated.
3. Mix flour and salt and add it into a large plastic bag.
4. Working on one okra piece at a time, drain the okra well by letting excess egg drip off, add it to the flour mixture, then seal the bag and shake well until okra is well coated.
5. Place the coated okra on a grease air fryer basket, coat remaining okra pieces in the same manner and place them into the basket.
6. Switch on the air fryer, insert fryer basket, spray okra with oil, then shut with its lid, set the fryer at 390 F and cook for 10 minutes until nicely golden and cooked, stirring okra halfway through the frying.
7. Serve straight away.

Nutrition:
Calories: 250
Fat: 9 g
Protein: 3 g
Carbohydrates: 4.1g

570. Creamed Spinach

Preparation Time: 10 minutes **Cooking Time:** 20 minutes **Servings:** 2

Ingredients:
- ½ cup chopped white onion
- 10 ounces frozen spinach, thawed
- 1 teaspoon salt
- 1 teaspoon ground black pepper
- 2 teaspoons minced garlic
- ½ teaspoon ground nutmeg
- 4 ounces cream cheese, reduced-fat, diced
- ¼ cup shredded parmesan cheese, reduced-fat

Directions:
1. Switch on the air fryer, insert fryer basket, grease it with olive oil, then shut with its lid, set the fryer at 350 F and preheat for 5 minutes.
2. Meanwhile, take a 6-inches baking pan, grease it with oil and set aside.
3. Place spinach in a bowl, add remaining Ingredients except for parmesan cheese, stir until well mixed and then add the mixture into prepared baking pan.

4. Open the fryer, add pan in it, close with its lid and cook for 10 minutes until cooked and cheese has melted, stirring halfway through.
5. Then sprinkle parmesan cheese on top of spinach and continue air fryer for 5 minutes at 400 degrees F until top is nicely golden and cheese has melted.
6. Serve straight away.

Nutrition:
Calories: 273
Fat: 23 g
Protein: 8 g
Carbohydrates: 5.1g

571. Eggplant Parmesan

Preparation Time: 20 minutes **Cooking Time:** 15 minutes **Servings:** 4

Ingredients:
- ½ cup and 3 tablespoons almond flour, divided
- 1.25-pound eggplant, ½-inch sliced
- 1 tablespoon chopped parsley
- 1 teaspoon Italian seasoning
- 2 teaspoons salt
- 1 cup marinara sauce
- 1 egg, pastured
- 1 tablespoon water
- 3 tablespoons grated parmesan cheese, reduced-fat
- ¼ cup grated mozzarella cheese, reduced-fat

Directions:
1. Slice the eggplant into ½-inch pieces, place them in a colander, sprinkle with 1 ½ teaspoon salt on both sides and let it rest for 15 minutes.
2. Meanwhile, place ½ cup flour in a bowl, add egg and water and whisk until blended.
3. Place remaining flour in a shallow dish, add remaining salt, Italian seasoning, and parmesan cheese and stir until mixed.
4. Switch on the air fryer, insert fryer basket, grease it with olive oil, then shut with its lid, set the fryer at 360 F and preheat for 5 minutes.
5. Meanwhile, drain the eggplant pieces, pat them dry, and then dip each slice into the egg mixture and coat with flour mixture.
6. Open the fryer; add coated eggplant slices in it in a single layer, close with its lid and cook for 8 minutes until nicely golden and cooked, flipping the eggplant slices halfway through the frying.
7. Then top each eggplant slice with a tablespoon of marinara sauce and some of the mozzarella cheese and continue air frying for 1 to 2 minutes or until cheese has melted.
8. When air fryer beeps, open its lid, transfer eggplants onto a serving plate and keep them warm.
9. Cook remaining eggplant slices in the same manner and serve.

Nutrition:
Calories: 193
Fat: 5.5 g
Protein: 10 g
Carbohydrates: 1.9g

572. Cauliflower Rice

Preparation Time: 10 minutes **Cooking Time:** 27 minutes **Servings:** 3

Ingredients:
For the Tofu:
- 1 cup diced carrot
- 6 ounces tofu, extra-firm, drained
- ½ cup diced white onion

For the Cauliflower:
- ½ cup chopped broccoli
- 3 cups cauliflower rice
- 1 tablespoon minced garlic
- ½ cup frozen peas
- 2 tablespoons soy sauce
- 1 teaspoon turmeric
- 1 tablespoon minced ginger
- 2 tablespoons soy sauce
- 1 tablespoon apple cider vinegar
- 1 ½ teaspoons toasted sesame oil

Directions:
1. Set the air fryer pan with olive oil, then shut with its lid, set the fryer at 370 F and preheat for 5 minutes.
2. Meanwhile, place tofu in a bowl, crumble it, then add remaining Ingredients and stir until mixed.
3. Open the fryer, add tofu mixture in it, spray with oil, close with its lid and cook for 10 minutes until nicely golden and crispy, stirring halfway through the frying.
4. Meanwhile, place all the ingredients for cauliflower in a bowl and toss until mixed.
5. When air fryer beeps, open its lid, add cauliflower mixture, shake the pan gently to mix and continue cooking for 12 minutes, shaking halfway through the frying.
6. Serve straight away.

Nutrition:
Calories: 258.1
Fat: 13 g
Protein: 18.2 g
Carbohydrates: 7g

573. Air-Fried Brussels sprouts

Preparation Time: 5 minutes **Cooking Time:** 10 minutes **Servings:** 2

Ingredients:
- 2 cups Brussels sprouts
- ¼ teaspoon sea salt
- 1 tablespoon olive oil
- 1 tablespoon apple cider vinegar

Directions:
1. Switch on the air fryer, insert fryer basket, grease it with olive oil, then shut with its lid, set the fryer at 400 F and preheat for 5 minutes.
2. Meanwhile, cut the sprouts lengthwise into ¼-inch thick pieces, add them in a bowl, add remaining Ingredients and toss until well coated.

3. Open the fryer, add sprouts in it, close with its lid and cook for 10 minutes until crispy and cooked, shaking halfway through the frying.
4. When air fryer beeps, open its lid, transfer sprouts onto a serving plate and serve.

Nutrition:
Calories: 88
Fat: 4.4 g
Protein: 3.9 g
Carbohydrates: 5g

574. Green Beans

Preparation Time: 5 minutes **Cooking Time:** 13 minutes **Servings:** 4

Ingredients:
- 1-pound green beans
- ¾ teaspoon garlic powder
- ¾ teaspoon ground black pepper
- 1 ¼ teaspoon salt
- ½ teaspoon paprika

Directions:
1. Switch on the air fryer, insert fryer basket, grease it with olive oil, then shut with its lid, set the fryer at 400 F and preheat for 5 minutes.
2. Meanwhile, place beans in a bowl, spray generously with olive oil, sprinkle with garlic powder, black pepper, salt, and paprika and toss until well coated.
3. Open the fryer, add green beans in it, close with its lid and cook for 8 minutes until nicely golden and crispy, shaking halfway through the frying.
4. When air fryer beeps, open its lid, transfer green beans onto a serving plate and serve.

Nutrition:
Calories: 45
Fat: 1 g
Protein: 2 g
Carbohydrates: 6.1g

575. Asparagus Avocado Soup

Preparation Time: 10 minutes **Cooking Time:** 20 minutes **Servings:** 4

Ingredients:
- 1 avocado, peeled, pitted, cubed
- 12 ounces asparagus
- ½ teaspoon ground black pepper
- 1 teaspoon garlic powder
- 1 teaspoon sea salt
- 2 tablespoons olive oil, divided
- ½ of a lemon, juiced
- 2 cups vegetable stock

Directions:
1. Switch on the air fryer, insert fryer basket, grease it with olive oil, then shut with its lid, set the fryer at 425 F and preheat for 5 minutes.
2. Meanwhile, place asparagus in a shallow dish, drizzle with 1 tablespoon oil, sprinkle with garlic powder, salt, and black pepper and stir.
3. Open the fryer, add asparagus in it, close with its lid and cook for 10 minutes until nicely golden and roasted, shaking halfway through the frying.
4. When air fryer beeps, open its lid and transfer asparagus to a food processor.
5. Attach the remaining Ingredients into a food processor and pulse until well combined and smooth.
6. Tip the soup in a saucepan, pour in water if the soup is too thick and heat it over medium-low heat for 5 minutes until thoroughly heated.
7. Ladle soup into bowls and serve.

Nutrition:
Calories: 208
Fat: 16 g
Protein: 6 g
Carbohydrates: 4g

576. Asparagus and Bacon Salad

Preparation Time: 5 minutes **Cooking Time:** 5 minutes **Servings:** 1

Ingredients:
- 1 hard-boiled egg, peeled and sliced
- 1⅔ cups asparagus, chopped
- 2 slices bacon, cooked crisp and crumbled
- 1 teaspoon extra virgin olive oil
- 1 teaspoon red wine vinegar
- ½ teaspoon Dijon mustard
- Pinch salt and pepper, to taste

Directions:
1. Set a pot of water to a boil. Add the asparagus and cook 2 to 3 minutes or until tender-crisp. Drain and attach cold water to stop the cooking process.
2. In a small bowl, whisk together, mustard, oil, vinegar, and salt and pepper to taste.
3. Set the asparagus on a plate, top with egg and bacon. Drizzle with vinaigrette and serve.

Nutrition:
Calories: 113
Fat: 7.2 g
Carbohydrates: 12.5 g
Protein: 1.9 g

577. Quinoa Tabbouleh

Preparation Time: 8 minutes **Cooking Time:** 16 minutes **Servings:** 6

Ingredients:
- 1 cup quinoa, rinsed
- 1 large English cucumber
- 2 scallions, sliced
- 2 cups cherry tomatoes, halved
- ⅔ cup chopped parsley
- ½ cup chopped mint
- ½ teaspoon minced garlic
- ½ teaspoon salt

- ½ teaspoon ground black pepper
- 2 tablespoon lemon juice
- ½ cup olive oil

Directions:
1. Plugin instant pot, insert the inner pot, add quinoa, then pour in water and stir until mixed.
2. Close instant pot with its lid and turn the pressure knob to seal the pot.
3. Select 'manual' button, then set the 'timer' to 1 minute and cook in high pressure, it may take 7 minutes.
4. Once the timer stops, select 'cancel' button and do natural pressure release for 10 minutes and then do quick pressure release until pressure nob drops down.
5. Open the instant pot, fluff quinoa with a fork, then spoon it on a rimmed baking sheet, spread quinoa evenly and let cool.
6. Meanwhile, place lime juice in a small bowl, add garlic and stir until just mixed.
7. Then add salt, black pepper, and olive oil and whisk until combined.
8. Set cooled quinoa to a large bowl, add remaining Ingredients, then drizzle generously with the prepared lime juice mixture and toss until evenly coated.
9. Taste quinoa to adjust seasoning and then serve.

Nutrition:
Calories: 85
Protein: 3g
Fat: 3g
Carbohydrates: 6g

578. Black Bean, Quinoa, and Mango Salad

Preparation Time: 10 minutes **Cooking Time:** 15 minutes **Servings:** 8

Ingredients:
- 1 small red or yellow pepper, seedless and hashed
- 2 cups (packed) of baby spinach, torn or sliced
- 1 cup (half 19 ounces/540 ml can) of black beans, rinsed and drained
- ¼ English cucumber, chopped
- 1 cup of quinoa
- 1 ripe mango, peeled and diced
- 2-3 green onions, chopped

Dressing:
- ½ teaspoon of curry powder or paste
- ¼ teaspoon of cumin
- 3 tablespoons of canola oil
- 2 tablespoons of white wine or white balsamic vinegar
- 2 teaspoons of honey

Directions:
1. Rinse the quinoa well under cool water. Drain well.
2. Over medium heat set in a large pot of boiling. Cook quinoa for about 15 minutes until tender but still firm to bite.
3. Drain well and return the quinoa to pot off the heat. Then cover with a tea towel. Set the lid and allow it to steam and produce fluffy quinoa as it cools.
4. Combine the mango, quinoa, pepper, spinach, cucumber, black beans, and onions in a large bowl.
5. Combine the vinegar, canola oil, curry, honey, and cumin in a jar or small bowl to make the dressing.
6. Shake to blend.
7. Set salad with dressing and toss until well coated. Serve and enjoy!

Nutrition:
Calories: 71
Fat: 4.8g
Carbohydrates: 6.6g
Fiber: 2.3g
Sugar: 2.9g
Protein: 2.5g

579. Low Fat Roasties

Preparation Time: 8 minutes **Cooking Time:** 25 minutes **Servings:** 2

Ingredients:
- 1lb roasting potatoes
- 1 garlic clove
- 1 cup vegetable stock
- 2tbsp olive oil

Directions:
1. Position potatoes in the steamer basket and add the stock into the Instant Pot.
2. Steam the potatoes in your Instant Pot for 15 minutes.
3. Depressurize and pour away the remaining stock.
4. Set to sauté and add the oil, garlic, and potatoes. Cook until brown.

Nutrition:
Calories: 53
Fat: 3.3 g
Carbohydrates: 4.9 g
Protein: 2.3 g

580. Roasted Parsnips

Preparation Time: 9 minutes **Cooking Time:** 25 minutes **Servings:** 2

Ingredients:
- 1lb parsnips
- 1 cup vegetable stock
- 2tbsp herbs
- 2tbsp olive oil

Directions:
1. Put the parsnips in the steamer basket and add the stock into the Instant Pot.
2. Steam the parsnips in your Instant Pot for 15 minutes.
3. Depressurize and pour away the remaining stock.
4. Set to sauté and add the oil, herbs and parsnips.
5. Cook until golden and crisp.

Nutrition:
Calories: 297
Fat: 4 g
Cholesterol: 276 mg
Sodium: 291 mg
Carbohydrate: 35 g

581. Lower Carb Hummus

Preparation Time: 9 minutes   **Cooking Time:** 60 minutes   **Servings:** 2

Ingredients:
- 0.5 cup dry chickpeas
- 1 cup vegetable stock
- 1 cup pumpkin puree
- 2tbsp smoked paprika
- salt and pepper to taste

Directions:
1. Soak the chickpeas overnight.
2. Place the chickpeas and stock in the Instant Pot.
3. Cook on Beans 60 minutes.
4. Depressurize naturally.
5. Blend the chickpeas with the remaining Ingredients.

Nutrition:
Calories: 228
Total Fats: 11.4g
Carbohydrates: 10.2g
Protein: 14.5g

---

582. Sweet and Sour Red Cabbage

Preparation Time: 7 minutes   **Cooking Time:** 10 minutes   **Servings:** 8

Ingredients:
- 2 cups Spiced Pear Applesauce
- 1 small onion, chopped
- ½ cup apple cider vinegar
- ½ teaspoon kosher salt
- 1 head red cabbage

Directions:
1. In the electric pressure cooker, combine the applesauce, onion, vinegar, salt, and cup of water. Stir in the cabbage.
2. Seal lid of the pressure cooker.
3. Cook on high pressure for 10 minutes.
4. When the cooking is processed, hit Cancel and quick release the pressure.
5. Once the pin drops, unseal and remove the lid. Spoon into a bowl or platter and serve.

Nutrition:
Calories: 175
Fat: 8g
Protein: 1g
Sugar: 5g
Carbohydrates: 4g

---

583. Pinto Beans

Preparation Time: 6 minutes   **Cooking Time:** 55 minutes   **Servings:** 10

Ingredients:
- 2 cups pinto beans, dried
- 1 medium white onion
- 1 ½ teaspoon minced garlic
- ¾ teaspoon salt
- ¼ teaspoon ground black pepper
- 1 teaspoon red chili powder
- ¼ teaspoon cumin
- 1 tablespoon olive oil
- 1 teaspoon chopped cilantro
- 5 ½ cup vegetable stock

Directions:
1. Plugin instant pots, insert the inner pot, press sauté/simmer button, add oil and when hot, attach onion and garlic and cook for 3 minutes until onions begin to soften.
2. Add remaining Ingredients, stir well, then press the cancel button, shut the instant pot with its lid and seal the pot.
3. Click 'manual' button, then press the 'timer' to set the cooking time to 45 minutes and cook at high pressure.
4. Once done, click 'cancel' button and do natural pressure release for 10 minutes until pressure nob drops down.
5. Open the instant pot, spoon beans into plates and serve.

Nutrition:
Calories: 50
Total Fat: 1.9 g
Carbohydrates: 10 g
Protein: 46 g

---

584. Cucumber and Kidney Bean Salad

Preparation Time: 10 minutes   **Cooking Time:** 0 minutes   **Servings:** 4

Ingredients:
- 3 cups diced cucumber
- 1 (15-ounce / 425-g) can low-sodium dark red kidney beans, drained and rinsed
- 2 avocados, diced
- 1½ cups diced tomatoes
- 1 cup cooked corn
- ¾ cup sliced red onion
- 1 tablespoon extra-virgin olive oil
- 1 tablespoon apple cider vinegar

Directions:
1. In a large bowl, combine the cucumber, kidney beans, avocados, tomatoes, corn, onion, olive oil, and vinegar.

Nutrition:
Calories: 205
Fat: 10.4g
Protein: 3.8g
Carbohydrates: 4.2g

---

585. Steamed Asparagus

Preparation Time: 3 minutes   **Cooking Time:** 2 minutes   **Servings:** 4

Ingredients:
- 1 lb. fresh asparagus, rinsed and tough ends trimmed
- 1 cup water

Directions:

1. Place the asparagus into a wire steamer rack and set it inside your Instant Pot.
2. Add water to the pot. Close and seal the lid, turning the steam release valve to the "Sealing" position.
3. Select the "Steam" function to cook on high pressure for 2 minutes.
4. Once done, do a quick pressure release of the steam.
5. Lift the wire steamer basket out of the pot and place the asparagus onto a serving plate.
6. Season as desired and serve.

Nutrition:
Calories: 53
Fat: 3.3 g
Carbohydrates: 4.9 g
Protein: 2.3 g

586. Squash Medley

Preparation Time: 10 minutes **Cooking Time:** 20 minutes **Servings:** 2

Ingredients:
- 2 lbs. mixed squash
- ½ cup mixed veg
- 1 cup vegetable stock
- 2 tbsps. olive oil
- 2 tbsps. mixed herbs

Directions:
1. Put the squash in the steamer basket and add the stock into the Instant Pot.
2. Steam the squash in your Instant Pot for 10 minutes.
3. Depressurize and pour away the remaining stock.
4. Set to sauté and add the oil and remaining Ingredients.
5. Cook until a light crust form.

Nutrition:
Calories: 735
Carbohydrates: 82 g
Fat: 45 g
Fiber: 3 g
Protein: 7 g

587. Eggplant Curry

Preparation Time: 15 minutes **Cooking Time:** 20 minutes **Servings:** 2

Ingredients:
- 3 cups chopped eggplant
- 1 thinly sliced onion
- 1 cup coconut milk
- 3 tbsps. curry paste
- 1 tbsp. oil or ghee

Directions:
1. Select Instant Pot to sauté and put the onion, oil, and curry paste.
2. Once the onion is soft, stir in remaining Ingredients and seal.
3. Cook on Stew for 20 minutes. Release the pressure naturally.

Nutrition:
Calories: 85
Fat: 3 g
Protein: 2.7 g
Carbohydrates: 3.2g

588. Lentil and Eggplant Stew

Preparation Time: 15 minutes **Cooking Time:** 35 minutes **Servings:** 2

Ingredients:
- 1 lb. eggplant
- 1 lb. dry lentils
- 1 cup chopped vegetables
- 1 cup low sodium vegetable broth

Directions:
1. Incorporate all the Ingredients in your Instant Pot, cook on Stew for 35 minutes.
2. Release the pressure naturally and serve.

Nutrition:
Calories: 224
Total Fats: 12.3g
Carbohydrates: 11.2g
Protein: 14.2g

589. Tofu Curry

Preparation Time: 15 minutes **Cooking Time:** 20 minutes **Servings:** 2

Ingredients:
- 2 cups cubed extra firm tofu
- 2 cups mixed stir fry vegetables
- ½ cup soy yogurt
- 3 tbsps. curry paste
- 1 tbsp. oil or ghee

Directions:
1. Set the Instant Pot to sauté and attach the oil and curry paste.
2. Once soft, place the remaining Ingredients except for the yogurt and seal.
3. Cook on Stew for 20 minutes.
4. Release the pressure naturally and serve with a scoop of soy yogurt.

Nutrition:
Calories 253
Protein 15g
Fat 20g
Carbohydrates: 2.1g

590. Lentil and Chickpea Curry

Preparation Time: 15 minutes **Cooking Time:** 20 minutes **Servings:** 2

Ingredients:
- 2 cups dry lentils and chickpeas
- 1 thinly sliced onion
- 1 cup chopped tomato
- 3 tbsps. curry paste

- 1 tbsp. oil or ghee

Directions:
1. Press Instant Pot to sauté and mix onion, oil, and curry paste.
2. Once the onion is cooked, stir the remaining Ingredients and seal.
3. Cook on Stew for 20 minutes.
4. Release the pressure naturally and serve.

Nutrition:
Calories: 40
Fat: 2.5g
Carbohydrates: 3.3g
Fiber: 0.9g

591. Split Pea Stew

Preparation Time: 5 minutes **Cooking Time:** 35 minutes **Servings:** 2

Ingredients:
- 1 cup dry split peas
- 1 lb. chopped vegetables
- 1 cup mushroom soup
- 2 tbsps. old bay seasoning

Directions:
1. Incorporate all the Ingredients in Instant Pot, cook for 33 minutes.
2. Release the pressure naturally.

Nutrition:
Calories 65
Protein 2g
Fat 1g
Carbohydrates: 2.4g

592. Kidney Bean Stew

Preparation Time: 15 minutes **Cooking Time:** 15 minutes **Servings:** 2

Ingredients:
- 1 lb. cooked kidney beans
- 1 cup tomato passata
- 1 cup low sodium beef broth
- 3 tbsps. Italian herbs

Directions:
1. Incorporate all the Ingredients in your Instant Pot, cook on Stew for 15 minutes.
2. Release the pressure naturally and serve.

Nutrition:
Calories: 735
Carbohydrates: 82 g
Fat: 45 g
Fiber: 3 g

593. Fried Tofu Hotpot

Preparation Time: 15 minutes **Cooking Time:** 15 minutes **Servings:** 2

Ingredients:
- ½ lb. fried tofu
- 1 lb. chopped Chinese vegetable mix
- 1 cup low sodium vegetable broth
- 2 tbsps. of 5 spice seasoning
- 1 tbsp. smoked paprika

Directions:
1. Combine all the Ingredients in your Instant Pot, set on Stew for 15 minutes. Release the pressure naturally and serve.

Nutrition:
Calories: 304
Total Fat: 18g
Carbohydrates: 31g
Protein: 38g

594. Chili Sin Carne

Preparation Time: 15 minutes **Cooking Time:** 35 minutes **Servings:** 2

Ingredients:
- 3 cups mixed cooked beans
- 2 cups chopped tomatoes
- 1 tbsp. yeast extract
- 2 squares very dark chocolate
- 1 tbsp. red chili flakes

Directions:
1. Combine all the Ingredients in your Instant Pot, cook for 35 minutes.
2. Release the pressure naturally and serve.

Nutrition:
Calories: 281
Protein: 4g
Fat: 23g
Carbohydrates: 5g

595. Brussels sprouts

Preparation Time: 5 minutes **Cooking Time:** 3 minutes **Servings:** 5

Ingredients:
- 1 tsp. extra-virgin olive oil
- 1 lb. halved Brussels sprouts
- 3 tbsps. apple cider vinegar
- 3 tbsps. gluten-free tamari soy sauce
- 3 tbsps. chopped sun-dried tomatoes

Directions:
1. Press the "Sauté" function on your Instant Pot, add oil and allow the pot to get hot.
2. Cancel the "Sauté" function and add the Brussels sprouts.

3. Stir well and allow the sprouts to cook in the residual heat for 2-3 minutes.
4. Add the tamari soy sauce and vinegar, and then stir.
5. Cover the Instant Pot, sealing the pressure valve by pointing it to "Sealing."
6. Select the "Manual, High Pressure" setting and cook for 3 minutes.
7. Once the cook cycle is done, do a quick pressure release, and then stir in the chopped sun-dried tomatoes.
8. Serve immediately.

Nutrition:
Calories: 88.4
Fat: 7.6 g
Carbohydrates: 3.9 g
Protein: 2.5

Appetizer

596. Calico Slaw

Preparation Time: 5 minutes **Cooking Time:** 5 minutes **Servings:** 8

Ingredients:
- 1 Red Delicious apple, cored and chopped
- 1 Golden Delicious apple, cored and chopped
- ½ teaspoon of fine sea salt
- 1 medium head green cabbage, shredded
- 3 carrots, shredded
- 2 tablespoons of apple cider vinegar
- 2 tablespoons of stevia
- 1 green bell pepper
- 1 red bell pepper
- 1 yellow bell pepper
- ground black pepper, to taste

Directions:
1. Combine carrots, cabbage, green bell pepper, red bell pepper, Red Delicious apple, and Golden Delicious apple in a bowl.
2. Whisk apple cider vinegar, sea salt, and stevia in a bowl; season with black pepper.
3. Pour vinegar mixture over cabbage mixture.
4. Stir gently to coat.
5. Seal the bowl and set to refrigerator for at least 30 minutes.
6. Serve and enjoy!

Nutrition:
Calories: 315
Fat: 11.3 g
Carbohydrates: 40.4 g
Protein: 15.1 g
Sodium: 469 mg

597. Simple Appetizer Meatballs

Preparation Time: 25 minutes **Cooking Time:** 25 minutes **Servings:** 24 pieces

Ingredients:
- ½ pound lean ground beef
- ½ pound lean ground pork
- ½ cup sodium-free chicken broth
- ¼ cup almond flour
- 1 tablespoon low-sodium tamari sauce
- ½ teaspoon ground cumin
- ¼ teaspoon freshly ground black pepper

Directions:
1. Preheat the oven to 375F.
2. Combine all the Ingredients together until completely incorporated in a large bowl.
3. Roll the mixture into ¾-inch balls and place them on a parchment-lined baking sheet.
4. Bake the meatballs until they are ready through and golden brown.
5. Serve.

Nutrition:
Calories: 125
Protein: 20g
Fat: 4g
Carbohydrates: 1.2g

598. Chicken Souvlaki Salad

Preparation Time: 20 minutes **Cooking Time:** 10 minutes **Servings:** 2

Ingredients:
- 2 cups of romaine lettuce, bite-sized
- ½ cup of cocktail or cherry tomatoes
- ¼ English cucumber, thickly sliced
- 1 teaspoon of dried oregano (divided)
- ¼ teaspoon of kosher salt
- 2 tablespoons of crumbled feta cheese
- ¾ pound of skinless and boneless chicken breast (divided into 1-inch cubes)
- zest from ½ lemon
- 1 tablespoon of freshly squeezed lemon juice (divided)
- 2 tablespoons of extra-virgin olive oil (divided)
- freshly ground pepper
- ¼ cup of Easy Instant Pot Yogurt (or store-bought yogurt)

Directions:
1. In a bowl, combine the lemon zest, chicken, ½ tablespoon lemon juice, ½ teaspoon oregano, ½ tablespoon olive oil, salt and a few grinds of pepper.
2. Let the chicken marinate for about 10 minutes.
3. Preheat a skillet over medium-high heat. Add ½ tbsp. of olive oil, then add the chicken.
4. Stir for about 8 minutes, then transfer to a plate lined with paper towels.
5. In another bowl, combine ½ tablespoon lemon juice, the yogurt, tablespoon olive oil, ½ teaspoon oregano and a few grinds of pepper.
6. In a bowl, mix the lettuce with a few tablespoons of dressing.
7. Divide the lettuce between two bowls and add the chicken, cucumbers, tomatoes, and feta cheese.
8. Serve and enjoy!

Nutrition:
Calories: 113
Fat: 7.2 g
Carbohydrates: 12.5
Protein: 1.9 g

599. Celery with Chickpea Feta Salad

Preparation Time: 15 minutes **Cooking Time:** 0 minutes **Servings:** 3

Ingredients:
For the salad:
- 5 ounces of small tomatoes (grape, cherry, etc.) halved or quartered
- ½ cup of feta cheese crumbled

For the dressing:
- 1 teaspoon garlic pepper
- 1 tablespoon balsamic vinegar
- 4 (3-inches) sprigs thyme
- 1 (15-ounces) can of chickpeas rinsed and drained
- 2 stalks celery sliced
- 2 tablespoons extra-virgin olive oil

Directions:
Making the dressing:
1. In a glass jar, mix the oil, vinegar, and pepper.

Making the salad:
1. In a bowl, combine the celery, chickpeas, and tomatoes.
2. Add the feta and seasoning.
2. Shake until well combined.
3. Add the leaves to the salad and discard the stems.
4. Distribute the chickpea salad in serving bowls. Serve and enjoy!

Nutrition:
Calories: 71
Fat: 4.8g
Carbohydrates: 6.6g
Fiber: 2.3g

600. Basil Vinaigrette with Summer Corn Salad

Preparation Time: 15 minutes **Cooking Time:** 0 minutes **Servings:** 6

Ingredients:
- 2 to 3 large spring onions thinly sliced (white part only)
- 1 cup of cucumber chopped
- 2 radishes thinly sliced into half-moons
- kosher salt
- ½ cup of avocado oil or extra-virgin olive oil
- 4 large ears of corn husks and silks were removed, cooked
- 1 large tomato seeded and chopped
- freshly ground black pepper
- 2 tablespoons of white wine vinegar
- ¼ cup of chopped fresh basil

Directions:
1. In a bowl, whisk together the vinegar, avocado oil, and basil
2. Add the corn to the bowl with the oil mixture.
3. Add the onion, tomatoes, cucumber, and radishes to the bowl.
4. Merge well and season with salt and pepper.
5. Serve immediately and enjoy. Or refrigerate for up to 24 hours.

Nutrition:
Calories: 40
Fat: 2.5g
Carbohydrates: 3.3g
Fiber: 0.9g

601. Lemon Vinaigrette with Sugar Snap Pea Salad

Preparation Time: 20 minutes **Cooking Time:** 2 minutes **Servings:** 3

Ingredients:
- 2 cups of alfalfa sprouts
- 2 tablespoons of fresh chives chopped
- 2 teaspoon of sugar snap peas
- 2 small radishes diced
- 2 tablespoons of Lemon Vinaigrette

Directions:
1. Set a pot of water to a boil.
2. Fill a bowl with ice water and place a small strainer in the bowl.
3. Attach the peas to the boiling water and cook for 2 minutes.
4. Drain the peas and lay them out on a clean dish towel, and dry.
5. Place the peas in a bowl and add the radishes.
6. Stir in 2 tablespoons of the dressing.
7. Divide sprouts among 4 salad plates: top with pea mixture.
8. Sprinkle with chives. Serve and enjoy!

Nutrition:
Calories: 53
Fat: 3.3 g
Carbohydrates: 4.9 g
Protein: 2.3 g

602. Green Dressing with Shrimp Avocado Salad

Preparation Time: 5 minutes **Cooking Time:** 5 minutes **Servings:** 4

Ingredients:

Green dressing:
- 3 tablespoons of extra-virgin olive oil divided
- ½ teaspoon of salt
- Freshly ground black pepper
- 2 oranges
- ½ cup of parsley
- 2 scallions roughly chopped
- ¼ cup of canned unsweetened coconut cream

Salad:
- ¼ cup of unsalted cashews toasted and roughly chopped
- 4 radishes thinly sliced
- 1 ½ pounds of large shrimp 31-40 count, peeled and deveined
- 12 cups of salad greens, you can use baby red and green romaine
- 1 avocado chopped

Directions:

Making the dressing:
1. Use a small knife to skin the orange starting at the top and cut along the orange's length.
2. Do this all the way around, making sure to remove the white pith. Repeat with other oranges.
3. Cut between the membranes of the orange to remove the segments again.
4. Squeeze the juice from the remaining orange membranes into a blender container.
5. If there is juice on your cutting board, add that to the blender as well. Discard the membranes.
6. Add the scallions, parsley, coconut cream, 1 tablespoon olive oil, salt, and a few pinches of pepper to the blender container.
7. Puree until smooth. Set aside.

Making the salad:
1. From a double layer of paper towels on a plate. Set aside.
2. Season shrimp with a few grinds of pepper. Warmth a wok over medium-high heat and add 1 tablespoon olive oil.
3. Attach half the shrimp and stir-fry until opaque, about 2 minutes.
4. Detach to plate and repeat with remaining shrimp and 1 tablespoon olive oil.
5. Attach salad greens to a large bowl and toss with some of the dressing. Set greens on 4 serving plates and add orange segments, avocado, cashews, radishes, and shrimp.
6. Set with remaining dressing and enjoy!

Nutrition:
Calories: 193
Fat: 5.5 g
Protein: 10 g
Carbohydrates: 1.9g

603. Beans with Pearl Couscous

Preparation Time: 10 minutes **Cooking Time:** 5 minutes **Servings:** 4

Ingredients:

For the dressing:
- ⅛ teaspoon of kosher salt
- 2 tablespoons of extra-virgin olive oil
- 3 tablespoons of cider vinegar
- 1 teaspoon of dried basil leaves
- 1 garlic clove finely minced

For the salad:
- 1 cup of grape or cherry tomatoes quartered
- ½ cup of chopped onion
- 14 ounces of beans (cannellini, Great Northern, black, kidney, or a mixture), rinsed and drained 1 can
- 1 ¼ cups of water
- 4 ounces of uncooked whole-wheat pearl couscous
- 1 hothouse cucumber diced
- 2 ounces of mozzarella cheese "pearls" or fresh mozzarella cheese diced

Directions:
1. In a bowl, whisk together basil, vinegar, garlic, and salt.
2. Continue whisking and attach the oil in a steady stream. Set aside.
3. Set water to a boil in a saucepan.
4. Attach the couscous, cover, and cook over low heat until tender.

5. Leak run under cold water and let drain again while you prepare the salad.
6. In a bowl, mix tomatoes, cucumbers, onion, beans, and cheese. Add cooled couscous and dressing.
7. Stir and serve immediately.

Nutrition:
Calories: 209
Fat: 17g
Protein: 6g
Sugar: 0.5g
Carbohydrates: 5g

604. Blackened Chicken Breast with Jalapeno Caesar Salad

Preparation Time: 8 minutes **Cooking Time:** 5 minutes **Servings:** 4

Ingredients:
- 1 small jalapeño pepper with some of the seeds, quartered
- 3 large cloves of garlic
- ¼ cup of grated Parmigiano-Reggiano cheese
- 1 large 18-ounces bunch of romaine lettuce, roughly chopped and chilled
- 2 tablespoons of Dijon mustard
- 1 pound of boneless skinless chicken breasts
- 1 ½ teaspoons of extra-virgin olive oil
- 1 teaspoon of freshly ground black pepper divided
- 1 ½ tablespoons of Worcestershire sauce
- 4 ounces of organic silken tofu drained (½ cup)

Directions:
1. Preheat the grill. Pound the chicken until about ½ inch thick.
2. Rub chicken with ½ teaspoon oil and sprinkle with ¾ teaspoon pepper.
3. Bake the chicken breasts on a baking sheet, about 8 minutes.
4. Let cooked chicken rest for at least 5 minutes, then slice into thin strips.
5. Add the garlic, jalapeño, cheese, mustard, Worcestershire sauce, tofu, and remaining ¼ teaspoon black pepper to a blender and blend.
6. Add 1 teaspoon oil and blend until smooth.
7. Mix the dressing with the chicken strips and lettuce and serve. Enjoy!

Nutrition:
Calories 253
Protein 15g
Fat 20g
Carbohydrates: 2.1g

605. Ginger Dressing with Kale Chicken Salad

Preparation Time: 5 minutes **Cooking Time:** 12 minutes **Servings:** 4

Ingredients:
- ¾ cup of light raspberry salad dressing
- 2 to 3 teaspoons of grated ginger root
- 1 pound of boneless skinless chicken breast
- 8 cups of packed spinach with baby kale greens

Directions:
1. Heat a skillet with medium-high heat.
2. Set chicken with cooking spray and sprinkle with a pinch of salt and pepper, if desired. Cook and allow to cool and thinly slice.
3. Arrange equal amounts of vegetables and chicken on four plates. Whisk together salad dressing and ginger until well blended.
4. Spoon equal amounts into the mixture. Serve.

Nutrition:
Calories: 228
Total Fats: 11.4g
Carbohydrates: 10.2g
Protein: 14.5g

606. Asian Cucumber Salad

Preparation Time: 5 minutes **Cooking Time:** 5 minutes **Servings:** 4

Ingredients:
For the dressing:
- ¼ cup of rice vinegar
- Dash of crushed red pepper
- 1 tbsp. of low-sodium tamari or soy sauce
- 2 teaspoons of sesame oil
- 2 teaspoons of honey

For the salad:
- 2 medium scallions (thinly sliced)
- 2 teaspoons black sesame seeds
- 1 pound English cucumbers (spiralized or sliced)
- 2 carrots (spiralized or grated)

Directions:
1. Spill together the tamari or soy sauce, sesame oil, honey, rice vinegar, and crushed red pepper in a large bowl.
2. Attach the sliced or spiralized cucumbers, spiralized or grated carrots, and sliced scallions.
3. Merge until the vegetables are well-coated
4. Garnish with sesame seeds.
5. Serve and enjoy!

Nutrition:
Calories: 50
Total Fat: 1.9 g
Carbohydrates: 10 g
Protein: 46 g

607. Pecans with Blackberry Ginger Beet Salad

Preparation Time: 60 minutes **Cooking Time:** 10 minutes **Servings:** 6

Ingredients:
- 1 tablespoon of whole-grain mustard
- 6 cups of mixed salad greens
- Coarse kosher salt
- Freshly ground black pepper
- 4 ounces of fresh goat cheese
- 1 pound of fresh beets washed and trimmed
- ⅓ cup + 2 tbsp. extra virgin olive oil plus for drizzling on beets before roasting
- 1 cup of whole pecans
- ¼ cup + 2 tablespoons blackberry ginger balsamic vinegar or any other fruity balsamic

Directions:
1. Preheat oven to 425F. Place beets on aluminum foil, drizzle with a little olive oil, and wrap tightly. Form the package on a baking sheet and roast for 1 hour or until the beets are tender. Allow cooling.
2. Next, heat a skillet over medium-high heat. Add pecans and stir until toasted. Remove from heat and allow to cool.
3. In another bowl, spill together the mustard and ¼ cup balsamic vinegar. Slowly spill in ⅓ cup olive oil, constantly whisking, until mixture has thickened.
4. In another bowl, whisk together 2 tablespoons olive oil and 2 tablespoons balsamic vinegar.
5. Skin the beets and cut them into thick slices.
6. Add to the vinegar/olive oil mixture.
7. Set the salad with some of the dressing and season with salt and pepper.
8. Arrange the greens on 4 individual serving plates. Add the beets, goat cheese, and toasted pecans. Serve.

Nutrition:
Calories: 224
Fat: 17.5g
Carbohydrates: 10g
Fiber: 3.4g

608. Blueberry Watermelon Salad

Preparation Time: 15 minutes **Cooking Time:** 0 minutes **Servings:** 4

Ingredients:
- zest from ½ lemon
- fresh mint chopped (optional)
- 1 pound of watermelon cut into small chunks (about half of a small melon)
- 1 cup of blueberries
- Kosher salt

Directions:
1. Set watermelon and blueberries in a large bowl.
2. Lightly drizzle with salt.
3. Merge gently enough that you won't nick the blueberries.
4. Brush with lemon zest and mint, if desired.

Nutrition:
Calories: 735
Carbohydrates: 82 g
Fat: 45 g
Fiber: 3 g

609. Orange Vinaigrette with Roasted Beets

Preparation Time: 20 minutes **Cooking Time:** 60 minutes **Servings:** 8

Ingredients:
- ¼ cup of squeezed orange juice
- 1 small shallot (minced)
- 1 clove garlic (minced)
- 2 tablespoons of rice vinegar
- ½ teaspoon of ground cumin
- ¼ teaspoon of ground coriander
- 1 pound of golden beets (washed and trimmed)
- 1 pound of red beets (washed and trimmed)
- ¼ cup of olive oil plus ⅓ cup (divided)
- ¼ teaspoon of kosher salt
- Freshly ground black pepper
- 1 teaspoon of Dijon mustard
- 1 tablespoon of parsley (chopped)

Directions:
1. Preheat oven to 350F.
2. Place the beets in a bowl. Attach the salt, pepper, and olive oil, then mix well.
3. Wrap each beet in aluminum foil, then place it on a baking sheet.
4. Bring in the oven and roast for about 1 hour or until the beets are soft.
5. Detach from oven and set aside to cool.
6. Place the shallots, orange juice, garlic, rice vinegar, cumin, and cilantro in a small saucepan over medium heat.
7. Set everything to a boil, then reduce the heat to medium-low and let the mixture simmer until its volume has reduced by half, about 10 minutes.
8. Remove from heat and allow cooling.
9. After about 5 minutes, attach the mustard to the mixture, olive oil while whisking constantly.
10. Remove the skins from each beet and discard.
11. Cut the beets into chunks, and then place them in a bowl and mix with the desired amount of dressing.
12. Garnish with parsley. Serve and enjoy!

Nutrition:
Calories: 71
Fat: 4.8g
Carbohydrates: 6.6g
Fiber: 2.3g

610. Blueberries with Nectarines Spinach Salad

Preparation Time: 15 minutes **Cooking Time:** 5 minutes **Servings:** 6

Ingredients:
- Freshly ground black pepper
- ¾ pound of fresh blueberries
- ¾ pound of fresh nectarines pitted and cut into ½-inch chunks
- 10 cups of baby spinach
- 2 tablespoons of balsamic vinegar, you can use blackberry ginger
- 3 tablespoons of extra virgin olive oil
- 1 shallot cut in half lengthwise and then thinly sliced
- 1 teaspoon of coarse kosher salt
- 1 cup of slivered almonds

Directions:
1. In a bowl, spill together oil, vinegar, shallots, salt, and pepper.
2. Add blueberries and nectarines and their juice.
3. Spill to coat and let sit for at least 10 minutes. Add the almonds, spinach and stir until the leaves are covered in the dressing.
4. Serve and enjoy!

Nutrition:
Calories: 258.1
Fat: 13 g
Protein: 18.2 g
Carbohydrates: 7g

611. Taco Slaw
Preparation Time: 20 minutes **Cooking Time:** 0 minutes **Servings:** 6
Ingredients:
- 1 carrot, chopped
- 1 tablespoon of chopped fresh cilantro
- 1 lime, juiced
- ½ small head cabbage, chopped
- 1 jalapeno pepper, seeded and minced
- ½ red onion, minced

Directions:
1. Mix the cabbage, carrot, cilantro, lime juice, jalapeno pepper, and red onion in a bowl. Serve!

Nutrition:
Calories: 45
Fat: 1 g
Protein: 2 g
Carbohydrates: 6.1g

612. Egg Fried Veg
Preparation Time: 10 minutes **Cooking Time:** 7 minutes **Servings:** 2
Ingredients:
- 4oz egg whites
- 1 cup mixed vegetables
- 2tbsp milk
- zero calorie spray
- herb and spice mix

Directions:
1. Spray a heat-proof bowl that fits in your Instant Pot with nonstick spray.
2. Whisk together the eggs, milk, and seasoning.
3. Pour into the bowl. Add the vegetables.
4. Place the bowl in your steamer basket.
5. Spill 1 cup of water into your Instant Pot.
6. Lower the basket into your Instant Pot.
7. Seal and cook on low pressure for 7 minutes.
8. Depressurize quickly.
9. Stir well and allow to rest, it will finish cooking in its own heat.

Nutrition:
Calories: 281
Protein: 4g
Fat: 23g
Carbohydrates: 5g

613. Bone Broth
Preparation Time: 10 minutes **Cooking Time:** 60 minutes **Servings:** 2
Ingredients:
- 1 chicken carcass and dripping OR 1 large marrow bone
- 1 chopped onion
- 1 stalk chopped celery
- 1tbsp minced garlic
- 1tbsp bouillon powder

Directions:
1. Place the chicken, onion, and celery in your Instant Pot.
2. Cover with 2 cups of water.
3. Seal and cook for 60 minutes.
4. Release the pressure naturally.
5. Strain the solids out.
6. Add the garlic and bouillon.

Nutrition:
Calories: 258.1
Fat: 13 g
Protein: 18.2 g
Carbohydrates: 7g

614. Cauliflower and Celeriac Soup
Preparation Time: 15 minutes **Cooking Time:** 10 minutes **Servings:** 2
Ingredients:
- 0.5lb cauliflower, chopped
- 4oz celeriac, chopped
- 1 chopped onion
- 2 cups vegetable stock
- salt and pepper

Directions:
1. Mix all the ingredients in your Instant Pot.
2. Cook on Stew for 10 minutes.
3. Depressurize naturally and blend.

Nutrition:
Calories: 40
Fat: 2.5g
Carbohydrates: 3.3g
Fiber: 0.9g

615. Mushroom and Eggs
Preparation Time: 10 minutes **Cooking Time:** 7 minutes **Servings:** 2
Ingredients:
- 4oz egg whites
- 1 cup chopped brown mushrooms
- 2tbsp milk
- zero calorie spray
- 1tsp mustard

Directions:
1. Spray a heat-proof bowl that fits in your Instant Pot with nonstick spray.
2. Whisk together the eggs, milk, and seasoning.
3. Pour into the bowl. Add the mushroom.
4. Place the bowl in your steamer basket.
5. Spill 1 cup of water into your Instant Pot.
6. Lower the basket into your Instant Pot.
7. Seal and cook on low pressure for 7 minutes. Depressurize quickly.
8. Stir well and allow to rest, it will finish cooking in its own heat.

Nutrition:
Calories: 85
Protein: 3g
Fat: 3g
Carbohydrates: 6g

616. Carrot and Cilantro Soup

Preparation Time: 15 minutes **Cooking Time:** 10 minutes **Servings:** 2

Ingredients:
- 2 cups chopped carrot
- 2 chopped onions
- 2 cups vegetable stock
- 1 cup chopped cilantro
- salt and pepper

Directions:
1. Mix all the ingredients in your Instant Pot.
2. Cook on Stew for 10 minutes.
3. Depressurize naturally and blend.

Nutrition:
Calories: 208
Fat: 16 g
Protein: 6 g
Carbohydrates: 4g

617. Tomato Eggs

Preparation Time: 10 minutes **Cooking Time:** 7 minutes **Servings:** 2

Ingredients:
- 4oz egg whites
- 2tbsp milk
- zero calorie spray
- 0.5 cup chopped cherry tomatoes
- 0.5 cup chopped bell peppers, mixed colors

Directions:
1. Spray a heat-proof bowl that fits in your Instant Pot with nonstick spray.
2. Whisk together the eggs, milk, and add a pinch of salt.
3. Pour into the bowl. Add the vegetables.
4. Place the bowl in your steamer basket.
5. Spill 1 cup of water into your Instant Pot.
6. Lower the basket into your Instant Pot.
7. Seal and cook on low pressure for 7 minutes. Depressurize quickly.
8. Stir well and allow to rest, it will finish cooking in its own heat.

Nutrition:
Calories: 185
Fat: 3.3g
Carbohydrates: 7.9
Protein: 11.4g

618. Herb Crusted Chicken

Preparation Time: 10 minutes **Cooking Time:** 10 minutes **Servings:** 2

Ingredients:
- 2oz chopped chicken breast
- 1 chopped sweet pepper
- 1 cup chopped sugar snap peas
- ¼ cup chopped fresh herbs
- 2tbsp olive oil

Directions:
1. Pat the chicken and vegetables dry and roll 1tbsp of the oil.
2. Roll in the herbs.
3. Put the other 1tbsp of oil into the Instant Pot.
4. Cook on Sauté for 10 minutes.
5. Let it cool before serving.

Nutrition:
Calories: 113
Fat: 7.2g
Carbohydrates: 12.5g
Protein: 1.9g

619. Carrot Hummus

Preparation Time: 15 minutes **Cooking Time:** 10 minutes **Servings:** 2

Ingredients:
- 1 small chopped carrot
- 2oz cooked chickpeas
- 1tsp lemon juice
- 1tsp tahini
- 1tsp fresh parsley

Directions:
1. Place the carrot and chickpeas in your Instant Pot.
2. Add a cup of water, seal.
3. Cook for 10 minutes on Stew.
4. Depressurize naturally.
5. Blend with the remaining ingredients.

Nutrition:
Calories 253
Protein 15g
Fat 20g
Carbohydrates: 2.1g

620. Mushroom Tofu Scramble

Preparation Time: 15 minutes **Cooking Time:** 7 minutes **Servings:** 2

Ingredients:
- 1 cup firm tofu
- 1 cup chopped mixed mushrooms
- 3tbsp mushroom soup
- 1tsp mixed herbs
- pinch of salt

Directions:
1. Spray a heat-proof bowl that fits in your Instant Pot with nonstick spray.
2. Chop the tofu finely.
3. Mix with the other ingredients. Pour into the bowl.
4. Place the bowl in your steamer basket.
5. Spill 1 cup of water into your Instant Pot. Lower the basket into your Instant Pot.
6. Seal and cook on low pressure for 7 minutes. Depressurize quickly.
7. Stir well and allow to rest, it will finish cooking in its own heat.

Nutrition:
Calories: 250
Fat: 9 g
Protein: 3 g
Carbohydrates: 4.1g

621. Lentil Soup

Preparation Time: 10 minutes **Cooking Time:** 20 minutes **Servings:** 2

Ingredients:
- 3oz dry lentils
- ¼ cup sliced leek
- 1 small chopped carrot
- 1 chopped celery stalk
- ¼ cup tomato sauce

Directions:
1. Set all the ingredients in your Instant Pot.
2. Seal and cook on Beans for 20 minutes.
3. Depressurize naturally.

Nutrition:
Calories: 175
Fat: 8g
Protein: 1g
Sugar: 5g
Carbohydrates: 4g

622. Stuffed Mushrooms

Preparation Time: 15 minutes **Cooking Time:** 5 minutes **Servings:** 2

Ingredients:
- 10 1-2" mushrooms, stalks removed
- 0.5 cup minced broccoli
- 0.5 minced onion
- 1 clove minced garlic
- salt and pepper

Directions:
1. Rinse the mushrooms.
2. Mix the other ingredients together and stuff them into the mushrooms.
3. Place the mushrooms carefully in your Instant Pot steamer basket.
4. Spill a cup of water into the Instant Pot and insert the steamer basket.
5. Cook on Steam for 5 minutes.
6. Depressurize naturally and serve right away.

Nutrition:
Calories: 123
Fat: 11 g
Protein: 4 g
Carbohydrates: 3g

623. Eggplant Tofu Scramble

Preparation Time: 15 minutes **Cooking Time:** 7 minutes **Servings:** 2

Ingredients:
- 1 cup firm tofu
- 1 cup roughly chopped eggplant
- 3tbsp low calorie stock
- 1tsp mustard
- pinch of salt

Directions:
1. Spray a heat-proof bowl that fits in your Instant Pot with nonstick spray.
2. Chop the tofu finely. Mix with the other ingredients. Pour into the bowl.
3. Place the bowl in your steamer basket.
4. Spill 1 cup of water into your Instant Pot. Lower the basket into your Instant Pot.
5. Seal and cook on low pressure for 7 minutes. Depressurize quickly.
6. Stir well and allow to rest, it will finish cooking in its own heat.

Nutrition:
Calories: 735
Carbohydrates: 82 g
Fat: 45 g
Fiber: 3 g

624. Spinach Dip

Preparation Time: 5 minutes **Cooking Time:** 2 minutes **Servings:** 2

Ingredients:
- 1oz chopped spinach
- 1oz low fat plain yogurt
- 1tbsp peanut butter
- 1tsp honey
- ¼tsp chili pepper

Directions:
1. Place the spinach, yogurt, and peanut butter in a heat-proof bowl.
2. Pour a cup of water into the Instant Pot.
3. Bring the bowl in the steamer basket and the basket in the Instant Pot.
4. Cook on Stew, low pressure for 2 minutes.
5. Release the pressure quickly.
6. Stir well and add the honey and chili.

Nutrition:
Calories: 123
Fat: 11 g
Protein: 4 g
Carbohydrates: 3g

625. Spinach and Orange Salad with Oil Drizzle

Preparation Time: 10 minutes **Cooking Time:** 0 minute **Servings:** 4

Ingredients:
- 4 cups fresh baby spinach
- 1 blood orange, coarsely chopped
- ½ red onion, thinly sliced
- ½ shallot, finely chopped
- 2 tbsp. minced fennel fronds
- Juice of 1 lemon
- 1 tbsp. extra-virgin olive oil
- Pinch sea salt

Directions:
1. In a bowl, toss together the spinach, orange, red onion, shallot, and fennel fronds.
2. Add the lemon juice, oil, and sea salt.
3. Mix and serve.

Nutrition:
Calories: 79
Fat: 2g
Carbohydrates: 8g
Protein: 10g

626. Fruit Salad with Coconut-Lime Dressing

Preparation Time: 5 minutes **Cooking Time:** 0 minutes **Servings:** 4

Ingredients:
For the dressing:
- ¼ cup full-fat canned coconut milk
- 1 tbsp. raw honey
- Juice of ½ lime
- Pinch sea salt

For the salad:
- 2 bananas, thinly sliced
- 2 mandarin oranges, segmented
- ½ cup strawberries, thinly sliced
- ½ cup raspberries
- ½ cup blueberries

Directions:
1. Spill all the dressing Ingredients in a bowl.
2. To make the salad: Add the salad Ingredients in a bowl and mix.
3. Drizzle with the dressing and serve.

Nutrition:
Calories: 141
Fat: 3g
Carbohydrates: 30g
Protein: 2g

627. Cranberry and Brussels sprouts With Dressing

Preparation Time: 10 minutes **Cooking Time:** 0 minute **Servings:** 4

Ingredients:
For the dressing:
- ⅓ cup extra-virgin olive oil
- 2 tbsp. apple cider vinegar
- 1 tbsp. pure maple syrup
- Juice of 1 orange
- ½ tbsp. dried rosemary
- 1 tbsp. scallion, whites only
- Pinch sea salt

For the salad:
- 1 bunch scallions, greens only, finely chopped
- 1 cup Brussels sprouts, stemmed, halved, and thinly sliced
- ½ cup fresh cranberries
- 4 cups fresh baby spinach

Directions:
1. To make the dressing: In a bowl, whisk the dressing Ingredients.
2. To make the salad: Add the scallions, Brussels sprouts, cranberries, and spinach to the bowl with the dressing.
3. Combine and serve.

Nutrition:
Calories: 267
Fat: 18g
Carbohydrates: 26g
Protein: 2g

628. Parsnip, Carrot, and Kale Salad with Dressing

Preparation Time: 10 minutes **Cooking Time:** 0 minutes **Servings:** 4

Ingredients:
For the dressing:
- ⅓ cup extra-virgin olive oil
- Juice of 1 lime
- 2 tbsp. minced fresh mint leaves
- 1 tsp. pure maple syrup
- Pinch sea salt

For the salad:
- 1 bunch kale, chopped
- ½ parsnip, grated
- ½ carrot, grated
- 2 tbsp. sesame seeds

Directions:
1. Merge all the dressing Ingredients in a bowl.
2. To make the salad, add the kale to the dressing and massage the dressing into the kale for 1 minute.
3. Add the parsnip, carrot, and sesame seeds.
4. Combine and serve.

Nutrition:
Calories: 214
Fat: 2g
Carbohydrates: 12g
Protein: 2g

629. Tomato Toasts

Preparation Time: 5 minutes **Cooking Time:** 5 minutes **Servings:** 4

Ingredients:
- 4 slices of sprouted bread toasts
- 2 tomatoes, sliced
- 1 avocado, mashed
- 1 teaspoon olive oil
- 1 pinch of salt
- ¾ teaspoon ground black pepper

Directions:
1. Blend together the olive oil, mashed avocado, salt, and ground black pepper.
2. When the mixture is homogenous – spread it over the sprouted bread.
3. Then place the sliced tomatoes over the toasts.
4. Enjoy!

Nutrition:
Calories: 125
Fat: 11.1g
Carbohydrates: 7.0g
Protein: 1.5g

630. Everyday Salad

Preparation Time: 10 minutes **Cooking Time:** 40 minutes **Servings:** 6

Ingredients:
- 5 halved mushrooms
- 6 halved Cherry (Plum) Tomatoes
- 6 rinsed Lettuce Leaves
- 10 olives
- ½ chopped cucumber
- Juice from ½ Key Lime
- 1 teaspoon olive oil
- Pure Sea Salt

Directions:
1. Set rinsed lettuce leaves into medium pieces and put them in a medium salad bowl.
2. Attach mushrooms halves, chopped cucumber, olives and cherry tomato halves into the bowl. Mix well. Pour olive and Key Lime juice over salad.
3. Attach pure sea salt to taste. Merge it all till it is well combined.

Nutrition:
Calories: 88
Carbohydrates: 11g
Fat: 5g
Protein: 8g

631. Super-Seedy Salad with Tahini Dressing

Preparation Time: 10 minutes **Cooking Time:** 0 minutes **Servings:** 1-2

Ingredients:
- 1 slice stale sourdough, torn into chunks
- 50g mixed seeds
- 1 tsp. cumin seeds
- 1 tsp. coriander seeds
- 50g baby kale
- 75g long-stemmed broccoli, blanched for a few minutes then roughly chopped
- ½ red onion, thinly sliced
- 100g cherry tomatoes, halved
- ½ a small bunch flat-leaf parsley, torn

Dressing:
- 100ml natural yogurt
- 1 tbsp. tahini
- 1 lemon, juiced

Directions:
1. Warmth the oven to 200C/fan 180C/gas 6. Set the bread into a food processor and pulse into very rough breadcrumbs. Set into a bowl with the mixed seeds and spices, season, and spray well with oil. Set onto a non-stick baking tray and roast for 15-20 minutes, stirring and tossing regularly.
2. Spill together the dressing Ingredients, some seasoning and a splash of water in a large bowl. Set the baby kale, broccoli, red onion, cherry tomatoes and flat-leaf parsley into the dressing and mix well. Set between 2 plates and top with the crispy breadcrumbs and seeds.

Nutrition:
Calories: 78
Carbohydrates: 6 g
Fat: 2g
Protein: 1.5g

632. Vegetable Salad

Preparation Time: 10 minutes **Cooking Time:** 0 minutes **Servings:** 1-2

Ingredients:
- 4 cups each of raw spinach and romaine lettuce

- 2 cups each of cherry tomatoes, sliced cucumber, chopped baby carrots and chopped red, orange and yellow bell pepper
- 1 cup each of chopped broccoli, sliced yellow squash, zucchini and cauliflower.

Directions:
1. Wash all these vegetables.
2. Mix in a large mixing bowl and top off with a non-fat or low-fat dressing of your choice.

Nutrition:
Calories: 48
Carbohydrates: 11g
Protein: 3g

633. Greek Salad
Preparation Time: 10 minutes **Cooking Time:** 0 minutes **Servings:** 1-2
Ingredients:
- 1 Romaine head, torn in bits
- 1 cucumber sliced
- 1 pint cherry tomatoes, halved
- 1 green pepper, thinly sliced
- 1 onion sliced into rings
- 1 cup kalamata olives
- 1 ½ cups feta cheese, crumbled

For dressing combine:
- 1 cup olive oil
- ¼ cup lemon juice
- 2 tsp. oregano
- Salt and pepper

Directions:
1. Lay Ingredients on plate.
2. Drizzle dressing over salad

Nutrition:
Calories: 107
Carbohydrates: 18g
Fat: 1.2 g
Protein: 1g

634. Alkaline Spring Salad
Preparation Time: 10 minutes **Cooking Time:** 0 minutes **Servings:** 1-2
Ingredients:
- 4 cups seasonal approved greens of your desired
- 1 cup tomatoes
- ¼ cup walnuts
- ¼ cup approved herbs of your choice

For the dressing:
- 3-4 key limes
- 1 tbsp. of homemade raw sesame
- Sea salt and cayenne pepper

Directions:
1. First, get the juice of the key limes. In a bowl, spill together the key lime juice with the homemade raw sesame "tahini" butter. Attach sea salt and cayenne pepper, to taste.
2. Cut the cherry tomatoes in half.
3. In a large bowl, merge the greens, cherry tomatoes, and herbs. Spill the dressing on top and "massage" with your hands.
4. Set the greens soak up the dressing. Attach more sea salt, cayenne pepper, and herbs on top if you wish. Enjoy!

Nutrition:
Calories: 77
Carbohydrates: 11g
Protein: 13g
Fat: 14g

635. Fresh Tuna Salad
Preparation Time: 10 minutes **Cooking Time:** none **Servings:** 3
Ingredients:
- 1 can tuna (6 oz.)
- ⅓ cup fresh cucumber, chopped
- ⅓ cup fresh tomato, chopped
- ⅓ cup avocado, chopped
- ⅓ cup celery, chopped
- 2 garlic cloves, minced
- 4 tsp. olive oil
- 2 tbsp. lime juice
- Pinch of black pepper

Directions:
1. Set the dressing by combining olive oil, lime juice, minced garlic and black pepper.
2. Merge the salad ingredients in a salad bowl and drizzle with the dressing.

Nutrition:
Calories: 212
Carbohydrates: 4.8g
Protein: 14.3g
Sugar: 1.1g

636. Roasted Portobello Salad
Preparation Time: 10 minutes **Cooking Time:** none **Servings:** 4
Ingredients:
- 1½ lb. Portobello mushrooms, stems trimmed
- 3 heads Belgian endive, sliced
- 1 small red onion, sliced
- 4 oz. blue cheese
- 8 oz. mixed salad greens

Dressing:
- 3 tbsp. red wine vinegar
- 1 tbsp. Dijon mustard
- ⅔ cup olive oil
- Salt and pepper to taste

Directions:
1. Preheat the oven to 450F.
2. Set the dressing by whisking together vinegar, mustard, salt and pepper. Slowly add olive oil while whisking.
3. Divide the mushrooms and set them on a baking sheet, stem-side up. Soak the mushrooms with some dressing and bake for 15 minutes.
4. In a bowl spill the salad greens with onion, endive and cheese. Sprinkle with the dressing.
5. Attach mushrooms to the salad bowl.

Nutrition:
Calories: 501
Carbohydrates: 22.3g
Protein: 14.9g
Sugar: 2.1g

---

637. Shredded Chicken Salad
Preparation Time: 5 minutes **Cooking Time:** 10 minutes **Servings:** 6

Ingredients:
- 2 chicken breasts, boneless, skinless
- 1 head iceberg lettuce, cut into strips
- 2 bell peppers, cut into strips
- 1 fresh cucumber, quartered, sliced
- 3 scallions, sliced
- 2 tbsp. chopped peanuts
- 1 tbsp. peanut vinaigrette
- Salt to taste
- 1 cup water

Directions:
1. In a skillet parboil one cup of salted water.
2. Attach the chicken breasts, cover and cook on low for 5 minutes. Detach the cover. Then discard the chicken from the skillet and shred with a fork.
3. In a bowl merge the vegetables with the cooled chicken, flavor with salt and sprinkle with peanut vinaigrette and chopped peanuts.

Nutrition:
Calories: 117
Carbohydrates: 9 g
Protein: 11.6 g
Sugar: 4.2 g

---

638. Broccoli Salad
Preparation Time: 10 minutes **Cooking Time:** none **Servings:** 6

Ingredients:
- 1 medium head broccoli, raw, florets only
- ½ cup red onion, chopped
- 12 oz. turkey bacon, chopped, fried until crisp
- ½ cup cherry tomatoes, halved
- ¼ cup sunflower kernels
- ¾ cup raisins
- ¾ cup mayonnaise
- 2 tbsp. white vinegar

Directions:
1. In a salad bowl combine the broccoli, tomatoes and onion.
2. Mix mayo with vinegar and sprinkle over the broccoli.
3. Add the sunflower kernels, raisins and bacon and toss well.

Nutrition:
Calories: 220
Carbohydrates: 17.3 g
Protein: 11 g
Sugar: 10 g

---

639. Cherry Tomato Salad
Preparation Time: 10 minutes **Cooking Time:** none **Servings:** 6

Ingredients:
- 40 cherry tomatoes, halved
- 1 cup mozzarella balls, halved
- 1 cup green olives, sliced

Dressing:
- ½ cup olive oil
- 2 tbsp. red wine vinegar
- 1 can (6 oz.) black olives, sliced
- 2 green onions, chopped
- 3 oz. roasted pine nuts
- 1 tsp. dried oregano
- Salt and pepper to taste

Directions:
1. In a salad bowl, merge the tomatoes, olives and onions.
2. Set the dressing by combining olive oil with red wine vinegar, dried oregano, salt and pepper.
3. Drizzle with the dressing and add the nuts.
4. Let marinate in the fridge for 1 hour.

Nutrition:
Calories: 32
Carbohydrates: 10.7 g
Protein: 2.4 g
Sugar: 3.6 g

---

640. Ground Turkey Salad
Preparation Time: 10 minutes **Cooking Time:** 35 minutes **Servings:** 6

Ingredients:
- 1 lb. lean ground turkey
- ½-inch ginger, minced
- 2 garlic cloves, minced
- 1 onion, chopped
- 1 tbsp. olive oil
- 1 bag lettuce leaves (for serving)
- ¼ cup fresh cilantro, chopped
- 2 tsp. coriander powder
- 1 tsp. red chili powder
- 1 tsp. turmeric powder

- Salt to taste

Dressing:
- 2 tbsp. fat free yogurt
- 1 tbsp. sour cream, non-fat
- 1 tbsp. low fat mayonnaise

Directions:
1. In a skillet set the garlic and ginger in olive oil for 1 minute. Attach onion and season with salt. Cook for 10 minutes over medium heat.
2. Attach the ground turkey and sauté for 3 more minutes. Add the spices (turmeric, red chili powder and coriander powder).

- 4 cups water
- 1 lemon, juiced
- 1 tsp. red chili flakes
- Salt and pepper to taste

3. Put 4 cups water and cook for 30 minutes, covered.
4. Set the dressing by combining yogurt, sour cream, mayo, lemon juice, chili flakes, salt and pepper.
5. To serve, line up the salad leaves on serving plates and place the cooked ground turkey on them. Top with dressing.

Nutrition:
Calories: 176
Carbohydrates: 9.1 g
Protein: 17.8 g
Sugar: 2.5 g

641. Celery Apple Salad
Preparation Time: 5 minutes **Cooking Time:** 10 minutes **Servings:** 4
Ingredients:
- 2 green onions, diced
- 2 Medjool dates, pitted and diced fine
- 1 honey crisp apple, sliced thin

Maple Shallot Vinaigrette:
- 1 tablespoon shallot, diced fine
- 2 tablespoons apple cider vinegar
- 1 tablespoon spicy brown mustard

- 2 cup celery, sliced
- ½ cup celery leaves, diced
- ¼ cup walnuts, chopped
- 1 tablespoon olive oil
- 2 teaspoon sugar-free maple syrup

Directions:
1. Heat oven to 375F (190C). Set walnuts on a cookie sheet and bake 10 minutes, stirring every few minutes, to toast.
2. Meanwhile, combine the ingredients for the vinaigrette in a small bowl. Stir to mix well.
3. When the baking is complete, in a large bowl, combine the baked walnuts with the remaining ingredients and toss to mix.
4. Drizzle vinaigrette over and toss to coat. Serve immediately.

Nutrition:
Calories: 52
Carbohydrates: 5.7 g
Protein: 1 g
Sugar: 3.1 g

642. Cauliflower Tofu Salad
Preparation Time: 10 minutes **Cooking Time:** 15 minutes **Servings:** 4
Ingredients:
- 2 cups cauliflower florets, blended
- 1 fresh cucumber, diced
- ½ cup green olives, diced
- ⅓ cup red onion, diced
- 2 tbsp. toasted pine nuts
- 2 tbsp. raisins
- ⅓ cup feta, crumbled
- ½ cup pomegranate seeds

- 2 lemons (juiced, zest grated)
- 8 oz. tofu
- 2 tsp. oregano
- 2 garlic cloves, minced
- ½ tsp. red chili flakes
- 3 tbsp. olive oil
- Salt and pepper to taste

Directions:
1. Flavor the processed cauliflower with salt and set to a strainer to drain.
2. Set the marinade for tofu by merging 2 tbsp. lemon juice, 1.5 tbsp. olive oil, minced garlic, chili flakes, oregano, salt and pepper. Set the tofu in the marinade and set aside.
3. Warmth the oven to 450F.
4. Bake tofu for 12 minutes.
5. In a salad bowl merge, the remaining marinade with onions, cucumber, cauliflower, olives and raisins. Add in the remaining olive oil and grated lemon zest.
6. Set with tofu, pine nuts, and feta and pomegranate seeds.

Nutrition:
Calories: 328
Carbohydrates: 34.1 g
Protein: 11.1 g.
Sugar: 11.5 g

643. Scallop Caesar Salad
Preparation Time: 5 minutes **Cooking Time:** 2 minutes **Servings:** 2
Ingredients:
- 8 sea scallops
- 4 cups romaine lettuce
- 2 tsp. olive oil

- 3 tbsp. Caesar Salad Dressing
- 1 tsp. lemon juice
- Salt and pepper to taste

Directions:
1. In frying pan warmth, the olive oil and cook the scallops in one layer no longer than 2 minutes per both sides. Season with salt and pepper to taste.
2. Set lettuce on plates and place scallops on top.
3. Spill over the Caesar dressing and lemon juice.

Nutrition:
Calories: 340
Carbohydrates: 14 g
Protein: 30.7 g
Sugar: 2.2 g

644. Chicken Avocado Salad

Preparation Time: 30 minutes **Cooking Time:** 15 minutes **Servings:** 4

Ingredients:
- 1 lb. chicken breast, cooked, shredded
- 1 avocado, pitted, peeled, sliced
- 2 tomatoes, diced
- 1 cucumber, peeled, sliced
- 1 head lettuce, chopped
- 3 tbsp. olive oil
- 2 tbsp. lime juice
- 1 tbsp. cilantro, chopped
- Salt and pepper to taste

Directions:
1. In a bowl spill together oil, lime juice, cilantro, salt, and a pinch of pepper.
2. Merge lettuce, tomatoes, cucumber in a salad bowl and toss with half of the dressing.
3. Spill chicken with the remaining dressing and combine with vegetable mixture.
4. Set with avocado.

Nutrition:
Calories: 380
Carbohydrates: 10 g
Protein: 38 g
Sugar: 11.5g

645. California Wraps

Preparation Time: 5 minutes **Cooking Time:** 15 minutes **Servings:** 4

Ingredients:
- 4 slices turkey breast, cooked
- 4 slices ham, cooked
- 4 lettuce leaves
- 4 slices tomato
- 4 slices avocado
- 1 tsp. lime juice
- A handful watercress leaves
- 4 tbsp. Ranch dressing, sugar free

Directions:
1. Top a lettuce leaf with turkey slice, ham slice and tomato.
2. In a bowl combine avocado and lime juice and place on top of tomatoes. Top with water cress and dressing.
3. Repeat with the remaining ingredients for 4. Topping each lettuce leaf with a turkey slice, ham slice, tomato and dressing.

Nutrition:
Calories: 140
Carbohydrates: 4 g
Protein: 9 g
Sugar: 0.5 g

646. Chicken Salad in Cucumber Cups

Preparation Time: 5 minutes **Cooking Time:** 15 minutes **Servings:** 4

Ingredients:
- ½ chicken breast, skinless, boiled and shredded
- 2 long cucumbers, cut into 8 thick rounds each, scooped out (won't use in a).
- 1 tsp. ginger, minced
- 1 tsp. lime zest, grated
- 4 tsp. olive oil
- 1 tsp. sesame oil
- 1 tsp. lime juice
- Salt and pepper to taste

Directions:
1. In a bowl combine lime zest, juice, olive and sesame oils, ginger, and season with salt.
2. Toss the chicken with the dressing and fill the cucumber cups with the salad.

Nutrition:
Calories: 116 g
Carbohydrates: 4 g
Protein: 12 g
Sugar: 0.5 g

647. Sunflower Seeds and Arugula Garden Salad

Preparation Time: 5 minutes **Cooking Time:** 10 minutes **Servings:** 6

Ingredients:
- ¼ tsp. black pepper
- ¼ tsp. salt
- 1 tsp. fresh thyme, chopped
- 2 tbsp. sunflower seeds, toasted
- 2 cups red grapes, halves
- 7 cups baby arugula, loosely packed
- 1 tbsp. coconut oil
- 2 tsp. honey
- 3 tbsp. red wine vinegar
- ½ tsp. stone-ground mustard

Directions:
1. In a small bowl, spill together mustard, honey and vinegar. Slowly pour oil as you whisk.
2. In a large salad bowl, mix thyme, seeds, grapes and arugula.
3. Drizzle with dressing and serve.

Nutrition:
Calories: 86.7g
Protein: 1.6g
Carbohydrates: 13.1g
Fat: 3.1g

648. Supreme Caesar Salad

Preparation Time: 5 minutes **Cooking Time:** 10 minutes **Servings:** 4

Ingredients:
- ¼ cup olive oil
- ¾ cup mayonnaise
- 1 head romaine lettuce, set into bite sized pieces
- 1 tbsp. lemon juice
- 1 tsp. Dijon mustard
- 1 tsp. Worcestershire sauce
- 3 cloves garlic, peeled and minced
- 3 cloves garlic, peeled and quartered
- 4 cups day old bread, cubed
- 5 anchovy filets, minced
- 6 tbsp. grated parmesan cheese, divided
- Ground black pepper to taste
- Salt to taste

Directions:
1. In a small bowl, whisk well lemon juice, mustard, Worcestershire sauce, 2 tbsp. parmesan cheese, anchovies, mayonnaise, and minced garlic. Season with pepper and salt to taste. Set aside in the ref.
2. On medium fire, place a large nonstick saucepan and heat oil.
3. Sauté quartered garlic until browned around a minute or two. Remove and discard.
4. Add bread cubes in same pan, sauté until lightly browned. Season with pepper and salt. Transfer to a plate.
5. In large bowl, place lettuce and pour in dressing. Toss well to coat. Top with remaining parmesan cheese.
6. Garnish with bread cubes, serve, and enjoy.

Nutrition:
Calories: 443.3g
Fat: 32.1g
Protein: 11.6g
Carbohydrates: 27g

649. Tabbouleh- Arabian Salad

Preparation Time: 5 minutes **Cooking Time:** 10 minutes **Servings:** 6

Ingredients:
- ¼ cup chopped fresh mint
- 1 ⅔ cups boiling water
- 1 cucumber, peeled, seeded and chopped
- 1 cup bulgur
- 1 cup chopped fresh parsley
- 1 cup chopped green onions
- 1 tsp. salt
- ⅓ cup lemon juice
- ⅓ cup olive oil
- 3 tomatoes, chopped
- Ground black pepper to taste

Directions:
1. In a large bowl, mix boiling water and bulgur. Let soak and set aside for an hour while covered.
2. After one hour, toss in cucumber, tomatoes, mint, parsley, onions, lemon juice and oil. Then set with black pepper and salt to taste. Toss well and refrigerate for another hour while covered before serving.

Nutrition:
Calories: 185.5g
Fat: 13.1g
Protein: 4.1g
Carbohydrates: 12.8g

650. Aromatic Toasted Pumpkin Seeds

Preparation Time: 5 minutes **Cooking Time:** 45 minutes **Servings:** 4

Ingredients:
- 1 cup pumpkin seeds
- 1 teaspoon cinnamon
- 2 packets stevia
- 1 tablespoon canola oil
- ¼ teaspoon sea salt

Directions:
1. Prep the oven to 300F (150C).
2. Combine the pumpkin seeds with cinnamon, stevia, canola oil, and salt in a bowl. Stir to mix well.
3. Pour the seeds in the single layer on a baking sheet, then arrange the sheet in the preheated oven.
4. Bake for 45 minutes or until well toasted and fragrant. Shake the sheet twice to bake the seeds evenly.
5. Serve immediately.

Nutrition:
Calories: 107
Carbohydrates: 18g
Fat: 1.2 g
Protein: 1g

Dessert

651. Strawberry Chiffon Pie

Preparation Time: 15 minutes **Cooking Time:** 45 minutes **Servings:** 4

Ingredients:
- 1 cup of crushed pineapple, unsweetened
- 12 strawberries
- 1 packet of O-Zenta strawberry gelatin
- 7 packages of artificial sweetener
- 1 cup of evaporated skim milk, chilled
- 1 tablespoon of lemon juice
- 1 ½ teaspoon of vanilla
- 1 teaspoon of almond extract

Directions:
1. Bring pineapple to a boil. Stir in gelatin, strawberries, and sweetener.
2. Stir until gelatin is completely dissolved.
3. Whisk milk and lemon juice in a cooled bowl until frothy.
4. Add the extracts and beat until stiff.
5. Slowly attach the gelatin mixture to the whipped milk.
6. Add to a 10-inch pie plate and refrigerate for a few minutes
7. Garnish with additional strawberries.
8. Serve and enjoy!

Nutrition:
Calories: 212
Carbohydrates: 4.8g
Protein: 14.3g
Sugar: 1.1g

652. Strawberry Fruit Squares

Preparation Time: 40 minutes **Cooking Time:** 45 minutes **Servings:** 4-6

Ingredients:
- 2 envelopes dietetic strawberry gelatin
- 1 cup of boiling water
- 1 cup of crushed pineapple in own juice
- 1 ripe banana, finely diced
- 6 ounces of plain yogurt
- 1 envelope Sweet and Low

Directions:
1. Set gelatin in boiling water.
2. Attach juice drained from pineapple with cold water.

3. Set cold water to equal 1 cup liquid.
4. Attach pineapple and banana. Pour ½ into a 1-quart bowl.
5. Chill until firm. Spread with plain yogurt mixed with a sugar substitute.
6. Place bowl in the freezer for 30 minutes until yogurt is firmer.
7. Pour remaining gelatin, very carefully, on top.
8. Chill until firm. Cut in squares.
9. Serve and enjoy!

Nutrition:
Calories: 250
Fat: 9 g
Protein: 3 g
Carbohydrates: 4.1g

653. Copper Penny Carrots

Preparation Time: 40 minutes **Cooking Time:** 45 minutes **Servings:** 15

Ingredients:
- 2 pounds carrots, cleaned and sliced thin
- 1 green pepper, thinly sliced

Sauce:
- ¼ cup of salad oil
- 1 teaspoon of Worcestershire sauce
- 1 (10 ounces of) can tomato soup, undiluted
- 1 medium onion, thinly sliced
- Salt and pepper as desired
- 1 teaspoon of yellow mustard
- ½ cup of vinegar
- 20 packets Equal

Directions:
1. Start cooking carrots in a covered pot in ½ inch of water, 11 minutes after boiling begins so carrots will be tender but not crispy.
2. Rinse in cold water to stop cooking. In a bowl, alternate layers of vegetables.
3. For the Sauce, mix all the ingredients.
4. Bring sauce ingredients to a boil. Remove from heat.
5. Cool for a few minutes. Add 20 equal packets. Place in blender and blend.
6. Pour sauce over vegetables while still hot. Cool.
7. Refrigerate at least 12 hours before serving.
8. Keep in refrigerator for several weeks in a covered plastic container.
9. To serve, use a slotted spoon. Serve!

Nutrition:
Calories: 48
Carbohydrates: 11g
Protein: 3g

654. Poached Pears

Preparation Time: 20 minutes **Cooking Time:** 1 hour 15 minutes **Servings:** 6

Ingredients:
- 6 medium ripe pears (about 2 pounds)
- 5 cups of white, unsweetened grape juice
- ¼ cup of fresh lemon juice
- 1 vanilla bean, split lengthwise
- 1-inch whole cinnamon stick
- ¼ cup of golden raisins

Directions:
1. The first thing to do is to skin the pears but leave the stems.
2. Mix the juices, vanilla bean, and cinnamon stick in a medium-sized pan and then cook over low heat.
3. Add the pears. Simmer uncovered for about 30 minutes, turning pears occasionally until tender when pierced with a knife.
4. Remove pears.
5. Reduce syrup for about 30 to 35 min to 1 ½ cups. Strain.
6. Stir in raisins and cool syrup to room temperature.
7. Serve pears in small glass compound bowls.
8. Spoon raisins and syrup over and around pears.

Nutrition:
Calories: 79
Fat: 2g
Carbohydrates: 8g
Protein: 10g

655. Carrot Cake

Preparation Time: 10 minutes **Cooking Time:** 40 minutes **Servings:** 18

Ingredients:
- Margarine and flour for pan
- 1 ½ cup of all-purpose flour
- ¼ cup of whole wheat flour
- 1 teaspoon of baking powder
- ½ teaspoon of baking soda
- ½ teaspoon of ground cinnamon
- ½ teaspoon of ground ginger
- 2 tablespoons of stevia; 2 eggs; vegetable oil.
- ¼ cup of unsweetened pineapple juice concentrate
- 1 teaspoon of vanilla extract
- 1 cup of shredded carrots
- ½ cup of golden raisins; salt
- ½ cup of unsweetened, crushed pineapple, drained

Directions:
1. Warmth oven to 350 F. Grease and flour a 9 X 5 X 3 inches loaf pan.
2. In bowl, merge flours, baking powder, baking soda, cinnamon, ginger, and salt.
3. In a second bowl, spill oil, stevia, eggs, pineapple juice, and vanilla.
4. Stir liquid into dry ingredients until smooth. Stir carrots, raisins, and pineapple.
5. Scrape into prepared pan. Bake for 35 to 40 minutes.
6. Set cake and ice with Cream Cheese Frosting. Cut into ½ inches slices to serve.

Nutrition:
Calories: 71
Fat: 4.8g
Carbohydrates: 6.6g
Fiber: 2.3g

656. Bran Muffins

Preparation Time: 10 minutes **Cooking Time:** 40 minutes **Servings:** 12

Ingredients:
- 1 cup of bran
- cup of buttermilk
- banana, mashed well
- 1 egg
- ¼ cup of oil
- ¼ cup of honey
- 1 cup of whole wheat flour
- 1 teaspoon of baking soda
- Finch of salt
- 2 tablespoons of margarine
- 2 tablespoons of honey

Directions:
1. Mix first 9 ingredients together. Place in microwave muffin pan.
2. Microwave 3 ½ mins. Mix last 2 ingredients together.
3. Spoon on each muffin and return to micro-wave for 1 minute.
4. Serve and enjoy!

Nutrition:
Calories 65
Protein 2g
Fat 1g
Carbohydrates: 2.4g

---

657. Frozen Mocha Milkshake

Preparation Time: 5 minutes **Cooking Time:** 0 minutes **Servings:** 1

Ingredients:
- 1 cup (240 ml) unsweetened vanilla almond milk
- 3 tbsp. (18 g) unsweetened cocoa powder
- 2 tsp. (4 g) instant espresso powder
- 1½ cups (210 g) crushed ice
- ½ medium avocado, peeled and pitted
- 1 tbsp. (15 ml) pure maple syrup
- 1 tsp. pure vanilla extract

Directions:
1. In a blender, combine the almond milk, cocoa powder, espresso powder, ice, avocado, maple syrup, and vanilla. Blend the ingredients on high speed for 60 seconds, until the milkshake is smooth.

Nutrition:
Calorie: 307
Fat: 20g
Protein: 6g
Carbohydrates: 33g
Sugars: 13g
Fiber: 13g
Sodium: 173mg

---

658. Baked Berry Cups with Crispy Cinnamon Wedges

Preparation Time: 25 minutes **Cooking Time:** 30 minutes **Servings:** 4

Ingredients:
- 2 tsp. stevia
- ¾ tsp. ground cinnamon
- Butter-flavor cooking spray
- 1 balanced carb whole wheat tortilla
- ¼ cup stevia
- 2 tbsp. white whole wheat flour
- 1 tsp. grated orange peel, if desired
- 1½ cups fresh blueberries
- 1½ cups fresh raspberries
- About 1 cup fat-free whipped cream topping

Directions:
1. Heat oven to 375F. In sandwich-size resealable food-storage plastic bag, merge 2 teaspoons stevia and ½ tsp. of the cinnamon. Set both sides of tortilla, about 3 seconds per side; divide tortilla into 8 wedges. In bag with cinnamon-sugar, attach wedges, seal bag. Shake to coat wedges evenly.
2. On ungreased cookie sheet, spread out wedges. Bake 7 to 9 minutes.
3. Meanwhile, spray custard cups or ramekins with cooking spray; place cups on another cookie sheet. In small bowl, spill ¼ cup stevia, the flour, orange peel and remaining ¼ teaspoon cinnamon until blended. In medium bowl, gently whisk berries with stevia mixture; divide evenly among custard cups.
4. Bake 15 minutes; stir gently.
5. To serve, set each cup with about ¼ cup whipped cream topping; serve tortilla wedges with berry cups. Serve warm.

Nutrition:
Calories: 735
Carbohydrates: 82 g
Fat: 45 g
Fiber: 3 g

---

659. Berry Smoothie Pops

Preparation Time: 5 minutes **Cooking Time:** 0 minutes **Servings:** 6

Ingredients:
- 2 cups frozen mixed berries
- ½ cup unsweetened plain almond milk
- 1 cup plain nonfat Greek yogurt
- 2 tablespoons hemp seeds

Directions:
1. Set all the ingredients in a blender and process until finely blended.
2. Pour into 6 clean ice pop molds and insert sticks.
3. Freeze for 3 to 4 hours.

Nutrition:
Calories: 70
Fat: 2g
Protein: 5g
Carbohydrates: 9g
Sugars: 2g
Fiber: 3g
Sodium: 28mg

660. Instant Pot Tapioca

Preparation Time: 10 minutes **Cooking Time:** 7 minutes **Servings:** 6

Ingredients:
- 2 cups water
- 1 cup small pearl tapioca
- ½ cup stevia
- 4 eggs
- ½ cup evaporated skim milk
- ¼ cup substitute sugar (like stevia)
- 1 teaspoon vanilla
- Fruit of choice, optional

Directions:
1. Combine water and tapioca in Instant Pot.
2. Secure lid. Press Manual and set for 5 minutes.
3. Perform a quick release. Press Cancel, remove lid, and press Sauté.
4. Whisk together eggs and evaporated milk. SLOWLY attach to the Instant Pot, stirring constantly so the eggs don't scramble.
5. Stir in the sugar substitute until it's dissolved, press Cancel, then stir in the vanilla.
6. Allow to cool thoroughly, then refrigerate at least 4 hours.

Nutrition:
Calories: 267
Fat: 18g
Carbohydrates: 26g
Protein: 2g

661. Oatmeal Cookies

Preparation Time: 5 minutes **Cooking Time:** 15 minutes **Servings:** 6

Ingredients:
- ¾ cup almond flour
- ¾ cup old-fashioned oats
- ¼ cup shredded unsweetened coconut
- 1 teaspoon baking powder
- 1 teaspoon ground cinnamon
- ¼ teaspoon salt
- ¼ cup unsweetened applesauce
- 1 large egg
- 1 tablespoon pure maple syrup
- 2 tablespoons coconut oil, melted

Directions:
1. Preheat the oven to 350F.
2. In a medium mixing bowl, merge the almond flour, oats, coconut, baking powder, cinnamon, and salt, and mix well.
3. In another medium bowl, combine the applesauce, egg, maple syrup, and coconut oil, and mix. Stir the wet mixture into the dry mixture.
4. Form the dough into balls. Bake for 12 minutes.
5. Using a spatula, remove the cookies and cool on a rack.

Nutrition:
Calories: 76
Fat: 6g
Protein: 2g
Carbohydrates: 5g
Sugars: 1g
Fiber: 1g
Sodium: 57mg

662. Raspberry Nice Cream

Preparation Time: 5 minutes **Cooking Time:** 0 minutes **Servings:** 3

Ingredients:
- 2 cups frozen, sliced, overripe bananas
- 2 cups frozen or fresh raspberries
- Pinch of sea salt
- 1-2 tablespoons coconut nectar or 1-1½ tablespoons pure maple syrup

Directions:
1. In a food processor or high-speed blender, combine the bananas, raspberries, salt, and 1 tablespoon of the nectar or syrup. Puree until smooth. Taste, and add the remaining nectar or syrup, if desired.
2. Serve immediately, if you like a soft-serve consistency, or transfer to an airtight container and freeze for an hour or more, if you like a firmer texture.

Nutrition:
Calorie: 193
Fat: 1g
Protein: 3g
Carbohydrates: 47g
Sugars: 24g
Fiber: 13g
Sodium: 101mg

663. Chocolate Baked Bananas

Preparation Time: 10 minutes **Cooking Time:** 10-15 minutes **Servings:** 8

Ingredients:
- 4-5 large ripe bananas, sliced lengthwise
- 2 tbsp. coconut nectar or pure maple syrup
- 1 tablespoon cocoa powder
- Couple pinches sea salt
- 2 tablespoons nondairy chocolate chips (for finishing)
- 1 tablespoon chopped pecans, walnuts, almonds, or pumpkin seeds (for finishing)

Directions:
1. Set a baking sheet with parchment paper and preheat oven to 450F.
2. Bring bananas on the parchment. In a bowl, merge the coconut nectar or maple syrup with the cocoa powder and salt. Whisk well to fully combine. Set the chocolate mixture over the bananas.
3. Bake for 8 to 10 minutes. Set on chocolate chips and nuts and serve.

Nutrition:
Calories: 146
Fat: 3g
Protein: 2g
Carbohydrates: 34g
Sugars: 18g
Fiber: 4g
Sodium: 119mg

664. Greek Yogurt Berry Smoothie Pops
Preparation Time: 5 minutes **Cooking Time:** 0 minutes **Servings:** 6
Ingredients:
- 2 cups frozen mixed berries
- ½ cup unsweetened plain almond milk
- 1 cup plain nonfat Greek yogurt
- 2 tablespoons hemp seeds

Directions:
1. Set all the ingredients in a blender and process until finely blended.
2. Pour into 6 clean ice pop molds and insert sticks.
3. Freeze for 3 to 4 hours.

Nutrition:
Calories: 70
Fat: 2g
Protein: 5g
Carbohydrates: 9g
Sugar: 2g
Fiber: 3g
Sodium: 28mg

665. Grilled Peach and Coconut Yogurt Bowls
Preparation Time: 5 minutes **Cooking Time:** 10 minutes **Servings:** 4
Ingredients:
- 2 peaches, halved and pitted
- ½ cup plain nonfat Greek yogurt
- 1 teaspoon pure vanilla extract
- ¼ cup unsweetened dried coconut flakes
- 2 tablespoons unsalted pistachios, shelled and broken into pieces

Directions:
1. Preheat the broiler to high. Arrange the rack in the closest position to the broiler.
2. In a shallow pan, arrange the peach halves, cut-side up. Broil for 6 to 8 minutes until browned, tender, and hot.
3. In a small bowl, mix the yogurt and vanilla.
4. Spoon the yogurt into the cavity of each peach half.
5. Sprinkle 1 tablespoon of coconut flakes and 1½ teaspoons of pistachios over each peach half. Serve warm.

Nutrition:
Calories: 102
Fat: 5g
Protein: 5g
Carbohydrates: 11g
Sugars: 8g
Fiber: 2g
Sodium: 12mg

666. Frozen Chocolate Peanut Butter Bites
Preparation Time: 5 minutes **Cooking Time:** 0 minutes **Servings:** 32
Ingredients:
- 1 cup coconut oil, melted
- ¼ cup cocoa powder
- ½ cup honey
- ½ cup natural peanut butter

Directions:
1. Spill the melted coconut oil into a bowl. Whisk in the cocoa powder, honey, and peanut butter.
2. Transfer the mixture to ice cube trays in portions about 1½ teaspoons each.
3. Freeze for 2 hours or until ready to serve.

Nutrition:
Calories: 80
Fat: 8g
Protein: 1g
Carbohydrates: 3g
Sugars: 2g
Fiber: 0g
Sodium: 20mg

667. Dark Chocolate Almond Butter Cups
Preparation Time: 15 minutes **Cooking Time:** 0 minutes **Servings:** 12
Ingredients:
- ½ cup natural almond butter
- 1 tablespoon pure maple syrup
- 1 cup dark chocolate chips
- 1 tablespoon coconut oil

Directions:
1. Set a 12-cup muffin tin with cupcake liners.
2. In a medium bowl, mix the almond butter and maple syrup. If necessary, heat in the microwave to soften slightly.
3. Spoon about 2 teaspoons of the almond butter mixture into each muffin cup and press down to fill.
4. In a double boiler or the microwave, dissolve the chocolate chips. Stir in the coconut oil and mix well to incorporate.
5. Drop 1 tablespoon of chocolate on top of each almond butter cup.
6. Freeze for at least 30 minutes to set. Thaw for 10 minutes before serving.

Nutrition:
Calories: 101
Fat: 8g
Protein: 3g
Carbohydrates: 6g
Sugars: 4g
Fiber: 1g
Sodium: 32mg

668. No-Bake Carrot Cake Bites
Preparation Time: 15 minutes **Cooking Time:** 0 minutes **Servings:** 20
Ingredients:
- ½ cup old-fashioned oats
- 2 medium carrots, chopped

- 6 dates, pitted
- ½ cup chopped walnuts
- ½ cup coconut flour
- 2 tablespoons hemp seeds
- 2 teaspoons pure maple syrup
- 1 teaspoon ground cinnamon
- ½ teaspoon ground nutmeg

Directions:
1. In a blender jar, combine the oats and carrots, and process until finely ground. Transfer to a bowl.
2. Add the dates and walnuts to the blender and process until coarsely chopped. Return the oat-carrot mixture to the blender and add the coconut flour, hemp seeds, maple syrup, cinnamon, and nutmeg. Process until well mixed.
3. Set the dough into balls about the size of a tablespoon.
4. Store in the refrigerator in an airtight container for up to 1 week.

Nutrition:
Calories: 68
Fat: 3g
Protein: 2g
Carbohydrates: 10g
Sugars: 6g
Fiber: 2g
Sodium: 6mg

669. Creamy Strawberry Crepes
Preparation Time: 10 minutes **Cooking Time:** 10 minutes **Servings:** 4
Ingredients:
- ½ cup old-fashioned oats
- 1 cup unsweetened plain almond milk
- 1 egg
- 3 teaspoons honey, divided
- Nonstick cooking spray
- 2 ounces (57 g) low-fat cream cheese
- ¼ cup low-fat cottage cheese
- 2 cups sliced strawberries

Directions:
1. In a blender jar, process the oats until they resemble flour. Add the almond milk, egg, and 1½ teaspoons honey, and process until smooth.
2. Heat a large skillet over medium heat. Spray with nonstick cooking spray to coat.
3. Add ¼ cup of oat batter to the pan and quickly swirl around and cook for 2 to 3 minutes.
4. Clean the blender jar, and then combine the cream cheese, cottage cheese, and remaining 1½ teaspoons honey, and process until smooth.
5. Set each crepe with 2 tablespoons of the cream cheese mixture, topped with ¼ cup of strawberries. Serve.

Nutrition:
Calories: 149
Fat: 6g
Protein: 6g
Carbohydrates: 20g
Sugars: 10g
Fiber: 3g
Sodium: 177mg

670. Swirled Cream Cheese Brownies
Preparation Time: 10 minutes **Cooking Time:** 20 minutes **Servings:** 12
Ingredients:
- 2 eggs
- ¼ cup unsweetened applesauce
- ¼ cup coconut oil, melted
- 3 tablespoons pure maple syrup, divided
- ¼ cup unsweetened cocoa powder
- ¼ cup coconut flour
- ¼ teaspoon salt
- 1 teaspoon baking powder
- 2 tablespoons low-fat cream cheese

Directions:
1. Preheat the oven to 350F (180C). Grease an 8-by-8-inch baking dish.
2. In a mixing bowl, set the eggs with the applesauce, coconut oil, and 2 tablespoons of maple syrup.
3. Stir in the cocoa powder and coconut flour and mix well. Sprinkle the salt and baking powder evenly over the surface and mix well to incorporate. Set the mixture to the prepared baking dish.
4. In a small, microwave-safe bowl, microwave the cream cheese for 10 to 20 seconds until softened. Add the remaining 1 tablespoon of maple syrup and mix to combine.
5. Drop the cream cheese onto the batter and use a toothpick or chopstick to swirl it on the surface. Bake for 20 minutes.
6. Store refrigerated in a seal container for up to 5 days.

Nutrition:
Calories: 84
Fat: 6g
Protein: 2g
Carbohydrates: 6g
Sugars: 4g
Fiber: 2g
Sodium: 93mg

671. Maple Oatmeal Cookies
Preparation Time: 5 minutes **Cooking Time:** 15 minutes **Servings:** 16
Ingredients:
- ¾ cup almond flour
- ¾ cup old-fashioned oats
- ¼ cup shredded unsweetened coconut
- 1 teaspoon baking powder
- 1 teaspoon ground cinnamon
- ¼ teaspoon salt
- ¼ cup unsweetened applesauce
- 1 large egg
- 1 tablespoon pure maple syrup
- 2 tablespoons coconut oil, melted

Directions:
1. Preheat the oven to 350F (180C).
2. In a medium mixing bowl, merge the almond flour, oats, coconut, baking powder, cinnamon, and salt, and mix well.

3. In another medium bowl, combine the applesauce, egg, maple syrup, and coconut oil, and mix. Stir the wet mixture into the dry mixture.
4. Set the dough into balls a little bigger than a tablespoon and place on a baking sheet. Bake for 12 minutes. Detach from the oven and let cool for 5 minutes.
5. Using a spatula, remove the cookies and cool on a rack.

Nutrition:
Calories: 76
Fat: 6g
Protein: 2g
Carbohydrates: 5g
Sugars: 1g
Fiber: 1g
Sodium: 57mg

672. Ambrosia

Preparation Time: 10 minutes **Cooking Time:** 0 minutes **Servings:** 8

Ingredients:
- 3 oranges, peeled, sectioned, and quartered
- 2 (4-ounce / 113-g) cups diced peaches in water, drained
- 1 cup shredded, unsweetened coconut
- 1 (8-ounce / 227-g) container fat-free crème fraîche

Directions:
1. In a large mixing bowl, merge the oranges, peaches, coconut, and crème fraîche.
2. Gently toss until well mixed. Cover and refrigerate overnight.

Nutrition:
Calories: 111
Fat: 5g
Protein: 2g
Carbohydrates: 12g
Sugars: 8g
Fiber: 3g
Sodium: 7mg

673. Banana Pudding

Preparation Time: 30 minutes **Cooking Time:** 20 minutes **Servings:** 10

Ingredients:
Pudding:
- ¾ cup Erythritol or other sugar replacement
- 5 teaspoons almond flour
- ¼ teaspoon salt
- 2½ cups fat-free milk
- 6 tablespoons prepared egg replacement

Meringue:
- 5 medium egg whites (1 cup)
- ¼ cup Erythritol or other sugar replacement
- ½ teaspoon vanilla extract
- 2 (8-ounce / 227-g) containers sugar-free spelt hazelnut biscuits, crushed
- 5 medium bananas, sliced
- ½ teaspoon vanilla extract

Directions:
Make the Pudding
1. In a saucepan, whisk the erythritol, almond flour, salt, and milk together. Cook until the sugar is dissolved.
2. Whisk in the egg replacement and cook for about 10 minutes, or until thickened.
3. Detach from the heat and stir in the vanilla.

Make the Meringue
1. Preheat the oven to 350F (180C).
2. In a bowl, set the egg whites for about 5 minutes, or until stiff.
3. Add the Erythritol and vanilla while continuing to beat for about 3 more minutes.
4. Spread the thickened pudding onto the bottom of a 3 × 6-inch casserole dish.
5. Set a layer of crushed biscuits on top of the pudding.
6. Place a layer of sliced bananas on top of the biscuits.
4. Set the meringue on top of the banana pudding.
5. Bring the casserole dish to the oven, and bake for 7 to 10 minutes, or until the top is lightly browned.

Nutrition:
Calories: 323
Fat: 14g
Protein: 12g
Carbohydrates: 42g
Sugars: 11g
Fiber: 3g
Sodium: 148mg

674. Pineapple Nice Cream

Preparation Time: 10 minutes **Cooking Time:** 0 minutes **Servings:** 6

Ingredients:
- 2 cups frozen pineapple
- 1 cup peanut butter (no added sugar, salt, or fat)
- ½ cup unsweetened almond milk

Directions:
1. In a blender or food processor, merge the frozen pineapple and peanut butter and process.
2. Add the almond milk, and blend until smooth.

Nutrition:
Calories: 301
Fat: 22g
Protein: 14g
Carbohydrates: 15g
Sugars: 2g
Fiber: 4g
Sodium: 39mg

675. Spiced Orange Rice Pudding

Preparation Time: 5 minutes **Cooking Time:** 35 minutes **Servings:** 6

Ingredients:
- 2 cups short-grain brown rice
- 6 cups fat-free milk

- 1 teaspoon ground nutmeg, plus more for serving
- 1 tsp. ground cinnamon, plus more for serving
- ¼ teaspoon orange extract
- Juice of 2 oranges (about ¾ cup)
- ½ cup Erythritol or other brown sugar replacement

Directions:
1. In an electric pressure cooker, stir the rice, milk, nutmeg, cinnamon, orange extract, orange juice, and Erythritol together.
2. Seal the lid and bring the pressure valve to sealing.
3. Select the Manual setting and cook for 35 minutes.
4. Once cooking is complete, quick-release the pressure. Carefully remove the lid.
5. Stir well and spoon into serving dishes. Enjoy with an additional sprinkle of nutmeg and cinnamon.

Nutrition:

Calories: 320
Fat: 2g
Protein: 13g
Carbohydrates: 61g
Sugars: 15g
Fiber: 2g
Sodium: 130mg

676. Strawberry Cream Cheese Crepes

Preparation Time: 8 Minutes   **Cooking Time:** 10 Minutes   **Servings:** 4

Ingredients:
- ½ cup old-fashioned oats
- 1 cup unsweetened plain almond milk
- 1 egg
- 3 teaspoons honey, divided
- Nonstick cooking spray
- 2 Ounces low-fat cream cheese
- ¼ cup low-fat cottage cheese
- 2 cups sliced strawberries

Directions:
1. In a blender jar, process the oats until they resemble flour. Add the almond milk, egg, and 1½ teaspoons honey, and process until smooth.
2. Heat a large skillet over medium heat. Spray with nonstick cooking spray to coat.
3. Add ¼ cup of oat batter to the pan and quickly swirl around to coat and cook for 2 to 3 minutes.
4. Transfer to a plate. Continue with the remaining batter, spraying the skillet with nonstick cooking spray before adding more batter. Set the cooked crepes aside, loosely covered with aluminum foil, while you make the filling.
5. Clean the blender jar, then combine the cream cheese, cottage cheese, and remaining 1½ teaspoons of honey, and process until smooth.
6. Fill each crepe with two tablespoons of the cream cheese mixture, topped with ¼ cup of strawberries. Serve.

Nutrition:

Calories: 149
Total Fat: 6g
Protein: 6g
Carbohydrates: 20g

677. Cream Cheese Swirl Brownies

Preparation Time: 10 Minutes   **Cooking Time:** 20 Minutes   **Servings:** 12

Ingredients:
- 2 eggs
- ¼ cup unsweetened applesauce
- ¼ cup coconut oil, melted
- 3 tablespoons pure maple syrup, divided
- ¼ cup unsweetened cocoa powder
- ¼ cup coconut flour
- ¼ teaspoon salt
- 1 teaspoon baking powder
- 2 tablespoons low-fat cream cheese

Directions:
1. Preheat the oven to 350F. Grease an 8-by-8-inch baking dish.
2. In a large mixing bowl, merge the eggs with the applesauce, coconut oil, and 2 tablespoons of maple syrup.
3. Stir in the cocoa powder and coconut flour and mix well. Sprinkle the salt and baking powder evenly over the surface and mix well to incorporate. Set the mixture to the prepared baking dish.
4. In a small, microwave-safe bowl, microwave the cream cheese for 10 to 20 seconds until softened. Attach the remaining tablespoon of maple syrup and mix to combine.
5. Drop the cream cheese onto the batter and use a toothpick or chopstick to swirl it on the surface. Bake for 20 minutes. Cool and cut into 12 squares.

Nutrition:

Calories: 84
Fat: 6g
Protein: 2g
Carbohydrates: 6g

678. Greek Yogurt Sundae

Preparation Time: 8 Minutes   **Cooking Time:** 0 Minutes   **Servings:** 1

Ingredients:
- ¾ cup plain nonfat Greek yogurt
- ¼ cup mixed berries (blueberries, strawberries, blackberries)
- 2 tablespoons cashew, walnut, or almond pieces
- 1 tablespoon ground flaxseed
- 2 Fresh mint leaves, shredded

Directions:
1. Spoon the yogurt into a small bowl. Top with the berries, nuts, and flaxseed.
2. Garnish with the mint and serve.

Nutrition:

Calories: 237
Fat: 11g
Protein: 21g
Carbohydrates: 16g

679. Cinnamon Baked Apples

Preparation Time: 5 Minutes **Cooking Time:** 15 Minutes **Servings:** 4

Ingredients:

- 4 large apples
- 2 teaspoons reduced-fat margarine
- ⅓ cup raisins
- 1 cup low-fat yogurt
- 1 teaspoon cinnamon
- 2 tablespoons sweetener
- ¾ cup boiling water

Directions:

1. Preheat the oven to 375F.
2. Cut a hole out of each apple, removing the core.
3. Mix the sweetener, raisins, and cinnamon in a bowl until well combined.
4. Stuff the apples with the prepared raisin mixture and place them in a baking dish.
5. Dot each apple with margarine.
6. Pour the boiling water into the dish and bake for 30-45 minutes or until the apples are tender but not mushy.

Nutrition:

Calories: 157
Carbohydrates: 32g
Fat: 1g
Protein: 6g

680. Lemon Berry Chiffon

Preparation Time: 14 minutes **Cooking Time:** 10 minutes **Servings:** 6

Ingredients:

- ⅓ cup fresh lemon juice
- ½ cup sweetener
- 4 large eggs, beaten
- 3 cup fresh berries, such as strawberries, blueberries, and blackberries

Directions:

1. Place lemon juice and sweetener in a small saucepan.
2. Warmth gently, stirring until all the sugar has dissolved. Remove from the heat and set aside to cool.
3. Whisk the lemon juice mixture into the eggs and return to the saucepan.
4. Whisk while cooking over low heat until the mixture thickens.
5. After around 5 minutes, the mixture should coat the back of a spoon.
6. Refrigerate for at least an hour.
7. Use the berries to top the lemon chiffon, or you can layer the berries into the serving glasses.

Nutrition:

Calories: 90
Carbohydrates: 11g
Fat: 4g
Protein: 5g

681. Flourless Chocolate Cake

Preparation Time: 10 Minutes **Cooking Time:** 45 Minutes **Servings:** 6

Ingredients:

- ½ cup of stevia
- 12 ounces of unsweetened baking chocolate
- ⅔ cup of ghee
- ⅓ cup of warm water
- ¼ teaspoon of salt
- 4 large pastured eggs
- 2 cups of boiling water

Directions:

1. Line the bottom of a 9-inch pan of a springform with parchment paper.
2. Heat the water in a small pot; then add the salt and the stevia over the water until wait until the mixture becomes completely dissolved.
3. Melt the baking chocolate into a double boiler or simply microwave it for about 30 seconds.
4. Mix the melted chocolate and the butter in a large bowl with an electric mixer.
5. Beat in your hot mixture, then crack in the egg and whisk after adding each of the eggs.
6. Pour the obtained mixture into your prepared springform tray.
7. Wrap the springform tray with foil paper.
8. Place the springform tray in a large cake tray and add boiling water right to the outside; make sure the depth doesn't exceed 1 inch.
9. Bake the cake into the water bath for about 45 minutes at a temperature of about 350°F.
10. Remove the tray from the boiling water and transfer it to a wire to cool.
11. Let the cake chill for an overnight in the refrigerator.

Nutrition:

Calories: 295
Carbohydrates: 6g
Fiber: 4g

682. Raspberry Cake with White Chocolate Sauce

Preparation Time: 15 Minutes **Cooking Time:** 60 Minutes **Servings:** 5

Ingredients:

- 5 Ounces of melted cacao butter
- 2 Ounces of grass-fed ghee
- ½ cup of coconut cream
- 1 cup of green banana flour
- 3 teaspoons of pure vanilla - 4 large eggs
- ½ cup of as Lakanto Monk Fruit
- 1 teaspoon of baking powder
- 2 teaspoons of apple cider vinegar
- 2 cups of raspberries

For the White Chocolate Sauce:

- 3 and ½ ounces of cacao butter
- ½ cup of coconut cream

Directions:
1. Warmth your oven to a temperature of about 280F.
2. Combine the green banana flour with the pure vanilla extract, the baking powder, the coconut cream, the eggs, the cider vinegar, and the monk fruit and mix very well.
3. Leave the raspberries aside and line a cake loaf tin with baking paper.
4. Spill the batter into the baking tray and scatter the raspberries over the top of the cake. Place the tray in your oven and bake it for about 60 minutes; in the meantime, prepare the sauce.

- 2 teaspoons of pure vanilla extract
- 1 Pinch of salt

5. Combine the cacao cream, the vanilla extract, the cacao butter, and the salt in a saucepan over low heat.
6. Mix all your ingredients with a fork to make sure the cacao butter mixes very well with the cream. Detach from the heat and set aside to cool a little bit, but don't let it harden. Drizzle with the chocolate sauce.
7. Scatter the cake with more raspberries.
8. Slice your cake, then serve and enjoy it!

Nutrition:
Calories: 323
Carbohydrates: 9.9g
Fiber: 4g

683. Lava Cake

Preparation Time: 10 Minutes **Cooking Time:** 10 Minutes **Servings:** 2

Ingredients:
- 2 oz. of dark chocolate; you should at least use chocolate of 85% cocoa solids
- 1 tablespoon of super-fine almond flour
- 2 oz. of unsalted almond butter
- 2 large eggs
- Half cup of sweetener

Directions:
1. Warmth your oven to a temperature of about 350F.
2. Grease 2 heat-proof ramekins with almond butter.
3. Now, melt the chocolate and the almond butter and stir very well.
4. Beat the eggs very well with a mixer.
5. Add the eggs to the chocolate and the butter mixture and mix very well with almond flour and the sweetener; then stir.
6. Pour the dough into two ramekins.
7. Bake for about 9 to 10 minutes.
8. Turn the cakes over plates and serve with pomegranate seeds!

Nutrition:
Calories: 459
Carbohydrates: 3.5g
Fiber: 0.8g

684. Roasted Mango

Preparation Time: 5 minutes **Cooking Time:** 10 minutes **Servings:** 4

Ingredients:
- 2 mangoes, sliced
- 2 teaspoons crystallized ginger, chopped
- 2 teaspoons orange zest
- 2 tablespoons coconut flakes (unsweetened)

Directions:
1. Preheat your oven to 350 F.
2. Add mango slices in custard cups.
3. Top with the ginger, orange zest and coconut flakes.
4. Bake in the oven for 10 minutes.

Nutrition:
Calories: 325
Carbohydrates: 6g
Fiber: 1g

685. Cake with Whipped Cream Icing

Preparation Time: 20 Minutes **Cooking Time:** 25 Minutes **Servings:** 7

Ingredients:
- ¾ cup Coconut flour
- ¾ cup of Swerve Sweetener
- ½ cup of Cocoa powder
- 2 teaspoons of baking powder

For Whipped Cream Icing:
- 1 cup of Heavy Whipping Cream
- ¼ cup of Swerve Sweetener

- 6 large eggs
- ⅔ cup of Heavy Whipping Cream
- ½ cup of melted almond butter

- 1 teaspoon of Vanilla extract
- ⅓ cup of Sifted Cocoa Powder

Directions:
1. Warmth your oven to a temperature of about 350F.
2. Grease an 8x8 cake tray with cooking spray.
3. Add the coconut flour, the Swerve sweetener, the cocoa powder, the baking powder, the eggs, the melted butter, and combine very well with an electric or a hand mixer.

For the Icing:
6. Whip the cream until it becomes fluffy; then add in the Swerve, the vanilla, and the cocoa powder.

4. Pour your batter into the cake tray and bake for about 25 minutes.
5. Detach the cake tray from the oven and let cool for about 5 minutes.

7. Add the Swerve; the vanilla, and the cocoa powder, then continue mixing until your ingredients are very well combined.
8. Frost your baked cake with the icing!

Nutrition:
Calories: 357
Carbohydrates: 11g
Fiber: 2g

686. Walnut-Fruit Cake

Preparation Time: 15 Minutes **Cooking Time:** 20 Minutes **Servings:** 7

Ingredients:
- ½ cup of almond butter (softened)
- ¼ cup of so Nourished granulated Erythritol
- 1 tablespoon of ground cinnamon
- ½ teaspoon of ground nutmeg
- ¼ teaspoon of ground cloves
- 4 large pastured eggs
- 1 teaspoon of vanilla extract
- ½ teaspoon of almond extract
- 2 cups of almond flour
- ½ cup of chopped walnuts
- ¼ cup of dried unsweetened cranberries
- ¼ cup of seedless raisins

Directions:
1. Warmth your oven to a temperature of about 350F and grease an 8-inch baking tin of round shape with coconut oil.
2. Beat the granulated Erythritol and the butter at high speed until it becomes fluffy.
3. Add the cinnamon, the nutmeg, and the cloves; then blend your ingredients until they become smooth.
4. Crack in the eggs and beat very well by adding one at a time, plus the almond extract and the vanilla.
5. Whisk in the almond flour until it forms a smooth batter, then fold in the nuts and the fruit.
6. Spread your mixture into your prepared baking pan and bake it for about 20 minutes.
7. Remove the cake from the oven and let cool for about 5 minutes.
8. Dust the cake with powdered Erythritol.

Nutrition:
Calories: 250
Carbohydrates: 12g
Fiber: 2g

687. Ginger Cake

Preparation Time: 15 Minutes **Cooking Time:** 20 Minutes **Servings:** 9

Ingredients:
- ½ tablespoon of unsalted almond butter to grease the pan
- 4 large eggs
- ¼ cup coconut milk
- 2 tablespoons of unsalted almond butter
- 1 and ½ teaspoons of stevia
- 1 tablespoon of ground cinnamon
- 1 tablespoon of natural cocoa powder
- 1 tablespoon of fresh ground ginger
- ½ teaspoon of kosher salt
- 1 and ½ cups almond flour
- ½ teaspoon of baking soda

Directions:
1. Warmth your oven to a temperature of 325F.
2. Grease a glass baking tray of about 8X8 inches generously with almond butter.
3. In a large bowl, whisk all together with the coconut milk, the eggs, the melted almond butter, the stevia, the cinnamon, the cocoa powder, the ginger, and the kosher salt.
4. Set in the almond flour, then the baking soda, and mix very well.
5. Spill the batter into the prepared pan and bake for about 20 to 25 minutes.
6. Let the cake cool.

Nutrition:
Calories: 175
Carbohydrates: 5g
Fiber: 1.9g

688. Orange Cake

Preparation Time: 10 Minutes **Cooking Time:** 50 Minutes **Servings:** 8

Ingredients:
- 2 ½ cups of almond flour
- 2 Unwaxed washed oranges
- 5 large separated eggs
- 1 teaspoon of baking powder
- 2 teaspoons of orange extract
- 1 teaspoon of vanilla bean powder
- 6 Seeds of cardamom pods crushed
- 16 Drops of liquid stevia; about three teaspoons
- 1 Handful of flaked almonds to decorate

Directions:
1. Warmth your oven to a temperature of about 350F.
2. Line a rectangular bread baking tray with parchment paper.
3. Place the oranges into a pan filled with cold water and cover it with a lid.
4. Bring the saucepan to a boil, then let simmer for about 1 hour and make sure the oranges are totally submerged.
5. Make sure the oranges are always submerged to remove any taste of bitterness.
6. Cut the oranges into halves, then remove any seeds, and drain the water, set the oranges aside to cool down.
7. Divide the oranges in half and remove any seeds, then puree it with a blender or a food processor.
8. Detach the eggs, and then whisk the egg whites until you see stiff peaks forming.
9. Add all your ingredients except for the egg whites to the orange mixture and add in the egg whites; then mix.
10. Spill the batter into the cake tin and sprinkle with the flaked almonds right on top.
11. Bake your cake for about 50 minutes.
12. Detach the cake from the oven and set it aside to cool for 5 minutes.

Nutrition:
Calories: 164
Carbohydrates: 7.1g
Fiber: 2.7g

689. Lemon Cake

Preparation Time: 20 Minutes **Cooking Time:** 20 Minutes **Servings:** 9

Ingredients:
- 2 medium lemons
- 4 large eggs
- 2 tablespoons of almond butter
- 2 tablespoons of avocado oil
- ⅓ cup of coconut flour
- 4-5 tbsp. of honey
- ½ tablespoon of baking soda

Directions:
1. Warmth the oven of 350F.
2. Crack the eggs in a bowl and set two egg whites aside.
3. Whisk the two whites of eggs with the egg yolks, the honey, the oil, the almond butter, the lemon zest, and the juice very well together.
4. Combine the baking soda with the coconut flour and gradually add this dry mixture to the wet ingredients and keep whisking for a couple of minutes.
5. Beat the two eggs with a hand mixer and beat the egg into foam.
6. Add the white egg foam gradually to the mixture with a silicone spatula.
7. Transfer your obtained batter to a tray covered with baking paper.
8. Bake your cake for about 20 to 22 minutes.
9. Let the cake cool for 5 minutes; then slice your cake.

Nutrition:
Calories: 164
Carbohydrates: 7.1g
Fiber: 2.7g

690. Cinnamon Cake

Preparation Time: 15 Minutes **Cooking Time:** 35 Minutes **Servings:** 8

Ingredients:
For the Cinnamon Filling:
- 3 tablespoons of Swerve Sweetener

For the Cake:
- 3 cups of almond flour
- ¾ cup of Swerve Sweetener
- ¼ cup of unflavored protein powder
- 2 teaspoon of baking powder
- ½ teaspoon of salt

For Cream Cheese Frosting:
- 3 tablespoons of softened cream cheese
- 2 tablespoons of powdered Swerve Sweetener
- 2 teaspoons of ground cinnamon
- 3 large pastured eggs
- ½ cup of melted coconut oil
- ½ teaspoon of vanilla extract
- ½ cup of almond milk
- 1 tablespoon of melted coconut oil
- 1 tablespoon of coconut heavy whipping cream
- ½ teaspoon of vanilla extract

Directions:
1. Warmth your oven to a temperature of about 325F and grease a baking tray of 8x8 inches.
2. For the filling, mix the Swerve and the cinnamon in a mixing bowl and mix very well; then, set it aside.
3. For the preparation of the cake, whisk all together with the almond flour, sweetener, the protein powder, baking powder, and the salt in a mixing bowl.
4. Add in the eggs, the melted coconut oil, and the vanilla extract and mix very well.
5. Add in the almond milk and keep stirring until your ingredients are very well combined.
6. Spread about half of the batter in the prepared pan; then sprinkle with about two-thirds of the filling mixture.
7. Spread the remaining mixture of the batter over the filling and smooth it with a spatula.
8. Bake for about 35 minutes in the oven.
9. Brush with the melted coconut oil and sprinkle with the remaining cinnamon filling.
10. Set the frosting by beating the cream cheese, the powdered erythritol, the cream, and the vanilla extract in a mixing bowl until it becomes smooth.
11. Drizzle frost over the cooled cake.

Nutrition:
Calories: 222
Carbohydrates: 5.4g
Fiber: 1.5g

691. Choco Peppermint Cake

Preparation Time: 5 Minutes **Cooking Time:** 10 Minutes **Servings:** 4

Ingredients:
- Cooking spray
- ⅓ cup oil
- 15 oz. Package chocolate cake mix
- 3 eggs, beaten
- 1 cup water
- ¼ teaspoon peppermint extract

Directions:
1. Spray slow cooker with oil.
2. Mix all the ingredients in a bowl.
3. Use an electric mixer on a medium speed setting to mix ingredients for 2 minutes.
4. Pour mixture into the slow cooker.
5. Seal the pot and cook on low for 3 hours.
6. Let cool before slicing and serving.

Nutrition:
Calories: 185
Carbohydrate: 27g
Protein: 3.8g

692. Ice Cream Brownie Cake

Preparation Time: 5 Minutes **Cooking Time:** 10 Minutes **Servings:** 4

Ingredients:
- Cooking spray
- 12 oz. No-sugar brownie mix
- ¼ cup oil
- 2 egg whites
- 3 tablespoons water
- 2 cups sugar-free ice cream

Directions:
1. Preheat your oven to 325F.
2. Spray your baking pan with oil.
3. Mix the brownie mix, oil, egg whites, and water in a bowl.
4. Pour into the baking pan.
5. Bake for 25 minutes.
6. Let cool.
7. Freeze brownie for 2 hours.
8. Spread ice cream over the brownie.
9. Freeze for 8 hours.

Nutrition:
Calories: 198
Carbohydrate: 33g
Protein: 3g

693. Strawberry Shortcake

Preparation Time: 9 Minutes **Cooking Time:** 25 Minutes **Servings:** 8

Ingredients:
- 1 ¾ cups whole-wheat pastry flour
- ¼ cup all-purpose
- 2 ½ teaspoons low-sodium baking powder

For the Topping:
- 6 cups fresh strawberries
- 1 tsp. sugar replacement (like stevia)
- ¼ cup trans-free margarine (chilled)
- ¾ cup fat-free milk (chilled)
- ¾ cup plain fat-free yogurt

Directions:
1. Preheat the oven to 425F.
2. In a mixing bowl, re-sift the flours, baking powder, and sugar replacement together. Divide the chilled margarine into the dry ingredients until the mixture resembles coarse crumbs. Attach the chilled milk and stir just until a moist dough form.
3. Set the dough onto a generously floured work surface and, with floured hands, knead gently 6-8 times. With a rolling pin, bend the dough into a rectangle ¼-inch thick. Cut into eight squares.
4. Set the squares onto the prepared baking pan and bake until golden, 10 to 12 minutes, or until golden brown.
5. Bring the biscuits onto individual plates. Set each with 1 cup strawberries and 1 ½ tablespoons yogurt. Set immediately.

Nutrition:
Calories: 225 Fat: 5g
Protein: 7g

694. Chocolate Cake

Preparation Time: 11 Minutes **Cooking Time:** 30 Minutes **Servings:** 8

Ingredients:
For the Cake:
- 2 cups Splenda
- 1 ¾ cups oat flour
- ¾ Unsweetened cocoa
- 1 ½ teaspoon baking powder
- 1 ½ teaspoon baking soda
- 1 teaspoon salt

For the Glaze:
- 3 tablespoon Splenda
- 1 tablespoon unsweetened cocoa
- 1 teaspoon cinnamon
- ½ cup liquid eggs (eggbeaters)
- 1 cup skim milk
- ½ cup extra virgin olive oil
- 2 teaspoon vanilla extract
- 1 cup boiling water
- 1 teaspoon cinnamon
- 4 teaspoons of water

Directions:
1. Heat the oven to 350F. Set a cooking spray and flour a 13x9 pan.
2. Spill together Splenda, flour, cocoa, baking powder, baking soda, cinnamon, and salt in a large bowl.
3. Attach eggs, milk, oil, and vanilla; beat on medium speed of mixer 2 minutes. Spill in boiling water. The batter will be thin. Pour the batter into the prepared pan. Bake 20-25 minutes.
4. Mix three tablespoons of Splenda, one tablespoon of cocoa, one teaspoon cinnamon, and four teaspoons of water. Drizzle over the cake.

Nutrition:
Calories: 138
Fat: 9g
Carbohydrates 16g
Protein: 5g

695. Berry Coffee Cake

Preparation Time: 8 minutes **Cooking Time:** 40 minutes **Servings:** 8

Ingredients:
- ½ cup skim milk
- 1 tbsp. vinegar
- 2 tbsp. canola oil
- 1 tsp. vanilla
- 1 egg
- ⅓ cup packed brown sugar
- 1 cup whole-wheat pastry flour
- ½ tsp. baking soda
- ½ tsp. ground cinnamon
- ⅛ tsp. salt

- 1 cup frozen mixed berries,
- ¼ cup low-fat granola

Directions:
1. Warmth the oven to 350F. Set an 8-inch round cake pan with cooking spray and coat with flour.
2. In a bowl, merge the milk, vinegar, oil, vanilla, egg, and brown sugar until smooth. Stir in flour, baking soda, cinnamon, and salt just until moistened. Gently bend half of the berries into the batter. Pour into the prepared pan. Sprinkle with the remaining berries and top with the granola.
3. Bake 25 to 30 minutes.

Nutrition:
Calories: 144
Fat: 4g
Carbohydrates 23g
Protein: 4g

696. Pound Cake

Preparation Time: 9 Minutes **Cooking Time:** 30 Minutes **Servings:** 18

Ingredients:
- Cooking spray
- 3 tbsp. dry breadcrumbs
- 4 cups sifted cake flour
- ¼ tsp. salt
- 1 ½ cups light sour cream
- 1 tsp. baking soda
- ¾ cup butter
- 2 ¾ cups sugar replacement (like stevia)
- 2 tsp. vanilla extract
- 3 large eggs
- 2 tbsp. fresh lemon juice

Directions:
1. Preheat the oven to 350F.
2. Set a 10-inch tube pan with cooking spray, dust with breadcrumbs.
3. Set flour into dry measuring cups, level with a knife. Merge flour and salt; stir with a whisk. Merge sour cream and baking soda; stir well.
4. Set the butter in a large bowl; set with a mixer at medium speed until light and fluffy. Gradually attach sugar and vanilla, beating until well blended.
5. Attach eggs, one at a time, beating well after each addition. Add juice; beat 30 seconds. Attach flour mixture alternately with the sour cream mixture to the sugar mixture, beating at low speed, beginning and ending with flour mixture.
6. Spoon batter into the prepared pan. Bake at 350F.
7. Cool in the pan and remove from the pan. Cool completely on the wire rack.

Nutrition:
Calories: 304
Fat: 10g
Carbohydrates: 36g
Protein: 4g

697. Dark Chocolate Cake

Preparation Time: 11 Minutes **Cooking Time:** 35 minutes **Servings:** 12

Ingredients:
- 1 ½ cup whole-wheat pastry flour
- 1 teaspoon baking soda
- ¼ teaspoon kosher salt
- 2 teaspoons chia seeds
- 2 tablespoons water
- 2 Ounces unsweetened dark chocolate
- 2 tablespoons unsalted butter, softened

Topping:
- 2 Ounces melted dark chocolate bar
- 12 Ounces strawberries, thinly sliced (optional)
- 2 tablespoons roasted mashed yam
- ¼ cup Splenda brown sugar, lightly packed
- ¼ cup unsweetened applesauce
- ¼ cup honey
- 1 ½ teaspoons vanilla
- ½ cup plain fat-free Greek yogurt
- ½ cup boiling water
- 2 teaspoons of cinnamon

Directions:
1. Heat the oven to 375F. Set a 9-inch round cake pan with cooking spray and flour lightly.
2. In a bowl, sift the flour, baking soda, and salt together. Set aside. In a bowl, merge chia seeds with water and set them aside to gel.
3. Slowly melt the unsweetened dark chocolate and then allow it to cool slightly.
4. In a bowl, set butter with yams, brown sugar, applesauce, and honey for 2 minutes. Attach chia gel and beat for an additional 2 minutes. Set in vanilla and then chocolate.
5. Gradually spill in half the flour mixture and then half the yogurt. Redo with the remaining flour mixture and yogurt. Slowly and carefully spill in the boiling water. Pour the batter into the cake pan.
6. Bake for about 20 minutes. Test the cake with a toothpick-it should come out wet but not gooey. Do not over-bake it.
7. Cool the pan on a rack for 20 minutes. Remove the cake from the pan and cut it into 12 pieces. Melt the chocolate bar, drizzle over the cake. Set on plates and brush with strawberries and cinnamon.

Nutrition:
Calories: 150
Fat: 6g
Carbohydrates: 24g
Protein: 4g

698. Berry Cobbler

Preparation Time: 8 Minutes **Cooking Time:** 45 Minutes **Servings:** 5

Ingredients:

For the Filling:
- 1 cup raspberries
- 1 cup blueberries

- 2 cups hashed apples
- 2 tbsp Splenda brown sugar
- ½ tsp. ground cinnamon

For the Topping:
- 1 large egg
- ¼ cup soy milk
- ¼ tsp. salt

- 1 tsp. lemon zest
- 2 tsp. lemon juice
- 1 ½ tbsp. cornstarch
- ½ tsp. vanilla
- 1 ½ tbsp. Splenda brown sugar
- ¾ cup whole-wheat pastry flour

Directions:
1. Preheat the oven to 350F. Lightly coat the ovenproof ramekins with cooking spray.
2. In a medium bowl, attach the raspberries, blueberries, apples, sugar, cinnamon, lemon zest, and lemon juice. Stir to mix evenly. Attach the cornstarch and stir until it dissolves. Set aside.
3. In a separate bowl, attach the egg white and spill until lightly beaten. Add the soy milk, salt, vanilla, sugar, and pastry flour. Stir to mix well.
4. Set the berry mixture evenly among the prepared dishes. Spill the topping over each. Arrange the ramekins on a large baking pan and place them in the oven.
5. Bake until the berries are crisp and the topping is golden brown.

Nutrition:
Calories: 136
Fat: 0g
Carbohydrates: 31g
Protein: 3g

699. Lemon Cheesecake

Preparation Time: 3 Hours **Cooking Time:** 0 Minutes **Servings:** 8

Ingredients:
- 2 tbsp. cold water
- 1 Envelope gelatin
- 2 tbsp. lemon juice
- ½ cup skim milk, heated almost to boiling
- Egg substitute equivalent to 1 egg, or 2 egg whites
- ½ cup sugar replacement (like stevia)
- 1 tsp. vanilla
- 2 cups low-fat cottage cheese
- Lemon zest

Directions:
1. Combine water, gelatin, and lemon juice in a blender container. Blend it at low speed for 1 to 2 minutes to soften the gelatin.
2. Add hot milk, processing until the gelatin is dissolved. Add egg substitute, sugar, vanilla, and cheese to the blender container. Blend on high speed until smooth.
3. Spill into a 9-inch pie plate or round flat dish. Refrigerate for 2 to 3 hours.

Nutrition:
Calories: 80
Fat: 1g
Carbohydrates: 9g
Protein: 9g

700. Banana Coffee Cake

Preparation Time: 11 Minutes **Cooking Time:** 30 Minutes **Servings:** 8

Ingredients:
- Cooking spray
- 1 ⅓ cups all-purpose flour
- ½ teaspoon salt
- ½ teaspoon baking powder
- ¼ teaspoon baking soda
- 1 cup mashed ripe banana
- ¾ cup granulated sugar replacement (or equivalent sugar substitute)
- 3 tablespoons vegetable oil
- 1 teaspoon vanilla extract
- ¼ teaspoon ground nutmeg
- 1 large egg
- ¼ cup packed Splenda dark brown sugar
- 1 tablespoon water
- 2 teaspoons margarine
- 2 tablespoons chopped macadamia nuts, toasted
- 2 tablespoons flaked sweetened coconut

Directions:
1. Preheat the oven to 350F.
2. Coat a 9-inch round cake pan with cooking spray, line the bottom of the pan with wax paper. Coat wax paper with cooking spray.
3. Set flour into dry measuring cups, level with a knife. Combine flour, salt, baking powder, and baking soda in a bowl, stirring with a whisk.
4. Combine banana and the next five ingredients (banana through egg) in a bowl.
5. Add the flour mixture to the banana mixture and beat until blended. Pour the batter into the prepared pan.
6. Bake at 350F. Cool in the pan; remove from the pan. Peel off the wax paper carefully.
7. Combine brown sugar, water, and margarine in a small saucepan; bring to a boil-cook 1 minute, stirring constantly. Remove from the heat; stir in nuts and coconut. Spread over the cake. Serve it warm.

Nutrition:
Calories: 189
Fat: 6g
Carbohydrates: 32g
Protein: 2g

701. Fruitcake

Preparation Time: 11 Minutes **Cooking Time:** 30 Minutes **Servings:** 12

Ingredients:
- 2 cups assorted hashed dried fruit, such as cherries, currants, dates, or figs
- ½ cup applesauce
- ½ cup crushed pineapple

- Zest and juice of 1 orange
- Zest and juice of 1 lemon
- ½ cup apple juice
- 2 tbsp. real vanilla extract
- ¼ cup sugar replacement (like stevia)
- ¼ cup flaxseed flour

Directions:
1. In a medium bowl, merge dried fruit, applesauce, pineapple, fruit zests and juices, and vanilla. Soak for 15 to 20 minutes.
2. In a large bowl, merge sugar, milled flax, oat flour, pastry flour, baking soda, and baking powder. Spill the fruit and liquid mixture

- ½ cup oat flour
- 1 cup whole-wheat pastry flour
- ½ tsp. baking soda
- ½ tsp. baking powder
- 1 egg
- ½ cup walnuts

into the dry ingredients and stir to combine. Add egg and walnuts and stir to combine.
3. Spill the mixture into a loaf pan lined with parchment paper and bake at 325F for 1 hour.
4. Let the fruitcake rest for 30 minutes.

Nutrition:
Calories: 229
Fat: 5g
Carbohydrates: 42
Protein: 4g

---

702. Angel Food Cake
Preparation Time: 9 Minutes **Cooking Time:** 30 Minutes **Servings:** 12
Ingredients:
- 1 cup sifted cake flour
- 1 ½ cups sugar replacement like stevia, divided (or sugar substitute equivalent)
- 12 large egg whites
- 1 teaspoon cream of tartar
- ¼ teaspoon salt
- 1 ½ teaspoons vanilla extract
- 1 ½ teaspoons fresh lemon juice
- ½ teaspoon almond extract

Directions:
1. Preheat the oven to 325F.
2. To prepare the cake, set flour into a dry measuring cup, level with a knife. Merge flour and ¾ cup sugar, stirring with a whisk.
3. Set egg whites in a large bowl; beat with a mixer at high speed until foamy. Attach cream of tartar and salt; beat until soft peaks form. Attach ¾ cup sugar, two tablespoons at a time, beating until stiff peaks form.
4. Beat in vanilla, juice, and almond extract. Set ¼ cup flour mixture over egg white mixture: fold in. Repeat with the remaining flour mixture, ¼ cup at a time.
5. Set the batter into an ungreased 10-inch tube pan, spreading evenly. Bake at 325F for 55 minutes or until cake springs back when lightly touched. Invert the pan; cool completely.
6. Loosen cake from the pan sides using a narrow metal spatula. Invert the cake onto a plate.

Nutrition:
Calories: 146
Fat: 1g
Carbohydrates: 31g
Protein: 4g

---

703. Chocolate Lava Cake
Preparation Time: 7 Minutes **Cooking Time:** 13 Minutes **Servings:** 8
Ingredients:
- ½ cup raw unsweetened cocoa powder
- ¼ cup butter, melted
- 4 eggs
- ¼ cup sugar-free and gluten-free chocolate sauce
- ½ teaspoon ground cinnamon
- ½ teaspoon sea salt
- 1 teaspoon pure vanilla extract
- ¼ cup raw stevia

Directions:
1. Pour one tablespoon of chocolate sauce into four cavities of an ice cube tray and freeze it.
2. Preheat the oven to 350F. Prepare four ramekins by greasing with oil or butter.
3. Spill together the cocoa powder, stevia, cinnamon, and sea salt in a small bowl.
4. Spill in the eggs, one at a time.
5. Add the melted butter and vanilla extract. Stir until well combined.
6. Fill each prepared ramekin halfway with the mixture.
7. Remove the chocolate sauce from the freezer and place one in each of the ramekins.
8. Cover the chocolate with the remaining cake batter.
9. Bake for 13 to 14 minutes until just set. Transfer from the oven to a wire rack and allow to cool for 5 minutes.
10. Carefully remove the cakes from the ramekins.
11. Enjoy your tasty and healthy chocolate lava cake by cutting into its molten center.

Nutrition:
Carbohydrates: 6g
Protein: 8g
Total Fat: 17g
Calories: 189

---

704. Decadent Three-Layered Chocolate Cream Cake
Preparation Time: 30 Minutes **Cooking Time:** 60 Minutes **Servings:** 8
Ingredients:
- 4 ounces unsweetened chocolate
- ½ cup (1 stick) butter
- 1 ½ cups powdered sweetener, divided
- 3 eggs
- ½ cup + 8 tablespoons raw unsweetened cocoa powder
- 1 Vanilla pod
- Pinch of sea salt
- 1 cup whipping cream
- Coconut whipped cream
- 1 Can of coconut milk, refrigerated overnight

Directions:

1. Preheat the oven to 325F. Spray a little cooking oil into a pan smaller than 8 inches.
2. Combine the chocolate and butter in a double boiler and melt them together. Spill in ½ cup of sweetener and keep on stirring over low heat until everything is well combined. Detach from the heat and let cool a little bit.
3. Separate the eggs and beat the whites until stiff peaks form. Add ¼ cup of sweetener little by little.

Cream:
1. To prepare the three types of filling, beat the whipping cream for about 6-7 minutes until it gets very thick. Slowly add ½ cup of sweetener.
2. Divide the cream into halves and place one half in a bowl. Divide the remaining cream into halves again and place in the other two separate bowls. You will have three bowls, one with ½ of the cream and two with ¼ of the cream.

Assembling:
1. Slice the cake horizontally in 3 equal slices using a very sharp knife.
2. Place the bottom part on a serving plate and cover with the middle-colored cream. Repeat with the second layer.

4. Whisk the yolks together with another ¼ cup of sweetener. Attach the chocolate mixture to the yolks and stir well. Mix in ½ cup cocoa, and then scrape the vanilla seeds from the pod and add to the mixture along with salt.
5. Fold in egg whites slowly to the chocolate mixture, but do not over mix.
6. Cook in the oven for 1 hour. Let it cool completely, and then remove it from the pan.

3. Take a bowl with ¼ cream, add one tablespoon of cocoa powder and mix well. This will be the lightest-colored cream.
4. Add ½ the cream to the bowl, add three tablespoons of cocoa powder. Mix until well distributed. This will be the middle-colored cream.
5. Attach 3-4 tablespoons of cocoa powder to the last bowl with ¼ cream. This will be the darkest cream.

3. Set with the third cake piece and spread the light-colored cream on top, followed by the darkest cream.
4. Cut in 8 slices and enjoy.

Nutrition:
Carbohydrates: 11g
Protein: 7g
Total Fat: 27g
Calories: 304

705. Carrot Cake with Cream Cheese Frosting

Preparation Time: 15 Minutes **Cooking Time:** 30 Minutes **Servings:** 6

Ingredients:

For the Carrot Cake:
- 1½ cups carrots, grated finely
- ¾ cups sugar substitute
- ¼ cup brown sugar substitute
- ½ cup coconut oil, melted
- 2 large eggs

For the Cream Cheese Frosting:
- 8 ounces cream cheese, softened
- 2 tablespoons pure Grade B maple syrup

- ¼ cup flax meal
- ½ teaspoon baking soda
- ½ teaspoon ground cinnamon
- ¼ teaspoon ground nutmeg
- ¾ cup almond flour

- ¼ teaspoon pure vanilla extract
- ¼ cup toasted walnuts, chopped (optional for garnish)

Directions:
1. Preheat the oven to 350F. Grease a 9-inch round cake pan with butter or oil.
2. Blend the sugars, coconut oil, and eggs together using a hand mixer.
3. Spill the dry ingredients together in a separate bowl until well combined.
4. Add the dry ingredients slowly and keep blending until no lumps remain.
5. Stir in the grated carrots and pour them into the prepared cake pan. Bake for 30 minutes or until a toothpick inserted comes out clean.
6. Remove from oven and allow to cool.
7. Merge the cream cheese, maple syrup, and vanilla extract until light and fluffy.
8. Top the cakes with the frosting, sprinkle with toasted walnuts, slices, and serve!

Nutrition:
Carbohydrates: 14g
Protein: 11g
Total Fat: 45g
Calories: 479

Index

Air Fryer Brussels sprouts; 138
Air Fryer Lemon Cod; 120
Air-Fried Brussels sprouts; 183
Alkaline Spring Salad; 200
Almond Berry Smoothie; 24
Almond Cheesecake Bites; 165
Almond Coconut Biscotti; 165
Almond Crusted Baked Chili Mahi Mahi; 128
Almond crusted chicken; 117
Almond Flour Crackers; 165
Amazing Overnight Apple and Cinnamon Oatmeal; 59
Ambrosia; 211
Angel Food Cake; 220
Apple and Pumpkin Waffles; 16
Apple Cinnamon Chia Pudding; 14
Apple Cinnamon Oatmeal; 57
Apple Leather; 160
Aromatic Toasted Pumpkin Seeds; 204
Asian Chicken Wings; 166
Asian Cucumber Salad; 193
Asian Frittata; 47
Asian Grilled Beef Salad; 90
Asparagus and Bacon Salad; 184
Asparagus and Salmon Quiche Cups; 21
Asparagus Avocado Soup; 184
Autumn Pork Chop with Red Cabbage and Apples; 60
Autumn Pork Chops; 77
Avocado and Egg on a Whole Wheat Toast with Chili Oil; 30
Avocado Smoothie; 169
Bacon and Chicken Patties; 63
Bacon and Fiddlehead Omelet; 53
Baked Berry Cups with Crispy Cinnamon Wedges; 207
Baked Cheese and Macaroni with Tomato; 48
Baked Eggplant with Marinara; 135
Baked Lamb and Spinach; 86
Baked Potato Topped with Cream cheese 'n Olives; 134
Baked Zucchini Recipe from Mexico; 133
Balsamic Turkey Breast; 116
Banana and Zucchini Bread; 19
Banana Cake; 172
Banana Coffee Cake; 219
Banana Crêpe Cakes; 17
Banana Nut Bread; 41
Banana Nut Cookies; 166
Banana Pepper Stuffed with Tofu 'n Spices; 134
Banana Pudding; 211
Barbecue Beef; 50
Barbecue Beef Brisket; 87
Barbecue Coleslaw; 171
Barbecue Turkey Burger Sliders; 95
Basic Bread Stuffing; 42
Basil Vinaigrette with Summer Corn Salad; 191
Basil-Parmesan Crusted Salmon; 119
Bean Beef Burritos; 46
Bean Salad with Balsamic Vinaigrette; 164
Beans with Pearl Couscous; 192
Beef and Butternut Squash Stew; 93
Beef and Mushroom Barley Soup; 83
Beef and Mushroom Cauliflower Wraps; 79
Beef and Pepper Fajita Bowls; 74
Beef and Red Bean Chili; 72
Beef Curry; 90
Beef Fajitas; 83
Beef Massaman Curry; 71
Beef steaks with green asparagus; 56
Beef Stroganoff; 78
Beef with Barley and Veggies; 86
Beef with Broccoli; 86
Beef, Tomato, and Pepper Tortillas; 85
Beets Dijon; 69
Bell Pepper-Corn Wrapped in Tortilla; 134
Bell Peppered Rings with Egg and Avocado Salsa; 14
Bell Peppers and Zucchini Stir Fry; 142
Berry Burrito; 45
Berry Cobbler; 218
Berry Coffee Cake; 217
Berry Mint Smoothie; 168
Berry Smoothie Pops; 207
Best Brown Rice; 151
Biryani; 49
Black Bean Burger with Garlic-Chipotle; 135
Black Bean, Quinoa, and Mango Salad; 185
Blackberry Baked Brie; 159
Blackberry Smoothie; 174
Blackened Chicken Breast with Jalapeno Caesar Salad; 193
Blended Berry Oats; 31
BLT Stuffed Cucumbers; 166
Blue Cheese Chicken Wedges; 66
Blueberries with Nectarines Spinach Salad; 194
Blueberry and Banana Breakfast Cookies; 25
Blueberry and Chicken Salad; 40
Blueberry Bake; 52
Blueberry Watermelon Salad; 194
Bok Choy and Mushroom Stir-Fry; 141
Bone Broth; 195
Braised Shrimp; 126
Bran Muffins; 207
Breakfast Cheddar Zucchini Casserole; 19
Breakfast Egg Bites; 33
Breakfast Grain Porridge; 20
Breakfast Homemade Poultry Sausage; 20
Breakfast Vegetable and Okra Hash; 26
Brie Quesadillas with Pears; 51
Broccoli Beef Stir-Fry; 73
Broccoli Cheese Breakfast Casserole; 34
Broccoli Omelet; 57
Broccoli Salad; 201
Broccoli with Bell Pepper; 141
Broth-Braised Cabbage; 68
Bruschetta Chicken; 97
Brussels Sprout with Fried Eggs; 27
Brussels sprouts; 188
Brussels sprouts with Balsamic Oil; 134
Buckwheat Crêpes; 16
Buckwheat Crêpes with Fruit and Yogurt; 36
Buffalo Bites; 166
Buffalo Cauliflower Wings; 181
Bunless Sloppy Joes; 90
Butter Glazed Carrots; 140
Buttery Lemon Chicken; 114
Cabbage and Carrot Stew; 145
Cabbage Wedges; 181
Caesar Salad; 46
Cajun Catfish; 121
Cajun Flounder and Tomatoes; 122
Cajun Shrimp; 120
Cajun Shrimp and Roasted Vegetables; 122
Cake with Whipped Cream Icing; 214
Calico Slaw; 190
California Wraps; 203
Candied Pecans; 161
Caprese Quiche; 29
Carrot and Cilantro Soup; 196
Carrot and Oat Pancakes; 26
Carrot and Zucchini Muffins; 139
Carrot Cake; 206
Carrot Cake with Cream Cheese Frosting; 221
Carrot Hummus; 196
Carrot Oat Pancakes; 33
Cauliflower and Beef Fajita; 79
Cauliflower and Celeriac Soup; 195
Cauliflower Hummus; 161
Cauliflower Mash; 164
Cauliflower Rice; 183
Cauliflower Tofu Salad; 202
Celery Apple Salad; 202
Celery with Chickpea Feta Salad; 191
Charred Bell Peppers; 179
Cheddar Bacon Burst; 63
Cheese and Onion Nuggets; 179
Cheese Crisp Crackers; 161
Cheeseburger Pie; 156
Cheesecake; 174
Cheesy Broccoli Bites; 167
Cheesy Cauliflower Fritters; 138
Cheesy Onion Dip; 161
Cheesy Pita Crisps; 162
Cheesy Spinach, Artichoke, and Egg Casserole; 28
Cheesy Taco Chips; 162
Chegg Salad Sandwich; 46
Cherry Tomato Salad; 201
Cherry-Glazed Lamb Chops; 92
Chewy Granola Bars; 162
Chicken and Bell Pepper Stew; 104
Chicken and Broccoli Bake; 98
Chicken and Broccoli Curry; 105
Chicken and Broccoli Kabobs; 103
Chicken and Cauliflower Curry; 104
Chicken and Grape Kabobs; 102
Chicken and Mushrooms; 155
Chicken and Spinach Curry; 105

Chicken and Spinach Stew; 103
Chicken and Sweet Potato Curry; 105
Chicken and Tomato Curry; 104
Chicken and Veggie Kabobs; 103
Chicken and Veggies Bake; 98
Chicken and Zucchini Kabobs; 102
Chicken and Zucchini Soup; 103
Chicken Avocado Salad; 203
Chicken Casablanca; 115
Chicken in Veggie Sauce; 101
Chicken in Wine; 114
Chicken Kabobs; 102
Chicken Liver Curry; 116
Chicken Meatballs Curry; 106
Chicken Salad in Cucumber Cups; 203
Chicken Sandwiches; 45
Chicken Souvlaki Salad; 191
Chicken Tikka Masala; 180
Chicken with Bell Peppers; 99
Chicken with Bok Choy; 99
Chicken with Broccoli and Mushroom; 100
Chicken with Cabbage; 100
Chicken with Caper Sauce; 97
Chicken with Carrot, and Kale; 112
Chicken with Cranberries; 101
Chicken with Mushrooms; 100
Chicken with Olives; 99
Chicken with Yellow Squash; 101
Chicken with Zucchini Noodles; 100
Chicken Zoodle Soup; 115
Chicken, Bean and Corn Salad; 170
Chili Lime Salmon; 176
Chili Lime Tortilla Chips; 162
Chili Sin Carne; 188
Chipotle Chili Pork Chops; 74
Choco Peppermint Cake; 216
Chocolate Baked Bananas; 208
Chocolate Cake; 217
Chocolate Cake Carrot; 172
Chocolate Chip Blondie's; 163
Chocolate Fudge; 51
Chocolate Lava Cake; 220
Chocolate Zucchini Muffins; 33
Cider Pork Stew; 72
Cilantro and Lime Broccoli Rice; 54
Cilantro Lime Grilled Shrimp; 122
Cinnamon Apple Chips; 163
Cinnamon Apple Popcorn; 167
Cinnamon Baked Apples; 213
Cinnamon Butternut Squash Fries; 139
Cinnamon Cake; 216
Cinnamon Nuts; 174
Cinnamon Walnut Granola; 32
Citrus and Chicken Salad; 40
Citrus Salmon; 125
Classic Stroganoff; 87
Clear soup with liver dumplings; 56
Coconut Berry Smoothie; 23
Coconut Meringue Cake; 41
Coconut Shrimp; 118
Coconut Spinach Smoothie; 168
Coffeed and Herbed Steak; 82
Coffee-Steamed Carrots; 176
Collard Greens; 177
Colorful vegetable casserole; 55
Copper Penny Carrots; 206
Corn on the Cob; 153
Corned Beef and Cabbage Soup; 93
Cottage Cheese Almond Pancakes; 35
Cottage Pancakes; 16
Couscous and Sweet Potatoes with Pork; 89
Crab and Spinach Dip; 167
Crab Curry; 125
Crab Frittata; 122
Cranberry and Almond Granola Bars; 157
Cranberry and Brussels sprouts With Dressing; 198
Cranberry Grits; 22
Cream Cheese Swirl Brownies; 212
Creamed Spinach; 182
Creamy Broccoli and Ham; 68
Creamy Spinach and Mushroom Lasagna; 136
Creamy Spinach Dip; 159
Creamy Strawberry Crepes; 210
Crispy Air Fryer Fish; 120
Crispy Eggplant Fries; 178
Crispy Fish Sticks; 119
Crispy Jalapeno Coins; 138
Crispy-Topped Baked Vegetables; 136
Crunchy Lemon Shrimp; 123
Cuban Pulled Pork Sandwich; 73
Cucumber and Kidney Bean Salad; 186
Curried Cauliflower Florets; 139
Curried Pork and Vegetable Skewers; 92
Curried Veggies Bake; 143
Dark Chocolate Almond Butter Cups; 209
Dark Chocolate Cake; 218
Decadent Three-Layered Chocolate Cream Cake; 220
Dill Pickle Dip; 42
Dilled Cucumbers; 171
Dried Bean and Cashew Salad; 170
Duck Breast; 110
Duck in Orange Sauce; 116
Easy and Creamy Grits; 26
Easy Beef Curry; 89
Easy Beef Roast with Green Peppercorn Sauce; 81
Easy Cauliflower Hush Puppies; 164
Easy Lime Lamb Cutlets; 88
Easy Pizza for Two; 163
Easy Pot Roast and Vegetables; 89
Easy Turkey Breakfast Patties; 29
Egg Fried Veg; 195
Egg Salad Sandwiches; 18
Eggplant Curry; 187
Eggplant Parmesan; 183
Eggplant Tofu Scramble; 197
Egg-Stuffed Tomatoes; 34
Everyday Salad; 199
Farro with Walnuts and Berries; 22
Fennel and Chickpeas; 150
Feta and Mushroom Frittata; 140
Feta Brussels sprouts and Scrambled Eggs; 26
Fiery Jalapeno Poppers; 62
Fish and Chips; 120
Fish Nuggets; 121
Flapjack; 48
Flourless Chocolate Cake; 213
French bread Pizza; 160
French Lentils; 175
Fresh Huevos Rancheros; 25
Fresh Pot Pork Butt; 76
Fresh Tuna Salad; 200
Fried Garlic Green Tomatoes; 180
Fried Tofu Hotpot; 188
Frozen Chocolate Peanut Butter Bites; 209
Frozen Mocha Milkshake; 207
Fruit Salad with Coconut-Lime Dressing; 198
Fruit Slush; 172
Fruitcake; 219
Funnel Cakes; 43
Garlic Cauliflower Tots; 180
Garlic Chicken Balls; 61
Garlic Galore Rotisserie Chicken; 113
Garlic Kale Chips; 178
Garlic Rosemary Grilled Prawns; 121
Garlic Salmon Balls; 178
Garlic Shrimp and Spinach; 130
Garlic Tomatoes; 179
Ginger Cake; 215
Ginger Dressing with Kale Chicken Salad; 193
Gingered Ground Chicken; 106
Glazed Bananas in Phyllo Nut Cups; 157
Glazed Carrots and Cauliflower; 68
Goat Cheese and Avocado Toast; 23
Golden Potato Cakes; 36
Gorgonzola Tofu Scramble; 44
Gouda Egg Casserole; 21
Grain-Free Berry Cobbler; 175
Greek Baklava; 157
Greek Chicken; 114
Greek Salad; 200
Greek Salad Kabobs; 158
Greek Yogurt and Oat Pancakes; 16
Greek Yogurt Berry Smoothie Pops; 209
Greek Yogurt Cinnamon Pancakes; 35
Greek Yogurt Sundae; 212
Green Beans; 184
Green Chicken and Veggies Curry; 106
Green Dressing with Shrimp Avocado Salad; 192
Green Goddess White Bean Dip; 158
Green Salad with Berries and Sweet Potatoes; 38
Greenie Smoothie; 168
Grilled Catfish; 53
Grilled Herbed Salmon with Raspberry Sauce and Cucumber Dill Dip; 129
Grilled Peach and Coconut Yogurt Bowls; 209
Grilled Salmon with Lemon; 121
Grilled Tuna Steaks; 123
Ground Chicken and Tofu Soup; 106
Ground Pork with Spinach; 65
Ground Turkey in Tomato Sauce; 108
Ground Turkey Salad; 201
Ground Turkey with Asparagus; 108
Ground Turkey with Pumpkin; 109
Halibut with Lime and Cilantro; 59
Halibut with Spicy Apricot Sauce; 129
Hamburger Muffins; 50
Herb Crusted Chicken; 196
Herbed Meatballs; 77
Herbed Salmon; 126
Herbed Whole Turkey Breast; 113
Herring and Veggies Soup; 130
Hollow Chicken Salad Supreme; 53
Honey Garlic Butter Roasted Carrots; 55
Honey-Glazed Salmon; 119
Hummus; 137
Ice Cream Brownie Cake; 217
Instant Pot Cinnamon Apricot and Pears; 69
Instant Pot Tapioca; 208
Irish Lamb Stew; 67

Italian Pork Chops; 84
Italian Roasted Vegetables; 150
Jamaican Jerk Pork; 84
Jarlsberg Lunch Omelet; 62
Jelly Cookies and Peanut Butter; 44
Jicama Fries; 138
Joseph's Bacon; 40
Kale and Cabbage Salad with Peanuts; 176
Kale with Carrot; 141
Kale with Cranberries and Pine Nuts; 141
Keto French fries; 180
Kidney Bean Stew; 188
Kohl Slaw; 45
Lamb and Chickpeas; 87
Lamb and Vegetable Stew; 92
Lamb Burgers with Mushrooms and Cheese; 92
Lamb Kofta with Cucumber Salad; 80
Lasagna Spaghetti Squash; 63
Lava Cake; 214
Lemon Berry Chiffon; 213
Lemon Cake; 216
Lemon Cheesecake; 219
Lemon Cilantro Chicken; 116
Lemon Cream Fruit Dip; 158
Lemon Pepper Salmon; 128
Lemon Sole; 127
Lemon Vinaigrette with Sugar Snap Pea Salad; 192
Lemonade; 173
Lemony Brussels Sprouts with Poppy Seeds; 152
Lemony Dijon Meat Loaf; 82
Lemony Kale; 140
Lemony Salmon; 124
Lentil and Chickpea Curry; 187
Lentil and Eggplant Stew; 187
Lentil snack with tomato salsa; 55
Lentil Soup; 197
Lime Fizz; 173
Lime-Parsley Lamb Cutlets; 75
Loaded Cottage Pie; 76
Low Carb Pumpkin Pie Pudding; 67
Low Fat Roasties; 185
Lower Carb Hummus; 186
Mango Pork Tenderloin; 81
Maple Oatmeal Cookies; 210
Marbled Cheesecake Muffins; 173
Marinated Green Beans; 169
Marinated Vegetable Salad; 169
Mashed Garlicky Potatoes; 49
Mashed Pumpkin; 177
Meat skewers with polenta; 74
Meatballs Barley Soup; 71
Mediterranean Burrito; 61
Mediterranean Fish Fillets; 124
Melon Cucumber Salad; 156
Mexican Turkey Tenderloin; 115
Mixed Chowder; 125
Mocha Spread; 173
Monkey Salad; 62
Mouth-Watering Egg Casserole; 58
Mu Shu Lunch Pork; 62
Mushroom and Eggs; 195
Mushroom Bread; 44
Mushroom Frittata; 17
Mushroom Pasta; 177
Mushroom Stew; 179
Mushroom Tofu Scramble; 197
Mushroom with Brussels Sprout; 142
Mushroom, Beef, and Cauliflower Rice in Lettuce; 83
Mushrooms Curry; 144
Mussels in Tomato Sauce; 125
Mustard Glazed Pork Chops; 91
Mustard Pork Chops; 80
No-Bake Carrot Cake Bites; 209
Nutella-Like Brioche Star; 50
Nutty Steel-cut Oatmeal with Blueberries; 57
Oat and Chia Porridge; 139
Oat Granola with Walnut; 24
Oatmeal Cookies; 208
Oats Coffee Smoothie; 168
'Oh, so Good' Salad; 66
Okra; 182
Old Fashioned Beef Soup with Vegetables; 71
Onion Rings; 178
Orange Cake; 215
Orange Carrot Smoothie; 169
Orange Vinaigrette with Roasted Beets; 194
Orange-Marinated Pork Tenderloin; 60
Oriental Coleslaw; 172
Oyster Stew; 41
Pancetta and Mushrooms; 52
Pan-Fried Trout; 158
Parmesan Cauliflower Mash; 152
Parmesan Golden Pork Chops; 80
Parmesan-Crusted Pork Chops; 91
Parmesan-Topped Acorn Squash; 153
Parsnip, Carrot, and Kale Salad with Dressing; 198
Pasta and Artichoke Heart Salad; 171
Pasta and Kidney Bean Salad; 171
Peaches with Creamy Chicken Salad; 47
Peanut Butter and Berry Oatmeal; 29
Peas with Mushrooms and Thyme; 148
Pecan-Oatmeal Pancakes; 42
Pecans with Blackberry Ginger Beet Salad; 193
Pesto Chicken Bake; 98
Pesto Veggie Pizza; 160
Pico de Gallo Navy Beans; 150
Pineapple Kabobs; 173
Pineapple Nice Cream; 211
Pinto Beans; 186
Poached Pears; 206
Popcorn Shrimp; 129
Pork Chops in Peach Glaze; 65
Pork Chops Pomodoro; 70
Pork Diane; 76
Pork Loin, Carrot, and Gold Tomato Roast; 82
Pork Medallions with Cherry Sauce; 70
Pork Rind Nachos; 84
Pork Salad; 64
Pork Souvlakia with Tzatziki Sauce; 85
Pork Tenderloin Roast with Mango Glaze; 91
Pork with Bell Peppers; 64
Portobello and Chicken Sausage Frittata; 18
Potato, Egg and Sausage Frittata; 32
Potatoes with Parsley; 148
Pound Cake; 218
Prosciutto Spinach Salad; 63
Prosciutto Wrapped Mozzarella Balls; 61
Pulled Pork Sandwiches with Apricot Jelly; 78
Pumpkin Apple Waffles; 36
Quick Breakfast Yogurt Sundae; 29
Quinoa Tabbouleh; 184
Rainbow Bean Salad; 39
Ranch Dump Style Pork Chops; 69
Raspberry Cake with White Chocolate Sauce; 213
Raspberry Choco Oatmeal; 15
Raspberry Nice Cream; 208
Ratatouille; 142
Ratatouille Baked Eggs; 35
Ravioli; 181
Red Cabbage Mix; 67
Red Clam Sauce and Pasta; 123
Red Pepper, Goat Cheese, and Arugula Open-Faced Grilled Sandwich; 165
Red Wine Pot Roast with Winter Vegetables; 65
Rice Breakfast Bake; 31
Ritzy Beef Stew; 88
Ritzy Jerked Chicken Breasts; 111
Roasted Beef with Peppercorn Sauce; 84
Roasted Beef with Shallot Sauce; 78
Roasted Beets, Carrots, and Parsnips; 151
Roasted Chicken with Root Vegetables; 111
Roasted Chickpea; 41
Roasted Cinnamon Celery Root; 151
Roasted Eggplant with Goat Cheese; 150
Roasted Mango; 214
Roasted Parsnips; 185
Roasted Persimmon Burrata Focaccia; 47
Roasted Pork Loin with Carrots; 77
Roasted Pork Shoulder; 64
Roasted Portobello Salad; 200
Roasted Root Vegetables; 137
Roasted Squash Puree; 137
Roasted Vegetable and Chicken Tortillas; 112
Rosemary Potatoes; 176
Rosemary-garlic Lamb Racks; 94
Salad with Salsa Verde Vinaigrette; 15
Salisbury Steaks with Seared Cauliflower; 66
Salmon and Asparagus; 128
Salmon Apple Salad Sandwich; 157
Salmon Cakes; 118
Salmon Cream Cheese and Onion on Bagel; 156
Salmon Curry; 131
Salmon Feta and Pesto Wrap; 156
Salmon Fillets; 120
Salmon in Green Sauce; 126
Salmon Milano; 123
Salmon Soup; 131
Salmon with Bell Peppers; 131
Sandwich Filling; 45
Sardine Curry; 127
Sausage and Pepper Burrito; 21
Sautéed Mixed Vegetables; 149
Savory Breakfast Egg Bites; 27
Scallop Caesar Salad; 202
Scalloped Potatoes; 30
Scrumptious Orange Muffins; 28
Seasoned Chicken Breast; 97
Seasoned Turkey Legs; 108
Shredded BBQ Cream Cheese Chicken; 68
Shredded Buffalo Chicken; 113
Shredded Chicken Salad; 201
Shrimp and Artichoke Skillet; 124
Shrimp and Veggies Curry; 132
Shrimp Burgers; 43
Shrimp Coconut Curry; 126
Shrimp Lemon Kebab; 129

Shrimp Peri-Peri; 59
Shrimp Salad; 131
Shrimp with Green Beans; 125
Shrimp with Scallion Grits; 19
Shrimps Saganaki; 44
Simple Appetizer Meatballs; 190
Simple Beef Roast; 55
Simple Cottage Cheese Pancakes; 24
Simple Grain-Free Biscuits; 27
Sloppy Joes; 82
Slow "Roasted" Tomatoes; 57
Slow Cooked Beef and Vegetables Roast; 88
Smoked Salmon and Cheese on Rye Bread; 157
Smothered Sirloin; 75
Spaghetti Squash Tots; 139
Spaghetti Squash with Sun-Dried Tomatoes; 149
Spiced Chicken Breast; 97
Spiced Leg of Lamb; 85
Spiced Nuts; 179
Spiced Orange Rice Pudding; 211
Spiced Quail; 110
Spicy Ahi Poke Salad; 47
Spicy Bruschetta; 163
Spicy Chicken Burger; 107
Spicy Garlic Pasta; 54
Spicy Pork on Whole Wheat Rolls; 30
Spicy Tuna Sandwich; 52
Spinach and Black-Eyed Pea Salad; 170
Spinach and Cheese Breakfast Tacos; 24
Spinach and Orange Salad with Oil Drizzle; 198
Spinach Dip; 197
Spinach Frittata; 46
Spinach with Tomatoes; 140
Split Pea Stew; 188
Squash Medley; 187
Steak and Broccoli Bowls; 79
Steak Sandwich; 81
Steamed Asparagus; 186
Stir Fried Veggie Noodles; 142
Strawberry Chiffon Pie; 205
Strawberry Cream Cheese Crepes; 212
Strawberry Fruit Squares; 205
Strawberry Shortcake; 217
Strawberry Smoothie; 168
Stuffed Bell Peppers with Quinoa; 61
Stuffed Mushrooms; 197
Sugar Free Strawberry Cheesecake; 43
Summer Veggie Scramble; 34
Sumptuous Lamb and Pomegranate Salad; 88
Sunday Pot Roast; 73
Sun-Dried Tomato Brussels Sprouts; 149
Sunflower Seeds and Arugula Garden Salad; 203
Sunny Poutine; 52
Super Grain Porridge; 23
Super-Seedy Salad with Tahini Dressing; 199
Supreme Caesar Salad; 204
Sweet and Sour Red Cabbage; 186
Sweet Potato and Spinach Stew; 145
Sweet Potato Cauliflower Patties; 182
Swirled Cream Cheese Brownies; 210
Swiss and Crab Melts; 48
Swiss chard Shakshuka; 21
Swordfish Steak; 127
Tabbouleh- Arabian Salad; 204
Taco Slaw; 195
Tacos with Pico De Gallo; 18
Tarragon Scallops; 130
Tempeh in Tomato Sauce; 154
Texas Goulash; 40
Thai Green Turkey Curry; 116
Thai Roasted Veggies; 137
Three Bean and Scallion Salad; 39
Toffee Nut Cookies; 50
Tofu and Bell Pepper Stew; 147
Tofu and Spinach Soup; 147
Tofu and Veggie Burger; 146
Tofu and Veggies Curry; 148
Tofu Curry; 187
Tofu Lettuce Wraps; 145
Tofu with Broccoli; 146
Tofu with Brussels Sprout; 147
Tofu with Kale; 146
Tofu with Peas; 147
Tomato and Broccoli; 37
Tomato and Roasted Cod; 181
Tomato Eggs; 196
Tomato Toasts; 199
Tomato Waffles; 20
Tomato-Herb Omelet; 58
Traditional Beef Stroganoff; 75
Tropical Fruity Steel Cut Oats; 22
Tropical Yogurt Kiwi Bowl; 17
Trout Bake; 127
Tuna Carbonara; 124
Tuna Sweet corn Casserole; 127
Turkey and Pumpkin Meatloaf; 110
Turkey and Quinoa Caprese Casserole; 96
Turkey and Spaghetti Squash; 115
Turkey and Veggie Salad; 107
Turkey Chili; 95
Turkey Divan Casserole; 96
Turkey Lettuce Wraps; 107
Turkey Loaf; 177
Turkey Meatball and Vegetable Kabobs; 112
Turkey Meatballs Kabobs; 109
Turkey Stuffed Zucchini; 109
Turkey with Mushrooms; 108
Turkey, Apple and Veggies Burgers; 109
Vanilla Coconut Pancakes; 28
Vegan Edamame Quinoa Collard Wraps; 135
Vegetable Curry; 152
Vegetable Medley; 151
Vegetable Salad; 199
Vegetables in Half and Half; 67
Vegetarian Chipotle Chili; 60
Veggie and Mustard Pasta Salad; 49
Veggie Casserole; 143
Veggie Fillets Omelets; 15
Veggie Kabobs; 144
Veggie Smoothie; 169
Veggie Stuffed Bell Peppers; 144
Veggies and Walnut Loaf; 144
Veggie-Stuffed Omelet; 31
Vietnamese Meatball Lollipops with Dipping Sauce; 159
Walnut-Fruit Cake; 215
Warm Barley and Squash Salad; 39
White chicken chili; 111
Whole Wheat Chapatti; 43
Wild Mushroom Frittata; 36
Wild Rice; 60
Wild Rice Salad with Cranberries and Almonds; 153
Yellow Squash and Bell Pepper Bake; 143
Yogurt and Parmesan Chicken Bake; 98
Yogurt Sundae; 32
Zhug Chicken; 51
Zoodles with Pea Pesto; 59
Zucchini Carbonara; 79
Zucchini Noodles with Lime-Basil Pesto; 149
Zucchini Parmesan Chips; 136

Conclusion

Type 2 diabetes is a severe disease - not something to treat lightly. As you learned from our 3 weeks to optimal blood sugar diet, a healthy lifestyle is a must if you want to control your diabetes. You need to realize that you can't just eat healthy foods to lose weight and control your blood sugar. You need to do the work if you want the results.

Now that you have read through our Type 2 Diabetes Cookbook, you know the basics of how to lose weight and control your blood pressure, cholesterol, and blood sugar. You can now take advantage of all these great benefits for yourself. You also need to realize that your age and weight will determine the time your body needs to adjust. Therefore, we propose sticking with the diet for three weeks. Not only will you feel greater, but your insulin levels will also begin to stabilize, and this will lower your chances of developing complications. Remember that the older you get, the more serious the condition. Therefore, those over 40 and overweight people should keep a close eye on their blood sugar and their medications.

This cookbook recipe section will show you how to transition your healthy lifestyle habits from a cookbook recipe method to a lifestyle guide. This guide is going to be very simple. It's going to be a day-by-day guide to help you begin your journey towards a healthier life. Let's start by talking about what you will need to be successful for this program to work. You will need something easy for you to stick with and something that you can stick with the rest of your life. The method of this is straightforward, and you will want to follow our lifestyle guide. Following the lifestyle guide will make your life healthier, happier, and more fulfilling. This book is planned to help you feel better, look better, and socialize better. It's simple. We are not trying to brainwash you with some weird cult ideals or anything like that. Our idea is that if it feels good for you, it must be suitable for your body. This book is designed to help you lose weight, lower your cholesterol, and lower your blood pressure. If you are seeking for a miracle cure to rid you of all these conditions at once, then this book may not be suitable for you. We don't expect everyone to follow our methods in the way we have laid them out for you. We hope that if you can open your mind to the possibilities, it will be easier for you to set up the diet plan that works well for your lifestyle. We want to help you take what we have learned and create your diet plan. You will need to take the information we have given you and mold it to fit your personal needs and wants.

It doesn't matter what category of diet plan you currently use. We all know that what we put into our body can either make it sick or make it feel good. We want to take what we learned from this book and help you form your recipe for healthy living.

This book has requested time and effort to be assembled and published.

If you have enjoyed it and it made some impact in your life, I would really be thankful if you can drop a review on the Amazon store, scanning with your phone camera the QR code below:

Thank you

Printed in Great Britain
by Amazon